KU-300-339

BAVARIA

Cadogan Books plc
London House, Parkgate Road, London SW11 4NQ, UK

Distributed in North America by
The Globe Pequot Press
6 Business Park Road, PO Box 833, Old Saybrook,
Connecticut 06475–0833

Copyright © Rodney Bolt 1995
Updated by Claudio Montani Adams
Illustrations © Brian Hoskin 1995

Book and cover design by Animage
Cover illustration by Povl Webb
Maps © Cadogan Guides, drawn by Thames Cartographic Ltd

Series Editors: Rachel Fielding and Vicki Ingle

Editor: Antony Mason
Proofreading: Jacqueline Chnéour
Indexing: Ann Hall

DTP: Linda McQueen and Jacqueline Lewin
Production: Rupert Wheeler Book Production Services

**A catalogue record for this book is available from the
British Library
US Library of Congress Cataloging-in-Publication-Data
available**

ISBN 0–94–7754–911

Output by Bookworm Ltd.
Printed and bound in Great Britain by Redwood Books Ltd. on Grosvenor
Woodfree supplied by McNaughton Publishing Papers Ltd.

The author and publishers have made every effort to ensure the accuracy of the information in the book at the time of going to press. However, they cannot accept any responsibility for any loss, injury or inconvenience resulting from the use of information contained in this guide.

About the Author

Rodney Bolt grew up in Africa, was educated at Cambridge University where he read English, and now lives in Amsterdam. He has travelled throughout Europe and has lived and worked in Greece, the Netherlands and Germany. He also writes and directs for the stage, and for some years ran a London pub theatre. In 1992 he set off in a battered Volkswagen van on a two-year-long journey through newly united Germany to research this book.

About the Updater

Claudio Montani Adams graduated from York and Cambridge Universities. Having worked as Head of Information for the German National Tourist Office in London for several years, he is now freelancing in the field of tourism promotion.

Author's Acknowledgements

I would like to thank Claudio Montani Adams for his help with updating and preparing material for this guide, and the German National Tourist Office and the various local tourist offices whose advice and assistance were invaluable. Once again, a big thanks to my editors Antony Mason and Vicki Ingle for their flexibility and support, and to Brian Hoskin for the great illustrations.

Please help us keep this guide up to date

We have done our best to ensure that the information in this guide is correct at the time of going to press. But places and facilities are constantly changing, and standards and prices in hotels and restaurants fluctuate. We would be delighted to receive any comments concerning existing entries or omissions. Significant contributions will be acknowledged in the next edition, and authors of the best letters will receive a copy of the Cadogan Guide of their choice.

Contents

The Arts and Culture 41–60

Munich 61–118

The Bavarian Alps 119–40

The Romantic Road 141–84

Introduction

Of all the tribes of Germany, none is fiercer about its singularity and independence than the Bavarians. A race of romantics whose national hero is a fantastical, dreamy 19th-century king, and who dismiss countrymen north of the border as spiritless *Saupreissen* (swinish Prussians), Bavarians often express their loyalties in a descending scale: 'Bavaria first, Europe second and Germany third'. The state capital, Munich, is twinned with Edinburgh in Scotland, and, like the Scots, many Bavarians cherish ideas of national independence though admittedly without quite the same degree of seriousness.

North Germans regard the southerners as rumbustious hedonists, pushy and uncouth. Foreigners expect (and often find) fat, *Lederhosen*-clad men with feathers in their hats, munching sausages and guzzling giant-sized measures of beer. The truth is that Bavaria packs between its borders a variety of spectacle and style that beats anywhere else in Germany. Here you'll find sleepy bucolic villages, chic highlife, cornerstones of European culture and (many say) the tastiest cooking in the land. In Munich you can plunge into what is arguably the country's best art collection, and its most Bacchanalian festival. Bayreuth and Oberammergau stage two of the most famous arts events in the world.

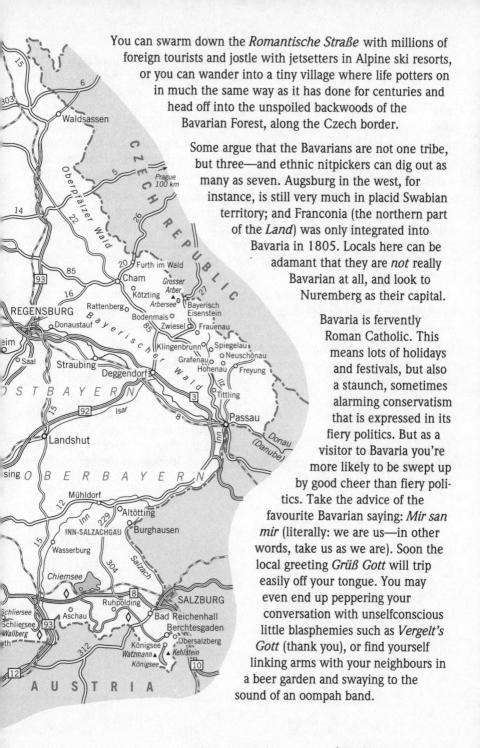

You can swarm down the *Romantische Straße* with millions of foreign tourists and jostle with jetsetters in Alpine ski resorts, or you can wander into a tiny village where life potters on in much the same way as it has done for centuries and head off into the unspoiled backwoods of the Bavarian Forest, along the Czech border.

Some argue that the Bavarians are not one tribe, but three—and ethnic nitpickers can dig out as many as seven. Augsburg in the west, for instance, is still very much in placid Swabian territory; and Franconia (the northern part of the *Land*) was only integrated into Bavaria in 1805. Locals here can be adamant that they are *not* really Bavarian at all, and look to Nuremberg as their capital.

Bavaria is fervently Roman Catholic. This means lots of holidays and festivals, but also a staunch, sometimes alarming conservatism that is expressed in its fiery politics. But as a visitor to Bavaria you're more likely to be swept up by good cheer than fiery politics. Take the advice of the favourite Bavarian saying: *Mir san mir* (literally: we are us—in other words, take us as we are). Soon the local greeting *Grüß Gott* will trip easily off your tongue. You may even end up peppering your conversation with unselfconscious little blasphemies such as *Vergelt's Gott* (thank you), or find yourself linking arms with your neighbours in a beer garden and swaying to the sound of an oompah band.

Guide to the Guide

Because cultural and religious boundaries do not always conform to the administrative ones, this guide is not divided into chapters devoted to each of the seven *Bezirke* (districts), but is structured around regions that have a common outlook or historical traditions, or which visitors are likely to tackle as a single piece. A trip down the Romantic Road, for instance, takes you through four different Bavarian *Bezirke*.

The first section focuses on the city of **Munich**, Bavaria's compact and cosmopolitan capital; but it also takes in the low-lying hinterland and attractive river of the Altmühl to the north, and the historic towns among rolling pastures of the Inn-Salzachgau to the east.

South of Munich lie the **Bavarian Alps**, with their sparkling lakes, mountains galore and clusters of Baroque churches and chapels. This is the stamping ground of the most rural and conservative Bavarians, who wear local *Trachten* (costume) with determination and pride. The route runs from the Alpine scenery of the upper Bavarian Alps in the east to the undulating pre-Alpine pastures and cosy towns of the Allgäu, as far as Lindau on Lake Constance.

Next comes Germany's most popular theme road, the **Romantic Road**, all 343km of it, travelling—as most people do—from north to south, with diversions sideways in forests and along the Danube.

The section on **Eastern Bavaria** begins with the Italianate cities of Regensburg and Passau on the Danube. The route moves eastward into the less accessible (but delightful) regions of the Bavarian and Upper Palatinate Forests, which is Bavaria at its sylvan best, luring hikers and bikers into its unspoilt, lonely wilderness.

Finally, across the top of the state stretches **Franconia**, Bavaria's largest and most recently acquired region. Franconia is a mixed bag, with Nuremberg (the unofficial capital of Germany in the Middle Ages), Bayreuth (home to the Wagner Festival) and Bamberg (a Baroque gem) thrown in with the rocky gorges of Franconian Swizerland and misty pine forests.

Travel

By Air

For travellers from outside mainland Europe, flying is often the most economical way to get to Bavaria—and indeed to Germany in general. Flights from Britain are fast and frequent and sometimes cheaper than long, sticky train journeys. The presence of US military bases in Germany has meant that the country is well served by American airlines. Despite military cutbacks, Germany is still one of the cheapest of trans-Atlantic destinations. Australians and New Zealanders, however, may find that it makes more sense to fly to London and buy a further ticket to Germany.

Bavaria's main international airport is Munich. Germany's largest international airport, Frankfurt, lies only 30km or so beyond Bavaria's border, and Stuttgart is similarly close.

From the UK and the Republic of Ireland

Flights to Munich with British Airways or Lufthansa begin at about £140 return; prices to Frankfurt or Stuttgart are normally £20 or so cheaper. A look through *Time Out* or the Sunday papers can sometimes uncover return flights for under £100 return, on a scheduled flight. Student and youth fares are unlikely to better any of the special deals you can find elsewhere. If you intend to travel around extensively, then a flight to Frankfurt in conjunction with a rail pass is the best bet.

Fares from Dublin work out at nearly double those from London, so it may well be worthwhile crossing to the UK for a cheaper flight.

There are flights to Germany from Heathrow, Gatwick and Stansted. (When comparing prices remember that trains to Gatwick and Stansted add another £16 or so to the cost.) The chief regional airports with connections to Germany are Manchester and Birmingham.

British Airways: 156 Regent St, London W1R 5TA, reservations ✆ (0345) 222 111.
Lufthansa: 10 Old Bond St, London W1, ✆ (0345) 737 747.
German Travel Centre: 8 Earlham St, London WC2, ✆ (0171) 836 4444.
Good air ticket bargains.
STA Travel: 86 Old Brompton Rd, London SW7, ✆ (0171) 938 4711.
Specializes in student and youth travel.

From the US and Canada

Some airlines fly direct to Munich (such as American Airlines, which offer direct flights out of Chicago), but by far the cheapest flights are on the New York–Frankfurt route. Off season you can pick up flights for under $400 return. Even in summer you can fly for around $500. Prices increase for flights from cities other than New York, but Delta offers off-season round-trips from any major US city to any of the main German airports for around $500 (though prices more than double in season). West Coast fares—from Los Angeles or San Francisco to Frankfurt—are about the same as East Coast ones off-season, but rise a bit at peak periods. The best deals are available through seat consolidators (scour the Sunday papers), with APEX rates on the major carriers coming a sorry second. All US fares are subject to airport taxes and surcharges.

Canadians can expect APEX fares of around CDN$800 from Toronto or Montreal, and pushing on CDN$1000 from Vancouver. Budget options are limited; your most economical alternative may be to fly to London and pick up a cheap connection.

Air Canada: 26th floor, Place Air Canada, 500 Dorchester Boulevard West, Montreal PQ H2Z 1X5, ✆ (0514) 879 7000.

American Airlines: P.O. Box 619 616, Dallas-Fort Worth Airport, Texas 75261-9616, ✆ toll-free number available locally.

British Airways: 530 Fifth Ave, New York, NY 10017, ✆ toll-free 800 247 9297; 1501 McGill College Avenue, Suite 1501, Montreal, PQ H3A 3M8, ✆ toll-free 800 668 1059; 1 Dundas St W, Toronto, ON M5G 2B2, ✆ (426) 250 0880.

Delta Air Lines: Hartsfield Atlanta International Airport, Atlanta, GA 30320, ✆ (404) 765 5000.

Lufthansa: 680 Fifth Ave, New York, NY 10017, ✆ 800 645 3880.

TWA: One City Center, 515 North Sixth Street, St Louis, Missouri, ✆ toll-free number available locally.

United Airlines: P.O. Box 66100, Chicago, Illinois 60666, ✆ 800 538 2929.

Virgin Atlantic Airways: 96 Horton St, New York, NY 10014, ✆ toll-free 800-862 8621.

By Train and Boat

Travelling by train and boat to Germany is time-consuming and (unless you're over 60 or under 26) usually more expensive than flying. Trains from London leave from Victoria Station (1hr 40mins channel crossing to Ostend) or Liverpool Street Station (6½hr crossing to Hook of Holland). The total journey time from London to Munich is about 14 hours.

Normal London–Munich return tickets cost £180 and are valid for two months. Students, and people aged under 26 or over 60, qualify for various discount schemes (details from any British Rail station). A small surcharge of £21 will convert the ordinary Senior Citizen Railcard into a **Rail Europ Senior** card, which gives you 30 per cent discount on rail and sea travel throughout Western Europe. An **InterRail Pass** (£249), not valid in France, Spain, Italy, Switzerland or Belgium, gives free travel on the continent and half-price travel on British trains, as well as discounts on some Channel crossings, to European residents under 26, for one month. The senior version of this pass (£269) offers the same deal to older travellers, minus the half-price British travel. German Rail also offer travel passes (*see* p.7) which will cut your costs substantially.

The Channel Tunnel offers prospects of much speedier train travel to all destinations in Europe. Already it is possible to reach Brussels from London (Waterloo) by the Eurostar Service in just 3¼ hours. At the outset of this service, however, travellers to Bavaria will not see any great advantage, as the connecting services do not appreciably reduce the journey time from that of the traditional train and boat across the Channel. Furthermore, the cost (about £260 from London to Munich return, £230 to Nuremberg return) is considerably more than the air fare. These circumstances may well change as the services develop. For onward journeys to Bavarian destinations from Brussels via the Channel Tunnel, contact Beyond Eurostar, ✆ (01233) 617 562 for information and ticketing.

By Coach

Journeys to Germany by coach don't compare favourably with cheap air travel either. At best the trip will be long and uncomfortable, at worst nightmarish, with stops every few hours, just as you are finally getting off to sleep. The main carrier from London is National Express/Eurolines, 52 Grosvenor Gardens, London SW1 0AG, ✆ (0171) 730 0202). Coaches leave two to five times a week for Munich (24 hours, single £60, return £99), and for Frankfurt (18 hours, single £49, return £83). Discounts of around 10 per cent are available for travellers between the ages of 13 and 25.

By Boat

By far the most pleasant way to arrive in Germany is on a Scandinavian Seaways overnight ferry from Harwich to Hamburg. You can while away the evening at the smorgasbord or in the bars, disco or casino, have a good night's sleep in a luxury cabin (at a price), then wake up to find yourself sailing gently up the Elbe past Hamburg's most luxurious villas. Prices start at £55 (one way), which includes the use of a couchette. Cabins cost £123. Add a further £58 if you want to take your car. Fares rise at weekends and at peak periods, but students get a whacking 50 per cent discount. However, if you are aiming to drive around Bavaria you will find it quicker to make a shorter ferry crossing to France or Belgium, and then to head for the border (*see* below).

By Car

Ferries plying the Channel from Dover, Folkestone or Ramsgate to Boulogne, Calais or Dunkerque in France or Ostend in Belgium—or from Harwich to the Hook of Holland or Felixstowe to Zeebrugge—all deposit you within 2–3 hours' drive of the German border. There is little difference in price between the main ferry operators. Crossings cost around £250 for a car and up to five people in high season, dropping to around £130 in low season. Bavaria is about 500km from the Channel ports—and you can travel by motorway all the way. British drivers using their own car need to take a valid driver's licence, insurance certificate (a Green Card is recommended), MOT and the vehicle's registration documents. You should fit small stickers that deflect the beam of your headlights. It is compulsory to carry a warning triangle in Germany, and your car (if British-registered) should have a GB label on the back. All of these accessories are available at British garages and motor shops.

Scandinavian Seaways: Parkeston Quay, Harwich, Essex CO2 4QG, ✆ (01255) 241 234; 15 Hanover St, London W1, ✆ (0171) 409 6060.
Sealink: Charter House, Park St, Ashford, Kent TN24 8EX, ✆ (01233) 64707.

P&O: Channel House, Channel View Rd, Dover, Kent CT17 9TJ,
✆ (01304) 203 388.

Sally Lines: 81 Piccadilly, London W1V 0JH, ✆ (0171) 409 2240.

Entry and Residence Requirements

European Union citizens, Americans, Canadians, Australians and New Zealanders do not need **visas** to visit Germany. A valid **passport** or British visitor's card will do. If you are arriving by road from another EU country you are likely to find border posts unstaffed, or (unless you appear deeply suspect) to be waved through without a second glance.

If you intend to stay for anything longer than 90 days, you should pay a visit to the local *Einwohnermeldeamt* (registration office) to register your address (*see* pp.22–3).

Customs Regulations and Currency Restrictions

Since the dissolution of internal borders in the EU there are no restrictions on the quantities of alcohol, tobacco and perfume that can be taken across EU borders, provided it has been bought duty-paid (i.e. not in a duty-free shop) within the EU and is for personal use only. You would have to have a good excuse—such as an imminent wedding reception—if you were found transporting a vanload of Liebfraumilch over the border.

American citizens may take up to 100 cigars and 200 cigarettes back into the USA. You may also take in one litre of alcoholic beverages. Most states restrict the import of alcohol and the laws of the state in which you arrive override Federal law—so it's worth checking up on this before you leave.

No currency restrictions are in operation. You can bring any amount of money into the country, and take as much as you want out.

Special-interest Holidays

From the UK

Bents Bicycle Tours, see p.9.

Major and Mrs Holt's Battlefield Tours (military history tours of Munich, Nuremberg and Berchtesgaden), 15 Market Street, Sandwich, Kent CT13 9DA, ✆ (01304) 612248.

Moswin Tours Ltd (wide range of independent and escorted holidays—themes include winter sports, cycling and rambling tours, language, music, history, archaeology, steam railways, Christmas markets, wine and beer festivals), Moswin House, 21 Church Street, Oadby, Leicester LE2 5DB, ✆ (01533) 714922.

Martin Randall Travel (art, music and Christmas tours), 10 Barley Mow Passage, Chiswick, London W4 4PH, ✆ (0181) 742 3355.

Travel for the Arts (opera and music tours, including Bayreuth Festival), 117 Regent's Park Road, London NW1 8UR, ✆ (0171) 483 4466.

From the Republic of Ireland

John Galligan Travel (castle holidays, Munich Oktoberfest), 29 Fitzwilliam Place, Dublin 2, ✆ (01) 661 9466.

From the USA

DER Tours (Christmas tours and Munich Oktoberfest), 11933 Wilshire Blvd, Los Angeles, CA 90025, ✆ (310) 479 41440.

Gerhard's Bicycle Odysseys (cycle tours), PO Box 757, Portland, OR 977207, ✆ (503) 223 2402.

Travcoa (medieval castles and towns), PO Box 2630, Newport Beach, CA 92658 2630, ✆ (714) 476 2800.

Viva Tours (Bayreuth), 12 Station Road, Bellport, NY 11713, ✆ (516) 286 2626.

For a complete list of US tour operators to Germany, contact **The German National Tourist Office**, 122 East 42nd Street, 52nd Floor, New York, NY 10168–0072, ✆ (212) 661 7200, @ 212 661 7174.

German Embassies Abroad

Australia: 119 Empire Circuit, Yarralumia AC, Canberra 2600, ✆ (062) 701 911.

Canada: PO Box 379, Post Station A, Ottawa, Ontario K1N 8V4, ✆ (0613) 232 1011.

Great Britain: 23 Belgrave Square, London SW1X 8PZ, ✆ (0171) 235 5033.

Republic of Ireland: 31 Trimelston Avenue, Booterstown, Blackrock, Co. Dublin, ✆ (01) 693 011.

New Zealand: 90–92 Hobson St, Wellington, ✆ (04) 736 063.

USA: 4645 Reservoir Rd NW, Washington 20007, ✆ (0202) 298 4000.

Getting Around

By Train

German Rail (*Deutsche Bundesbahn*) can whizz you around Bavaria—even to remote corners—with speed and awesome efficiency, and it is well worth considering the train as your principal mode of travel.

For longer journeys, the **InterCityExpress** (**ICE**, Germany's answer to France's TGV) reaches speeds of up to 250kph, while passengers recline in sleek, air-conditioned carriages. The main ICE line connects Hamburg to Frankfurt and Munich, and there is another via Würzburg and Nuremberg. Unless you are travelling on a German Rail Pass (*see* below) you will need to pay a surcharge for this speed and comfort. You also need to pay a supplement (DM9) for the next notch down, the **InterCity** (IC) and **EuroCity** (EC) (international) express trains. If you are not in a real hurry, you'll find these just as good a means of city-hopping as ICE. For journeys between smaller centres there are the

InterRegio trains, or you can meander about on the local D-Zug (normal service) or E-Zug (slow) trains.

Thomas Cook publish an indispensable **Timetable Summary** (£3), which you can buy from local agencies in Britain. (It comes free with a German Rail Pass.) Over weekends and during the holiday periods trains can get very crowded, and it is advisable to book a seat (for which there is a small extra fee). If you are travelling long distances overnight you can bite the bullet and sit the whole way, or share a couchette (4-berth, 6-berth, not sex-segregated), or lord it in a sleeper. Prices vary according to distance travelled, for example: Ostend–Munich 4-berth couchette £16.70, 6-berth £11.90, double sleeper £50.20, single sleeper £107.80.

Ticket (*Fahrkarte*) prices are based on the distance travelled, so a return journey is no cheaper than two singles. This does mean, however, that you can break your journey along the way. Tickets are valid for two months. Children under 4 travel free, those from 4 to 11 travel at half-price. If you are thinking of doing any amount of rail travel at all, it is worth considering a **Euro Domino Pass** (adult pass for 3 days £138, 5 days £154, 10 days £229; youth pass (under 26) for 3 days £103, 5 days £114, 10 days £171). These are available only to non-residents of Germany, and should be bought before you leave. (German Rail offices and some travel agents can supply you.) With a rail pass you can travel on everything from the humblest E-Zug to the ICE, without surcharge. It also allows you to travel up the Rhine and the Mosel on boats of the Köln-Düsseldorfer Line, on bus services run by German Rail (to places not served by trains and along tourist routes such as the Romantic Road) and on local **S-Bahn** (suburban railway) trains.

> **UK:** German Rail Services Suite 4, The Sanctuary, 23 Oakhill Grove, Surbiton, Surrey KT6 6DU, ✆ (0181) 390 0066.

> **USA:** German Rail DER Tours Inc., 9501 W. Devon Avenue, Rosemont, LI 60018–4832, ✆ (708) 692 6300.

By Car

During the 1930s Germany built the world's first **motorways**. Today's *Autobahn* network is still one of the most extensive and best maintained on the Continent, and there are no charges for using them. Regional roads ('B' roads) and country routes (in the west) are also impressive. There is no speed limit on open stretches of motorway and driving on them requires nerves of steel. If you do not have the mechanical means or the psychological mettle to overtake at supersonic speeds, then stick to the slow lane. Otherwise a giant Mercedes or BMW will bear down on you out of nowhere, lights flashing furiously, and travel within inches of your rear bumper until you get back to where you belong. On B roads outside of built-up areas there are **speed limits** of 80–100kph. In towns the limit is 50kph, and these rules are dutifully adhered to.

If you have an **accident** in Germany you must wait until the police arrive. Failure to do this can result in prosecution. It is not enough simply to swap insurance details. If your car **breaks down**, then you should move it to the side of the road and place a warning triangle a few metres behind it. The German motoring organization, the **ADAC**, will give you free help (and sometimes even repair your car) if you break down on a main road. However, you will have to pay for parts and towing. You can call the ADAC on orange emergency telephones by asking for *Strassenwachthilfe*, or by telephoning direct on 19211. If you are a member of the AA or RAC in Britain, you should make enquiries about reciprocal deals before you leave. If you take your car to a garage to be repaired, you are legally required to leave the registration documents with it.

In Germany you **drive on the right** and overtake on the left. As in Britain, cars already travelling around a roundabout have right of way. Be especially careful in cities with trams. **Trams** always have right of way, even crossing roundabouts or junctions. Often they travel up and down the centre of wide roads, but the stops are on the pavement, so tram-users have to cross the flow of traffic to reach the tram. When a tram stops in such places, cars are not allowed to overtake, and must leave access to the doors clear. Often there is a line on the street coincident with the back of the tram to show you where to stop, but sometimes there is no marking at all.

In many of the larger cities and historical towns, the centre is closed to motor traffic. There are usually ample garages and **car parks** around the periphery. These are invariably well signposted, sometimes even with electronic signs telling you how many spaces are left. Park-and-Ride facilities (marked P+R) are usually further out, but with direct public transport connections to the centre. Parking here is cheaper, and may be free. Street parking is either metered or works on the 'pay and display' system (you put your money in a central machine and leave the ticket it prints out on the inside of your windscreen). Sometimes parking is free, but subject to a time limit. This is indicated by a blue P sign with a dial underneath. Here you should leave an indication on the dashboard of when you arrived (you can buy cardboard clocks that do this at petrol stations).

The major **car hire** firms—Avis, Budget and Hertz—have branches all over Bavaria. It is cheaper to book a car in advance from an office in your home country than to rent it in Germany, though local firms may offer rates that undercut the big names.

Perhaps the cheapest way of all to get around Bavaria is by making use of the *Mitfahrzentralen*—lift agencies. For a small fee the agency will put you in touch with a motorist driving to your destination. After that all you pay is a contribution to the petrol costs. (This is also a way of cutting costs for the motorist.) Usually the *Mitfahrzentrale* recommends a price—a fraction of the cost of any other means of travel. Drivers have to leave their address and registration number at the *Mitfahrzentrale*, and you usually meet at the agency itself, so the system is quite safe.

By Bus

There is no national German bus network—there is little need for one with such an efficient rail service. German Rail itself runs buses to many areas not served by trains (train tickets and rail passes are valid on these routes). Otherwise local buses can be useful for visiting more out-of-the-way sights and travelling between villages. Such long distance coaches that do exist are usually privately run and aimed at the tourist market (such as the one from Frankfurt to Munich, which travels along the Romantic Road with sightseeing stops along the way, *see* p.142).

By Air

Lufthansa offers a good internal service between major German cities, but flights are expensive (for example Berlin–Munich one way £162.40, return £212.00). Student discounts apply only to people living and studying in Germany. If you buy all your tickets before you leave, you can often get a cheaper rate, but have to stick with the dates you have chosen.

By Boat

Much of Bavaria can be visited by boat, and several of the trips are among the most romantic river journeys in Bavaria. Local cruise liners and ferries make a slow but delightful travel alternative, and sometimes afford the best views of all. Particularly recommended is the route along the easternmost stretch of the Danube (p.200) and along the Altmühl valley (p.105).

Bicycling and Hiking

The Bavarians are enthusiastic walkers and cyclists, and both activities are well catered for. Often a bike is by far the most sensible, convenient and economical means of transport in a town. Most towns, especially in the west, have well-laid-out **cycle paths**, which makes getting around easy and safe. You will also find cycle paths alongside regional roads and criss-crossing the countryside between villages. In cities the pavement is often divided into two, with the cyclists' part marked by paving stones of a different shape or colour. Pedestrians should remain on their half, or risk being mown down by a mountain bike.

If you have a valid train ticket, you can **hire bicycles** from most rail stations for only DM10 a day (ask at the left luggage counter). German Rail Pass holders get a further 50 per cent discount. In rural areas you are sometimes even allowed to take the bike on to the next station and leave it there. Commercial bicycle hire firms are listed under the separate 'Getting Around' sections for each city—or you'll find them in the phone book under *Fahrradverleih*. (Most of these require your passport or around DM50 as a deposit.) To take your **bicycle on a train** you will have to buy a ticket for it (*Fahrradkarte*) and put it in the luggage van yourself. (InterCity and EuroCity trains and some local trains don't allow bicycles, so it is always a good idea to check first.) A number of firms offer **organized bicycling holidays** (transporting your luggage to the next inn for you). One of the friendliest and best organized of these is the British-based Bents Bicycle Tours (The Priory, High Street, Redbourn, Herts AL3 7LZ, ℡ (01582) 793 249), which specializes in Bavarian tours.

Country areas are webbed with well-marked **hiking trails**. Few of them are very arduous, and over weekends and holidays they swarm with healthy marchers (many of whom really *do* wear knee-breeches and bright woollen socks). Even the longer trails are liberally punctuated by shelters, villages and inns, so there is rarely any danger of starving, or of dying a lonely death on a mountainside. Nevertheless it is a good idea to carry an adequate **map** (the local tourist office can generally oblige), as signposting sometimes isn't clear.

Trams and **buses** make up the backbone of public transport in many Bavarian cities. When you have the choice, you'll find trams the quicker and more frequent of the two. Munich has an **U-Bahn** (*Untergrundbahn*, underground railway) which also runs overground, while an **S-Bahn** (*Stadtbahn*, town railway) is a suburban railway.

Tickets are usually dispensed by automatic machines at stations and stops and are valid on all forms of public transport (subject to zone restrictions). Rail Passes and Deutsche Bundesbahn (DB) tickets are valid on the S-Bahn but on none of the others. In some cities tobacconists and newsagents also sell tickets. Single journeys can be expensive, but a day pass (*Tageskarte* or *24-Stunden-Karte*), which offers unlimited travel on whatever the city has to offer, is always good value. Keep an eye open also for special deals over weekends and for families. Whatever form of ticket you buy, you must validate it, before or as you board, by sticking it in the franking machines on trams and buses and at the entrance to station platforms.

Travellers with Disabilities

Travellers with disabilities will find themselves well catered for in Bavaria. Buses can be a problem, but many of the newer trams have low steps to assist people of limited mobility. Rail stations that are not fully converted for wheelchairs have eagle-eyed attendants waiting to help. (If you find you do need assistance, look out for someone with a *Bahnhofsmission* armband.)

In Germany the **Touristik Union International** (TUI, Postfach 610280, D–30602 Hannover, ✆ (0511) 5670) has a list of hotels with facilities that cater for special needs. The list ranges from the humblest pensions to the poshest Grand Hotels. The organization also provides advice and assistance on travelling in Germany. When cities offer special facilities for the disabled they have been listed here under the relevant 'Tourist Information' or 'Getting Around' sections. Otherwise look in the phone book under *Behinderter* (Disabled). In Britain you can get advice, and information on specialized holidays, from RADAR (25 Mortimer Street, London W1M 8AB, ✆ (0171) 637 5400).

Practical A–Z

Addresses

In Germany the street name is written before the number. *Straße* (street, abbreviated to Str.) is joined on to it, unless the name is an adjective (usually a town name ending in *er*), hence Fauststraße, but Berliner Straße. Other common terms are *Platz* (square), *Gasse* (alley), *Ufer* (quay/bank) and *Ring* (ring road). Politicians, dead or alive, make favourite street names, as do other towns (don't be surprised to find a Berliner Straße tucked away in some corner of Bavaria.

Business Travel

Bavaria is the largest *Land* in Germany, a showcase of post-war Teutonic prosperity. Bavarian industry employs over 5.6 million people or 20 per cent of Germany's total workforce. There are two international airports (Munich and Nuremberg) and a large and efficient public transportation network, both on the road and on rail. Its wide variety of success stories include Mercedes-Benz, Audi, Siemens, and recent ventures into high-tech manufacturing. The dynamic economic backdrop and beautiful scenery make Bavaria a popular conference destination. There are around 95 existing convention and conference sites, ranging from modestly priced, no-frills hotels to major, full-service convention centres. Planners can call on the free resources of the branches of the **German Convention Bureau** in Frankfurt (Lufthansa-Basis/Gebäude 303, D–60546 Frankfurt/M, ✆ (069) 695 1092/1093, ✉ (069) 695 1192) and New York (1640 Hempstead Turnpike, East Meadow, NY 11554, ✆ (516) 7941632, ✉ (516) 7948487).

Children

The Germans are the first to talk anxiously about the nation's *Kinderfeindlichkeit* (antipathy to children). In public, children are generally well disciplined—all part of civic duty, reinforced by public notices addressed to parents to remind them of their responsibilities. A rabble of noisy foreign brats will be looked on very coolly indeed.

Before unification West Germany had the lowest birthrate in Europe and was in many respects a very adult-orientated society. Bavaria, too, followed this pattern. (The situation was always rather different in the East, where people married young, had large families and access to free crèche facilities.)

That said, it is easier to find somewhere to eat and drink as a family in Bavaria than it is, for example, in Britain, where attitudes to children are supposed to be more sympathetic. Children, accompanied by adults, are welcome in inns and cafés. Many city museums (especially scientific or technological ones) are especially aimed at younger visitors, with lots of hands-on exhibits and displays.

Climate and Packing

Bavaria is in the Central European Temperate Zone, but that does not mean that it has a uniform climate. In fact there is a considerable climatic difference between regions. The south has cold but bracing winters. In the north the winters are damp and soggy.

Spring comes to Lindau on Lake Constance at the beginning of May, a good six weeks earlier than to the heart of the Allgäu Alps, just a few kilometres away. Around this time you can still ski in the Alps, then nip down to Lake Constance for an invigorating first swim of the season. However, a good summer can seem positively Mediterranean, with long scorching days and sultry nights throughout Bavaria. Misty autumn is the perfect time to visit forest areas, which dissolve into shades of gold, and wine-growing regions, where you can soak in the infectious energy of the harvest, then sit in warm taverns drinking the cloudy, newly fermented grape juice.

					Temperature Chart in °C			
Munich	**January**		**April**		**July**		**October**	
	max	min	max	min	max	min	max	min
	2	−5	13	3	23	2	17	9

If you are travelling around the region it is a good idea to pack your winter woollies as well as your summer cottons and silks at most times of the year. Take an umbrella, too. Rain falls throughout the year. In summer especially there may be sudden storms.

Business **dress codes**, especially at a senior level, tend to be conservative, with dark suits the norm for men and neatly tailored clothes preferred by women. Some very exclusive restaurants demand a collar and tie, but otherwise dress in restaurants tends to be informal but smart. New clothes are one of the ways in which West Germans in particular display their wealth, and your favourite old coat or faded cotton shirt may leave you feeling distinctly out of place.

It is also a good idea to pack a few **books**. German bookshops in larger cities do carry a range of English titles, but they tend to be very expensive. You may also need adaptors or **special plugs** for electrical equipment (*see* 'Electricity' below). Throw in a box of **aspirins**, too. In Germany you can only buy them in pharmacies, at about four times what they would cost at home.

Crime and the Police

See also 'Emergency Numbers' below.

Bavaria does not have a particularly bad crime problem. Provided you take the normal precautions (lock your car, hang on to your handbag, don't keep your wallet in your back pocket, and avoid dodgy areas at night), you shouldn't be troubled by petty theft. If you are robbed, then report the incident to the **police** immediately. This will plummet you into the usual morass of bureaucracy, but is essential if you are going to make any insurance claims.

You are required to have some form of **identification** with you at all times (preferably a passport). If you are found to be without one, you may be subject to prosecution.

If you end up on the wrong side of the law, get in touch with your consulate at once—

though you are unlikely to receive much sympathy in drug-related offences. The possession of any **illegal drugs** is a punishable offence, for which the penalty is a prison sentence or deportation.

Electricity

The supply in Germany is 220 volts, so all UK appliances (which require 240 volts) will work. American equipment will need a transformer. The plugs are the two-pronged kind, standard in much of Continental Europe. Adaptors are available from electrical suppliers in Germany and can also be found in travel and specialist electrical shops outside Germany.

Embassies and Consulates

Bonn

Australia: Godesberger Allee 119, Bad Godesberg, ✆ (0228) 81030.
UK: Friedrich-Ebert-Allee 51, ✆ (0228) 234 061.
Canada: Friedrich-Wilhelm-Str. 18, ✆ (0228) 231 061.
New Zealand: Bonn-Center, ✆ (0228) 214 021.
USA: Deichmanns Ave 29, Bad Godesberg, ✆ (0228) 3391.

Munich

UK: Bürkleinstr. 10, ✆ (089) 211 090.
USA: Königinstr. 5, ✆ (089) 28880.
Canada: Tal 29, ✆ (089) 222 661.

Emergency Numbers

You can reach the **police** by dialling **110**; for an **ambulance**, or the **fire brigade**, call **112**. Other emergency numbers are listed under the separate city entries.

Etiquette

Germany is still a very formal society, especially in the world of business. Work colleagues—even of the younger generation—still tend to use *Herr* (Mr) and *Frau* (Mrs/Ms) instead of first names, and often use the formal *Sie* rather than *du* form of 'you'. This can be the case even among people who have worked in the same office for decades. Leaping the chasm between *Sie* and *du* is a tricky exercise, even for Germans themselves. Generally the rule is always to use *Sie* with a stranger or new acquaintance, until you mutually agree not to. The older or more senior person will suggest this first. The transition is often made quite formally—and is sometimes even marked with a toast. Younger people meeting in informal situations—such as bars or discos—usually use *du*, but the borders can be hazy.

If someone has a title, use it when addressing him or her: *Herr Professor*, *Frau Doktor*, for example. Women get lumbered with their husband's title as well. Gone are the days when you would even call your baker *Herr Bäcker*—though you will still hear older people summoning a waiter with *Herr Ober!* (Mr waiter).

Festivals and Events

The Bavarian calendar is crammed with festivals, from the formal national and religious holidays to riotous local romps, usually with pagan roots. Local festivals are listed under the towns where they occur, but here is an overview.

Date	Place	Event
February (lead-up to Shrove Tues)	All round the region, particularly Munich, Bavarian Swabia, Franconia	Fasching (Shrovetide carnival)
Sundays between Easter and September	Rothenburg	Shepherds' Dance
Whit weekend	Rothenburg	Mayor's wine-quaffing and fancy-dress
Corpus Christi	All round the region	Street processions
May/June	Region-wide	Spring/summer festivals
June/July (1996, 1999)	Landshut	Landshut Wedding
Aug/Sept/Oct	Wine-growing regions	Summer and harvest festivals
Sept/Oct	Munich	*Oktoberfest*
Advent	Region-wide (especially Nuremberg, Munich, Rothenburg)	Christmas markets

The most important festival across the country is **Christmas**, a time of candle-light and gingerbread, relaxed chats over *Glühwein* around the fire and magical Christmas markets. Christmas decorations are less tacky, and festivities less forced, than in most parts of the English-speaking world. **Fasching** is essentially a southern, Roman Catholic form of carnival, but it is beginning to catch on in the Protestant areas of Franconia as well. Although the main events take place over the weekend and week leading up to Shrove Tuesday, celebrations may be set in motion as early as January. Festivities include costume parades, feasts, and general clowning about and hilarity.

The Bavarian Olympics

This is Bavaria's equivalent of Scotland's Highland Games. Unlike its Gaelic counterpart, however, no fixed venue has yet been established, and the competitors traipse all over Upper Bavaria to take part in the various rounds. Throughout the summer you can watch beery men dust off their old *Lederhosen* and impress spectators with fierce contests of finger-wrestling, tree-stump-sawing, beer-stein-lifting or snuff-sniffing. All this takes place against a bacchanalian backdrop and to the sounds of many an oompah band. The Bavarian Tourist Board in Munich (Prinzregentenstr. 18/IV, D-80538 München, © (089) 2123970, @ (089) 293582, holds listings of the individual annual competitions.

Food and Drink

Eating is a serious business in Bavaria. There are strong local culinary traditions and tremendous variation between regions. Franconia has one of the best reputations for food of all Germany. People eat out frequently and plentifully, feeding is the focal activity of most fairs, and drinking the *raison d'être* of many festivals.

Basic German cookery is a meat-and-one-veg affair, and in Bavaria the essential pattern is no different. Potatoes and cabbage (the latter boiled, pickled as *Sauerkraut*, or cooked with apples to make *Apfelrotkohl*) are the favourite vegetables. 'Meat' almost invariably means pork. The Germans get through 50kg of it per head each year, and eat every conceivable part of the pig, cooked in all imaginable ways. Nowadays, especially in newer restaurants, the heavy, fatty meat dishes are offered together with a contrasting array of well-prepared fresh salads and a more imaginative selection of vegetables.

Vegetarians will have a difficult time. Pork appears quite without warning—a sausage floating in bean soup, or bacon mixed in with a side-dish of potatoes. Often the only 'vegetarian meal' on the menu involves fish. Until recently 'salads' meant pickles, or meat and tinned vegetables smothered in mayonnaise. (This is still true in some traditional eateries.) In the larger cities you will find specialist vegetarian restaurants, while the mainstream ones will also offer more of a choice to vegetarians. Keep an eye open also for *Reformladen* (**health food shops**), and *Naturcafés*, which sell wholefood (but again not necessarily purely vegetarian fare).

The prospect of such hearty, meat-based grub might be daunting, but Bavarian dishes are often subtle and delicious. Standards are high, and portions generous. ('It looked an infamous mess,' remarked one 18th-century traveller of the meal set before him in Nuremberg, 'but tasted better than passable.')

Soups range from clear broths populated by plump dumplings to purée-thick mixtures of potatoes or beans. An ideal autumnal tummy-warmer is an *Eintopf* (literally: one pot), a cross between a soup and a stew, containing anything the cooks could lay their hands on. (*Eintopf* on the main part of the menu means casserole.) You can have extra sausages chopped into it if you wish. Another favourite, adapted from the Hungarian original, is a thick, peppery *Gulaschsuppe*.

Sausages come in all colours and thicknesses. Most are made with pork. White ones (*Weißwurst*) are popular south of Frankfurt (the River Main is nicknamed the *Weißwurst* equator), and contain veal and brains. Black ones are made with blood. The most popular of all is the *Bratwurst* (literally; grilled sausage, though often it is deep fried), which is served with a bread roll and a dollop of mild mustard. Some of Germany's most celebrated sausages come from Nuremberg, where they are cooked over wood grills. You'll find sausages at fast-food stalls, in beer halls and in taverns. Bavaria even has specialized *Wurstküchen* (sausage kitchens) that can boast Michelin ratings.

Apart from sausages, the most ubiquitous pork dishes are *Schweinshaxen* (huge knuckles of pork that look as if they belong on a medieval banqueting table), and *Schweinebraten* (roast pork, often sprinkled with ground coriander). **Veal**, **chicken** and **game** (especially venison, boar and hare) make their way on to many menus. Venison is often cooked in fruity sauces and served with wild mushrooms, or simmered in a mouthwatering stew. **Goose** and **turkey** are common, even out of the festive season. **Beef** makes its appearance mainly as steak. **Lamb** is more of a rarity, confined mainly to Turkish and Middle Eastern restaurants. Bavaria's lakes provide an abundance of **fish**: the favourites are carp, salmon, trout and perch. Fish is cooked with delicacy and flair, though it is usually more expensive than other items on the menu.

Potato **dumplings** (*Knödel*)—or light, crinkly **noodles** (*Spätzle*) in Bavarian Swabia—come with almost everything. Dumplings may also be made from stale bread (*Semmelknödel*) or with liver (*Leberknödel*). A variation on the stringy noodles is the Swabian *Maultasche*, a sort of giant ravioli.

Desserts are fairly run-of-the-mill, though *Bayerische Creme* (a sweet sauce best served with a tangy mush of various red fruits and berries) makes an invigorating palate cleanser. *Dampfnudeln* (steamed dumpling, smothered in sweet, fruity sauce) is a meal in itself. You can also indulge your sweet tooth by joining in the great pastime of *Kaffee und Kuchen* (coffee and cake)—the German equivalent of English afternoon tea. *Kaffee und Kuchen* can be the end-point of a Sunday afternoon excursion, the excuse for a good gossip in the local café, or a genteel means of whiling away the morning. *Apfelkuchen* (apple pie) is a reliable standard and *Hefeteignudeln* or *Ausgezogne* (sweetened yeast pastries) can be found all over the region—but you are more likely to be tempted by the splendid, calorie-charged creations of a local baker supremo.

Meals

Breakfast, in all but the stingiest of hotels, involves coffee and fruit juice, cold meats, cheeses (including *Quark*—curd cheese a little like yoghurt), jams, fruit and a bewildering variety of **breads**. German bread is one of the great pluses of the cuisine. Even small local bakeries are cornucopias of thirty or so different varieties—ranging from damp, heavy *Schwarzbrot* (black bread) and healthy granary loaves to crusty white rolls. The famous *Pumpernickel*—a rich, black rye bread—is by no means the only *Schwarzbrot*. You can get variations with hazelnuts and all sorts of other additions. Brown breads can be made with combinations of three, four or six different types of grain, and are often pepped up by the addition of sunflower seeds, onion or spices. A sandwich made with a good, grainy brown loaf can keep you going all day.

Lunch is still the main meal of the day for most Bavarian families (though this doesn't preclude eating out in restaurants at night). The **evening meal** usually takes the form of a light supper (*Abendbrot*), similar in style to breakfast but with the addition of salads and sometimes a soup. Late afternoon or evening entertaining may take place over cakes and wine.

For a quick snack or take-away there is the ubiquitous **Imbiß**. There are two main categories of *Imbiß*: traditional (mainly sausages), and foreign (mainly Turkish doner kebabs or Italian pizzas)—though sometimes there are inspired regional variations, such as stalls serving fried forest mushrooms or delicate noodle dishes. In an *Imbiß* you usually order at the counter, pay on delivery and eat standing up, or at one of a scattering of plastic tables. Sausages, hamburgers and meatballs are the usual fare, though some *Imbisse* are more sophisticated and offer modest meals. *Halbes Hähnchen* (spit-roast chicken, unceremoniously hacked in two) is usually good value at around DM4.

Another place for a quick lunch or snack is the **Stehcafé** (literally: standing café). These are usually attached to bakeries or butchers, or found in stations or busy shopping areas. You buy your food at the counter then devour it standing up at elbow-high tables nearby. It is perfectly acceptable behaviour to get your bread roll at one shop, your cream cake at another and polish them off in a third which sells coffee. Often a number of establishments will share a group of tables so you can do just that.

At the other end of the scale are classy **restaurants**, good enough to rival any in the world. Often, though, you end up paying well over the odds for food that isn't particularly special. Bavarians seem best at cooking variations of their own cuisine, rather than imitating others. Recently, though, a **New German Cuisine** has emerged. This blends traditional ingredients and techniques with a lighter, French-influenced approach—subtle sauces and imaginative combinations of flavours—with delicious results.

For a tasty, good-value meal by far the best option is to head for a *Gaststätte*, *Gasthaus*, *Brauhaus* or *Wirtschaft*—inns that serve *gutbürgerliche Küche* (good solid cooking). Standards are higher than you would expect in similar establishments in Britain or the USA: food is often simple, portions are generous and you will rarely eat a bad meal.

You can join in the ritual of *Kaffee und Kuchen* in a **café** or **Konditorei** (cake shop)— some are quite trendy, others the realm of redoubtable old ladies in severe hats. A *Konditorei* will usually have a better selection of cakes, and often hand-made chocolates too. The usual practice is to choose your cake at the counter, tell the attendant, then order your coffee from the waitress at your table. She will then bring everything together.

Restaurant and bistro prices given in this guide are for a three-course meal for one with a glass of wine.

expensive	over DM65
moderate	DM20–65
inexpensive	under DM20

In cafés and inns most main dishes (often with vegetables or salad) are around DM10. In general, prices are reasonable by European standards.

Drinking

The distinction between restaurants and bars is less rigidly drawn in Germany than in most English-speaking countries. At a **café**, **Weinstube** (wine bar) or **Bierstube**, you can also usually get good, freshly cooked food. Nobody complains, though, if you want only a beer or a cup of tea.

Bars that are mainly for drinking are called **Bierkeller** or **Bierstadel**. Even here, people seldom stand and drink, as they do in an English pub. If there is no table free, it is perfectly acceptable to join a table of strangers. You might even end up chatting to each other for the rest of the evening. Regulars will have a private table—a *Stammtisch*—in one corner of the pub. Sometimes this is marked by a small sign. Even if it isn't, you'll soon be told if you sit at the *Stammtisch* by mistake.

beer

Germany's annual beer consumption averages 150 litres a head for every man, woman and child in the country (more than their consumption of milk, wine and soft drinks together). Tourists do their bit to add to the statistics, but there can be little doubt that beer is Germany's favourite drink. The nation has over a third of the world's breweries — more than half of them in Bavaria. The beer-drinking reputation of Bavaria is enhanced by the massive Munich Oktoberfest, but this is by no means the only big beer-drinking beano: there are spring and autumn beer festivals in virtually every town in Bavaria. Even in the wine-producing northern part of Bavaria beer is seen not as just a drink, but as part of the German way of life—with all the associated tradition. Beer and *Abendbrot* (snacks) is an evening pastime and it is still common to see colourful horse-drawn dray-carts delivering wooden barrels of beer to pubs around town.

There is a distinct genre of German painting devoted to portraying people drinking beer—from impressionist studies of ladies sipping out of small glasses under chestnut trees, through jolly tavern scenes to the pictures of fat, greedy-eyed monks with foaming tankards by the painter Eduard Grützner (1846–1925). Beer-drinking paraphernalia, such as the carved and painted stone beermugs with pewter lids, make valued collectors' items.

Controversies centred on beer can incite fervent passion. In the 19th century rioters stormed and sacked breweries in Munich when the government tried to raise a tax on beer. Today even the most devoted European federalist will bridle if you mention the *Reinheitsgebot* (Purity Law), legislation which dates back to 1516, but which was first put forward in Bavaria as early as 1487. Its strict regulation of standards of beer production (which preclude the use of any chemicals) were rigidly adhered to for centuries, but recently EU bureaucrats ruled that the law amounted to an illegal restriction on trade. Beer from other countries is full of preservatives—foam stabilizers, enzymes, and additives such as formalin and tannin—and so could not be imported to Germany. The German government was forced to back down, but feeling still runs high. Over 95 per cent of the populace believed that the *Reinheitsgebot* should have been maintained—and all Bavarian breweries still obey its strictures.

Much of the beer brewed in Bavaria is aimed primarily at the home market. Sampling a region's, or a town's, beer is as crucial a part of a visit as tasting the local cuisine. Many towns have excellent local breweries, with a **Brauhaus** (drinking tavern) on the premises—often a good place for a hearty meal and rousing evening. Bamberg is known for a smoky beer that gets its taste from beechwood burned during the brewing process. In

Neustadt (near Coburg) the beer also gets a fine, smoky flavour after hot stones are plunged into the brew to caramelize the malt. Munich is one of the top European beer-producing cities. It offers a wide range of brews from light lagers to various *Bocks*, the strongest beer type. Kulmbach (near Bayreuth) comes up with the strongest beer in the world, at 22 per cent proof.

Beer in Bavaria is either bottom-fermented (the process most common in other countries, whereby beer is made with yeast that has sunk to the bottom of the fermentation tank) or top-fermented (an age-old process, recently revived, made with yeast from the top of the tank). Top-fermented beer tends to have more body, and be more characterful than beer made by the easier, more modern method—though *Pils*, a bottom-fermented beer high in hop content, is the most popular brew.

Beer is usually served in a *Maß*—a challenging litre-tankard. Whether you are gulping down a *Maß* in a rowdy beer tent, or sipping it in a smoky cellar, or drinking alongside the huge copper vats in a local *Brauerei*, or sailing down the River Isar propped up against your own barrel (a popular Bavarian springtime activity, *see* p.28), your encounters with beer in Germany may well number among the most memorable moments of your visit.

wine

Don't be put off by the sickly sweet German wines that are generally offered in Britain or the United States. Many German wines are dry and delicious. The same applies to the wines of Bavaria, which because of climatic conditions are produced mainly in Franconia, in a small but outstanding belt of land that runs between Frankfurt (in Hesse) and Nuremberg. The leading grape in Bavaria is Müller-Thurgau, alas, which all too often produces bland wines. Traminer, however, makes a tangy, spicy wine, while Silvaner is milder and more full-bodied. The fruity Bacchus and Scheurebe are other varieties worth looking out for. Whites feature more strongly than reds because red-wine grapes don't ripen easily in northern climates. All Franconian varieties are sold in traditional flagon-shaped bottles called *Bocksbeutel.*

Tafelwein is basic plonk, **Landwein** is just a step up from that (like the French *vin de pays*). Better quality wines are labelled **Qualitätswein**, and *really* good wines will have an additional *Prädikat* or *Kabinett* (grower's reserve) on the label. Better quality wines may also be labelled according to the timing and manner of the harvest. *Spätlese* (late-picked) wines are full and juicy, while for *Auslese* (specially selected) brands the grapes are picked separately to produce a rich, ripe, honey-sweet nectar. (Wines are discussed in more detail in the section on Franconia.) In addition to bottled wine, restaurants often sell half- and quarter-litre carafes of a wide selection of wines—not just the house plonk. It is also acceptable practice for people eating together to order their own glasses or mini-carafes to go with a meal. In summer many prefer a refreshing *Schorle*—wine with mineral water or soda.

warmth and spirit

Even in the humblest *Imbiß* **coffee** is likely to be freshly brewed and filtered. Cafés and restaurants will also offer espresso and cappuccino. **Tea** is usually taken black. Herb and fruit teas are becoming popular, and some cafés have long tea 'menus'.

In the winter, street-side stalls pop up selling *Glühwein* (hot, spicy mulled wine) and *Feuerbohle* (a similar brew that has had a rum-soaked sugar cone melted over it). Common **spirits** include **Schnapps** (often drunk with beer as a chaser). There is also a wide range of sticky, fruity liqueurs, such as *Obstler* and the gentian-based *Enzian*.

The Gay Scene

Conservative Roman Catholic Bavaria has somewhat mixed feelings towards the gay scene (in German the word for gay is *schwul*). The main centre of gay and lesbian life is Munich, where the atmosphere is busy and friendly. Elsewhere, especially in rural areas, public attitudes can be intolerant. A recent law in Bavaria introduced mandatory AIDS testing for people 'suspected of being HIV positive'.

The international publication *Spartacus* (available in gay bookstores) lists clubs and discos in Bavarian cities, or you could buy the glossy German magazine *Männer* (available in pubs and some bookstores). These publications are aimed mainly at gay men, though they contain information relevant to lesbians too. Germany's main lesbian magazine is the *UKZ-Unsere Zeitung*.

Munich: Sub Info Laden, Müllerstr. 38, ✆ (089) 260 3056.

Berlin: Bundesverband Homosexualität, ✆ (030) 581 8306 (central gay organization). **Deutsche AIDS-Hilfe**, Dieffenbachstr. 33, D–10967, ✆ (030) 690 0870.

Geography

The Free State of Bavaria (*Bayern*) is the largest *Land* in the Federal Republic of Germany and comprises seven administrative districts: Upper Bavaria (*Oberbayern*), Lower Bavaria (*Niederbayern*), Swabia (*Schwaben*), Upper Palatinate (*Oberpfalz*), Upper Franconia (*Oberfranken*), Central Franconia (*Mittelfranken*) and Lower Franconia (*Unterfranken*). Together they cover 70,532 sq km. The state borders on the German *Länder* of Baden-Württemberg to the west, Hesse to the northwest and Thuringia and Saxony to the north, and has international borders with the Czech Republic in the east and Austria in the south.

The landscape of the northern part of Bavaria consists primarily of extensive plains and ranges of hills. The ridge of high ground that delineates Franconia drops away gently away into the Danube depression and the flat landscape that skirts the Alpine foothills, then rises suddenly and dramatically into the towering Alps of the south. There are some notable forested mountain ranges along the way, such as the Franconian Forest, the Upper Palatinate Forest and the Bavarian Forest. Vigorous rivers criss-cross the countryside. The Inn and Isar flow northeast from the Alps and stream into the Danube, which sweeps from west to east across the middle part of the state. In the north, the Main winds its way westwards through Franconia.

Munich is the biggest city, with a population of 1.2 million. Then comes Nuremberg (493,000), Augsburg (255,000), Würzburg (127,000) and a host of other cities with populations of 80,000–120,000—11 million people in total.

Insurance and Medical Matters

EU nationals are entitled to free medical care in Germany—but you must carry a form **E111** (fill in application form SA30, available from DSS branches or post offices). Theoretically you should organize this two weeks before you leave, though you can usually do it over the counter in one visit. Citizens of other countries have no such privileges, and the E111 does not insure personal belongings. For these reasons, all travellers are advised to take out some form of **travel insurance**. Consult your insurance broker or travel agent, and shop around for a good deal. Also check out any existing policies you have, as you might already be covered for holidays abroad. Many travel insurance packages include not only medical cover, but lost luggage, theft and ticket cancellation. If you do suffer any of these misfortunes, check the small print for what documentation—police reports, medical forms or receipts—you require to make a claim.

You get prescription drugs from an *Apotheke*. A list of duty emergency pharmacies, which stay open after normal working hours, is posted on the door of all *Apotheken*. Even emergency pharmacies may look closed; ring the doorbell and the pharmacist will emerge from an inner recess and serve you through a hatch in the glass.

The Germans are a litigious bunch, and losers in court have to pay the opponent's **legal costs** as well. If you are involved in a motor accident, scratch somebody's car with your shopping trolley or knock over something in a shop, you could find yourself involved in a costly court action. If you are staying in Germany for any length of time, or doing much bicycling, it is a good idea to take out **personal liability insurance** (*Haftpflichtversicherung*). In Germany nearly everybody does this, and policies are cheap (around DM70 a year). Most travel insurance also includes cover for third-party liabilities.

Laundry

Most hotels provide efficient, if pricey, laundry services. Launderettes/laundromats (*Wäscherei*), however, are a rarity, even in the biggest cities. Over 80 per cent of Germans have their own washing machine. When you do find a launderette (try the Yellow Pages under *Wäscherei*), a single load will cost you around DM7. Dryers will cost at least another DM4. **Drycleaners** are more plentiful, but also expensive. Look out for signs advertising *Reinigung* (literally: cleaning).

Living and Working in Germany

If you intend to stay for longer than 90 days, you should visit the local *Einwohnermeldeamt* (registration office) to register your address. You will also need to show proof of some income (non-EU nationals must have a job *before* they come into the country) in order to get a **residence permit** and a **work permit**. Set aside a good two days and take some Valium. You are likely to be shuffled between at least three different offices at opposite ends of town, and will experience grinding German bureaucracy at its most Kafkaesque. Be prepared to wait for hours in a queue simply to be handed a form to fill in (three minutes' work), then shunted to the back of the queue in order to hand your form in again. Anything slightly out of the ordinary in your story will have you tangled up in this process indefinitely. Come with every possible personal document you can lay your hands on. The only way to survive the ordeal is to beat them at their own game.

Accommodation in Bavaria is at a premium, especially in lower rent-brackets. Even in provincial towns apartments can be very hard to come by. A *Mitwohnzentrale* can arrange medium-term lets, or find you room in shared accommodation until you find your feet, but be prepared to pay over the odds.

The **Goethe Institute**, which exists to promote German culture, offers reasonably priced language courses, usually of a high standard. There are branches in Bavaria as well as in most major cities around the world.

Maps

The ADAC offer excellent route maps (free to members and at a minimal charge to others). They also publish a simplified tourist map of Bavaria. This shows only motorways and main roads, but gives information (in German) on the interesting towns. Far more useful is the detailed 37-part **Generalkarte** series—clear, individual maps covering the whole of Germany in sections and printed in great detail. The handiest and most up-to-date city maps are published by Falk.

If you want to buy a map before you leave, look for one published by Falk, RV, or Kümmerly und Frey. In Britain, Stanfords (12–14 Long Acre, London WC2 9LP, ✆ (0171) 836 1321) has the best selection. In the US try the Complete Traveler (199 Madison Ave, New York, NY10016, ✆ (0212) 685 9007). The best source of **specialist hiking and cycling maps** is the tourist office in the relevant region.

Media

Newspapers in Germany tend to be regional rather than national, in focus and distribution. The main respectable exception is the Munich-based *Süddeutsche Zeitung*, which is read all over Germany, as are the *Frankfurter Allgemeine Zeitung* (popular with the business community), its liberal counterpart the *Frankfurter Rundschau*, and the left-wing Berlin paper, the *Tageszeitung*, known as the *Taz*. The best-selling papers are the right-wing *Die Welt* and the notorious, sleazy, sensationalist *Bild Zeitung*—both products of the publishing empire of the late Axel Springer. The three most prominent **magazines** are the leftish *Der Spiegel*, the recently founded Munich-based *Focus* and the right-of-centre weekly *Die Zeit*, all of which include serious and informative reportage. The once fairly respectable *Stern* has never recovered from the humiliation of publishing (as genuine) the forged Hitler diaries a few years ago, and has now joined the ranks of the populist press. In most cities and larger towns, leading **British and American newspapers** are on sale on the day of publication. Railway station newsagents are the surest places to find them.

There are two main national **television** channels—*ARD* and *ZDF*—as well as a host of regional stations and satellite channels, but there is little on any of them to warrant staying in at night. A more informative alternative is **BBC Radio**. You can get the World Service on 604 kHz MW and on 90.2 FM in the Munich area, and Radio 4 on 198 LW.

Money and Banks

> *The Reichs Doller of Germany is worth foure shillings foure pence, and the silver Gulden is accounted three shillings and foure pence English. Twenty Misen silver Groshes, 32 Lubecke shillings, 45 Embden stivers, foure Copstocks and a halfe, 55 groates, 36 Maria grosh, 18 spitz-grosh, 18 Batz, make a Reichs Doller. Two seslings make a Lubecke shilling: foure Drier a silver grosh: two dreyhellers a Drier: two schwerd grosh a schneberger: foure creitzers a batz: foure pfennig a creitzer.*

A travel guide of 1617

Today things are a touch simpler. There are 100 Pfennigs to a Deutschmark (DM), and the currency is valid over the whole country, east and west. At the time of writing there are about 2.5 DM to the pound and roughly 1.6 DM to the US dollar.

Germany is very much a cash society. **Eurocheques** are sometimes used in place of cash and some hotels only accept Eurocheques and cash. You cannot take it for granted that restaurants and shops (especially those not on the tourist circuit) will accept **credit cards**: many don't. However, petrol stations, larger hotels and upmarket restaurants will take plastic. **Travellers' cheques** in dollars, sterling or marks are the safest way to carry around your money; banks will give you the best rates for changing them into cash.

Banks are generally open Mon–Fri 9–12.30 and 1.30–3.30. On Thursdays some remain open until 6pm, but all are shut on Saturdays and Sundays. Banks with extended hours and commercial **Bureaux de Change** can be found near railway stations and airports. 'Hole-in-the-wall' money-changing machines are also beginning to make an appearance. EU card holders can also draw money from machines at banks, provided they know their personal number.

Museums

Bavaria has an extraordinary array of high-quality museums. For centuries Bavaria was a loose amalgamation of independent political entities. Each ruler built up an art collection, and most collections have stayed put, so that even the smaller towns can have museums of a surprisingly high standard. Opening hours vary, but many museums are closed on a Monday. Smaller museums may close for lunch; opening hours in winter may be shorter. In some towns museums stay open until 8pm on a Wednesday or a Thursday night.

Bavaria has three museums that rank among the best in Germany (*see* also 'The Best of Bavaria', inside back cover):

Alte Pinakothek (Munich, pp.76–8): one of the world's great art galleries, with an outstanding collection of German masters.

Germanisches Museum (Nuremberg, pp.217–8): a shrine to the artefacts of German civilization throughout the ages.

Deutsches Museum (Munich, p.79): the country's top technological museum.

Opening Hours: Business and Shopping

Germany has the most irritating and inconvenient shopping hours in Europe. Shops close at 5.30 or 6pm on weekdays and between 12.30 and 1pm on Saturdays. After that you can buy *nothing*, not even in major cities, unless you are prepared to trek to the main railway station or airport where there will be a poorly stocked and over-priced supermarket. Petrol stations also sell a few meagre provisions, though by law they should only serve passing motorists. To make matters worse, staff begin to wind down a full hour before closing time. Meat and fresh produce are packed away early and, just as office workers are tearing into the store for the brief 30 minutes they are allotted to stock up on provisions, the check-out staff pack up and go home, leaving one or two brave souls to cope with queues that snake back through the entire shop.

Saturday mornings are hell. This is the only time that anyone with an office job can do the weekly shopping. You have to fight for a supermarket trolley, bakeries run out by 11am, fruit and vegetables disappear by 12 noon and the same rule of diminishing checkout attendants applies. Saturday afternoons have a depressing, eerie stillness. Everywhere is closed and the populace creeps home to sleep off the horrors of the day. This is not all. Except in the very centre of the largest cities, all shops and businesses take a **lunch hour**. (This includes banks, post offices and even most tourist offices.) Lunch hour is a misnomer. Businesses are closed for 1½–2 hours, sometimes longer. This lunch break may begin at 12, 12.30 or 1pm—so unless you know the exact idiosyncrasies of all the shops you want to go to, you might as well write off the hours of 12–3. You'll find very few shops open before 9 or 9.30 in the morning.

Once a month (usually the first or last Saturday) shopworkers will steel themselves for a *Langer Samstag* (literally: Long Saturday) and bravely work on until around 4pm. Some businesses do this on a Thursday too (*Langer Donnerstag*, when they stay open until 6 or 7pm), but you can never be sure.

Many office workers (especially in the public services) quite officially go home at lunchtime on Fridays. The suggestion of a business appointment for a Friday afternoon is likely to be met with stunned silence. If one of the numerous public holidays falls a day's gap away from the weekend, it is taken as read that the intervening day will be taken off, and that you will go home at lunchtime of the day before the long weekend.

Post and Telephones

Post offices are open Mon–Fri 8–6 and Sat 8/9–12-noon. Some cities have extended or 24-hour services—usually at the post office nearest the station. You can send **telegrams** from a post office or by phoning 1131. Different counters have different functions (look at the sign above the clerk's head), though most sell stamps (*Briefmarken*) and accept parcels

(*Pakete*). You can also change money at a post office. Larger post offices operate a **Poste Restante** service—letters should be clearly marked *Postlagernde Sendungen*.

Most **public telephones** now operate on the **phonecard** system. You can buy a card (*Telefonkarte*) from a post office for DM12 or DM50, and it is a good idea to carry one. Coin-operated phones require a minimum of 30 Pfennigs. **Hotels** charge well over the odds for use of room telephones, but have to advertise the rate on the same card as the room rate (usually pasted on the back of the door). You can **call abroad** from most public telephones, and **receive calls** on those that display a picture of a bell on the booth. If you can't find a call box, try a café—many have telephones with meters for public use, but may charge a little more than the going rate.

> Operator **03**
> Directory enquiries **1188**
> International enquiries **00118**
>
> **International dialling codes**
>
> Britain: **00 44**
> USA and Canada: **00 1**
> Australia: **00 61**
> New Zealand **00 64**

Public Holidays

New Year's Day (*Neujahr*, 1 Jan)
Epiphany (*Heilige Drei Könige*, 6 Jan)
Good Friday (*Karfreitag*, changes annually)
Easter Monday (*Ostermontag*, changes annually)
May Day (*Maifeiertag*, 1 May)
Ascension Day (*Christi Himmelfahrt*, changes annually)
Whit Monday (*Pfingstmontag*, changes annually)
Corpus Christi (*Fronleichnahm*, changes annually)
Feast of the Assumption (*Mariä Himmelfahrt*, 15 Aug)
Day of German Unity (*Tag der Deutschen Einheit*, 3 Oct)
All Saints Day (*Allerheiligen*, 1 Nov)
Day of Prayer and National Repentance (*Buß- und Bettag*, variable date in Nov)
Christmas Day (*Erster Weihnachtstag*, 25 Dec)
Boxing Day (*Zweiter Weihnachtstag*, 26 Dec)

Religious Affairs

There is no state religion in Germany, but, that said, Bavaria is staunchly Roman Catholic. At the latest census 67 per cent of the population registered as Catholic and 27 per cent (mainly in Franconia) as Protestant.

As you are entering a city you will see the times of church services posted on boards beside the road. Bavarians are not particularly avid churchgoers, though in rural Roman Catholic regions the religious festivals are very much part of community life, and are celebrated by everyone. Most Bavarians pay a church tax (an additional 5 per cent of their normal tax bill). This money is used to support various church charities. Payment is not compulsory, but you have to go down to the town hall and 'de-register' yourself if you don't want to pay it, and most people don't bother.

Before the Holocaust there were over 530,000 Jews living in Germany. Today less than 2 per cent of Bavarians live in Jewish communities, mostly in Munich and Nuremberg. There are about 45 Jewish congregations scattered throughout the region. You can get further information from the **Zentralrat der Juden** in Deutschland, Fischerstr. 49, VD–40477 Düsseldorf.

Despite the sizeable Turkish population in Bavaria, there is little evidence of **Muslim** places of worship. Mosques tend to be makeshift affairs in private homes or obscure buildings.

Sports and Activities

There is an old local joke that when two Germans meet they shake hands, when three meet they form a society. This certainly holds true for Bavaria in the field of sport. Every third inhabitant is a member of a **sports club**. Public sports facilities are good—but you are likely to find courts, fields or lanes reserved for organized club activities.

Soccer is by far the most popular sport. The most famous team is Bayern München, though recently München 1860 have been making a mark. Thousands attend matches in season (Bavaria isn't plagued by hooliganism to the extent that the UK is). League matches are usually held on Saturday afternoons, while European Cup games usually take place on Wednesday evenings.

Gymnastics and **tennis** are fairly distant runners-up to soccer in the popularity stakes. But German champions Boris Becker and Steffi Graf are the focus of pop-star-like adulation and have made tennis a very popular spectator sport.

The Bavarians are an outdoor folk. Most towns, even in colder parts of the region, will have a *Freibad* (open-air swimming pool) that opens for the summer months. Many of the rivers, and most of the lakes, are clean enough to swim in and **watersports**—especially windsurfing—are becoming increasingly popular.

Hiking and **cycling** are two great national enthusiasms and are practised with vigour. Marked hiking trails abound, especially in mountain resorts.

Bavaria offers some of the best **skiing** in Germany. The Bavarian Alps offer the best resorts (*see* pp.126–7), but smaller ranges such as the Franconian Forest are also popular (and generally cheaper). The upland areas around Garmisch-Partenkirchen and Berchtesgaden in the Upper Bavarian Alps and Oberstdorf in the Allgäu Alps are punctuated with lifts and runs. High season normally runs from mid-December to mid-January. Local tourist offices provide information on regional skiing and lifts. Ski passes for *Abfahrt* (downhill skiing) are not cheap (DM35–40 per day), but many resorts grant discounts to guests at local hotels and guesthouses. There are graded slopes for skiers of all levels as well as carefully prepared *Loipen* (tracks) for *Langlauf* (cross-country skiing), especially in the region around Berchtesgaden and Oberstdorf.

Rafting: some 22 local operators offer river trips of an unusual kind in Bavaria: on massive log rafts, similar to those used in the Middle Ages. Jaunts range from hair-raising rapid-shooting to more leisurely cruises on 18-log rafts complete with barrels of beer, oompah bands and 60 passengers. The following operators will provide further information.

Hölzl Floßfahrten, Mittenmühlweg 23, D-85049 Ingolstadt, ✆ (0841) 33700.

Isar-Floßfahrt, Kalkofenstr. 14, D-83646 Arzbach, ✆ (08042) 1220.

Students

Bavaria has a thriving university culture, and a significant percentage of its youth in higher education. Most museums, and some theatres and concert halls offer reduced prices on production of a student card. In addition, some universities will allow you to eat in the *Mensa* (student cafeteria)—though it is best to check with the cashier first. (For reduced fares, *see* p.3 and p.7)

Time

In essence Germany's time is GMT plus one hour. However, clocks go an hour forward at the end of March to GMT plus two hours, and back an hour at the end of October.

Tipping

Tips are included in restaurant bills, but it is customary to round up the amount to the nearest Mark, or to the nearest five if the bill is large. Additional tips for exceptionally good service never go amiss. Taxi drivers and hairdressers also expect an extra Mark or two.

Toilets

The availability of public loos varies tremendously from town to town. Some will have just one or two (usually on the market place), others seem to have one on practically every corner. Look out for signs reading WC. *Herren* means Gents, and *Damen* is the Ladies. You are usually expected to pay for the privilege of use—anything from 25 to 80 Pfennigs. It is also possible to use the lavatories in cafés—though in touristy areas the proprietors are sometimes not too keen on this, and it is wise to ask first.

Tourist Information

There is a comprehensive network of tourist offices in Bavaria—even small villages are likely to have one. The most usual locations are in or near the main railway station or on the market square. Ask for the *Verkehrsamt*, or simply Tourist Information, or for the *Kurverwaltung* at spas. Most offer **room reservation** services with local hotels (for a booking fee of around DM3), and can also help you find accommodation in private homes (*see* 'Where to Stay', below). The offices are also well-stocked with brochures and maps, and staff can give you information about local events and guided tours.

For information about Bavaria before you leave, contact one of the branches of the German National Tourist Office:

Australia: Lufthansa House, 12th floor, 143 Macquarie Street, Sydney,
✆ (02) 221 1008.

Britain: Nightingale House, 65 Curzon Street, London W1Y 8NE,
✆ (0891) 600100.

Canada: Place Bonaventure, Montreal, Quebec, H5A 1B8,
✆ (0514) 8778 9885.

USA: 747 Third Avenue West, New York, NY 10017,
✆ (0212) 308 3300.

Where to Stay

Eighteenth-century travellers through southern Germany complained of having to undress in front of the landlord and share their quarters with cows and hogs. A travel guide of the time advised visitors to push furniture against the door at night and to make an extravagant display of their firearms before retiring.

Today, life in Bavaria's inns and hotels could hardly be more different. Standards are uniformly high. You are unlikely to have to share your room with even the most harmless of local fauna, the beds will be spotless and comfortable, and the only accusation you are likely to level would be one of dullness.

German hotels are graded on a scale of nearly 80 classifications, which is ironic as (apart from the luxury end of the market) standards are pretty even. Certainly this makes any corresponding star system out of the question. In the broad bracket of moderate-priced hotels, you will find rustic ones (with wooden beams and folksy knick-knacks), others stuck in a 1970s time warp (decorated in purple, brown and orange) and smart new ones with plastic-coated furniture chosen from a catalogue. An *en suite* bathroom or shower is standard, except at the lower end of the market. You are also likely to find a TV and phone in the room. Service is usually efficient and often friendly.

Most of the hotels mentioned in this book have been chosen because they offer something exceptional—in atmosphere, location or service. Prices are for one night in a double room with bathroom or shower *en suite*, including breakfast. For single rooms, reduce the price by 30 to 40 per cent. It is worth bearing in mind that festivals and trade fairs can double prices and devour available accommodation.

Inexpensive alternatives to hotels are **pensions** (which also keep high standards) and **private rooms**. The latter are a good bet in country areas. Look out for signs advertising *Fremdenzimmer* or *Zimmer frei*. Here you can simply walk up and knock on the door.

Local tourist offices carry lists of private landlords and landladies offering rooms, and the staff can often make a reservation for you.

The first **youth hostel** (*Jugendherberge*) in the world was in Germany, and youth hostels in Bavaria still provide cheap and reliable dormitory accommodation for all people under the age of 27. Most hostels are members of the International Youth Hostel Association, and to use them it is necessary to become a member. You can sign up at the first hostel you visit (you'll need a passport photograph), but it is cheaper to join at a branch of your own national association before leaving home. Many hostels close for the winter months.

For a fraction of the normal cost of an overnight stop (as little as DM30 per person for bed and breakfast) you can take your pick from around 1500 rustic dwellings, which form part of the **farm holidays** scheme. The houses range from the characteristic sloping-rooved farmhouses of traditional Allgäu farms to the tiered farmsteads of the Franconian heights. You'll get a taste of Bavarian farm life, meet local people—and you might even pick up a few tips on Bavarian cooking—but you generally do need to book ahead at the individual farm, and to stay for at least three nights. Detailed brochures on farm holidays (in German only) have been produced for four separate areas (Upper Bavaria, Allgäu, Eastern Bavaria, Franconia) and are available from the German National Tourist Office or the following agency in Germany:

> **Landesverband 'Urlaub auf dem Bauernhof in Bayern' e.V.**, Max-Joseph-Str. 9, D-80333 München, ℂ (089) 55873165, @ (089) 55873505.

Wildlife and Flora

From May to July the Alpine pastures are awash with anemones, cyclamen, rhododendron, gentian, orchids and edelweiss, while in autumn the white limestone rocks of the valleys are offset by the penetrating greens and golden hues of the conifers and shrubs. The pre-Alpine landscape abounds in red deer, hare, martens and polecats, while foxes, chamois bucks and marmots roam the upland plateaux of the Alps. Overhead, you may see various birds of prey, including the rare golden eagle. It should be said, however, that many of these animals are seldom seen from the designated hikers' trails—and gamekeepers and foresters don't encourage you to wander.

History

Beginnings

As with Scotland and Brittany, the first glimmers of a Bavarian history became visible through a Celtic twilight. Celtic tribes first settled the lands that comprise modern Bavaria around 800 BC. By 400 BC the deft iron-workers had become Europe's dominant culture. They left behind some 200 **Keltenschanzen** (barrows) chock-full of fine pottery, gold jewellery and decorated weapons, as well as a string of place and river names still in use today.

By 200 BC **Germanic tribes** migrating south from Jutland and northern Polish regions had come up against **Roman armies** marching north. In 113 BC two of these tribes, the *Cimbrii* and the *Teutones*, had the effrontery to defeat a Roman army in the Alps. In turn, they and their kind were very nearly annihilated by the great Roman general Marius.

The Romans

By 15 BC Roman armies had forced their way into the land between the Alps, Dolomites and the Danube, securing Rome's northern frontier and garnering the riches of Celtic iron and salt mines in the process. They divided the southern part into the provinces of **Raetia** and **Noricum**, but the defeat of two Roman legions by **Arminius**, chief of the *Cheruscii*, in the Teutoburg Forest in AD 9 foiled any more expansionist moves across the Danube. The fortified settlements that the Romans built along the banks of the river behind the ramparts of their imperial border formed the foundation blocks of many a present-day Bavarian town. Augsburg (Augusta Vindelicorum), Kempten (Kambodounon), Regensburg (Radasbona) and Passau (Batavis) were important outposts of the empire, and you can find . Roman ruins throughout the land south of the Danube.

For the next two hundred years the Romans kept an uneasy peace with the tribes across the Danube. It was at this time that the Roman historians **Strabo** and **Tacitus** first began to mention one Germanic tribe, the *Baiuvarii*, establishing for posterity the name of the Bavarians. The Latin *Baiuvarii* probably comes from a Celtic word meaning 'those from Boihaemum', modern-day Bohemia. Recent research suggests that this tribe descended from the Celtic *Boier*. The *Baiuvarii* appear to have belonged to non-Roman Germania, a vague and uncharted territory that covered much of eastern Europe. After about AD 488 and after constant battering, the Roman defences finally gave in, and the *Baiuvarii* swept across the waters from the north and east to establish lands for themselves south of the Danube.

Tribal Duchy

In the chaos of the collapsing Roman Empire the Franks, under King Clovis (*c.* 466–511), emerged as the most powerful tribe in northern Europe. Clovis established the Christian Merovingian dynasty, which ruled over nearly all of France and the Low Countries, as well as most of western and southern Germany, for more than two and a half centuries. The Merovingians claimed the land north of the Danube (roughly approximating to modern-day Franconia) as royal crown land in the early 8th century. South of the Danube they installed the Burgundian Agilolfing family to rule over the mix of invading Germanic tribes and the remaining Celts and Romans. The family stayed from about 555 to 788, establishing their main seat at Regensburg. Later, though, they began to get uppity, befriending the Lombards (in present-day Italy) and Christianizing the Slavs to the south in an attempt to secure their own power base. They failed to establish more than a transitory presence in what is now Austria, but succeeded mightily in displeasing their Merovingian overlords. In AD 788 the last of the Agilolfing dukes, **Tassilo III**, was deposed by Charlemagne and the Bavarian duchy was absorbed into the Carolingian Empire.

Charlemagne's empire collapsed after the death of his successor, Louis the Pious, in AD 840, and was partitioned into three separate kingdoms. Bavaria came under the suzerainty of **Louis the German**, king of the eastern Franks, becoming part of what was later referred to as the **Holy Roman Empire of the German Nations**, though it retained its own dukes. Louis appointed **Luitpold** as Margrave, who founded the **Schyren dynasty** and slowly set about consolidating his power base. But he was unable to check incursions by marauding bands of Slavs. At the **Battle of Pressburg** in AD 907 the Magyars of Hungary inflicted a disastrous defeat on Luitpold, who was slain in the conflict. Two years later, his son **Arnulf** quashed the belligerent eastern tribes and drove them out of the land, but when, in AD 937, he made a bid for his own independence, Emperor Otto I clipped his wings and reduced him to ruling over his ancestral margravate. From then on Bavaria became a battleground for the Welf and Staufian dynasties, reflecting the power games played out by these two rival families elsewhere in Germany. Eventually, in 1158, **Emperor Frederick Barbarossa** gave the duchy to his cousin **Henry the Lion**, the powerful Saxon duke who had founded **Munich** (*see* p.65).

The Wittelsbachs

But Henry the Lion overreached himself, and upset his imperial cousin by refusing to give him military help. Barbarossa retaliated in 1180 by handing Bavaria over to the Count Palatine **Otto of Wittelsbach**, a descendant of the margraves of Schyren. Thus began a dynasty that was to last, unbroken, until 1918. By the time the first Wittelsbach came to power Bavaria covered the lands between the Bohemian Forest in the north, the Rivers Inn and Lech to the east and west, and the Alps to the south. The focus of the Wittelsbach power, however, was their extensive ancestral domains around Kelheim, the home town of the early Wittelsbachs.

The real founder of the dynasty was Otto's son, Duke Ludwig. He took a leading part in the affairs of the Holy Roman Empire, and through some astute politics, inheritance, feudal acquisitions and force extended his domains, especially to the north and east. Towns, monasteries and abbeys, such as Cham, Landau, Landshut and Straubing, founded by Ludwig played an important role in the colonization of the country and soon became centres of cultural life. Duke Ludwig also won control of the Palatinate of the Rhine in 1214, and secured succession to the **County of Bogen** by marrying the widowed countess, adding the white and blue diamonds of its coat of arms to that of his own family (blue and white are still Bavaria's national colours). His bright career came to a rather sudden end in 1231 when he fell victim to a crazed assassin on the bridge at Kelheim. The killer was lynched by incensed members of the duke's entourage and no one thought of questioning his motives. The most likely explanation for the crime is that it was set up by followers of Emperor Frederick II, who feared the duke's growing power.

The affairs of the duchy were quickly put back on the straight and narrow by Ludwig's son, **Otto II** (the Illustrious), who, in an effort to put his father's murder behind him, decided to relocate his residence to the newly founded Landshut. Duke Otto set about expanding his territory even further, though he relied on purchase rather than conquest, picking up small patches of land that were strategically useful to the defence of his expanding borders.

On his death in 1253 the Wittelsbachs fell to bickering over the family fortune. Personal rifts between Otto's sons led to **territorial divisions** that, for the next 250 years, nurtured by family feuds and petty squabbles, sapped the power of the dynasty and all but undid their earlier successes. Initially just the duchies of Upper Bavaria and Straubing went their separate ways. By the late 14th century, however, the family's various branches had fragmented into a cluster of four separate duchies (Landshut, Straubing, Ingolstadt, Munich). The prosperous Landshut branch outshone everyone else in wealth and aspirations. In 1475 they found a way to flaunt their superior status, hosting the extravagant **Landshut Wedding** between Duke Georg and Jadwiga, daughter of the king of Poland.

While the nobles played out their own dynastic struggles, the new merchant class was steadily building up its wealth and power—both in the Franconian towns such as **Nuremberg**, and in towns such as **Augsburg** and **Regenburg** on the busy southern trade routes. The most powerful trading towns became **Free Imperial Cities**, responsible only to the emperor. Outside of these civic strongholds, however, Bavaria was backward, chaotic and violent. Neighbouring states encroached upon its borders, and the lesser nobles fought each other for land and ignored the authority of the dukes. At the time, the **Landtag**, an assembly of representatives from all the land's estates instituted at the beginning of the 14th century, oversaw much of the day-to-day administrative and financial affairs of state. It maintained a veneer of stability in Bavaria and gradually began to acquire political clout.

Consolidation and the Electorate

This state of affairs lasted until 1506, when **Duke Albrecht IV** (the Wise) of the Munich branch of the Wittelsbachs made the first tentative steps to re-establish a unified Bavarian duchy under his rule. Albrecht put the brakes on further fragmentation of territory by introducing a system of inheritance through primogeniture into the Bavarian domains and elevated Munich to his capital. Under his son, **Duke Wilhelm IV**, the **Reformation** began to have an impact on Bavaria, but the Wittelsbachs were fervent Catholics, and under the Dukes Albrecht V and Wilhelm V the **Counter-Reformation** gathered momentum. The religious movement had political consequences as the neighbouring princes of the Palatinate—the Rhineland, Baden, Württemberg and Hesse—somewhat forcefully espoused Protestantism. Despite the **Peace of Augsburg** of 1555, which preached religious tolerance and *cuius regio, eius religio* (that subjects assumed their monarch's faith), Bavaria's Protestants were subjected to increasing persecution. Teaming up with the equally devout Catholic Habsburgs, the Wittelsbach dukes began forcibly to convert Bavaria to Catholicism by pursuing a ruthless crusade against all heretics and purging the land of Protestant communities, save in the Free Imperial city of Regensburg. By 1609 Germany had split into a **Protestant Union** led by the Palatinate and a **Catholic League**, founded by the Wittelsbach **Duke Maximilian I**, which centred on Bavaria. Bigotry and persecution were rife, and by 1618 the situation erupted into one of the most pointless and destructive conflicts Europe has known—the **Thirty Years' War**. France, Spain, Denmark and Sweden were sucked into the fray. For three decades armies plundered and pillaged the land, swapping sides at will and losing any sense of what they were fighting for (apart from self-gain). Whole towns and villages were destroyed, vast areas of land were devastated, millions were slaughtered, trade and agriculture collapsed and famine reduced some people to cannibalism.

Eventually the armies of King Gustav Adolphus of Sweden swept across Bavaria to defeat the notoriously cruel **Johann Tilly**, the reformer of the Bavarian forces and military champion of the Catholic armies. Both Augsburg and Munich were briefly occupied by the Swedes in 1632.

Bavaria needed some 40 years to recover from the social and economic deprivation that the war brought about, but the Wittelsbachs were amply rewarded for their pains. Duke Maximilian had gained the **Upper Palatinate** and was given the hereditary title of **Elector**, putting him on a par with the much older grandees who had formal powers to mint their own coinage, build fortresses, extract tolls and operate their own legislature and judiciary.

The Wittelsbachs now set about the massive task of rebuilding a battered Bavaria, finding in the exuberant, sensuous Baroque style the perfect antidote to sober Protestantism. Towns, castles, churches and monasteries were finally rebuilt, often by the best architects and artists the movement had to offer, such as the virtuoso duos of the Asam and Zimmermann Brothers. The passion for new building reached its zenith during the reign of **Max II Emmanuel**, who cultivated an unbridled Bavarian Baroque.

But once again the Wittelsbachs hawkishly began to eye land other than their own. Neighbouring states began to get twitchy. Splits emerged with Austria, an erstwhile ally, when Bavaria challenged her authority by making claims against Habsburg territories. In 1701 the pugnacious Habsburg Leopold I openly turned against his prosperous northern neighbour and unleashed the **War of the Spanish Succession**, which again brought havoc to the Bavarian lands. In 1704 Prince Eugene of Savoy and the Duke of Marlborough led a coalition of Habsburg and British troops to victory over the French and Bavarians at the **Battle of Blenheim** (for which Marlborough received the Bavarian town of Mindelheim in the Allgäu as a reward). For ten years, despite popular unrest, Bavaria was under the control of the Habsburg Emperors. Another 35 years on and once again the Wittelsbachs found themselves at the receiving end of a devastating war, and again under Austrian occupation. The young, fastidious **Maximilian III Joseph** withdrew from the **War of the Austrian Succession** by making peace with Austria, renouncing many of his hereditary titles, and instead concentrating on vital reforms at home. More of a thinker than a warrior, he set up the Munich-based **Academy for the Arts and Sciences** and oversaw the abolition of the increasingly conniving Jesuit order in Bavaria. It was left to Frederick the Great of Prussia, a brilliant military strategist, to halt Austrian inroads into Bavaria during the 1778 **War of the Bavarian Succession** and ensure the territory of the Wittelsbach Electors.

The Kingdom of Bavaria

Following successive waves of Imperial Austrian and French Revolutionary occupations across the region in the late 1790s, **Elector Maximilian IV Joseph** decided to throw in his lot with Napoleon. He was one of the few princes in Germany to switch his allegiance. Napoleon remembered his friends, and in 1805 Bavaria was doubled in size by the **Treaty of Pressburg**, acquiring, at the expense of Austria, approximately the boundaries it now has. The largest chunks it gained were most of the secular and ecclesiastical principalities of **Franconia** to the north and several **Swabian** territories to the east. (Later, in 1837, the use of Franconia's name was revived by King Ludwig I, who created the provinces of Upper, Middle and Lower Franconia.) The treaty also elevated the Bavarian duchy to the status of a **kingdom**. Although the fledgling monarchy was drawn into Napoleon's expansionist activities, the internal stability it enjoyed under the Emperor's wing proved good ground for laying the foundations of a **modern state**: by 1808 serfdom was abolished, universal taxation and equality before law were established; municipal governments were strengthened and the secularization of various monasteries was pushed forward regardless of the vigorous objections of Bavaria's Church establishment.

However, after some 30,000 troops from Bavaria were casualties of Napoleon's futile Russian campaign, **King Maximilian I** once again changed the course of his foreign policy and between 1813 and 1815 became an ally of the **Germanic Confederation**. This switch ensured that Bavaria emerged politically and territorially virtually unscathed from the **Congress of Vienna** in 1815, becoming the third largest German state after Austria and Prussia.

The Bavarian kingdom is still recalled as Bavaria's **Golden Age**. On Maximilian's death in 1825, his son **Ludwig I** took over the helm of state and introduced further, much needed administrative and religious reforms. During his brief rule Bavaria's international prestige soared and this led to a blossoming of **Bavarian nationalism**, at a time when other Germans were beginning to entertain the wider idea of an all-embracing German nation state. Ludwig was committed to the promotion of commerce and a patron of the arts. It is him we have to thank for many of Munich's most graceful Neoclassical buildings, put up under the guidance of his court architect **Leo von Klenze**. Yet, in 1848, Ludwig was forced to abdicate following the waves of popular unrest (now known as the 1848

Revolts), but also as a result of a scandalous affair with a dancer, Lola Montez (*see* p.179). Ludwig's son **Maximilian II** carried on the good work, forging alliances with Saxony, Hannover and Württemberg, chiefly to establish a strong third force to put a check on the growing power of Austria and Prussia. There was no love lost between Bavaria and the wily Prussian **Prince Otto von Bismarck**, and Maximilian subsequently tended to support Austria against Prussia.

In 1864 the famed **Ludwig II** (*see* pp.179–83) became king of Bavaria, showing much the same reluctance towards Bismarck's attempts to incorporate his kingdom into a German state under Prussian leadership. However, in the swift **Seven Weeks' War** (1866) Prussian victory over the Austrian armies dislodged Austria as a main player on the German field, and established Prussia in its place. This left Bavaria the final stumbling block on the road to a united Germany. Shrewdly, Bismarck didn't punish Bavaria for siding with Austria. Rather, Ludwig II was forced to assent to what was called a **defensive alliance** under Prussian domination. Bismarck's conciliatory approach towards Bavaria at one stage even went so far as offering Ludwig II the Imperial throne of a unified Germany. It needed another carefully engineered, victorious war with France, the **Franco-Prussian War** (1870–71), in which Bavarian troops fought side by side with the Prussians, finally to coax Bavaria into a greater **German Reich**. In January 1871 Bismarck persuaded Ludwig II to invite—on behalf of his fellow princes—Wilhelm I of Prussia to accept the Imperial crown. When the empire was proclaimed in the *Galerie des glaces* at the **Palace of Versailles** on 18 January, Ludwig was conspicious by his absence. Records show that his decision finally to give in to Bismarck was propelled more by the latter's promise of generous grants for Ludwig's building schemes than by any devotion to German unity. The Iron Chancellor raised the funds by creaming off some of the proceeds of the sale of the recently seized Welf dynasty treasury.

With Germany now under Prussian dominance, Bavaria was now a monarchy in name only, though under the **German Constitution of 1871** it was granted a greater degree of independence than other German states. Bavaria was allowed to keep an autonomous diplomatic service, military administration, post and telegraph service and its own railways. Undercurrents of resentment ran strong on both sides. While Prussian scholars exploded that Bavaria was a 'political deformity that is unfit to survive', Berlin was commonly referred to by Munich's bourgeoisie as the 'glorified garrison town'.

Under the Weimar Republic and the Nazis

Germany's defeat in the **First World War** spelt an ignominious end to Bavaria's Golden Age. On the eve of 8 November 1918 Kurt Eisner, the leader of the Independent Socialists in Bavaria, deposed Ludwig III, the last of the Wittelsbachs, and proclaimed Bavaria a **republic**, bringing the 738-year-old dynasty to a close. What followed was a short-lived Soviet-style republic, with revolutionary councils spearheading some Bolshevik-inspired 'Red Terror' in the streets of Munich. By May 1919, however, the left-wing uprising had been quelled by units of the infamous *Freikorps*, volunteers comprising mainly ex-officers and right-wing extremists, who relished the task of stamping out any opposition to the government in a ruthless 'White Terror'. Under the new Bavarian constitution of August 1919 Bavaria became a parliamentary state in the **Weimar Republic**. The Weimar years were a tumultuous period of political unrest throughout Germany. Munich quickly turned into a hotbed of reactionary movements, with unsuccessful right-wing coups in 1920 and 1921.

It is perhaps no coincidence that ex-Austrian **Adolf Hitler** (1889–1945)—one-time corporal and failed postcard painter—centred so much of his activity on Munich, later calling the city 'the Capital of our Movement'. In 1919 he joined the Munich-based German Workers' Party, whose assets amounted to a resounding 7.50 Marks (about £2) at the time and whose membership didn't even reach three figures. But Hitler went to work immediately. In 1920 he renamed the party the **National Socialist German Workers' Party** (NSDAP); members were soon to be referred to as **Nazis**. He adopted the ancient good-luck symbol, the swastika, and established the brown-shirted **SA**, short for *Sturmabteilung* (Stormtroopers), a group of armed heavies that lined the walls at meetings and beat up opponents. The colour brown was chosen because the party could lay their hands on a large quantity of unused, low-priced colonial uniforms of the defunct Imperial Army.

In 1923 Hitler had enough confidence in his private army to make a grab at power himself. Backed by some 600 followers he staged the **Munich Beerhall Putsch**, storming into a beerhall, firing into the air and capturing the Bavarian state leaders. (He wanted to persuade them to lead a march on Berlin.) The next day he held a mass demonstration, but the police turned out in force and opened fire. Sixteen Nazis and three policemen were killed, and Hitler and his cronies were arrested. He was tried for high treason and sentenced to five years' imprisonment at **Landsberg Prison**—though he was released after only nine months (an indication of prevailing right-wing sympathies in the Bavarian state government). He used his time to dictate his manifesto **Mein Kampf** (*My Struggle*), in which he outlined his strategy for world domination and set out his anti-semitism.

When Hitler finally came to power in 1933, bringing an end to the Weimar Republic, Bavaria was already a bastion of Nazism. Bavarian cities carry with them some of the darkest associations of the Nazi period. Nuremberg was the scene of the *Reichsparteitage*, the stage-managed **Nazi Party Conventions** that pandered to Hitler's delusion of grandeur, and in 1935 provided the platform for the declaration of the *Nürnberger Rassengesetze* or **Racial Purity Laws**, the anti-semitic legislation that provided the framework for the Holocaust. **Dachau** was the site of the first of the **concentration camps** that swallowed up the scapegoats for all of Germany's ills—the Jews, plus Communists and other dissenters, gypsies and homosexuals. Even the sleepy, picture-postcard Alpine resort of **Berchtesgaden** was blackened by Nazi connotations: the **Eagle's Nest**, perched awesomely on the Kehlstein mountain, became Hitler's personal mountain retreat. The nearby *Berghof* residence, now razed to the ground, was the site of Neville Chamberlain's last-ditch attempt at peace which resulted in the infamous **Munich Agreement** of 1938. As negotiations were conducted in Bad Godesberg on the Rhine and Berchtesgaden, the term is somewhat misplaced.

Despite all these unsavoury associations with the Third Reich, Bavarians, fired perhaps by their sense of Bavarian rather than German nationalism, put up some resistance against being incorporated into the over-centralized Nazi nation state. But a considerable number of Bavarians had become adherents of National Socialism, and the Nazis had quickly established party control over every institution in the state, including the police, universities and professional associations. Munich University was one of the few places where resistance flickered on. In the course of 1942 and 1943, a clandestine circle of friends centred on the student siblings Hans and Sophie Scholl, and, calling themselves the **White Rose Society**, printed and circulated a number of underground pamphlets on the university premises. When they were finally caught, they were tried for 'civil disobedience' and brutally executed.

During the **Second World War**, Bavarian labour and industry amply fuelled Hitler's war effort—most notably at Augsburg, where the famous Messerschmidts were made. Bavaria offered safe locations well behind Germany's air defences, but from mid-1944 on, British and American planes carpet-bombed Bavarian cities night and day, reducing the region to ash and rubble. In March 1945 the first US troops rumbled through Bavaria, crushing last-ditch resistance and liberating the desolate concentration camps before marching on the capital.

A Free State in Post-War Germany

After the war, Bavaria became part of the US zone of occupation. The Palatinate was merged into the new *Land* of Rhineland-Palatinate and the island of Lindau became part of Baden Württemberg (though it later reverted to Bavaria). The rest of the state remained intact. Because of its indelible associations with the Nazis, Nuremberg was chosen by the Allies for their **war crimes trials**. In Bavaria, as elsewhere in Germany, the Allies began a desperate search for leaders untainted by Nazi affiliations to take control of a new federal state and put the region back on its feet. But more pressing needs were occupying the minds of the war-torn populace: not only did they have to struggle with the rebuilding of their land and industry, they also had to find new homes and employment for literally thousands of displaced refugees as Bavaria was flooded with German-speaking people expelled from the Sudetenland, now in the Czech Republic.

In 1946 a constituent assembly gave the new Federal **Land** of Bavaria its post-war constitution. However, Bavarian bloody-mindedness and separatism again reared its head when, by referendum, a majority of Bavarians refused to ratify the Basic Law, the constitution of the Federal Republic (the only federal state in Germany to do so). As a result, Bavaria was declared a Free State, with its own constitution.

Since its inception, the State government has been firmly under the control of the right-wing **Christian Social Union** (CSU), from 1978 ruled over by unofficial 'king' of Bavaria **Franz-Josef Strauss**. In 1980, against the advice of his political associates in the rest of West Germany, of the Christian Democrats, Strauss declared his candidacy for the office of chancellor of the Federal Republic, but failed to win approval on a national level. When he died without a successor in 1988, numbers of party members switched their allegiance to the extreme-right *Republikaner* party, which was led by an ex-SS officer. The State government has been responsible for some draconian legislation—such as the recent law sanctioning mandatory blood tests on anyone suspected of being HIV positive, and arrest and indefinite detention for people carrying the AIDS virus who don't follow a code of 'proper behaviour'.

The 1990 reunification of East and West Germany came as something of a mixed blessing to Bavaria. On the one hand, northern Bavaria, notably Franconia, has again found itself in the centre of a unified Germany, with all the political and economic gains that were expected from the union. On the other hand, the finely tuned political balance between the Federal Government in Bonn and its **Länder** has been put to a severe test of will. During the parliamentary debate of 1991 on whether the Federal seat of government should return to Berlin, members of the Bavarian CSU were among the most outspoken opponents, inadvertently admitting that Bavaria stood to see a diminishment of its status as part of an enlarged Germany.

The Arts and Culture

The princelings, archbishops, kings, dukes and electors who parcelled up Germany into states, then ran their domains with all the pomp and splendour they could muster, left a trail of grand palaces, beautiful churches and rich art collections right across the country, particularly in Bavaria. Wealthy burghers in the merchant towns joined in with competitive zeal, and the result is a prodigious, widespread artistic heritage. Local princes kept a tight hold on their collections, so Germany's treasures haven't all filtered down to one capital city, or been carried off to foreign museums. (This is one of the reasons that German art is so little known abroad.) The fierce sense of *Heimat* and (in the 19th century) a growing Romantic nationalism meant that local works of art stayed put, so small-town museums still come up with big-time surprises. Post-war prosperity, the federal system and fat arts subsidies have helped to maintain this tradition, and German children seem to grow up with a more deeply developed sense of *Kultur*, and more first-hand experience of great art and architecture, than their English or American counterparts.

The petty rulers and their protégés were conservative, however, and took a while to get to grips with new ideas. Artists kept a self-effacing anonymity long after their colleagues in other countries were signing works, and are known to us by the names of their major achievements (such as the Master of the Bartholomew Altar). The Gothic style arrived later and stayed on longer than elsewhere in Europe, and the first shoots of the Renaissance in Germany appeared nearly a century after Italy was already blossoming. Of course you can see French, Italian and Netherlandish influences at work, especially in border regions, but schools and movements usually centred on one or two of the tiny states, developing a distinctive style, though often with little international recognition or impact. In their own day, many of Germany's greatest artists were local heroes only.

German art has, however, had at least two Golden Ages—one in the 16th century, with Cranach, Dürer, Grünewald and Holbein as the stars, and another early this century, when the German Expressionists developed a powerful individual style, and the Bauhaus group (quite literally) changed the shape of 20th-century architecture.

Early Days

Apart from a few **Roman** buildings such as the superb remains at Trier, Germany's earliest surviving architecture dates back to the **Carolingian Period** (9th century). Charlemagne saw himself as a direct successor to the Caesars, and energetically set about imitating things Roman. He imported southern building techniques and design for his huge palace chapel at Aachen, and established the prototype for what was later to develop into the Romanesque style (*see* below). The secluded upper floor—from which the emperor could watch the goings-on at the high altar without being seen by the masses below—became the basis for later *Doppelkirchen* ('double churches') throughout Germany.

Although he could barely read himself, Charlemagne was an enthusiastic collector of books, and imported whole libraries from Italy and Byzantium. The lavish illustrations in these tomes must have astonished the hitherto rather inept northern painters, who were stimulated into a frenzy of **manuscript illumination**—much of it deft, vibrant and extraordinarily sophisticated. Germany's first acknowledged great painter, known as the **Master of the Registrum Gregorii**, was an illuminator—you can see his *Codex Egberti* in Trier. Charlemagne also commissioned the renowned scholar Alcuin of York to renovate the alphabet, which had collapsed into an illegible scrawl through centuries of semi-literate scribes copying out the pages of the Bible. The letters on this page are descended from the alphabet worked out by Alcuin and his followers at Tours in France.

Charlemagne's empire survived him by a mere 30 years. Plundering Vikings and Magyars plunged the land into desolation and confusion. But a new dynasty of German emperors, the **Ottonians**, emerged in the mid-10th century and managed to salvage Carolingian culture. During the Ottonian period there were even greater advances in manuscript illumination and architecture. The massive St Michael's in Hildesheim is the finest of surviving Ottonian churches.

Romanesque Art

Between the 10th and the 12th centuries medieval Europe stopped looking back over its shoulder at Imperial Rome, and began to explore new directions for itself. Church building became an obsession, even (wrote Raoul Glaber, an 11th-century monk) when congregations were 'not in the least need... It was as if the whole earth, having cast off the old... were clothing itself in the white robe of the church.' Nineteenth-century historians called the style that emerged 'Romanesque', in the mistaken belief that it was an imitation of Roman monumental building, and just a flawed step on the way to Gothic perfection. They were wrong—Romanesque architecture has a spirit all of its own.

The new generation was determined to build in stone. They could still remember the earlier wooden-roofed buildings going up in smoke as barbarians had burned their way through the land. Enterprising masons came up with groin vaults that supported daringly large stone ceilings. The churches they put up were solid, blocky masses of geometric shapes—rectangles, cubes, cylinders and semi-circular arches. Less successful Romanesque churches are heavy and ponderous, but the best ones are sublime. The rhythmic patterns of rounded arches and columns have a soothing, meditative effect—a purity and simplicity closer to Islamic than to later Christian architecture.

Decorative elements are confined to repetitive carving on the columns and around portals, some chunky relief work and sculpture, and **frescoes**. Fresco cycles—picture-bibles for an illiterate congregation—developed into a major art form in Romanesque churches. The achievements of the 11th and early 12th centuries were Germany's first and (until the Bauhaus in the 20th century) last major contributions to international architectural design.

The Gothic Period

Renaissance critics, who revered classical antiquity, first used the term 'Gothic' as a derisive label for a style they thought violated the standards of Greece and Rome, and so simply must have come from the nasty, barbaric Goths. 'May he who invented it be cursed,' wrote one outraged historian. The exuberant, decorative style does seem cheerfully to ignore most good and true classical norms, but it has its roots in a change of mood that was permeating Europe. 'The air of the city is the breath of freedom' went the slogan.

The insecurities of rural, feudal life were disappearing. A middle class of wealthy merchants and professionals, safe in their walled towns, could keep the aristocracy in check. Soaring Gothic cathedrals expressed this new confidence. They were real images on Earth of the Heavenly Jerusalem, often (in Germany at least) paid for by public subscription rather than aristocratic largesse. Burghers proudly called these new churches that towered over their towns *opus modernum* (modern work).

The attitude to women was changing too. The heroes of earlier ballads waxed rhapsodic about their swords, those of the Gothic minnesingers (lyric poets and musicians) swoon over their ladies. This was the time of gallant knights and courtly love. The church eased its restrictions on representing women in art, and the cult of the Virgin Mary burgeoned all over Europe. Romanesque painting and carving had dwelt on severe themes such as the Last Judgement. Gothic work favours gentler subjects, often centring on the Madonna.

Architecture

The pointed arches, flying buttresses, high towers and delicate tracery that characterize Gothic architecture are not merely decorative but the result of complicated new building ideas. Pointed arches led to a lighter and far more flexible system of vaulting, opening up possibilities for a more varied ground plan and much bigger windows. Buttresses helped carry the weight of the supporting masonry, so cathedrals could shoot up to impressive heights. Filigreed stonework gave support, yet also helped architects to realize their ambitions of building almost diaphanous structures. **Stained glass** flourished as an art form.

New Gothic styles had begun to appear in France around 1140, but nearly a century passed before they took hold in Germany. Early Gothic churches can seem prosaic in comparison to contemporary French achievements. But soon German builders were imitating the Gallic flair, and by 1250 had embarked on their supreme achievement, the cathedral at Cologne. Many German builders, though, favoured the more sober **Hallenkirche** (hall church—a church with nave and aisles of the same height, sometimes with a flat roof), which had its origins in the design of monasteries for the austere Cistercian order. The Liebfrauenkirche in Munich is one of the most famous.

Sculpture

Early Gothic stone-carving, especially in Thuringia and Saxony, was in the aptly named **Zackenstil** ('jagged style'). Hard, angular lines of cloth covered the scarcely perceptible anatomy of the figures. Soon French influence was felt here, too. In around 1300 masons began to carve in the so-called **Soft Style**—soft, flowing robes, draped over perfectly moulded limbs and bodies: they were obviously working from live models. Along with this move towards naturalism came far more subtle characterization. Intense, anguished facial expressions became a speciality, and the *Man of Sorrows* was a favourite subject. Christ's face on crucifixes began to show real suffering. **Portraiture** began to emerge as an art form, and patrons often appeared in works they had commissioned.

Tilman Riemenschneider (1460–1531), arguably the greatest sculptor of the late-Gothic period, worked mainly in wood. His restless, flamboyant carvings crop up all over Germany, but especially in and around his native Würzburg. The other great wood-carver of the period was **Veit Stoss** (*c.* 1447–1533), a talented old rascal (*see* p.217) who spent most of his working life in Nuremberg turning out exquisite, realistic masterpieces.

Panel Painting

When artists began to paint on wooden panels (in Germany around 1300), art became portable and saleable, and styles began to spread more quickly. Painting had evolved out of manuscript illumination. Early painters were seen as craftsmen, trained and controlled by powerful guilds. The guild got them commissions, and made sure that the work was well paid. It was only later, during the Gothic period and early Renaissance, that artists began to emerge as individuals and personally sign their work. In Germany this took a long time, as the guilds were more powerful than elsewhere in Europe.

Most early panel paintings were intended as altarpieces. Initially, the pictures were quite static. Backgrounds were of gold leaf or covered in ornament, and figures related to each other with stylized gestures. Later, the Soft Style (which is also known as the International Style) took over here too. Painters created little scenes; people talk to each other, there is far more realism and a stronger narrative element than before. **Master Bertram** (*c.* 1345–1415), a Hamburg painter and the first German artist we know by name, liked to paint narrative cycles on small panels that he would group around a sculpture. **Conrad von Soest** (active *c.* 1394–1422) did appealing, brightly coloured pieces with fine attention to detail. **Conrad Witz** (*c.* 1400–46) did much to move German painting towards a greater sense of realism, though his work is very much in a blunt, sculptural 'hard' style. It was **Jan Joest** of Kalkar (*c.* 1455–1519) and **Hans Pleydendurff** (*c.* 1420–72) who were most influenced by Netherlandish naturalism. Pleydendurff's panels especially show a richness of colour and careful composition reminiscent of the Flemish painter Dirk Bouts. Pleydendurff was the first German to paint landscapes (rather than patterns or cities) into the background of his works. Painters of the **Danube School** based in Passau and Salzburg refined this technique towards the end of the 15th century, filling out their panels with lush Danube country scenes.

Artists working in the south, such as Conrad Witz (who spent much of his life in Switzerland) and the Tyrolean **Michael Pacher** (*c.* 1435–98) came under Italian influence. Pacher painted with hard, bright colours. A harsh light shines on his subjects, casting strong, clear shadows. (You can see examples in the Alte Pinakothek in Munich.) Painters in Cologne, on the other hand, followed the trends in the neighbouring Netherlands. In the 15th century they developed such a distinctive style that later art historians have grouped them together as the Cologne School.

The Cologne School

The first to paint in this softer, more realistic Cologne style was the **Master of St Veronica** (*c.* 1420). He is named after a painting (now in the Alte Pinakothek in Munich) of St Veronica holding up the Sudarium (a cloth she had offered to Christ on the road to Golgotha to wipe the sweat from his brow, and which was handed back with the Lord's face miraculously imprinted on it). The large-scale image of Christ's countenance, and Veronica's gentle features are said to have sent Goethe into raptures.

The supreme artist of the school, if not of the entire German Soft Style, was **Stefan Lochner** (c. 1410–51). He paints with loving detail, and his works are subtly shaded, often with a glowing ethereal quality. (You can see many of his paintings in the Alte Pinakothek or in Cologne, where his masterpiece, the *Epiphany Triptych*, is in the cathedral.) Later artists of the Cologne School, such as the **Master of the Life of the Virgin** (active c. 1460–85) and the **Master of the St Ursula Legend** (active c. 1490–1505), developed a more narrative style and filled their panels with anecdotal detail. The School's last great practitioner was also its most idiosyncratic. The **Master of the St Bartholomew Altarpiece** (active c. 1470–1510) handles colour in a more sophisticated way than even Lochner, but includes quirky details. In the St Bartholomew altarpiece his fashionably dressed, bejewelled women look like anything but the saints they are meant to depict. Strung behind them, a brocade backdrop recalls the gold backgrounds of earlier paintings; over the top of it, you can see a more modern dreamy landscape.

The Renaissance

Architecturally, Germany was immersed in the Gothic until well into the 16th century, though in sculpture and painting new forces were already stirring in the late 1400s. At the turn of the century this new energy burst into a brief but brilliant Golden Age of German painting. By 1528, with the death of the main exponents, Dürer and Grünewald, the force seemed spent and the Golden Age fizzled out just as quickly as it had begun. The exact reason for the sudden decline is not clear—though the religious wars that racked the land and the rise of Protestantism no doubt played a part.

Painting and Graphics

The new movement was triggered by a conscious desire to copy what was going on in Italy at the time. Wealthy merchants in south Germany had close contact with Venice, and Germany's humanists were in touch with scholars in Florence. Italian engravings circulated throughout northern Europe, and led to a corresponding German interest in **graphic arts** (i.e. line drawing, illustration and printmaking). The most skilled and adventurous German engraver was **Martin Schongauer** (c. 1450–91). His subtle metal-engraving technique became a standard for German graphic artists, and his blending of realism with delightful innovation, and choice of exotic (even demonic) subjects, have led art-historians to call him the father of the German Renaissance.

The name that overshadows all others of the period is that of the Nuremberg artist **Albrecht Dürer** (1471–1528). He is Germany's complete Renaissance Man—an artist, scientist, mathematician and thinker—the 'Leonardo of the North'. Dürer was the first northerner to travel to Italy expressly to study art. He worked with tremendous energy and was the first artist outside Italy to become internationally famous in his own time. His engravings—many of them of popular subjects at a price ordinary people could afford—spread his renown, and made him a rich man. Many say that he is at his best as an engraver—the versatility, luminosity and dramatic power of his woodcuts have never been surpassed. He could also show a sensitive and delicate touch, and is equally celebrated for beautiful watercolour nature studies (though the fading originals of these are rarely exhibited). His later paintings, such as the *Four Apostles* (1526) in the Alte Pinakothek in Munich, show a subtlety of touch and extraordinarily strong characterization. Dürer's paintings and woodcuts surface in museums all over Germany, but his best work can be seen in Munich and Nuremberg.

Matthias Gothardt-Niethardt, known as **Grünewald** (*c.* 1480–1528), another artist of highly original genius, worked for the archbishops of Mainz as court painter, architect and hydraulic engineer before fleeing Germany in 1525, having been on the wrong side in the ill-fated Peasants' Revolt. Unlike Dürer, he was largely forgotten until recent years. His reputation rests mainly on an enormous polyptych, the *Isenheim Altarpiece* (1510–15), which many regard as the supreme achievement of German art. The original altar is in Colmar (now in France), but there is a gruelling version of the *Crucifixion* panel in Karlsruhe—perhaps the most memorable interpretation of the subject ever. It is a taut, agonized picture, painted in dissonant colours and angular shapes.

Albrecht Altdorfer (*c.* 1480–1538) was the kingpin of the **Danube School** (*see* above), which continued to flourish into the Renaissance, and is credited with the first landscape in Western art painted for its own sake. He was a talented and unorthodox colourist, especially when it came to light and atmospheric effects, and had a penchant for depicting fantastic buildings (he was also an architect). His most important work, the enormous *Battle of Issus* (1529, in the Alte Pinakothek) swarms with insect-like soldiers, each finished with a miniature-painter's precision. At least half the canvas is taken up by a dramatic landscape that gives the onlooker a god's-eye view across the Alps to Cyprus and Egypt.

Lucas Cranach the Elder (1472–1553), another artist of the Danube School, is best known for his later works. These are usually on humanist rather than religious themes (mythology, history and portraits) and feature nudes, which Cranach paints with disarming, almost naïve charm. A strain of humorous, rather wicked eroticism runs through his paintings. In the latter part of his life, in answer to a summons from the Elector of Saxony, he settled in Wittenberg. Here he became a friend of Luther, and established a workshop that churned out paintings at an alarming rate. His son **Lucas Cranach the Younger** (1515–86) carried on the work, a worthy imitation of his father, but without much original flair. The period's quirkiest painter was **Hans Baldung** (1484–1545), known as **Grien** because he always wore green clothes. He studied under Dürer, from whom he learnt his fine colouring technique. His choice of subject matter and even his treatment of conventional themes is delightfully (almost wilfully) bizarre. Baldung's works are scattered throughout Germany, but you can easily spot them. In the Early German galleries of a museum, if your eye is caught by an odd painting of an evil-looking cupid, a bewitched child or a weird woman, it is sure to be by Baldung.

Augsburg, as seat of the Hapsburg court and home to the powerful Fugger family (*see* pp.173–4), was an influential centre of the Renaissance in Germany. The most notable artists to rise from this milieu were **Hans Burgkmair** (1473–1531), a master of opulent Italianate decoration, and **Hans Holbein the Younger** (1497–1543), best known for his firm, faultless portraits. When Holbein upped sticks for England in 1531, he left the German Renaissance in its dying throes.

While it lasted, it was primarily a boom in painting and graphics. Developments in **architecture** came later and were more episodic. In Augsburg **Elias Holl** (1573–1646) took Italian models to heart, and put up buildings that have little of Germany about them at all. Most survivors of the period are civil or domestic buildings—ornate Rathäuser or high-gabled merchants' houses decorated with scrolls, obelisks and statues.

Baroque and Rococo

There is no clear dividing line between Renaissance and Baroque. The Renaissance was an age of innovation and discovery, but its images were relatively static. Baroque art moves. Artists tested the new ground their predecessors had laid out, took a few shaky steps, then ran riot. Art historian Helen Gardner described the era as 'spacious and dynamic, brilliant and colorful, theatrical and passionate, sensual and ecstatic, opulent and extravagant, versatile and *virtuoso*'. Façades are sinuous and irregular. Interiors writhe with twisted pillars, horseshoe vaulting and stucco. The dome, oval and circle are the underlying shapes of design. Bumps are gilded, and flat surfaces covered in bright painting. Witty *trompe l'œil* abounds, often combined with clever 3-D stucco trickery. Stained glass is banished and churches are flooded with light—often from hidden sources that throw up contrasting patterns of shade. Enthusiasm for the Virgin and the saints was redoubled, and altarpieces became monumental. Later, as Baroque broke into the lighter, airier and even more fantastic Rococo, stucco-work became less intense, but even more irregular. Asymmetrical cartouches and cake-icing licks of dazzling white plaster are spread with happy abandon.

Early Baroque painting in Germany is fairly unremarkable: the glory days were in the latter part of the 17th and early 18th centuries, as late Baroque became Rococo. After about 1660 abbots and bishops in the south of the country—back in place after the Counter-Reformation—set about rebuilding their churches with exuberance. Most couldn't resist a show of triumph and commissioned top, fashionable architects who came up with the most ambitious plans their patrons could afford. Today Germany's most spectacular Baroque and Rococo art is to be seen in the frescoes, decoration and design of these southern churches and palaces. The responsibility for most of the best work lies with a brilliant few who seldom restricted themselves to one skill but designed, painted frescoes and often did the stucco work too.

The Big Names in Architecture

Balthasar Neumann (1687–1753) was the era's supremo. He started work in Würzburg as a bell-founder, took up architecture as a hobby and was soon snapped up by the powerful Schönborn family to build churches and palaces throughout Germany. His complicated designs have such energy and intricate detail, and there is such a flowing pulse between space and massive structure, that at least one art critic likens them to a Bach fugue—as 'frozen music'. Neumann relished meetings with other architects and enriched his own style with what he learnt from great French, Viennese and Italian artists of the time. Grand, sweeping staircases were a speciality (you can see fine examples in Würzburg and Brühl), and his churches can be breathtaking—the Vierzehnheiligenkirche near Bamberg being one of the best.

The **Asam Brothers**—sculptor Egid Quirin Asam (1692–1750) and painter Cosmas Damian Asam (1686–1739)—formed a team, first to decorate existing churches, later to undertake entire projects of their own (such as the Asamkirche in Munich). The brothers studied in Rome and were never seduced from their stately, southern High Baroque style into the frivolities of Rococo. Cosmas Asam became particularly well known for his tricks with perspective and vast dome paintings of the open heavens.

The Rococo period was dominated by two other siblings, architect **Dominikus Zimmerman** (1685–1766) and his fresco-painting brother **Johann Baptist Zimmerman** (1680–1785). Together they worked on the Wieskirche in 1750 (*see* p. 000), which many hold to be Germany's supreme achievement in the style. Johann Baptist also worked with another great architect of the time, the Belgian **François Cuvilliés** (1695–1767), on the Munich Residenz and Schloß Nymphenburg. The diminutive Cuvilliés was originally employed by Elector Max Emmanuel as a court jester, and only began working as an architect in his thirties. His theatre in the Munich Residenz and the Amalienburg in the Nymphenburg park are Rococo at its most delightful.

Neoclassicism

Frederick the Great's Berlin became the focus for growing moves towards a more restrained Neoclassicism, which later also became fashionable in Munich and around Mainz and Cologne. Neoclassicism was a more stringent and academic revival of Greek and Roman architecture. Buildings became plainer, with simple pediments and colonnaded porticoes in front of the entrances. Interiors were muted, with the odd Rococo flourish, or decorated in the styles of Greece and Rome. (Excavation of Pompeii, which began in 1748, fired enthusiasm for this, and threw new light on ancient design.) German architects favoured colder Doric styles, and the desire for symmetry became obsessive. In some churches a false pulpit was even erected to counterbalance the functional one. Leading architect of the day was **Karl-Friedrich Schinkel** (1781–1841), whose work is above all associated with Berlin.

Neoclassical painting tended to be skilful, though cold—or subject to nationalistic fervour. One painter who did introduce some warmth into his canvases was **Johann Heinrich Wilhelm Tischbein** (1751–1829), the youngest of a dynasty of Neoclassical artists. His idyllic landscapes were a source of great inspiration to Goethe, whose portrait Tischbein painted, lounging in an Italian setting.

The 19th Century

> We desire to surrender our whole being, that it may be filled with
> the perfect bliss of one glorious emotion.
>
> Goethe's romantic hero, Werther

Eighteenth-century gallants thought it in bad taste to be 'original' or 'enthusiastic' (read 'eccentric' or 'sincere'). Stony, sober Neoclassicism vanquished the artifice and frivolity of Rococo, and banished emotion even further from polite society. Yet, almost at the same time, after 1750, another quite different mood was filtering through Europe. It became quite fashionable to swoon, languish in unrequited love and weep. All of this was done with gusto by the heroes and heroines of a new literary phenomenon that was sweeping the continent—the novel (German: *Roman*). German critics were the first to call this flowering of sensibility 'Romantic'—to distinguish what they saw as peculiarly 'modern' traits in the arts from the old values of Neoclassicism.

In Germany the Romantic movement, which reached its peak in the first half of the 19th century, was felt primarily in music and literature, and to a lesser extent in painting. In architecture Neoclassicism held out until around 1830, when it was routed by **Neo-Gothic**. For the Romantics the Gothic style epitomized their dreamy ideal of Old Germany, and many great Gothic cathedrals received their finishing touches in the 1800s, seven centuries after they had been started. (The famous spires on Cologne's cathedral were topped off only in 1880.) Fake Gothic—and some classical—'ruins' popped up in the grounds of grand homes all over the country. In Bavaria King Ludwig II outdid everyone with his series of fairytale castles (*see* pp.183, 184 and 116–17).

The year 1850 saw the beginning of the **Gründerjahre** (Founders' Period), when wealthy industrialists put up showy mansions (design invariably coming second to size in their priorities) and filled the rooms with reproduction medieval furniture. The middle classes contented themselves with **Biedermeier**—lighter, comfortable, cushioned furniture characterized by simple, flowing lines, elegant wood veneers and glass-fronted cabinets.

Romantic Painting

In **Caspar David Friedrich** (1774–1840) you can see Romantic painting in its very essence. He is perhaps the one 19th-century German painter whose works are widely popular and familiar outside of his own country. His highly original pictures of mist-shrouded Gothic ruins, winter-blasted landscapes and violent, windswept seas hauntingly reveal the Romantic obsession with death and isolation, and prints of these adorn the walls of sensitive and suicidal youth throughout the Western World. Human figures (if they feature at all) are tiny, often seen from the back, and overwhelmed by powerful Nature.

Few other German artists of the time can match Friedrich's stature. The architect **Karl-Friedrich Schinkel** (*see* above), who took to painting to earn extra money, managed to slip easily into a more Romantic style and came up with spectacular architectural fantasies. **Philipp Otto Runge** (1777–1810) is best known for his portraits of chubby-cheeked children (usually his own), but at the time of his early death was collaborating with Goethe on a project involving vast paintings, poetry and music with which he hoped to recover the lost harmony of the universe. Only studies of the paintings—*The Times of Day*—remain. **Anselm Feuerbach** (1829–80), an artist rather neglected outside Germany, painted big, Italianate canvases and is at his best with powerful, brooding portraits of women. The Swiss-born **Arnold Böcklin** painted delightful, fey pictures on mythological or fairytale themes. **Hans Thoma** (1839–1924), the erstwhile director of the Karlsruhe art museum, could come up with sensitive, moving paintings, but often lapsed into gooey sentimentality.

In an abandoned monastery in Rome **Johann Friedrich Overbeck** (1789–1869) founded the **Nazarene Brotherhood**—a group of German artists who painted detailed, idealistic, rather enchanted canvases in a style later taken up by the Pre-Raphaelites in England. Overbeck lived out his life in Italy, but other painters—including **Peter von Cornelius** (1783–1867) and **Wilhelm Schadow** (1788–1862)—returned to Germany, where their activity centred on the **Düsseldorf Academy**. Here the style of the school degenerated into vast, pompous historical paintings. The painters were popular, however, and their frescoes are emblazoned on the walls of public buildings across the country.

Other 19th-century Painters

During the 19th century Munich and Berlin became centres of the arts, each developing avant-garde groups that rebelled against powerful, conservative institutions such as the Düsseldorf Academy. In Berlin painters formed the **Secession movement**, headed by **Max Liebermann** (1847–1935), but it was in the Schwabing quarter of Munich that the most adventurous artists gathered (*see* pp.75–6). At the centre of the Munich movement was **Franz von Stuck** (1863–1928), a highly individual artist whose dark, mysterious paintings seem an odd mixture of Pre-Raphaelite style and Expressionist violence.

Portraiture was in popular demand and obliging artists such as **Franz von Lenbach** (1863–1904) moved in the highest society, making themselves very rich. (Lenbach painted Bismarck no fewer than 80 times.) **Realism** returned as a style later in the century. **Adolf Menzel** (1815–1905) was one of the first painters to capture scenes from the newly industrialized cities on canvas, while **Wilhelm Liebl** (1844–1900) is especially renowned for his studies of Bavarian peasants, painted from life. **Impressionism** made very little impact on Germany—perhaps the bright colours and light touch just didn't appeal to the national temperament. The only really exciting German Impressionist was **Lovis Corinth** (1858–1925)—though his large, gentle pictures often seem rather cold.

Jugendstil

Towards the end of the 19th century a reaction set in against the blunt, hard shapes that were the aesthetic by-product of industrialization. Influenced by the flowing lines of Japanese prints, and by William Morris's intricate, interwoven designs and radical views which put handicraft back on its medieval pedestal, a new style emerged, centred mainly in Paris and Vienna. The French called this ornamental style of graceful, serpentine lines and organic forms Art Nouveau. In Germany it was known as Jugendstil—the style named after the journal which promoted it, *Jugend* (Youth). Architecture, sculpture, painting and especially the applied arts (furniture, ceramics, glassware and even jewellery) were swept up into an enormously popular movement that lasted until the First World War. Early Jugendstil architecture in Germany shows its Neoclassical ancestry. Houses are symmetrically and solidly built, but graced with flowing decoration—often with fruit and flower motifs or wistful women's faces. Later, lines became stronger and more dramatic and seem to prefigure Expressionist and Bauhaus styles. German furniture makers and glass-blowers excelled themselves, and exquisite examples of their work crop up in museums all over the country. Look out for jewellery by Patriz Huber, glassware by Peter Behrens and stylish household goods by Joseph M. Olbrich.

The 20th Century

It was France that led European painting into the 20th century. Germany lagged rather sorrowfully behind. Impressionism hardly made a mark east of the Rhine, but when the Fauves (French for 'wild beasts') under the leadership of Henri Matisse hit Paris in 1905, German artists began to stir again. The Fauves' shocking colours and bold patterns were far more appealing. The Germans began to turn out intense, savage canvases, lashed with vigorous brushwork, blazing with clashing colours and strongly expressive of personal feeling. The movement, which became known as **Expressionism**, also affected literature (especially drama) and film, and produced the first German art for centuries to make an impact on the outside world. German Expressionism was still going strong in the 1930s when Hitler labelled the movement 'degenerate'. Works were banned, a lot was destroyed, and many of the artists fled the country. Some of the painters who come under the Expressionist umbrella were also part of simultaneous movements—such as the anarchic **Berlin Dadaists** and **Neue Sachlichkeit** (*see* below), a 'post-Expressionist trend' which began years before Expressionism was exhausted. The **Bauhaus** school—which grew out of Jugendstil and the British-inspired Arts and Crafts movement—attracted some major Expressionist artists, but developed an individual style that was to set the pace for 20th-century architecture and design.

The German Expressionist Painters

Although the Expressionist movement was ignited by the Fauves it burned on solid German fuel. The strong colour, hard line, emotional subject matter and even the otherworldly overtones are direct descendants of earlier German painting and engraving. The Expressionists organized themselves into two schools: **Die Brücke** ('The Bridge'—uniting nature and emotion) and **Der Blaue Reiter** ('The Blue Rider'—after a picture by Kandinsky).

Die Brücke was founded in Dresden in 1905 by three disgruntled architecture students who had taken to painting—**Ernst Ludwig Kirchner** (1880–1938), **Erich Heckel** (1883–1970) and **Karl Schmidt-Rottluff** (1884–1976). They revived the woodcut as an art form and put such emphasis on colour that it became as much a component of their paintings as the subject itself. Soon after it was founded the group (with some new members tagging along behind them) moved from Dresden to Berlin, left off painting gaudy landscapes and turned to scenes from city life. They broke up to follow their individual careers in 1913, Kirchner having the most sustained success.

Der Blaue Reiter was formed in 1911 by two artists scorned by the powerful Munich establishment—**Wassily Kandinsky** (1866–1944) and **Franz Marc** (1880–1916). Later they were joined by (amongst others) **August Macke** (1887–1914) and the Swiss painter **Paul Klee** (1879–1940), and *Der Blaue Reiter* became a more loosely knit group, aimed at promoting Modernism in all the arts. Colour, line and shape became more important than subject matter—a brave and imaginative step that set painting well on the way to pure abstraction. Kandinsky was already being called an 'abstract Expressionist' in 1919. He divided his work into *Compositions* (consciously planned and ordered geometrical shapes) and *Improvisations* (spontaneous arrangements of colour). Marc's work was more representational; he loved painting animals. He was beginning to move towards a more abstract, geometrical style when he was killed in the First World War. Macke (who also died in the war) painted gentle scenes—often of slender, brightly dressed figures floating through parks or down quiet streets. Before he died his work began to show a Cubist influence. Klee was the oddest of the four. His paintings and drawings are usually small—subtle, whimsical figures of men, animals and fantastical creatures drawn with child-like brevity. They seem to lift the lid on a sensitive, very personal view of a mysterious universe.

Many of Germany's most renowned Expressionists, however, belonged to neither school. The most individualistic of these (though he was for a time a member of *Die Brücke*) was **Emil Hansen** (1867–1956), known as **Nolde** after his birthplace. His distorted, violent canvases are very much reminiscent of Grünewald, or the Flemish painter Hieronymus Bosch. **George Grosz** (1893–1959) was a prominent member of the anarchic Berlin Dadaists (*see* below), and is best known for the savage, indignant caricature-like drawings with which he lambasted capitalist society, and the decadent Weimar Republic in particular. **Käthe Kollwitz** (1867–1945), one of the leading women artists of the 20th century, took the woodcut and engraving to heights not reached since Dürer. Her wrenching black and white images are usually powerful, poignant cries against the horrors of war. After her son was killed in the First World War she became preoccupied with a Mother and Child theme, and when her grandson was killed in the Second World War her woodcuts and sculptures became howls of the deepest tragedy. **Ernst Barlach** (1870–1938) produced haunting sculptures with sharp, smoothly planed lines that show medieval influence. **Max Beckmann** (1884–1950) was an independently minded painter who bridged the gap to *Neue Sachlichkeit* (*see* below). His bitter paintings of distorted figures accentuated by hard, black lines reflect the horrors of the First World War and of Nazi oppression. Often he paints himself as a clown, king or convict—the artist buffeted by his times.

Bauhaus

In 1906 the Belgian Jugendstil designer **Henry van de Velde** (1863–1957) started a School of Arts and Crafts in Weimar. When he left Germany at the outbreak of the First World War he recommended a young architect, **Walter Gropius** (1883–1969), as his successor. In 1919 Gropius took over the directorship, changed the name of the school to Das Staatliche Bauhaus Weimar, redesigned the curriculum and eventually (in 1925) moved the whole caboodle to a sparkling new building in Dessau. The new Bauhaus, which immediately attracted artists such as Kandinsky and Klee as teachers, was rooted in the Arts and Crafts tradition of the previous century in that it offered a broad range of disciplines from architecture to drama and basket weaving. However, it set itself squarely in post-war Germany and, unlike the Arts and Crafts movement in Britain, it was prepared to exploit modern mass-production techniques to solve problems in areas such as housing and urban planning. Bauhaus wanted to unite art and technology and had two main aims—to work '*am Bau*' (in connection with a real building, rather than just theoretically), and to come up with inventive but practical prototypes for industry.

In 1911 the American architect Frank Lloyd Wright (1867–1959) held a tremendously influential exhibition in Berlin. Around the same time the Swiss architect Charles Edouard Jeanneret-Gris (1887–1965, known as Le Corbusier) was designing rectilinear 'functional' houses—'machines for living'. Both men used the new invention of prestressed concrete to revolutionize building design, and became leading exponents of the **International Style**—a 'machine-age' architecture of clean, straight lines, open-plan interiors and no decoration at all. (One architect went so far as to call decoration a 'crime'.) The Dessau Bauhaus not only fitted into this climate, but firmly established the principles of the International Style. Indeed Gropius designed the skeleton of concrete slabs held up by steel pillars that was to be the heart of Le Corbusier's buildings and which still forms the basic structure of much of 20th-century architecture. Buildings designed by Gropius and other Bauhaus architects, such as the superbly imaginative **Ludwig Mies van der Rohe** (1886–1969, designer of New York's Seagram Building), became touchstones of modern architecture. A number of Bauhaus architects went to the USA in the 1930s. Their enormous influence on the design world there helped to make the USA the leader of architectural and design style in the immediate post-war era.

Neue Sachlichkeit

Neue Sachlichkeit is usually translated into English as 'New Objectivity'—a loose term which is really only right when you take objectivity to mean neutrality or 'matter-of-fact-ness'. The name describes a small trend that grew up in opposition to Expressionism around 1923. *Neue Sachlichkeit* artists painted with a ruthless realism, often with a harsh almost sadistic touch and an acid left-wing political comment. Though many of the painters in this new movement had come through a period of Expressionism, they now renounced what they regarded as Expressionism's emotional excess and lack of control. The *Neue Sachlichkeit* painters, as had many of the Expressionists, used the city as subject matter, but their focus was hard and (they believed) without sentiment. 'Man is good' had been the Expressionist dictum. 'Man is a beast' retorted George Grosz at the beginning of the 1920s. George Grosz and Max Beckmann were both associated with the style for a time, but its most famous practitioner was **Otto Dix** (1891–1969). His meticulous, at times rather vicious pictures show grotesque, larger-than-life characters and dwell on human suffering and the decadence of city life.

Oddly, *Neue Sachlichkeit* and Bauhaus had little to do with each other, though the no-frills, tidy approach characteristic of both schools has led to the work of some later Bauhaus artists being given a *Neue Sachlichkeit* label. Later *Neue Sachlicheit* work spills over into complete abstraction with the work of **Willi Baumeister** (1889–1955) and **Oskar Schlemmer** (1888–1943), a mercurial artist who flits between styles and schools. He is perhaps most famous for the ballets he designed for students at the Bauhaus.

The Dadaists

The zany, irreverent, nihilistic Dada movement (which was based mainly in Zurich, Barcelona and New York) had its followers in Germany too. Dada art was intentionally disruptive and ephemeral. **Kurt Schwitters** (1887–1948), however, did contribute some more lasting works. He made collages from rubbish and scrap paper, which he called *Merz Pictures*. (*Merz* is a syllable from the German word for 'commercial', and caught Schwitters' attention one day when he was cutting up newspapers). **Max Ernst** (1891–1976) began as a Dadaist, also making collages, but in the 1920s he left Germany for America and France, where he turned more towards Surrealism.

After the War

In 1937 the Nazis had held an exhibition of *Entartete Kunst* ('Degenerate Art') in Munich. Most of the prominent artists of the day were featured, and their work was later banned or destroyed. It is not surprising that after this, and the horrors of the Second World War, German artists wanted to start afresh. In 1957 Heinz Mack (b.1931), Günther Uecker (b.1930) and Otto Piene (b.1928) formed **ZERO**. Their aim was to strip away all the elements by which art was traditionally defined and reduce it to pure absolutes—space and colour. Their anti-individualist manifesto had an influence all over Europe, and in the 1960s artists began to come up with completely blank monochrome canvases.

Other German artists, working in more individual ways, have also made a mark on the international scene. **Georg Baselitz** (b.1938) is the most easily recognizable, as he hangs his bright, energetic, rather primitive paintings upside down in an attempt to make you redefine the way you see things. **Sigmar Polke** (b.1941) began by painting abstract designs onto boards, blankets and odd bits of cloth, but has recently become intrigued by colour, producing thinly coated pastel-shaded panels. **Anselm Kiefer** (b.1945) wants to counter the power of American culture by appealing to the traditions of Old Europe. He works on a monumental scale employing good, old-fashioned painterly skills in new ways. His vast paintings would seem to hark back to the styles of the Renaissance, but are filled with modern surprises such as tacked on bits of paper and the odd hole in the canvas. **A. R. Penck** (b.1939) paints giant stick figures interspersed with symbols from different epochs—from mythological signs to technical designs.

The movement of art over the past few decades—away from painting and towards installation, performance and constructed sculpture—is seen by many to have its origins in the work of **Joseph Beuys** (1921–85). Beuys has been called the father of the European avant-garde. His piles of fat and felt and esoteric statements on man and nature are to be found all over Germany, and are imitated in art colleges around the world. His 'action art'—walks or water journeys, planting oak trees in Kassel—have become the core of much recent ecologically focused work.

The work of **Gerhard Richter** (b.1932) is more accessible and is becoming increasingly popular. He begins with photographs (often of animals, the sky, or family snaps), blows them up and lightly stylizes them, frequently in shades of grey and blue paint. **Jörg Immendorf** (b.1945) is best known for his grotesque carvings, and nightmarish paintings that would seem to owe a debt to Otto Dix. Like Dix, he takes his politics seriously and his works often carry an overt political message.

The destruction wrought by Allied bombers led to a building boom in the 1950s and 1960s. Much of the work was hurried, functional and ugly. The trend towards

Brutalism—an austere style that had its origins in the Bauhaus and is characterized by its emphasis on the building materials (especially bare concrete) and unconcealed service pipes—did little to improve the situation. The one area where there was interesting innovation was in **church architecture**, and more recently inventive designs for shiny glass hotels, office blocks, museum buildings and concert halls have been popping up in cities all over Germany, including Bavaria, assisted by healthy federal budgets.

Literature: A Concise Chronology of Bavarian Writing

The Middle Ages

Not counting a fragment of the nine lines of the 8th-century *Wessobrunn Prayer*, the beginning of German literature in Bavaria is usually seen as the *Abrogans*, a glossary of German words from medieval Latin dating from *c.* AD 765, preserved in the Bavarian State Library in Munich. Later, Bavarian monasteries spawned a rich heritage of religious lectionaries and sacred poetry. In 1050 a monk in the abbey at Tegernsee eulogized the adventures of a young Christian knight in the *Ruodlieblied* (only fragments of which still exist). In the 12th century the abbey was the source of the **mystery plays** that became the bedrock of popular Christian instruction. Close contact with French culture during long marches to the Holy Land in the 12th century fired crusaders with an enthusiasm for ballads and narrative poems and led to the evolution of the *Minnesang* (*see* 'Music' p.58). At the same time writers began to record sagas and anthologies from Germany's rich oral tradition. One of these, the *Carmina Burana*, originates from the abbey at Benediktbeuren around 1250 (*see* 'Music' p.58).

c. **1250: Wernher der Gartenaere.** A Franciscan friar most famed for the rustic tale of *Meier Helmbrecht* about an idle farmer's son, who left his village near the River Inn to lead the life of a wanderer.

1477–1534: Aventin. Lanky, red-haired innkeeper's son, who took up the name of his Bavarian birthplace (Abensberg) and became a best-selling author of his time, in spite of his secret leanings towards emerging Lutherism. His Latin textbooks and Bavarian Chronicle of 1522 led to a flourishing of early German printed books in Bavaria.

Jesuit Plays

In the 17th century the Catholic Wittelsbachs took it upon themselves to champion the cause of the Counter-Reformation through a number of mystery and morality plays produced under the aegis of the Jesuit order. The plays set the Virgin and saints firmly back on their pedestals and led to a burgeoning of religious drama that has survived to this day in the form of rural **passion plays** such as the one at Oberammergau.

1578–1639: Jacob Bidermann. A professor of rhetoric at Munich, Bidermann developed a kind of educational drama that served to teach morality and the transience of human greatness—as in his most illuminating play, *Cenodoxus, Doctor of Paris* (1609).

The Golden Age

The heyday of Bavarian literature was during Bavaria's Golden Age in the second half of the 19th century, when Munich came to play a major role in the intellectual life of a recently united Germany. The triumph of nationalism, and the growth-pains of the Industrial Revolution, led to the emergence of much politically inspired literature. Stylistically, apart from the odd experimenter, writers favoured a more earthy, naturalistic approach, in reaction to the Romanticism of the previous decades.

1830–1914: Paul von Heyse. Poet and poet laureate of King Maximilian II. Together with fellow lyricist **Emanuel Geibel** (1815–84) he presided over a celebrated literary circle, known as Maxililian II's *Tafelrunde* (Round Table). Heyse received the Nobel Prize for literature in 1911.

1855–1920: Ludwig Ganghofer. Having spent most of his adult life as dramatist in Vienna, Ganghofer returned to Munich to compile an anthology of Bavarian folk tales inspired by popular local oral culture.

1867–1921: Ludwig Thoma. A lawyer from Dachau turned writer. He is known for his politically engaged articles in the satirical periodical *Simplicissimus* (writing under the pseudonym of Peter Schlemihl). He later upset his fellow Bavarians with wry yarns about the incestuous, small-minded village life in his native Upper Bavaria.

1881–1920: Lena Christ. Bavaria's most illustrious female novelist wrote two doleful psychological novellas, *Rumpelhanni* and *Erinnerungen einer Überflüssigen* (Recollections of an Unwanted Person) based on her own humiliating childhood memories (she was an illegitimate child). Later she committed suicide in one of Munich's cemeteries.

1882–1948: Karl Valentin. Bavaria's answer to Charles Chaplin. A performing comedian as well as a humorist, the lanky Valentin drew heavily on his experience on the Variety stage. His collection of quirky sketches was a great inspiration to Germany's surrealist movement (*see* p.71).

1894–1967: Oskar Maria Graf. In his *Bayerisches Dekameron*, a collection of erotic tales, and his novel *Wir sind Gefangen* (We are Prisoners), Graf, a politically active socialist, captures a strong sense of ambivalence and duality. When his books weren't banned by the Nazis, Graf grumpily announced, from his Austrian exile, that they deserved to be burnt too. Then he emigrated to the United States.

Music

Germany has produced some of the world's greatest composers. (Many—such as Mozart—were, in fact, Austrian, but this is a pedantic quibble.) For centuries Vienna and Leipzig were the twin vortices of European music, and in each major period German musicians have been among the great movers and shakers in their field. Even the briefest of overviews of the development of German music leaves you wondering if there was anyone of note left who *wasn't* German.

Beginnings

Discounting ancient military horns whose chief function was to make a stirring racket, we can trace the beginnings of German music back to the early Middle Ages, and to two main sources—the church and the court. The first manuscripts of **ecclesiastical music** (such as the *Carmina Burana*) date back to the 12th century, and as early as the 11th century courtiers were entertained by wandering troubadours. These minstrels developed a form of lyrical ballad known as the **Minnesang** (from the German for love song). Most famous of all minnesingers was **Walther von der Vogelweide** (1170–1228)—some of his songs have survived, and devotees still decorate his grave in Würzburg with flowers (*see* p.147). By the 15th and 16th centuries the minnesingers had organized themselves into guilds, and were recognized as master craftsmen—local supremos being granted the title of *Meistersinger* (master-singer). The inventiveness and spontaneity that had characterized the Minnesang, however, was strangled by rigid and complicated rules enforced by the guilds. Top-ranking *Meistersinger* of all time was **Hans Sachs** (1494–1576), a Nuremberg cobbler who produced some 6000 works. In the 19th century Richard Wagner—who, like his Romantic contemporaries, was fascinated by Germany's medieval past—celebrated Sachs and his colleagues in the opera *The Mastersingers of Nuremberg*.

Early Music and the Baroque Period

For a long time court and church music developed alongside each other. In the churches the **part-song** flourished, and led to the growth of motets and masses. The earthier, more popular hymns that came into fashion in Protestant churches during the Reformation had repercussions in Roman Catholic church music too, developing into chorales and cantatas. After the banquet and around the hearth the movement was more towards instrumental and dance music. The main domestic instrument was the lute, though later small orchestras were formed and from the 15th century onwards independent instrumental forms—such as the sonata and the concerto—began to emerge. Also at around this time the organ began to be used as a solo instrument in churches.

The Thirty Years' War put a stop to most cultural activity across the whole country. The Germany that emerged after the war was a very different place. Old feudal structures had been severely shaken, and local merchants were becoming more powerful. When a musical revival came, it happened in town orchestras, choirs, student *Collegia Musica* and opera houses. (Germany's first opera houses opened in the second part of the 17th century in Dresden, Munich and Hamburg.) Two rival musicians emerged during this period— **Georg Philipp Telemann** (1681–1767) and **Johann Sebastian Bach** (1685–1750). At the time Telemann was considered the superior of the two. Bach's work as a composer was all but forgotten after his death. Even though he had given new depth and impetus to forms such as the cantata and oratorio, and propelled chamber music to new heights, this was only acknowledged in the 19th century when his great works—such as the *Brandenburg Concertos* and the *St Matthew Passion*—were rediscovered. Another innovative composer of the time, an early master of opera and oratorio, was **Georg Friedrich Händel** (1685–1759). Händel eventually settled in England, where he changed his name to Handel and composed the famous *Messiah* (1741).

The Classical Period

The second half of the 18th century saw the blossoming of new musical genres, notably the symphony. Many of these new forms, as well as older ones such as the sonata and concerto, were given their classical shape by composers **Joseph Haydn** (1732–1809) and the man many consider to be the greatest musical genius of all time, **Wolfgang Amadeus Mozart** (1756–91). Mozart also took German opera to a new summit, while **Ludwig van Beethoven** (1770–1827) is usually considered to be the most powerful exponent of the symphony. He gave the three dominant forms of the classical period—the symphony, the string quartet and the piano sonata—dramatic new expression; his tremendous, moody later symphonies set the tone for the Romantic movement of the 19th century.

Romantic and 19th-century Music

The success of the French Revolution seemed to inspire artists to a celebration of humankind's freedom and power, which was accompanied by a loosening of classical restraints on form. Early 19th-century instrumental music—such as that by **Felix Mendelssohn-Bartholdy** (1809–47) and **Robert Schumann** (1810–56)—is still bound by classical structure, but the final operas of **Carl Maria von Weber** (1786–1826), and music by **Anton Bruckner** (1824–96) and **Johannes Brahms** (1833–97) align German music with the Romantic movement that was sweeping the country.

The grand master of the Romantic opera is undoubtedly **Richard Wagner** (1813–83). Wagner drew on heroic tales from German mythology, wrote his own libretti and involved himself in all aspects of staging. He wanted his 'musical dramas' to be spiritually uplifting *Gesamtkunstwerke* (total works of art), and brought a new psychological density to opera. Musically, his approach was also revolutionary—especially in his use of the *Leitmotiv*, a recurring theme used to depict a character, or evoke an idea or change in psychological state. Wagner's name is closely associated with Bavaria, through the passionate patronage of King Ludwig II, and through Bayreuth, which Wagner made his home, and which stages the famous Wagner Festival every year.

Two further developments occurred in the 19th century that are still felt today. The German *Lied*, which had had its foundations in song-cycles by **Franz Schubert** (1797–1828), became an independent form that was to keep its popularity with composers into the 20th century. Also, people began to make a clearer distinction between serious and light music, though the latter had perfectly respectable champions in German-born **Jacques Offenbach** (1819–80)—best known as the composer of *Orpheus in the Underworld*, the music used for the can-can—and in the father and son whose name is synonymous with the waltz: **Johann Strauss** Senior (1804–49) and Junior (1825–99).

Into the 20th Century

Gustav Mahler (1860–1911), who carried the torch for the symphonic form, and **Richard Strauss** (1873–1946), whose operas such as *Salome* and *Der Rosenkavalier* are very much constructed on groundwork laid out by Wagner, move German music into contemporary times. In the 20th century Germany has had its share of inventive, though traditionally orientated, composers—such as **Paul Hindemith** (1895–1963) and **Carl Orff** (1895–1982), whose energetic *Carmina Burana* is one of the most widely listened to of all modern 'serious' compositions. More adventurous experimenters include **Arnold Schönberg** (1874–1951), whose **twelve-tone system** completely redefined musical frontiers, and the Cologne-based **Karlheinz Stockhausen** (b.1928) whose performances continue to delight and perplex.

Cinema

Thanks to the patronage of the Wittelsbachs and Munich-based financiers at the beginning of the 20th century, cinema quickly developed into a respected art form in Bavaria. As early as the 1920s film-makers from around the world came to Munich, the centre of the region's film industry, lured by excellent studios and technical equipment. A then unknown **Alfred Hitchcock** made an appearance in 1925 with his *The Pleasure Garden*, and *Mountain Eagle* followed a year later. Even in the bleak years of the Second World War a series of insipid escapist movies were shot here, most notably under the talented direction of **Helmut Käutner**, who had started his career as an actor and comedian.

Following the post-war division of Germany, Munich's studios benefited greatly from the fact that their main rivals around Berlin remained off-limits for West-German film-makers, and they soon became the centre of the revival of German art cinema. In 1959 the **Bavaria Film Studios**, which had begun production in 1920, were reorganized at Geiselgasteig on the southern edge of town. Here the young German directors tended to work as *auteurs*, often producing the film and writing the screenplay as well, giving the work a distinctive personal imprint. The 1970s were the heyday of this **new German cinema**, with the big three directors (**Fassbinder**, **Wenders** and **Herzog**) producing a string of Munich-based, award-winning films and commercial successes.

As a consequence, Munich became known as the 'Los Angeles of the Isar Valley', and increasingly drew international film-makers into its orbit. As early as 1957 **Stanley Kubrick** filmed the interior sets for *Paths of Glory* at the Bavaria Studios. Actors of the calibre of Dirk Bogarde, Gregory Peck and Kirk Douglas (for Richard Fleischer's *The Vikings*) worked here. In 1971 **Bob Fosse** made a name for himself in Munich with the production of *Cabaret*, and the **Monty Python** team also filmed in Munich.

By the late 1970s Munich had spawned a new generation of German directors, fascinated with recent Hollywood successes. **Wolfgang Petersen** shot to fame in 1981 with his epic wartime drama *The Boat*, one of the costliest film productions ever attempted in Germany and filmed almost entirely at Munich's Bavaria Studios. The series of worldwide successes continued with the productions of *The NeverEnding Story* (1983), *Enemy Mine* (1985) and most recently *Stalingrad* (1993) (*see* also p.83).

Munich

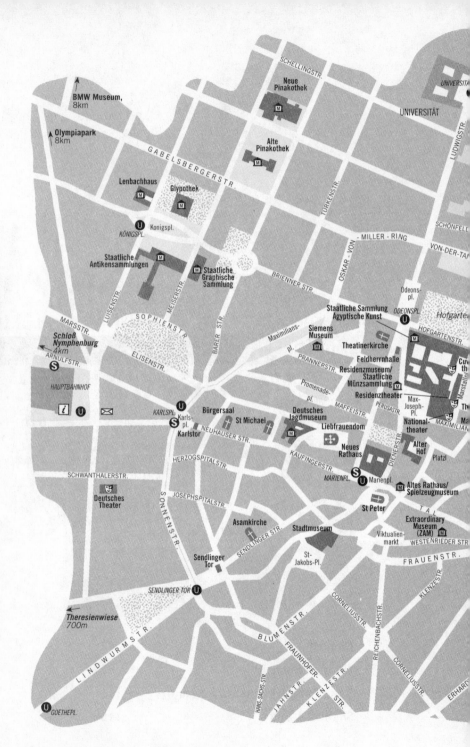

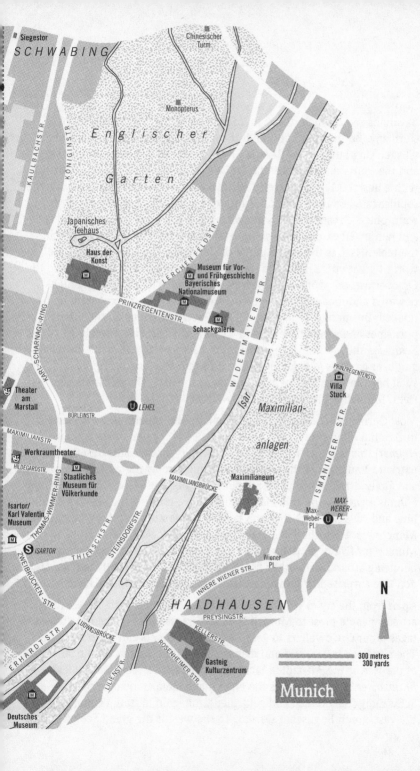

Siegestor

SCHWABING

Chinesischer
Turm

Monopterus

E n g l i s c h e r

KAULBACHSTR.

KÖNIGINSTR.

G a r t e n

Japanisches
Teehaus

Haus der
Kunst

LERCHENFELDSTR.

Museum für Vor-
und Frühgeschichte
Bayerisches
Nationalmuseum

PRINZREGENTENSTR.

Schackgalerie

WIDENMAYERSTR.

Isar

PRINZREGENTENSTR

Villa
Stuck

KARL-SCHARNAGL-RING

Theater
am
Marstall

BÜRLEINSTR.

LEHEL

Maximilian-

anlagen

ISMANINGER STR.

MAXIMILIANSTR.

Werkraumtheater

HILDEGARDSTR.

Staatliches
Museum für
Völkerkunde

THOMAS-WIMMER-RING

MAXIMILIANSBRÜCKE

Maximilianeum

Max-
Weber-
Pl.

*MAX-
WEBER-
PL.*

Isartor/
Karl Valentin
Museum

ISARTOR

THIERSCHSTR.

STEINSDORFSTR.

ZWEIBRÜCKEN-STR.

Wiener
Pl.

INNERE WIENER STR.

HAIDHAUSEN

PREYSINGSTR.

KELLERSTR

ERHARDTSTR.

LUDWIGSBRÜCKE

LILIENSTR.

ROSENHEIMER STR.

Gasteig
Kulturzentrum

N

Deutsches
Museum

300 metres
300 yards

Munich

'Der Deutsche Himmel.'

('It's the German Heaven', Thomas Wolfe)

'Voilà une capitale.'

(Charles de Gaulle, on his first visit)

Bavarians see Munich (German: *München*) as the 'secret capital' of Germany. Berliners sniffily call it the *Millionendorf*, a big provincial village. King Ludwig I of Bavaria proclaimed it the 'Athens on the Isar', and the tourist brochures settle for *'Weltstadt mit Herz'* (the metropolis with a heart). Munich herself can't make up her mind whether she is the sophisticated courtier, or boisterous village wench. Her architectural wardrobe is a resplendent, somewhat too grand array of royal cast-offs, and her jewelbox dazzles—yet one whiff of hops and she's dancing on the table. Here is the stratosphere of German high society, one of the world's great opera houses, a transcendent collection of art—and also the Oktoberfest, the world's beeriest beano. Munich is fast-moving, high-powered and modern, yet everyone seems fresh-faced, exuberant and relaxed. Businessmen dart out of flashy new office blocks, shed their pinstripes and sunbathe by the River Isar. In smart cafés, wealthy *Schickies* show off designer versions of Bavarian *Tracht*, while in cellars and beer gardens jolly families in real *Lederhosen* and feathered hats swill beer and try to drown out the oompah band. The Berliners are right. Munich *is* parochial. That is what makes it so enticing.

Most Germans dream of living in Munich. The popular press (especially in Bavaria) often prints polls showing that (if they had to leave their *Heimat*) this is the city most Germans would choose. This despite the patriotic smugness of the locals—Munich is simply the best in everything and *Zugereiste* (newcomers) remain so for decades—and the Föhn. The Föhn is a warm wind that blows off the Alps, clearing the sky to a crystal blue and causing headaches and bolshie bad-temper in otherwise cheery Münchners. Even the Föhn is wary of *Zugereiste*. You have to live in Munich for five or so years before you begin to feel its effect. So if you're bouncing around with other happy visitors on an apparently perfect day, don't be surprised by growling barmen and snappy shop assistants.

Apart from the style, conviviality and super-elegant architecture, what attracts people most to Munich is its setting and size. In the time that it takes other city-dwellers to get to work, Münchners can be in the Alps. The city itself is compact and manageable. In the centre, on the left bank of the Isar, is the Altstadt, a racing heart of swish streets and rollicking *Brauhäuser*. To the north is the erstwhile bohemian quarter of Schwabing (now tamed and gentrified), the main museum complex and the vast, green Englischer Garten. To the west is the grand Schloß

Nymphenburg. Across the river and to the south you'll find the quirkier corners, pockets of immigrants and artists and the biggest technical museum in the world.

History

In 1158 the Emperor Frederick Barbarossa was called on to settle a dispute between his uncle, Bishop Otto von Freising, and his cousin, Henry the Lion. Otto had controlled a very profitable toll bridge across the Isar—directly on the lucrative salt route. With his customary leonine ferocity, Henry had simply burnt the bridge down, and built his own further along the river. He called the settlement that subsequently sprang up 'Munichen', after the monks who had built a new church nearby. A cautious Barbarossa decided in favour of his cousin, though in 1180 Henry fell from grace (for refusing military help to the emperor) and power was handed over to the Wittelsbach family. They ruled Bavaria continuously right up until 1918.

At first the capital of the region was Regensburg. The first Wittelsbach to set up home in Munich was Duke Ludwig the Severe, who built a suitably plain Residenz in 1255. By the beginning of the 16th century Munich was capital and the official family seat.

The salt trade boomed, and Munich got fat. Even the Thirty Years' War, which devastated the rest of Germany, left the town relatively undiminished. (King Gustavus Adolphus of Sweden called it 'the golden saddle on a scraggy nag'.) In the 18th century, Baroque style blossomed here as hardly anywhere else north of Italy. Then, in 1806, Napoleon made Bavaria a kingdom. The first king, Ludwig I, with his penchant for Neoclassical architecture, set about creating his Athens of the north, but a love affair with the Spanish dancer Lola Montez caused a scandal which eventually led to his abdication. Ludwig's son, Maximilian II, also had the building bug, and Munich grew even grander. The next king, Ludwig II, brought Wagner to Munich (*see* p.180), but hated the capital and spent most of his time in the mountains, dressing up and building fantastical castles.

In the 1900s, under Prince Regent Luitpold, Munich became one of the centres of European intellectual life. Jugendstil germinated here, and during the first part of the century, in smoky cafés in the Schwabing district, you could have met the likes of Trotsky and Thomas Mann, the painters Marc, Kandinsky and Klee or the playwright Bertolt Brecht.

Hitler put an end to this Golden Age. In 1919 he established his Nazi party headquarters in Munich, and though his 1923 putsch failed (*see* p.38), he made Munich the 'Capital of our Movement'. It was here that Chamberlain signed the agreement he was sure meant 'peace in our time' in 1938. Within months war was declared. Munich was the centre of a gallant anti-Nazi resistance movement, the White Rose, but the organization was crushed and the leaders executed. In the last years of the war, heavy Allied bombing destroyed 40 per cent of the city centre. However, most of the Baroque buildings (and, alas, some of Hitler's monstrosities) survived. Restoration work has been careful and sensitive, and there are few high-rise blocks or ugly concrete sprawls.

Today Munich still has a flourishing artistic life. There are more theatres here than in any other city in Germany, and it is the centre of the German film industry (*see* p.82–3). Fassbinder lived and worked here for years. Nearly one fifth of the city's population are scholars or students, and there is a busy publishing industry.

Above a bohemian undercurrent lies a glossy layer of prosperous bankers, insurance brokers and hi-tech industrialists. The twinkle in Munich's social sheen is still the Wittelsbach family. They are an unofficial local royalty. Bavarians still address the Duke of Bavaria as 'Your Royal Highness', and the Wittelsbach parties at Schloß Nymphenburg are the *ne plus ultra* of the Munich social calendar.

Getting Around

by air

Munich's spanking new **Franz Josef Strauß Airport** (✆ (089) 97 52 13 13) has non-stop flights to New York (8hrs), London (2hrs) and most other European capitals. Line S8 on the S-Bahn gets you to the Hauptbahnhof in 39 minutes, for only DM10. The Airport Bus also goes to the Hauptbahnhof (Arnulfstraße entrance). It takes 45 minutes and costs DM12. Both services leave every 20 minutes.

by train

Munich's cavernous **Hauptbahnhof** deposits you just west of the city centre, and immediately locks into the extensive metro system. Munich is a hub of rail travel, and Europe's fastest trains will speed you all over Germany and across its borders. For train information ✆ (089) 1 94 19, for reservations ✆ (089) 12 23/23 33.

by car

Munich is also a major node on Germany's *Autobahn* system, though the Munich–Berlin route barely copes with post-unification traffic. Pedestrians rule in the middle of town and, though some parking is available, it's better to use one of the parking lots south of the centre, or around the Bahnhof, and rely on public transport.

Car hire: Europcar, Schwanthalerstr. 10a, ✆ (089) 594 723.

Mitfahrzentrale: Lämmerstr. 4, ✆ (089) 59 45 61.

public transport

A fast and efficient system of trams, buses and S-Bahn and U-Bahn trains will whisk you all over the city between 5am and 1am. A single ticket costs DM2.50, but you may find it more cost effective to buy a *Tageskarte* (Day Ticket; DM8 for central zone, DM16 for entire metropolitan area). This entitles two adults, three children and a dog to unlimited travel from 9am on one day to 4am on the next. There is no expiry date on a *Streifenkarte* (Strip Ticket; DM10 for 20 strips). Two strips are valid for travel (with appropriate hops and changes) for two hours in any one direction. *Streifenkarten* and single tickets must be validated at the beginning of each journey, and *Tageskarten* should be stamped before setting out on your first journey. (Validating punches are found on buses and trams and at the entrance to stations.) You can buy tickets from dispensing machines at the stops, tobacconists and newsagents with a white K in the window, or on buses and trams. For bus and tram information ✆ (089) 23 80 30 (for S-Bahn information ✆ (089) 55 75 75).

Taxi: ✆ (089) 21610 or (089) 19410.

by bicycle

If you take the S-Bahn out into the countryside around Munich, you'll find that many railway stations also operate an inexpensive bicycle rental service (ask at the parcels counter). Radius Touristik, Arnulfstr. 3, ✆ (089) 59 61 13, near the Hauptbahnhof, rents out bikes at DM15 per day (DM45 per week) and also offers guided cycle tours.

Tourist Information

Tourist information offices: Hauptbahnhof, Bayerstraße entrance, ✆ (089) 23 91 256/7 (*daily 8am–10pm*); Airport, ✆ (089) 97 59 28 15 (*Mon–Sat 8.30am–10pm, Sun 1pm–9pm*); Rindermarkt, Pettenbeckstraße (*Mon–Fri 9.30–6*). They supply brochures and maps, and for DM5 will book you a room (no phone bookings).

Post office: Opposite the Hauptbahnhof (*open 24 hours*). It has ranks of telephones and fax machines, and a good **bureau de change**.

American Express: Promenadeplatz 6, ✆ (089) 2 19 90, and you'll find main branches of most German **banks** in the immediate vicinity.

Ambulance: ✆ 1 92 22.

Emergency medical service: ✆ (089) 55 86 61.

Emergency pharmacy service: ✆ (089) 59 44 75.

Police: ✆ 110.

consulates

American: Königinstr. 5, ✆ (089) 2 88 80.

British: Bürkleinstr. 10, ✆ (089) 21 10 90.

Canadian: Tal 29, ✆ (089) 22 26 61.

Festivals

The first thing to note about the famous **Oktoberfest** is that it takes place in September. In just over two weeks (from mid-September to the first Sunday in October), crowds of revellers get through over five million litres of beer, half a million sausages, 650,000 chickens, 70,000 knuckles of pork and usually around 70 oxen. Most of the drinking is done in enormous beer tents on the Theresienwiese (the 'Wies'n'—a vast fairground just behind the Hauptbahnhof), under the watchful eye of the towering statue of Bavaria. Those who have had their fill of beer and oompah bands spill out of the beer tents to whoop it up on the dodgems, big dippers and various other stomach-churning spins and rides in the surrounding funfair. The autumn air is pungent with the smell of roasting meat, spilt beer and toasted almonds.

During the Oktoberfest there are balls and parties all over town, and two spectacular parades. The **Opening Parade** of landlords and brewers starts at 11am on the first day of the *Fest*. Landlords and their families ride to the fairground in ornate carriages or prettily decorated horse-drawn drays. You can jostle with the crowds in Schwanthalerstraße, or get a better view from the grandstand in Sonnenstraße (tickets DM36 from the tourist office). On the first Sunday of the festival there is a two-hour-long **procession** of bands, coaches, decorated floats, people in traditional dress, thoroughbred horses, prize oxen and even the odd goat. The route goes from the Max II Denkmal, through the city centre to the fairground. Grandstand seats will set you back DM55, but there's an enclosed standing area at Odeonsplatz where you can avoid the worst of the crush for DM16 (tickets from the tourist office).

Rather wisely, there is **no parking** around the Oktoberfest grounds, so people are encouraged to use public transport. The **U-Bahn** to Theresienwiese (Lines 4 and 5) is very crowded; Lines 3 and 6 to Goetheplatz or Poccistraße are easier going and deposit you a short walk from the southern end of the grounds.

Munich's **Stadtgründungsfest** (City Anniversary, mid-June) is a much smaller affair, but in many ways more fun. This is the festival the locals keep for themselves. From Marienplatz to Odeonsplatz and in the courtyards of the Rathaus you'll find food stalls, long beer tables and *ad hoc* cafés. Lots of people dress up in traditional *Tracht*, and even those who don't are prone to bouts of folk-dancing. Aromas of pretzels, fresh chocolate, crispy pork and countless other local and foreign foods fill the air. Oompah bands, local choirs and visiting musicians keep up a steady beat. There is an intimate, birthday-party atmosphere, no uncomfortable crush and only a scattering of tourists.

Those with a liking for fleamarkets should keep an eye open for the **Auer Dult**, an outdoor fleamarket on Mariahilfplatz that takes place three times a year (for eight days at the ends of April, July and October). The **Christkindlmarkt**, Munich's Christmas market, is on Marienplatz from the end of November. Stalls sell gifts, kitsch and trivia, but also charming German handmade decorations and lots of *Glühwein* and food. Every evening at 5.30pm you can hear live Christmas music.

Munich has its own lively carnival tradition—here the celebration is called **Fasching**. Hi-jinks last from mid-January to Shrove Tuesday, with rounds of Costume Balls and jolly doings at the Viktualienmarkt on the final day.

On the cultural side there is the **Münchner Opernfest**, an opera festival of world renown which takes place from mid-July until the beginning of August. Tickets are hard to come by, so it is a good idea to contact the tourist office or the Nationaltheater, ℰ (089) 221 316, long before the event if you wish to attend. During the festival there are also special concerts held all over town.

Marienplatz and the Southern Altstadt

Marienplatz has been the centre of Munich since the town began. It started life as a corn market, then became a public execution site and jousting arena. In 1315 Emperor Ludwig the Bavarian affably decreed that the square should never be built on, so that it would remain 'all the more jolly, attractive and leisurely for gentlemen, citizens and friends'. And so it has—though today it is a touch more frenetic than leisurely.

There is no motor traffic in 'Munich's parlour' (as locals call it), just two types of people: those criss-crossing the square with purpose, and those sitting about in randomly scattered white metal chairs, chatting sociably or cricking their necks to look up at the points and pinnacles of the Neo-Gothic **Neues Rathaus**.

The Neues Rathaus, which fills the entire northern edge of Marienplatz, was built between 1867 and 1909 to supersede the far more graceful, real Gothic **Altes Rathaus** (built in 1475, on the east side of the square). The modest tower of the Altes Rathaus contains a small **Toy Museum** (*see* 'Museums' below). The tower of the 19th-century upstart is a full 80m high, and sports an elaborate *Glockenspiel*. Every day, at 11am (*May–Oct also noon and 5pm*), carved figures re-enact the wedding festivities of the 16th-century lovers Duke Wilhelm V and Renata von Lothringen. At a few minutes past the hour (marked with reckless lack of synchronization by all the bells of the city), the *Glockenspiel* creaks and jangles into life. The carillon hammers out a haphazard and tinny tune as trumpeters, banner-waving citizens and jousting knights jerk past the impassive couple. Below them, figures revolve in the *Schäfflertanz* (coopers' dance)—a joyful jig from 1517 that celebrated the end of the plague. Finally a cock pops out and crows thinly, and it's all over. A trickle of applause runs through the crowd, and they divert their gaze to the buskers on the square.

Just beyond the Altes Rathaus, on Platzl, the famous **Münchner Hofbräuhaus** (literally: Court Brewery) roars and trumpets its way well into the night (*see* 'Bars and Cafés' below). Nearby is **Alter Hof** (Old Court), built up from the sparse ruins of Ludwig the Severe's 13th-century Residenz, but requiring quite a feat of imagination to endow it with any medieval atmosphere.

Just off the south-east corner of Marienplatz, looking loftily out over the town, is **St Peter's**, Munich's oldest church. First records appear in 1169, though most of the present structure was built between the 15th and 17th centuries. The church is no architectural stunner, but locals love it. They call it *Alter Peter* (Old Peter) and come in their hundreds for weddings and Sunday services (after which, in good Munich fashion, they file out for a quick drink in one of the surrounding bars). Visitors can clamber up the tower for a fine view over the city.

South of St Peter's, the **Viktualienmarkt** (produce market) sprawls between ancient chestnut trees. The wooden stalls are daily piled high with bright fruit and flowers. There are choice cuts of game, exotica such as banana leaves and dried worms, and more types of sausage than you could dream of. As you thread between the barrels of wine, piles of eggs and Winnie-the-Pooh honeypots, you get whiffs of freshly baked bread, tangy spices, cheeses and ground coffee. Everything is very much under the control of rosy-cheeked women vendors, renowned for their earthy wit, but notoriously grumpy if you handle their wares. The little alleys (such as Heiligestraße) around the market are lined with long-established family food shops, and are great fun to explore. The Viktualienmarkt is a favourite lunchtime feasting spot for Münchners. In good weather people sit in the midst of it all, drinking beer under the dense shade of the chestnut trees—or duck off into one of the many surrounding Gaståtte (*see* 'Eating and Drinking' below).

East of the market, in Westenrieder Straße, are Munich's quirkiest museums. Seven of them are collected under one roof at **ZAM**, *Das Zentrum für Aussergewöhnliche Museen* (The Centre for Unusual Museums) (*daily 10–6; adm DM8 for the lot*). The **Corkscrew Museum** and the **Padlock Museum** are cabinet-sized and merit but a quick glance; the others are more intriguing. Two millenia's worth of potties fill the **Chamber Pot Museum**—Roman ones with dumpy handles, Chinese porcelain ones with lids, pompous Royal Doulton and nifty Art Deco ones, humble workers' potties and some that met very grand royal bottoms. The **Bourdalou Museum** features the delicate porcelain containers, shaped rather like gravy boats, that discreetly served the needs of 18th and 19th-century society ladies trapped for long hours in toiletless courts. Children can skip off to the **Easter Bunny Museum** (thousands of the creatures), but you'll probably want to join them in the **Pedal Car Museum**. Pedal cars hit the streets soon after the first horseless carriages. There are bone-shaking contraptions from the 1880s; flash mini-Bugattis, Buicks and Morgans; Noddy cars, pert little French numbers and solid British bangers. The **Sisi Museum** is not what English speakers might expect, but a shrine to one of Bavaria's heroines, Elizabeth ('Sisi'), the favourite cousin of Ludwig II, who married the Emperor of Austria.

Elizabeth, Empress of Austria ('Sisi')

 Sisi is the nation's most revered tragic royal, a sort of 19th-century Princess Di. She was born in 1837 to Duke Max in Bayern and his wife Ludovika, sister of the Grand Duchess of Austria. She was a plain child (with the looks of a peasant maid, her aunt complained), but made up for it in sweetness, charm and good humour. By the time she was 16, the ugly duckling had grown into a graceful, rather fetching young woman—so much so that when she bumped into her cousin, Emperor Franz Joseph of Austria, one summer evening in the spa resort of Bad Ischl, he fell head over heels in love with her. The emperor was just seven years Sisi's senior. The match seemed ideal, and it wasn't long before an engagement was announced—despite Sisi's private misgivings. (She kept these doubts to herself, though spelled them out in sorrowful poems in the *Versbüchlein* she kept.)

Sisi's caution was justified. Her aunt and mother-in-law, the domineering Grand Duchess Sophie (perhaps the most politically powerful woman in Europe since Maria Theresa), developed an antagonism to the young bride and made her life at court unbearable. Her relationship with her new husband was also not a success. Sisi began to put herself through punishing fasts. Soon the 1.72m-high empress weighed just 50kg and had a waist measurement of 50cm. She developed fevers and coughs, which immediately disappeared once she was away from Vienna, her husband and her mother-in-law. Publicly, though, Sisi was wildly popular. She had blossomed into an exceptionally beautiful woman, was spirited and sympathetic, and spent her time visiting hospitals and old people's homes. When family pressure got too much for her, she would take herself off to Italy or Greece for 'rest cures' lasting months on end, until the emperor arrived to take her back home. But even these long absences didn't alienate her subjects, who continued to adore their nobly suffering empress.

In 1872 Grand Duchess Sophie died (Sisi nursed her through her final illness and was continually at her bedside), but this did not really ease the lot of the hapless empress. In 1886 her cousin, and one of her closest friends, King Ludwig II of Bavaria drowned in mysterious circumstances (*see* p.183). Then in 1889 her son the Crown Prince Rudolph and his mistress were found dead in an apparent joint suicide. From now on Sisi wore only black, and sank into a deep melancholy. When she was cautiously asked if she didn't feel a sense of rebellion against her fate, she replied coolly '*Nein, ich bin von Stein*' ('No, I'm made of stone'). On 10 September 1898 while, heavily veiled, she was taking an evening walk, she was fatally stabbed by an Italian anarchist who had, in fact, mistaken her for someone else.

Today, like her cousin Ludwig, Sisi has a cult following (especially among Germany's gay community). The museum of her memorabilia in Munich has a shrine-like atmosphere, cafés have been named in her honour and a recent TV series on her life broke viewing records.

Westenrieder Straße leads up to the **Isartor**, one of the three remaining medieval town gates. Here, in one of the towers, is an even odder collection, the **Karl Valentin Museum** (*Mon, Tues, Fri and Sat 11.01–17.29, Sun 10.01–17.29; adm 299 Pfennigs, children and fools [sic] 149 Pfennigs*). Karl Valentin (1882–1948) was the German Charles Chaplin and still has a cult following. His spindly statue in the Viktualienmarkt always has fresh flowers in its hand and little offerings about its feet. Brecht and Hermann Hesse were fans, but Valentin's humour can leave foreigners a little perplexed. His most famous joke is: 'Why does St Peter's have eight clocks?' 'So that eight people can tell the time at once.' The tower is chock-a-block with memorabilia, cartoons and jokey exhibits such as a melted snowman and a nest of unlaid eggs, but the labels are all in German. Right at the top is the cosiest café in town (*see* below).

If you wander back through the Viktualienmarkt and out off its western side you'll come to the more conventional **Stadtmuseum** in St Jakobs-Platz (*Tues–Sun 10–5, Wed until 8.30pm; adm DM5*), housed in a late-Gothic arsenal. The heart of the museum is an excellent local history collection, where you can see Erasmus Grasser's vibrant *Moriskentänzer* (Morris Dancers, 1485) carved for the ballroom of the Altes Rathaus. The turn of an ankle, a fold of cloth and the angle of the hands give the wooden figures uncanny life and grace. These statues alone make a visit worthwhile, but the Stadtmuseum has a brood of other collections under its wing. The **Museum of Musical Instruments** is of world renown, though unimaginatively presented. (Look out, though, for periodic concerts, when you can hear the instruments in use.) The **Puppet Museum** has around 25,000 exhibits from all over the world, ranging from life-size marionettes to quaint creatures cobbled together out of junk (though, again, rather statically presented). As well as the expected shelves of historical equipment, the **Photography Museum** has some interesting old pictures of Munich. Ludwigomanes can delight in some rarely seen photographs of the eccentric king. Film buffs should keep an eye open for the daily-changing programme of rare movies. The temporary exhibitions are usually superb and, appropriately for Munich, there is also a **Brewery Museum**.

Beyond the Stadtmuseum is Sendlinger Straße, which leads up to **Sendlinger Tor**, another of the medieval town gates. Halfway along the street is the florid Rococo **Asamkirche** (1746), designed by the brothers Cosmas and Egid Quirin Asam (*see* p.49), and considered a highpoint of their long partnership.

The third medieval gate, **Karlstor**, is to the north on Karlsplatz, a vast but seedy square where shifty adolescents hang out around a modern fountain. Locals call Karlsplatz 'Stachus' (supposedly for one Eustachius Föderl who had a beer garden here long ago)— and nowadays even underground train-drivers say *Stachus* when they announce the stop.

Munich's busiest shopping precinct connects Karlsplatz and Marienplatz. In the midst of the pedestrian hubbub the **Liebfrauendom** (or 'Frauenkirche') points two knobby towers skywards. The two steeples date from 1525. Their tops look rather like beer mug lids, and have become something of a city symbol. The church itself is a huge, but disappointingly plain, Gothic hall, built between 1468 and 1494. It contains the oldest Wittelsbach vault, and a mysterious black footprint (reputedly that of the Devil) burned into the marble floor.

The more interesting Wittelsbachs (including 'mad' King Ludwig II) are buried in **St Michael's** church, a little further along on Neuhauser Straße. The church was built between 1583 and 1597 for Duke Wilhelm V (he of the *Glockenspiel*). In a niche on the strong Renaissance façade, the Archangel Michael delivers the finishing blow to the forces of Evil (a satyr). The capacious interior is primly dressed with white stucco and covered by a barrel vault second in size only to St Peter's in Rome. Nearby is the **Bürgersaal**, an 18th-century oratory. The church itself is upstairs; at ground level there is a dimly lit hall where you'll invariably find a handful of people lighting candles at the grave of Father Rupert Mayer. This popular priest was packed off to a concentration camp for his brave resistance to the Nazis, but his congregation created such an uproar that he was later released and kept under house arrest at Kloster Ettal (*see* p.123). He survived to preach a few more times at the Bürgersaal, but died in 1945.

The Northern Altstadt and the Residenz

In the 19th century, three successive Wittelsbach rulers turned the patch north of Marienplatz into one of the most sustainedly elegant suites of squares and boulevards of any city in the world. It all began at the turn of the century, when King Max I Joseph laid out Max-Josef-Platz and built the Opera House, raising the enormous sums required by imposing a local beer tax. His son, King Ludwig I, returned from a seven-month tour of Italy and Greece so struck with classical architecture that he declared he would not rest 'until Munich looked like Athens' (a more comprehensible ambition in the 19th century than it would be today). By the time he died, he had done so much to achieve his aim that his son, King Max II, cautiously wondered: 'Do you think I am allowed to build something different?' Max was not plagued by self-doubt for long, but hatched the graceful 'Maximilian style', and in 1851 built **Maximilianstraße**, now Munich's grandest shopping boulevard.

Maximilianstraße sweeps away to the east of Max-Josef-Platz, over the Isar and up the opposite bank to the **Maximilianeum**—a striking pile of pale, glimmering stone and home to the Bavarian State Parliament. From a perch on the roof, an archangel loftily surveys the *crème de la crème* of Munich society gliding in and out of the classic boutiques and exclusive cafés. The **Vier Jahreszeiten**, one of the world's most prestigious hotels, stands in their midst with quiet composure.

Max-Josef-Platz itself is boxed in by the Doric colonnade of the Hauptpost (originally a 19th-century family palace), the imposing classical façade of the Opera House and the mighty **Residenz**—once the Wittelsbach family home, but now a splendid museum (*Tues–Sun 10–4.30; adm DM4*). The palace is so large that guided tours manage only half of it at a time (you come back later in the day for the other part). Even if you wander about in your own time, you would be advised to set aside at least half a day for the visit, and to invest in the *Residenz Guidebook*, an exhaustive room-by-room guide available from the ticket office. (Note that you'll need to buy further tickets for admission to other museums in the complex.)

When the Swedes conquered Munich during the Thirty Years' War, King Gustav Adolf looked over the Residenz and sighed, 'If only it had wheels!' Luckily for Münchners, he could not take it back to Sweden with him, and left it pretty much intact. Today, the Residenz is considered one of the finest Renaissance palaces in Europe, though the buildings that cluster around the seven inner courts in fact date from the 16th to the 19th centuries, and are a jumble of Renaissance, Rococo and Neoclassical styles. After Second World War bomb damage, the complex had to be almost entirely rebuilt—but most of the sumptuous furniture was saved and is on display.

The oldest part of the palace is the **Antiquarium**, a cavernous barrel-vaulted hall, wildly decorated with views of Bavaria, grotesques and grumpy putti. It was built in 1571 (though the décor came a decade or so later) to house the Wittelsbachs' collection of antiquities. The Antiquarium leads off the **Grotto Court**, one side of which is a playful cavern of volcanic rock inset with mussel shells and colourful chunks of crystal. Duke

Wilhelm V had the grotto built in 1586 as a 'secret pleasure garden'. Other highlights on the ground floor include the **Nibelungen Halls** (to the left of the main entrance) decorated for Ludwig I between 1827 and 1867 with glossy paintings of the Nibelung legends; the **Ancestral Gallery** (along the northern side of Königsbauhof), a rich Rococo corridor lined with (often imaginary) portraits of past Wittelsbachs; and a 17th-century **Court Chapel**. The rooms around the Grotto Court house a dazzling collection of **porcelain**.

Most spectacular of all are the aptly named **Rich Rooms** on the upper floor—Rococo extravaganzas designed by François Cuvilliés (*see* below). They lead through to Duke Maximilian I's tiny **Secret Chapel** (*c.* 1615), an outrageous nook of marble and lapis lazuli, flecked with gold tendrils and coloured stone. In an adjoining room you can see the duke's impressive collection of reliquaries, including those containing the heads of John the Baptist and his mother.

You need another ticket for the **Schatzkammer** (*same times; adm DM4*). Here you can see the Bavarian crown jewels, other crowns dating back to the year 1000 and a striking collection of jewellery and precious objects—golden stags with coral antlers, carved rhino-horn drinking vessels and beautifully inlaid boxes. Look out especially for Duke Wilhelm V's private altar (1580), carved from ebony, and laden with gold, enamel, precious stones and pearls; and the breathtaking Statuette of St George (1590). St George sits astride an agate stallion (draped with rubies and diamonds) and slays an emerald dragon with a crystal sword. If you could lift up his bejewelled visor, you would see a tiny painted face.

Yet another ticket is needed for the **Altes Residenztheater** (or Cuvilliés-Theater), entrance off the Brunnenhof (*Mon–Sat 2–5, Sun 10–5; adm DM2.50*), a Rococo triumph by the erstwhile court jester, François Cuvilliés. Elector Max Emmanuel spotted the Belgian dwarf's talent as a designer soon after he arrived at court, and sent him off to Paris to study. Cuvilliés returned to give Rococo flair and flourish to buildings all over Germany. In 1943 all the boxwood panels of the plush, gilded interior were dismantled and safely stored. Later, after Allied bombs had burnt out the old building, a modern **Neues Residenztheater** was built within the walls; the old interior was reconstructed on the present site.

François Cuvilliés

 When Elector Max III Joseph of Bavaria (1745–77) decided to build a new palace theatre in 1750, he chose as an architect the deputy head of his Office of Works, François Cuvilliés. Cuvilliés was born in Hainault in Belgium in 1695, and had joined the Elector's grandfather's court as a dwarf jester at the age of 11. Later, *le nain Cuvilliés*, became a cadet and made such a mark that, despite his small stature, he was promoted to the Elector's own regiment in 1717. Here he proved especially clever at mathematics and the theory of fortification—so much so that the emperor personally paid for him to be sent to study court architecture at the Académie Royale in Paris (though Cuvilliés himself would have preferred to be drafted to the Hungarian front).

When he arrived back in Germany in 1726, design commissions flowed in thick and fast, including one to decorate the interior of the palace at Brühl near Cologne (1728, for Prince Bishop Clemens August, brother of the Elector of Bavaria), and for the Amelienburg in Munich's Nymphenburg Park (1734, *see* p.81). Cuvilliés, now approaching middle age, was at the forefront of a golden age of Rococo which was just beginning in Bavaria. When Max III Joseph approached him to build the new Residenztheater he was at the zenith of his career, and produced what is still one of the most splendid interiors to be seen in Munich.

The Residenz also accommodates the **Staatliche Münzsammlung** (State Coin Collection) (*Tues–Sun 10–4.30; adm DM2.50*), the largest and oldest of its kind in Germany. To the north of the palace is a stiffly formal **Hofgarten**, once the royal park.

The Hofgarten opens out onto **Ludwigstraße**. At the beginning of the 19th century this was a vegetable garden. King Ludwig I flattened it with a broad, grand avenue that runs in a dead straight line from Odeonplatz to the solid eminence of the **Siegestor**, a triumphal arch built in 1850 to honour all Bavarian armies. Odeonplatz is dominated by the **Feldherrnhalle** (1841) an insufferably pompous monument to Generals Tilly and von Wrede (of the Thirty Years' and Napoleonic Wars respectively). It was here that 14 Nazis were shot dead during Hitler's unsuccessful 1923 putsch. The gay yellow Rococo façade and twirly-topped towers of the **Theatinerkirche** (designed by Cuvilliés in 1768) brightens the mood of the square, but the rest of Ludwigstraße is very much four-square and solid. Suitably, the stately buildings that line the street house such august institutions as the state archives and library, the government offices and the university.

Beyond the Siegestor the mood changes completely. Tall trees line the street, cafés spill out onto the pavement, and knots of students and *Schickies* chatter under the bright umbrellas, or wander in and out of the trendy shops and galleries. This is **Schwabing**, no longer the shocking hotbed of Bolsheviks and bohemians it was at the turn of the century, but still vibrant and fun to explore. It is one of the most fruitful areas in town for cafés, restaurants, fringe theatres and night life (*see* listings below). The central axis is Leopoldstraße. Here you'll find the glitzier cafés. The student bars, quirky shops and cheaper restaurants are mainly to the west of Leopoldstraße. Hopeful young artists ply their wares, and snack bars double as galleries. The east of Leopoldstraße, towards Wedekindplatz and Münchner Freiheit, is more the province of black clothes, sharp hair-cuts and pounding discotheques.

In its heyday Schwabing was a honeypot to artists, writers and thinkers from all over Germany. From collaboration around a *Stammtisch* in the Alte Simpl café came *Simplicissimus*, the leading satirical magazine of the time. Another local publication, *Jugend* (Youth), gave its name to Jugendstil, the German equivalent of Art Nouveau. The novelist Thomas Mann, the poet Rainer Maria Rilke and the painter Lovis Corinth, as well as countless other lesser-known artists, all lived and worked here. Even Lenin put in a brief appearance (calling himself Meyer) between 1900 and 1902. (There was later a Bolshevik revolution in Munich, in 1918, and for a few months Bavaria was declared a republic.) Many of the artists became famous and moved to grander parts of town.

Hopefuls, would-bes and property speculators moved in. Nowadays Schwabing is fashionable but expensive, and has lost its edge. The truly trendy are to be found in Haidhausen (*see* 'Bars and Cafés' below).

The Museum Quarter

Munich has more museums than any other city in Germany, and the quality of the collections puts even Berlin in the shade. The credit (or blame) for this lies with the pillaging Wittelsbachs. All around Bavaria and the Palatinate (which was ruled by a branch of the family), museum directors will sulkily reel off lists of treasures that went south to Munich.

Most of the important museums are clustered north of the Altstadt. The Alte Pinakothek (14th–18th-century masterpieces), the Neue Pinakothek (18th- and 19th-century), the Glypothek (Classical sculpture), the Staatliche Antikensammlungen (Greek, Roman and Etruscan art) and the Lenbachhaus (Munich painters from Gothic to contemporary) are distinguished neighbours in the area west of Ludwigstraße. East of the boulevard, along Prinzregentstraße, are the Haus der Kunst (20th-century art), the Bayerisches National Museum (Wittelsbach booty from the Middle Ages onwards), the Schack Galerie (19th-century painting) and the Villa Stuck (Jugendstil). There is enough to keep you here for days. All state museums are free on Sundays and public holidays; otherwise a *Verbundeintrittskarte* (joint entrance ticket) makes a good investment at DM20.

The **Alte Pinakothek** (*Tues–Sun 9.15–4.30; adm DM7*) ranks easily among the world's top art collections. An incomparable array of early German Masters will give you the clearest art history lesson on the period you're ever likely to get; the few Italian paintings are pearls; and there is more Rubens than you can find in one spot anywhere else. Yet, despite its eminence, this is a quirky collection, reflecting the tastes and foibles of the Wittelsbachs who put it together over a period of nearly 400 years. Elector Maximilian I (1597–1651) had a penchant for Dürer, and tracked down pieces all over the country. His court artists could imitate the master impeccably, and 'corrected' smaller paintings to a size deemed more appropriate for the vast Residenz walls. Elector Max Emmanuel, who was Governor of the Spanish Netherlands from 1692 to 1701, is responsible for acquiring many of the Flemish works. It took Brussels dealers, and the Bavarian treasury, some time to recover from one spending spree in which Max Emmanuel allegedly got through 200,000 francs in half an hour. A century later, King Ludwig I brought crates of paintings back from his Italian journey. He also spent a fortune on contemporary art.

The Early German collection is in the left wing on the lower floor, and overflows into a few rooms upstairs. The lower right wing is taken up by paintings (from all countries) between the Renaissance and Baroque. Upstairs, working from left to right (after the Early German and Early Netherlandish rooms) you will find Italian, Flemish and Dutch works, and finally painting from France and Spain. Confusingly, room numbering begins afresh upstairs, and is done in a mixture of Roman and Arabic numerals.

Highlights on the ground floor left wing include *The Golden Age* (1530, Room IIa) by Lucas Cranach the Elder. Cranach, one of the first German artists to dare to paint naked figures, fills an Eden-like garden with frolicking nudes. Look out also for Bernhard Strigel's warmly realistic *Guard with a Crossbow* (1521, Room IIb) and Wolf Huber's dramatically charged *Christ Taken Prisoner* (1530) hanging nearby. Jesus is set upon by a relentlessly ugly mob (one of whom seems intent on reporting on what he can see up the Saviour's robe). This dramatic realism was the result of the influence of Netherlandish painters, and is used with powerful effect in the vividly coloured *Kaisheim Altar* (1502) by Holbein the Elder and *Crucifixion* (1450) by the Master of the Benediktbeueren Crucifixion, both in Room III.

The line between Flemish and German painting is sometimes hard to draw. One of the leading artists of the Late-Gothic Cologne School, Bartholomew Bruyn, was, in fact, Flemish. You can see Bruyn's work, as well as more fine Cologne School painting (such as *St Veronica* (1420) by the Master of St Veronica) in Cabinets 1–3. But to see the best work from the Cologne School (by Stefan Lochner, and the Masters of the Bartholomew Altarpiece and of the Life of the Virgin) you should go to Room III upstairs. South German painters were more under the influence of the Italians—as you can see from the harsh light and clear shadows of Michael Pacher's altarpiece hanging in the same room.

Albrecht Dürer was the first European artist to paint self-portraits. In Room II upstairs you can see his Christ-like *Self-Portrait with Fur-Trimmed Robe* (1500), which he inscribes with delightful self-assurance: 'Thus I, Albrecht Dürer of Nuremberg, painted myself in imperishable colours at the age of 28.' Room II is a treasure trove, with many of Dürer's finest works such as *The Four Apostles* (1526) and also superb paintings by his contemporaries. Look out for Hans Burgkmair's exotic *Altarpiece of St John the Evangelist* (1518), populated by monkeys and colourful birds; Albrecht Altdorfer's seething *Battle of Issus* (1529); and Matthias Grünewald's intricately worked *Saints Erasmus and Maurice* (1520).

A wander through the Italian rooms takes you past choice paintings by Botticelli, Fra Filippo Lippi and Raphael, including his tender *Tempi Madonna* (1507), which King Ludwig I battled for 20 years to own. You can see Leonardo's earliest known painting— the *Madonna with a Carnation* (1473)—and superlative works by Titian and Tintoretto.

The vast Rubens collection fills the rooms at the heart of the upper floor. The 65 pieces on display range from hasty *modellos*, run off for his workshop, to enormous canvases of the Last Judgement (Room VII). Look out especially for *Drunken Silenus* (1616, Room VII), where a flabby old Silenus (Bacchus's tutor) stumbles about in bleary intoxication, and is mocked by his retinue and goosed by a Moor. The Flemish and Dutch collections continue with paintings by Van Dyck, Rembrandt and the much-neglected Jan Steen.

After a glimpse of some frothy French painting by François Boucher and Nicolas Lancret (Room XII), and the darker moods of El Greco and Murillo (Room XIII), you can pop back downstairs to see Pieter Breughel's witty *Land of Cockaigne* (1566). Three fat men lie sprawled on the ground in this Promised Land of Gluttons (they would have had to chomp their way through a mountain of buckwheat porridge to get there), while around them are fences made of sausages, pigs that come equipped with a carving knife, and ready-capped eggs that run about on little legs waiting to be eaten. Nearby is Jan Breughel's densely populated *Harbour Scene* (1598).

Across the way from the museum is the shiny modern **Neue Pinakothek** (*same times and price, or DM7 for both*), lean fare after the banquet of the Alte Pinakothek, but still worth a visit. The collection begins with artists (such as David, Gainsborough, Goya and Turner) who broke with Baroque traditions and set the style for 19th-century painting, but it is the Germans who get the strongest look-in. Keep an eye open for Arnold Böcklin's dreamy *Pan in the Reeds* (1859), Anselm Feuerbach's statuesque *Medea* (1870), the murky, mysterious paintings of Hans von Mareés and the huge translucent Greek and Italian landscapes produced by Ludwig I's court artists. There is a respectable range of French work, including Manet's *Breakfast in the Studio* (1868) and Degas' *Woman Ironing* (1869)—a change from the usual ballet dancers. You can also see a version of Van Gogh's *Sunflowers* and familiar works by Gauguin, Egon Schiele and Gustav Klimt.

Nearby, the **Glypothek** (*Tues, Wed, Fri–Sun 10–4.30, Thurs noon–8.30pm; adm DM3.50*) and **Staatliche Antikensammlungen** (*Tues and Thurs–Sun 10–4.30, Wed noon–8.30; adm DM3.50; joint ticket for both museums DM6*) occupy two daunting Neoclassical piles on either side of an otherwise barren Königsplatz. King Ludwig I commissioned the buildings to house his collection of antiquities. The Glypothek is the more interesting of the two, with an entire pediment plundered from the Aphaia Temple in Aegina, the outrageously erotic *Barberini Faun* and fine statues from the Hellenistic period. The chief attraction of the Antikensammlungen is the glittering array of Greek and Etruscan gold jewellery.

Directly across Luisenstraße is the **Lenbachhaus** (*Tues–Sun 10–6, Thurs to 8pm; adm DM5*), the elegant, Italianate villa of the highly paid 'painter prince', Franz von Lenbach (1836–1904). Many of the rooms keep their original fittings and furnishing, but most of the villa is now the Municipal Museum. The main reason for a visit is the extensive collection of paintings by Kandinsky and fellow members of the *Blaue Reiter*, such as Klee, Marc and Macke (*see* p.52). Ironically, the conventional, established von Lenbach was the group's greatest foe. Most of the works on show here were part of a secret hoard stashed away for years by Gabriele Münter, Kandinsky's jilted mistress. The Russian-born Kandinsky had to leave Munich at the outbreak of the First World War, and left everything he owned in her charge. While he was away he met and married someone else. Years later Gabriele gave him back his furniture, but held onto all the artworks he had left behind. Well into her eighties, she handed the lost collection over to an astonished city council, who, in the search for somewhere large enough to display all the works, came up with the Lenbach villa. The museum often also holds good exhibitions of contemporary German work.

Over on Prinzregentstraße you'll find the **Haus der Kunst**, a nasty 1930s building that still has swastikas carved into the stone above the doorways. The State Gallery of Modern Art, usually housed in the west wing, is indefinitely closed for renovation. In the meantime, parts of the superb collection of 20th-century art pop up as temporary exhibitions in other museums around town.

The **Bayerisches Nationalmuseum** (*Tues–Sun 9.30–5; adm DM3*) is almost next door. The core of the sprawling museum is once again a Wittelsbach collection—this time of art and artefacts from all around Europe. Highlights are sculptures by Tilman Riemenschneider (*see* p.147) and a collection of nativity scenes dating from the 17th to 19th centuries. Another division of the museum contains folk art. Another has applied art, with especially good displays of porcelain and clocks.

A little further down the street is the **Schack-Galerie** (*daily except Tues 9.15–4.40; adm DM2.50*), a cosy little museum very much worth a visit for its excellent collection of works by 19th-century artists Anselm Feuerbach, Arnold Böcklin, Franz von Lenbach and Moritz von Schwind—painters often unfairly ignored outside of Germany.

Just over the river, past the glittering **Angel of Peace** high on her stone column, and across Europaplatz is one of Munich's gems, the **Villa Stuck**, Prinzregentstr. 60 (*Tues–Sun 10–5, Thurs to 9pm; adm DM2*), home and studio of the painter Franz von Stuck (1863–1928). Perhaps his greatest gift was for interior design, and the villa is a monument to Jugendstil, with patterned parquet floors, richly painted walls and stylish furniture.

The Englischer Garten and the Isar

The **Englischer Garten** is an enormous park stretching for over 5km along the Isar, north of Prinzregentstraße. Icy brooks criss-cross its broad meadows, and skip along through thick forests and past cultivated lawns. At times all you can hear is birdsong and splashing water—and you can't see the city at all. It is easy, indeed pleasant, to get lost. People stroll about, play ball games and sunbathe (completely naked in the grass around the Eisbach), but the Garten is most famous for its large, shady **beer gardens** (*see* below).

The idea for the park came in the late 18th century from an American, Benjamin Thompson, inventor of the cast-iron stove, and later made Count Rumford by a grateful Elector Karl-Theodor, who was entranced with the garden. Near the south entrance there is a **Japanese Teahouse** built in 1972 (*traditional tea ceremonies second and fourth weekends of the month, Sat and Sun 3pm, 4pm and 5pm*). Further into the park you'll find the **Monopterus** (a 19th-century temple with a fine view back over the city) and the **Chinesischer Turm**, a fragile pagoda in the middle of the most popular beer garden.

South of the Englischer Garten, you can follow the Isar past rows of grand 19th-century buildings and some very elegant old bridges. In summer the sandy banks are spread with more sunbathers, and between Wolfrathausen and Thalkirchen enormous log rafts float gently downstream, laden with revellers, beer barrels and sometimes even small bands and portaloos. On Museumsinsel, just past the Ludwigsbrücke is the **Deutsches Museum** (*daily 9–5; adm DM8*), a gigantic museum of science and technology (you would have to walk over 16km to take in everything).

You can see a model of a bow drill from the fourth millenium BC and a space capsule; the first German submarine, the original Puffing Billy and a Wright Brothers aeroplane. You can go down a coal mine or sit under the stars in the Zeiss Planetarium. There are sections on metallurgy, hydraulic engineering, carriages and bicycles, telecommunications, new energy techniques, physics and photography—and that's just for starters. The Aeronautics and Space Travel exhibitions are the most interesting, but even Power Machinery can come up with intriguing surprises. You can clamber in and out of many of the exhibits, and even operate a few. Children love it. The museum shop is a treasure trove of models, toys for boffins and splendidly illustrated books—and they also sell a very necessary floor guide.

The Deutsches Museum also has a separate aircraft section called **Flugwerft** (*daily 9–5; adm DM13*), located in a hangar at Schleißheim, 13km north of Munich proper. More than 7000 square metres of glassed-in exhibition space, it displays some 50 original aircraft, ranging from early reconstructed gliders and a Heinkel He III bomber to a post-war Starfighter jet and a full-size Europa-Rocket.

Nymphenburg

When, after ten years of hoping, the Electress Henriette Adelaide finally gave birth to a son in 1662, her husband celebrated by building her a small palace 5km to the west of the city. She called the Italianate villa *Castello delle Ninfe*. Later generations of Wittelsbachs added a succession of symmetrical wings, and as **Schloß Nymphenburg** (*Tues–Sun 9–12.30 and 1.30–5; adm DM2.50 for Schloß, DM6 including pavilions and Amelienburg; Tram 12, Bus 41*) it became their favourite summer residence.

This stately palace is set in acres of Versailles-style park. Inside, the rooms are suitably lavish—mainly Rococo and High Baroque. In the notorious *Schönheitengalerie* (Gallery of Beauties) there are 36 portraits of women who took King Ludwig I's fancy between 1827 and 1850, including one of his scandalous mistress, Lola Montez. (The king cherished his favourites, chatted to them during the sittings, and even selected husbands for a few.)

Staatliche Porzellan-Manufaktur Nymphenburg

For most people, fine German porcelain *objets d'art* mean one thing—sought-after wares in the classic Meißen tradition. For those in the know, however, Wittelsbach patronage did as much for the craft as did the Wettins of Dresden. For over 230 years now the factory at Nymphenburg has been producing excellent porcelain, today identified by its green armorial trademark.

It was the last Prince-Elector of the ancestral line of the Wittelsbachs, Max III Joseph, who in 1747 founded the first porcelain manufactory at the diminutive Neudeck palace on the outskirts of

Munich. Then in 1761 the workshops moved to the Schloßrondell to the east of Nymphenburg palace, where new premises, complete with their own mill and kiln (still used in the manufacturing process), had been built. Virtuoso pieces of porcelain have been emerging from this Wittelsbach summer residence ever since.

The factory had its first golden age when the services of the most talented artist ever employed here, the Italian-born **Franz Antom Bustelli**, were secured in 1754. In less than nine years he sculpted about 150 Rococo pieces, including the much-acclaimed set of 16 figurines from the *Commedia dell'arte*. Meanwhile glittering dinner services painted by the adroit floral and landscape artist Joseph Zächenberger were produced at the workshops.

Bustelli's successor, **Dominikus Jakobus Auliczek**, is famed for a series of sculptures of the Greek gods and goddesses, and his *Perl Service*, which became the Wittelsbach household's dinner service (*Bayerisches Königs-Service*). In 1799 the Palatine Frankenthaler porcelain factory merged with the one at Nymphenburg, and in 1815 King Ludwig I promoted the factory to a royal academy with a special emphasis on ceramic painting. The famous *Onyx Service*, its designs based on paintings in the Alte Glyptothek, dates from this period.

In 1888 the business magnate **Albert Bäuml** took over the management of the porcelain factory, introduced new techniques, and concentrated on contemporary designs and reproductions of the factory's own 18th-century classic pieces. In 1975 control of the factory returned to descendants of the Wittelsbachs, and is now operated by a family foundation.

Close on 20,000 individual, hand-painted articles have been produced at the Nymphenburg workshops and are now scattered all over the world. Painstaking attention to detail ensures that only a very limited number of items is added to this total every year. Most of the finest pieces are still in Munich, in the collection of the **Porzellan-Sammlung Bäuml** in the Marstallmuseum, the **Verkaufs- und Ausstellungspavillion** (shop and showroom) at Schloßrondell's (*Mon–Fri 8.30–12, 12.30–5; adm free*), the **Residenz** (*see* p.73) and the **Bayerisches Nationalmuseum** (*see* p.79). The **factory shop** at Odeonsplatz in Munich offers fine reproductions and modern originals for sale.

The interiors of the **Amelienburg** (a hunting lodge behind the south wing of the palace, designed by Cuvilliés) surpass anything in the main building. Cuvilliés gives the dinky lodge the sumptuousness and splendour of a grand palace, but with a refined lightness of touch. He even manages a diminutive Hall of Mirrors without violating the boundaries of good taste.

As you wander about the park, keep an eye open for the **pavilions**: the **Magdalenenklause** (1728), a 'ruined' hermitage retreat with a grotto; the **Pagodenburg** (1719), a chinoiserie party house; and the **Badenburg** (1721), a Baroque bathing house where the pool has handy underwater benches.

Munich's Other Museums

This is one city where you will never be at a loss for something to do on a rainy day. Here is but a selection of some of the other museums you can find around town.

Staatliche Sammlung Ägyptische Kunst, Hofgartenstr. 1 (*Tues–Sun 9–4; adm DM2.50*). Mummies, Coptic robes and artworks from the Wittelsbachs' Egyptian phase.

Staatliche Graphische Sammlung, Meiserstr. 10, © (089) 55 91 490 (*Mon–Wed 10–1 and 2–6.30, Thurs to 6pm, Fri 10–12.30; adm free*). An enormous selection of drawings, woodcuts and etchings—not all are on display, but may be viewed in the Study Hall by prior arrangement. Particular strengths are the collections of 15th-century German woodcuts and graphics by German Expressionists.

Deutsches Jagdmuseum, Neuhauserstr. 53 (*daily 9.30–5; adm DM4*). Equipment, clothes and end-products of huntin', shootin' and fishin'. This is the place to come to see the world's largest collection of fish-hooks.

Museum für Vor- und Frühgeschichte, Lerchenfeldstr. 2 (*Tues–Sun 9–4; adm DM2.50*). Bits and bobs from Bavarian households from prehistoric times to the early Middle Ages.

Staatliches Museum für Völkerkunde, Maximilianstr. 42 (*Tues–Sun 9.30–4.30; adm DM5*). Well-stocked ethnological museum with good Asian and Oriental collections.

Siemens Museum, Prannerstr. 10 (*Mon–Fri 9–4, Sat and Sun 10–2; adm free*). Hi-tech, hands-on electronics museum.

BMW Museum, Peteulring 130 (*daily 9–5; DM4.50*). Massive public relations job for the car company. Flash modern exhibits rather than vintage oddities.

Spielzeugmuseum, Altes Rathaus (*daily 10–5.30; adm DM4, children DM1, family card DM8*). A towerful of cases crammed with toys from carved Futurist figures to Barbie dolls.

Bavaria-Filmstadt

Have you ever wondered how they did those rip-roaring special effects for the movie *The Boat*? The Bavaria-Filmstadt at Geiselgasteig, 10km south of Munich's Hauptbahnhof, provides riveting insights into a special-effect-laden chapter of Germany's film history. (*U-Bahn line 1 or 2 to Silberhornstraße, then tram 25 to Bavariafilmplatz*). With 356,000 square metres of production area, the studios constitute the largest film-making and post-production centre in Europe and Bavaria's answer to Hollywood (*see* 'Cinema', p.60).

The first motion picture made here was shot in 1919 (recently the owner of the studios, Bavaria Film, staged a lavish spectacle to commemorate their 75th anniversary). The then unknown Alfred Hitchcock used the production facilities to set up his early films *The Pleasure Garden* (1925) and *The Mountain Eagle* (1926). After the war, highlights of the long line of successes emerging from these studios were *The Great Escape* (1962) and *Cabaret* (1971). Then in the late 1970s the German director Wolfgang Petersen set up base here, producing his internationally acclaimed wartime epic *The Boat* (1981), rapidly followed by his fantasy blockbuster *The NeverEnding Story* (1983) and the sci-fi feature film *Enemy Mine* (1985). Latter-day big screen accomplishments include Joseph Vilsmaier's anti-war drama *Stalingrad* (1993), as well as a myriad serial productions for German TV.

Since August 1981 **Bavaria Film Tour**, a subsidiary of Bavaria Film, has mounted an exhibition of the sets and props of several of these films. You can also join the throngs on a 90-minute **guided tour** (*March–Oct daily 9-4; DM14*), to see behind-the-scenes film-maker's wizardry in a theme-park setting. If at all possible, avoid visiting at weekends or holiday periods, and arrive first thing: the numbers of visitors here have soared in line with the successes of German film productions. On your way through the halls you can clamber through Wolfgang Petersen's U-Boat, walk around the mock-up of a pre-war street in Berlin, make friends with the fantasy characters from *The NeverEnding Story*, lower your-self into the *Drac* spacecraft from *Enemy Mine* and take cover from a Russian T-34 tank from *Stalingrad*. The live exhibition also includes a 30-minute **stunt show** (*variable times; adm DM8*) in which an expert team engages in a *tour de force* of simulated brawls, fire fights and death-defying plunges. A highly realistic ride through a deserted silver mine, viewed from the safety of a seat in the **Showscan cinema** (*variable times; adm DM7*), is made possible by the latest US computer-animation techniques. For serious would-be actors the organisers offer a special, bookable tour, during which you can even acquire a new face, applied by professional make-up artists.

Shopping

Along Maximilianstraße even the shops have crystal chandeliers. Here you'll find the Chanels, Cartiers and Cardins. By contrast, in Schwabing, the rents are lower and the fashion shops trendier. Happy consumer-culture department-store shop-ping goes on in the pedestrian walkways of Neuhauser Straße and Kaufingerstraße, and along Sendlinger Straße. Just behind the Rathaus, in Dienerstraße, is a 300-year-old delicatessen, Dallmayr's, which still supplies the Wittelsbachs with teas and coffees from its wooden chests, sticky sausages from its racks and lobster and caviar from beneath its gushing fountain. For even headier tastes and aromas try the Viktualienmarkt (*see* p.70). At Loden-Fry in Maffeistraße, you can buy Bavarian hats and *Lodentracht*, hardy green Alpine wear. Nearby, in the Wallach-Haus, it can cost up to DM700 for a hand-made dirndl, though you could run up your own from hand-printed textiles at around DM80 a metre. The humbler Hans-Sachs-Straße (south of the centre, near Sendlinger Tor) is a quaint street of ethnic stores, secondhand shops, galleries and quirky clothes shops, and in Schellingstraße there are *two* English bookshops (Anglia's at No.3 and Words Worth's at No.21a).

Activities

Jogging, walking and cycling in the Englischer Garten is a favourite Munich activity. You could also join the locals for a swim in one of the lakes or rivers in the park (they are quite clean enough). In colder weather try the **Volksbad** (*variable* *opening times*), a graceful turn-of-the-century indoor swimming pool just across the Ludwigsbrücke.

To the northwest of Schwabing, just off the Georg-Brauchle-Ring (U-Bahn Line 3 or 8, S-Bahn Line 8) is the **Olympiapark**, a vast complex of sports facilities created for the 1972 Olympic Games including an enormous swimming pool, an ice rink and a cycle track. The buildings are set in landscaped parkland beside an artificial lake and are also used for concerts and festivals in the summer.

Where to Stay

expensive

Hotel Vier Jahreszeiten Kempinski, Maximilianstr. 17, ✆ 23 03 90, 🖷 23 03 96 93 (DM548–628). From its classic wood-panelled lobby to the glass-walled, roof-top swimming pool, this is the Grand Duchess of the world's top hotels. An exalted guest list (the Windsors and Gorbachevs have been here before you), palatial period suites, smart modern rooms and award-winning restaurants come together with a genuine warmth of atmosphere and discreet, impeccable attention to your every need. This is the one hotel in Germany to splash out on, even if your budget doesn't usually stretch so far.

Hotel Insel-Mühle, Von-Kahr-Str. 87, ✆ 8 10 10, 🖷 8 12 05 71 (DM250–380). A converted 16th-century mill on a gushing stream in a leafy spot just beyond Schloß Nymphenburg. Run with love and flair. The rooms are cosy, and most look out over a small park.

Queens Hotel, Effnerstr. 99, ✆ 92 79 80, 🖷 98 38 13 (DM310–345). Glitzy modern hotel, peacefully detached from the throb of the city, but only 10 minutes away by car. Business visitors will find swift service and hi-tech back-up. The 'Bavarian Suites' are decked out in country-cottage nouveau, with pine four-posters and repro tiled stoves.

moderate

Hotel Olympic, Hans-Sachs-Str. 4, ✆ 23 18 90, 🖷 231 89199 (DM165–240). Centrally located in a trendy street just to the south of the Altstadt. It hugs a pretty little garden courtyard—and most rooms get a peek. The proud new owners give it a friendly, personal touch.

Hotel Am Markt, Heiliggeiststr. 6, ✆ 22 50 14 (DM120–140). Tucked away in an alley beside the Viktualienmarkt. The owner has plastered the walls with photographs of his favourite opera singers, and runs his establishment with appropriate verve. The rooms are comfortable, but not diva-sized.

Hotel Dollmann, Thierschstr. 49, ✆ 23 80 80, 🖷 23 80 83 65 (DM165–225). A sober 19th-century patrician mansion with pastel colours, soft lighting and hushed guests. Situated near the Isar, in a peaceful street just off Maximilianstraße.

Hotel Lettl, Amalienstr. 53, ℰ 28 30 26, ⊕ 2 80 53 18 (DM165–210). A touch 1970s, this hotel occupies a quiet court in the heart of Schwabing. Rather grumpily managed.

Hotel Nymphenburg, Nymphenburger Str. 141, ℰ 18 10 86, ⊕ 18 25 40 (DM180). Well-appointed rooms and a pocket-sized garden. Away from the Alstadt bustle, on the road to Schloß Nymphenburg.

Gästehaus Englischer Garten, Liebergesellstr. 8, ℰ 39 20 34 (DM152–172). Idyllic, creeper-covered *Pension* on the edge of the Englischer Garten. Avoid the Annexe, though, where the rooms are quite spartan.

Hotel Galleria, Plinganserstr. 142, ℰ 723 3001, ⊕ 724 1564 (DM170–240). An elegant Jugendstil villa, with spacious rooms, just 10 minutes south of the centre (S-Bahn, Line 7 to Mittersendling).

inexpensive

Pension Am Kaiserplatz, Kaiserplatz 12, ℰ 34 91 90 (DM67–75). Good-value *Pension* run by a sweet old lady with a very individual flair in interior design.

Pension Frank, Schellingstr. 24, ℰ 28 14 51 (DM80–90 without private bath). A haven for cheery backpackers in the heart of Schwabing. Big rooms and a helpful management.

Pension Carolin, Kaulbachstr. 42, ℰ 34 57 57 (DM110–118). Friendly, well-run *Pension* just behind the university.

Pension Steinberg, Ohmstr. 9, ℰ 33 10 11 (DM98–125). Bright Schwabing *Pension* with a well-founded reputation for its slap-up breakfast.

Youth Hostels: DJH München, Wendl-Dietrich-Str. 80, ℰ 13 11 56 (DM19) (age limit 27); Jugendgästehaus München, Miesingstr 4, ℰ 723 6550 (DM24) (age limit 27); Haus International, Elisabethstr. 87, ℰ 12 00 60 (DM40) (no age limit).

Eating and Drinking: Restaurants and Taverns

expensive

Aubergine, Maximilianplatz 5, ℰ 59 81 71 (DM 150–200). Perennially Munich's top restaurant. Lavender rather than aubergine décor, an intimate atmosphere and top-class cooking by gourmet chef Eckhart Witzigmann.

Grüne Gans, Am Einlaß 5, ℰ 26 62 68 (DM100). Private-dinner-party atmosphere in tiny restaurant, personally supervised by cooks Julius and Inge Stollberg. Delicious classic cuisine, without fuss or pretension.

Kay's Bistro, Utzschneiderstr. 1, ℰ 2 60 35 84 (over DM100). Above your head minute fairylights glitter between drapes of muslin. Around you are bits of Neoclassical paraphernalia, nobs, snobs and wealthy tourists. Rich sauces abound, and you get the impression that this restaurant rides a little on its reputation of being one of the city's most chic.

Deutsche Eiche, Reichenbachstr. 13 (central). A cosy old-fashioned *Gaststätte* that was Fassbinder's local. It attracts an arty crowd, and the matronly owner cooks splendid, simple meals—occasionally surprising customers with duck or curry.

Halali, Schönfeldstr. 22, ✆ 28 59 09 (central). A rarity: rustic Bavarian décor that isn't kitsch, and a chef who experiments with local cuisine and comes up with wonders. Wild boar, venison and strange local mushrooms abound.

Weichandhof, Betzenweg 81, ✆ 811 1621 (Obermenzing, S-Bahn Line 2). Folksy ambiance, riverside setting and standard Bavarian fare. Tuck into a hearty *Hirschragout* (venison stew) or *Böfflamott* (from *Bœuf à la Mode*, a Napoleonic boil-up of beef, herbs and wine).

Augustiner-Großgaststätten, Neuhauser Str. 16, ✆ 551 99 257 (central). In the big, domed middle-room, quaintly decorated with seashells and hunting trophies, you can devour mounds of *Weißwurst* (boiled veal sausages) and pretzels. *Weißwurst* is *the* south-Bavarian speciality. They must be fresh (one of the ingredients is brain) and you shouldn't eat the skin.

Gaststätte Leopold, Leopoldstr. 50, ✆ 39 94 33 (Schwabing). Good, old-fashioned *Gaststätte* with walls browned by decades of tobacco and cooking smoke. Try the *Leberkäs mit Ei*—meatloaf with egg (ordered by the 100g), eaten with pretzels.

Weinhaus Neuner, Herzogspitalstr. 8, ✆ 260 3954 (central). Through the door on the left is a well-stocked wine bar, on the right there is a busy restaurant serving good, tasty food.

Haxnbauer, Münzstr. 8, ✆ 22 19 22 (central). Strictly for carnivores. Enormous grilled knuckles of pork disappear with astonishing rapidity down the throats of even the frailest-looking customers.

Amaranth, Steinstr. 42, ✆ 448 7356 (Haidhausen). Upmarket vegetarian restaurant with adventurous, herby risottos and crêpes.

Osteria Italiana, Schellingstr 62, ✆ 272 0717 (Schwabing). The best of Munich's many Italian restaurants, popular with academics, film people and para-mafiosi.

Shida, Klenzlestr. 32, (Haidhausen). Popular Thai restaurant with a mouthwatering menu of spicy soups, delicate curries and fish dishes.

Nürnberger Bratwurst Glöckl am Dom, Frauenplatz 9, ✆ 29 52 64 (central). Home of the grilled *Bratwurst*. You order them in pairs with sweet mustard and bread rolls, and eat them out under the trees beside the Frauenkirche in summer, or in the snug wood-panelled *Stüberl* in winter.

Bratwurstherzl, Heiliggeiststr. 3, ✆ 22 62 119 (central). Quick-stop beer-and-*Brotzeit* pub with mounds of delicious sausages, *Leberkäse* and *Obaazta* (a classic snack made with mature Camembert, peppers and spices).

Crêperie Normande, Pariserstr. 34, ✆ 48 69 39 (Haidhausen). Crêpes and galettes with flair (try the Roquefort-and-apple compote flambéed with Calvados). Also more conventional fillings.

Anti, Jahnstr. 36 (central). Gaudy décor, bouzouki music, Greek ex-pats and food that takes you right back to that idyllic island holiday.

Primo, Maximilianstr. 30 (central). Stand-up *Imbiß par excellence*, with superb wines, deli-delights and a posh clientele.

The **Viktualienmarkt**, Blumenstraße 7–11, is the best place of all for a cheap snack. Try a *Wurstsemel* (roll with sliced sausage) or a *Schinkensemml* (with ham) direct from one of the butchers, or steaming soup from the Münchner Suppenküche. Lots of booths sell Bratwurst and Weißwurst, which you can then take along to the beergarden. The *Ausgezogene* (heavy doughnuts, a.k.a. *Schmalznudeln*) at Café Frischut, on the market, are reputedly the best in town.

Bars and Cafés

Central

Hofbräuhaus, Platzl 9. Munich's most famous beerhall bursts at the seams with raucously singing Australians, Americans and Germans from the provinces. Everyone sways to the resonant oompah band, and many feel moved to dance. The Hofbräuhaus is the subject of a drinking-song that is almost the Bavarian national anthem, but few locals go anywhere near the place.

Schumann's, Maximilianstr. 36. Perennial favourite of the rich and famous, with suitably arrogant waiters and inflated prices. Keep an eye open for Boris Becker and assorted megastars. *Stammtische* here are holy territory, and will remain empty even when the rest of the bar resembles the U-Bahn at rush hour.

Nachtcafé, Maximiliansplatz 5. Bright, buzzing and open until 6am. Full of bleary disco flotsam, fashion victims and high-fliers who never sleep. There is also good live music, and snacks to appease late-night hunger pangs.

Heiliggeiststuberl, Heiliggeiststraße. A minute, cosy wooden box of a bar, tucked away in a little alley beside the Viktualienmarkt.

Jahreszeiten Bar, Maximilianstr. 17. Rich mahogany, enveloping leather chairs and live piano music surround incurable romantics and journalists on expense accounts.

Café Luitpold, Brienner Str. 11. Traditional cakes-and-coffee café. Aunties' favourite.

Café Kreuzkamm, Maffeistr. 4. A defeating array of delicious cream cakes and *haute couture*. There's a flicker of excitement in the atmosphere—as if coffee drinking were still a vice.

Schwabing

Pavement cafés line Leopoldstraße, Wedekindplatz and Münchner Freiheit, but at weekends Schwabing loses any vestige of its past bohemian atmosphere. BMWs with spoilers and jazzed-up Opels line the streets; their sunbed-bronzed owners fill the bars. Old Schwabing does make a gallant attempt to fight back, but most of the real trendies are in Haidhausen on the other side of town.

Alter Simpl, Türkenstr. 57. The pub where the satirical magazine *Simplicissimus* was germinated, where Thomas Mann stood on a chair to read from his novels and Frank Wedekind sang to a lute accompaniment. Children and grandchildren of the original clientele come back to enjoy a living-room atmosphere that has somehow survived the commercialization of the rest of Schwabing.

Café Extrablatt, Leopoldstr. 7. Owned by gossip columnist Michael Graeter, and once *the* café in Schwabing. Nowadays it is populated by glamour goblins and aspiring media stars who haven't done their research properly. (Their hoped-for Svengali, no doubt, being already half-sozzled in the Augustiner-Keller.)

Munich, Leopoldstr. 9. Another wannabe showroom. Lots of cheek-pecking and darting glances.

Café an der Uni, Ludwigstr. 24. Cosier café with agreeable student crowd.

Drugstore, Feilitzschstr. 12. It has never quite forgotten its 1960s heyday, but now this gives it a nostalgic charm for a new wave of young trendies.

Haidhausen and Further Afield

Glimpse through the windows in Haidhausen and you'll see Bavarian kitsch, Turkish textiles and bright new canvases. Immigrants, artists and ageing Munich originals live side by side in one of the liveliest quarters in town. Between the Isar and the Ostbahnhof, in the streets around Wiener Platz and Max-Weber-Platz, and in the 'French Quarter' around Orleansplatz and Rosenheimer Platz, you'll find galleries, good restaurants, bars and cafés galore. A walk of just a few yards down Wörthstraße is a good example of what the area has to offer. You can have a slap-up breakfast for around DM10 in a trendy café (**Café Voilà** at No.5), down a beer in a workers' bar (**No.7**), bop to live music in the **Snoopy Music Club** (No.9), or visit a **Café Theatre** and winebar (No.11).

Café Giesing, Bergstr. 5. Owned by a local pop star, who programmes good live music for a young, arty, friendly crowd of drinkers.

Casino, Kellerstr. 21. Solid blue walls throw faultless haircuts and bright Caribbean cocktails into stark relief. Perfect for posing.

Café Größenwahn, Lothringerstr. 11. A party atmosphere prevails. Drunken musicians break into impromptu performances, and crowds of thirty-somethings have a jolly good time.

Café Wiener Platz, Innere Wiener Straße. Nothing special to look at, but it has one of the warmest atmospheres of any café in the district. The crowd is a mixed bag of actors, students and local shopkeepers.

Hofbräukeller, Innere Wiener Str. 19. Thundering beerhall full of big round tables and big round men.

Ballhaus, Klenzestr. 71. Odd chandeliers flicker with electric candles and wistful couples nibble at plates of sushi in a downbeat but carefully trendy café.

Café Stöpsel, Preysingstr. 16. Comfy hideaway for afternoon tea and a good read.

Those who are too up-to-the-minute even for Haidhausen head west to the battered concrete suburb of **Neuhausen**.

Café Freiheit, Leonrodstr. 20. Currently Munich's 'in' café. Crowded, unpretentious and friendly, but subject to poisonous exhaust fumes from the hectic Mittleren Ring.

Ruffini, Orffstr. 22–24. A quieter alternative, famed for its soups and Sunday breakfasts (when you have to arrive early to get a seat).

Beer Gardens

The entire population of Ingolstadt (all 110,000 of them) could descend on Munich in one swoop, and each find a seat in a beer garden. Münchners—with a little help from their visitors—get through prodigious quantities of beer annually (five million litres during the Oktoberfest alone). In great beer tents during festivals, out under the trees in the summer, and in noisy halls and cellars the whole year round good burghers, grannies, *Schickies* and punks rub shoulders and down hefty *Maße* (litre mugs) of beer. Clusters of tourists join in, curious as to whether the fat men in feathered hats are for real (they are), and all too often destined to become one of the *Bierleichen* (beer corpses) that litter the ground at the end of the evening. You can get hearty helpings of Bavarian nosh in most beer gardens (sausages, roast pork and grilled fish are the standard fare), and it is perfectly acceptable to take your own picnic. Kick-off time is around 10am, and the hardy keep going to midnight and beyond. In bad weather you can usually retreat into an adjacent beerhall. What follows is a selection of watering holes to start you off. A little knowledge of local terminology is also useful:

Maß (a.k.a. *Helles*):	A litre of conventional beer.
Dunkles:	Strong malt beer, popular at festivals.
Weißbier:	Beer made from wheat instead of barley, and served with a slice of lemon.
Radler-Maß:	A 50/50 lager and lemonade shandy.

Russn-Maß:	*Weißbier* shandy.
Isar-Maß:	Mixture of *Weißbier*, apple juice and Blue Curaçao. Not for delicate constitutions.
Stammtisch:	Table for regular customers.

Central

Franziskaner-Garten, Perusastr. 5. A good place for a beer-and-sausage breakfast, right in the heart of town. There's been an inn on the site for 500 years, and Emperor Franz Joseph had a *Stammtisch* here.

Augustiner-Keller, Arnulfstr. 52. A leafy surprise off a tatty street behind the station, much favoured by staff from *Bayerischer Rundfunk* (the Bavarian TV station). If you sit at one of their *Stammtische* just near the entrance, the waiters will give you short shrift. The house-brewed beer is excellent, and the aroma of *Steckerlfisch* (char-grilled skewered fish) fills the neighbourhood.

The Englischer Garten

Chinesischer Turm, southern end of the Englischer Garten. Known to locals as the 'China-Turm'. On sunny days you'll find more students here than at the university, and cheery bands of young tourists too.

Aumeister, Sondermeierstr. 1; north end of the Englischer Garten. The best place for a picnic under the chestnut trees. Anything you bring to eat will be better than the food on sale, but the beer is a tasty Hofbräuhaus brew.

Seehaus, on the Kleinhesseloher See. Respectably quiet lakeside garden, full of dewy-eyed couples barely noticing the sunset.

Osterwald-Garten, Keferstr. 12. Hairy academics and paunchy Schwabing diehards drink slowly and have grumbly conversations. For once the food is good—try the *Schweinsbraten* (roast pork) which comes with giant dumplings.

Further Afield

Kloster Andechs, just east of the Ammersee (*see* 'South of Munich,' pp.116–17). The local monks brew potent beers, which you can drink on a terrace overlooking the valley below the monastery. In deference to the surroundings, there are signs commanding *Singen und Lärmen nicht gestattet* (No noise or singing allowed). The *Bock-Bier* is so powerful that it is now only served during the week—over weekends it caused too many motor accidents. The Kloster kitchens come up with delicious fare (try the creamy Beer Soup).

Schloßgaststätte Leutstetten, Altostr. 10, Leustetten (off the A95, or train in Starnberg direction). In a small village south of Munich. The real thing, with waitresses in traditional dress, FC Bayern football team at their *Stammtisch* and the best *Schweinsbraten* (roast pork) for miles.

Waldwirtschaft Großhesselohe (A bit of a mouthful which locals shorten to *Wawi*, Georg-Kalb-Str. 3, Großhesselohe (S-Bahn Line 7, 27). A large beer garden on the Isar with a jazz band usually in full swing by mid-afternoon. This is the best place to sample *Ausgezogene*—alcohol-absorbent doughnuts, fried in lard and dipped in sugar. The *Stecklerlfisch* (char-grilled skewered fish) ranks with the best.

Entertainment and Nightlife

Munich has possibly the best opera company in Germany, two top-class orchestras, over 40 theatres, a vibrant film industry, the country's leading theatre school, two excellent music academies and a lively jazz and modern music scene. The local listings magazines *Münchner Stadtmagazin* (available from newsagents) and *In Munich* (free from cafés and theatres) will guide you through the maze.

opera and classical music

The **Opera House** on Max-Joseph-Platz has an advance ticket sales office on Maximilianstr. 11, ✆ 22 13 16 (*Mon–Fri 10–1 and 3.30–5.30, Sat 10–12.30pm*). Operas often sell out well in advance, but you can get standing room and student tickets from DM5 at the box office in the Opera House one hour before the performance. The **Opera Festival** in July and August ranks with those in Salzburg and Bayreuth. The **Staatstheater am Gärtnerplatz**, ✆ 201 67 67 (*Mon–Fri 10–1 and 3.30–5.30, Sat 10–12.30pm*) presents a frothier programme of operetta, ballet and musicals, with similar last-minute ticket offers. Classical concerts take place in churches all over town, in the **Herkulessaal** (Residenz, ✆ 29 06 71) and in the Gasteig (*see* below). Keep an eye open also for concerts in the beautiful Cuvilliés Theatre. The best place to buy advance tickets is at the central **Theater-und Konzertkasse** (Neuhauserstr. 9, ✆ 12 04 0). The *Münchner Philharmonie* (under the baton of Sergui Celibidache, a front-rank conductor who refuses to record) and the *Bayrischer Rundfunk Sinfonie Orchester* (under Sir Colin Davis) are Munich's leading orchestras, but the *Münchner Kammerorchester* and ensembles from local academies also keep a high standard. Munich's largest concert hall is the Philharmonie Hall, part of the new **Gasteig Kulturzentrum**, Rosenheimerstr. 5, ✆ 4 80 98 614 (*general box-office open Mon–Fri 10.30–2 and 3–6, Sat 10.30–2*). Amidst much controversy, the city recently built this huge, incongruous, glass-and-brick arts centre just across the Isar at a cost of 350 million Deutschmarks. It is now the focal point of much of the city's best music and theatre, and also hosts the annual film festival.

theatre and cinema

Munich has eleven major theatres, as well as a plethora of fringe and cabaret venues (amply supplied by out-of-work actors from the national drama academy). Performances are almost always in German and, even if your German is good, the cabaret (which relies heavily on in-jokes and dialect) can be glumly incomprehensible. The outer reaches of the avant-garde, on the other hand, are equally confusing to all, no matter what your mother-tongue is. Hardy perennial Alexeij Sagerer continues to bewilder the establishment with performances involving live pigs, mud and lots of noise. The **Deutsches Theater** (Schwanthalerstr. 13, ℂ 51 44 360) sometimes imports foreign musical and dance companies. Mainstream local theatre is to be seen at the **Residenztheater** (Max-Joseph-Platz, ℂ 22 57 54). **Werkraumtheater** (Hildegardstr. 1, ℂ 23 72 1328) and **Theatre im Marstall** (Marstallplatz, tickets from Residenztheater box-office) stage more experimental work, and the most established cabaret venue is the **Münchner Lach-und Schiesgesellschaft** (Ursulastr. 9, ℂ 39 19 97). **Hai** (Rosenheimerstr. 123–5), in Haidhausen, is the liveliest venue to head for at present, with a bar, exhibitions, occasional discos, cabaret—and often Alexeij Sagerer. The annual Munich Film Festival in June and July gives you the opportunity to see new cinema from around the world. Failing that, head for **Museum-Lichtspiele** (Lilienstr. 2, ℂ 48 24 03), a complex of three cinemas that shows films in the original language (usually English)—a rarity in Germany.

nightlife and live music

The *Münchner Jazz-Zeitung* (available in music shops and jazz clubs) will tell you what's on in town. Avant-garde jazz and improvised music are particularly strong in Munich—**Unterfahrt** (Kirchenstr. 96) in Haidhausen being the venue for the adventurous. More mainstream fare can be had at **Alltoria** (Türkenstr. 33). Madonna and Prince-sized rock concerts are held in the **Olympiahalle** (Olympia-Park) and the **Circus-Krone-Bau** (Marsstr. 43), with tickets on sale at agencies around town (such as the one in the Marienplatz U-Bahn concourse). For up-and-coming German bands and the best visitors from abroad, check the programme at **Backstage** (Graubünderstr. 100, ℂ 18 33 30—good on rap, reggae and Afro), **Theaterfabrik** (Föhringer Allee 23, ℂ 950 56 56) and **Café Giesing** (*see* 'Bars an Cafés' above). The **babalu club** (Leopoldstr. 19) is currently the most popular dance spot, with US rap teams, Techno sounds and the best local DJs. During the summer you can bop about in the open air at **Sound Garden** (Schleißheimer 393) to everything from punk to sixties oldies. **Station West** (Berduxstr. 30) presents a mixed-bag of discos, live concerts and curious theatre, but the chicest place to dance is the **Park-Café** (Sophienstr. 7)—though here you can pay up to DM20 just to get in. Early in the week many clubs offer free or reduced admission, otherwise you can expect to pay around DM10 to get in, and often the same again for a drink.

North of Munich

Dachau

About 20km north-west of Munich is the **Dachau Concentration Camp Memorial** (*Tues–Sun 9–5; adm free; S-Bahn Line 2 to Dachau, then Bus 722 to the* Gedenkstätte (Memorial); *Autobahn 8 Exit Dachau/Fürstenfeldbruck, then follow signs to KZ, Konzentrationslager*). Dachau was the Nazis' first concentration camp, set up in March 1933 on the site of an old munitions factory. It was used mainly for political prisoners, so, unlike Auschwitz and Belsen, was not primarily a 'death camp'. Nevertheless, a visit is a sombre, disturbing and eye-opening experience.

The camp is a bleak, windswept expanse of gravel and concrete (Allied soldiers razed the wooden barrack huts to the ground in 1945). Next to the entrance gate, which bears the cynical motto *Arbeit macht Frei* (Work brings Freedom), is the old kitchen and laundry, now a **museum**. Here there is a display of photographs and documents relating to the camp that is at once chilling and depressing, and a short but harrowing **documentary** film is shown (*11.30 and 3.30 in English*). Across from the museum are two reconstructed **barrack huts**. Each hut was built to accommodate 208 prisoners, with only two wash-rooms between them. By 1938 up to 1600 people were crowded into each barrack. Inside you can see how the original prisoners' bunks were redesigned to become wooden three-tiered shelves on which the inmates slept, crammed against each other and stacked to the ceiling. The sites of the other 28 barracks are marked by neat gravel oblongs. At the end of the row is a Jewish Temple, an International Memorial, and Catholic and Protestant Churches. A path from the far corner of the camp takes you to the ovens and crematorium, and the gas chamber—camouflaged as a shower room. Lethal gas was to be surreptitiously channelled in through holes in the ceiling. You can still see the holes, though the gas chamber was never used. Dachau prisoners selected for gassing were transported to Hartheim Castle near Linz in Austria, where 3166 were executed between 1942 and 1944 alone.

Schleißheim

If your taste is for Baroque architecture, or if you like looking at paintings and pottering around museums, you should take your cue from the 17th- and 18th-century dukes of Bavaria, and break your journey at Schleißheim, 15km north of the centre of Munich, on the outskirts of the city (S-Bahn 1 towards Freising: Oberschleißheim). The **Altes Schloß** (Old Palace) (*Tues–Sun 10–5; adm DM5*) began as a modest hermitage completed for the devout Duke Wilhelm V in 1597. In 1616 Duke Maximilian I acquired the estate from his father and the retreat grew into an Italianate Renaissance palace. Sadly, today's palatial complex is a pale image of what it used to be like before bombs destroyed it during the Second World War. A skilful reconstruction of the 17th-century original buildings, it now contains a permanent exhibition of domestic Christian *objets d'art*, such as nativity cribs, depictions of the Passion and Eastern European Easter eggs.

The earlier residence is very much in the shadow of the much grander **Neues Schloß** (New Palace) (*Tues–Sun 10–12.30 and 1.30–5; adm DM2*). As early as 1693 Elector Maximilian II Emanuel decided to build an extension to the existing castle. The War of the Spanish Succession put a stop to the building work until 1719, when Joseph Effner was commissioned to re-start the project, following new designs.

The state rooms are paean to Baroque opulence. Architectural big guns of the time—such as François Cuvilliés, Johann Baptist Zimmermann and Cosmas Damian Asam (*see* p.49)—employed by Effner, became locked in a frantic competition to outdo each other, and it shows. The Augsburg woodcarver Ignatz Günther draped the eastern portal's panels with mythological allegories. Amid all this Baroque splendour is the **Großer Saal** (Large Hall), whose dazzling brightness is outshone only by its stunning painted dome, which rises through scenes from the history of the Wittelsbachs. The Neues Schloß also houses the **Barockgalerie** (picture gallery) (*at time of writing closed for renovation*), a spin-off from the Bavarian state collection of Baroque paintings in Munich's Alte Pinakothek (*see* p.77).

A stroll through the landscaped gardens offers little respite. Arabesques of blossoms and coloured pebbles, geometric hedges and a canal with cascades adorn the French-style formal gardens for over 330m. The **Gartenschloß Lustheim** (garden palace) (*Tues–Sun 10–12.30 and 1.30–5; adm DM3*) to the east predates the completion of the Neues Schloß by some 30 years; it was built as a wedding present to the Elector's wife, Maria Antonia, and designed by Enrico Zuccalli, who was cheated of seeing the project through because the War of the Spanish Succession so depleted the Electors' coffers. Fewer people make it up to Lustheim, but its light and delicately designed rooms make it worth the walk. Since 1968 it has contained the stunning collection of Meißen porcelain which integrates supremely with the Baroque interior.

Freising

In the shadow of Munich's sparkling new airport lies Freising, one of Bavaria's oldest towns. There has been an episcopal diocese in Freising since the 8th century and under Otto von Freising (*c.* 1115–58), uncle of Emperor Frederick Barbarossa, the see began an early spiritual and cultural boom. The town grew up around the bishopric, whose local dignitaries became powerful secular princes, remaining so until the beginning of the 19th century.

Getting Around

By car: Freising is 35km northeast of Munich on the B11.

By train: Freising is connected to Munich's S-Bahn network. Take Line 1 for a 25-minute jaunt to the terminus at Freising. All the main sights are within easy walking distance of the Bahnhof.

Tourist Information

The **tourist information office**, © (08161) 54122, is at Marienplatz 7, bang in the middle of the Altstadt.

The Domberg

Perched casually on top of the low hill called the Domberg in the upper part of town is Freising's pre-eminent ecclesiastical monument, the **Mariendom**. From outside it's no beauty, stumpily fashioned out of blank masonry. A twin-towered basilica, it was originally built during the Romanesque period, and on entering the Dom you can see an animated stone sculpture of the Emperor Barbarossa, one of the church's early benefactors, gazing down from the left-hand side of an arched portal. The interior, however, is in surprisingly opulent contrast to the exterior—a sumptuous feast of Baroque and Rococo architecture. In 1724 Johann Eckher set about countering severe Reformation aesthetics with new, sinuous forms that provided splendid backdrops for the pomp and ceremony of popular worship. The result of the bishop's fervour is the sparkling white interior by Egid Quirin Asam, with energetic ceiling *trompe l'œil* by his brother, Cosmas Damian. In his depiction of the Second Coming, above the nave, little figures float up into the sky, swirling ever higher through the clouds. Contemporary with these frescoes is the Rococo decoration of the church's late Gothic cloisters. The crypt is the oldest surviving part of the building. It contains the empty tomb and the refashioned, gold shrine (1863) of St Korbinian, the founder and patron-saint of the church which preceded the Dom. Among the 24 columns is the mysterious **Bestiensäule** (Beast Column), one of the most distinguished pieces of early medieval sculpture in Bavaria. Its eccentric, yet highly skilled carvings consist of an entwined mass of men and beasts, symbolizing the struggle between the powers of darkness and light.

Abutting the Mariendom to the west is the 15th-century **Dombibliothek**. The library dates from the early days of the diocese in the 8th century, and this is where one of the oldest books in the German language, the *Abrogans*, was drafted by monastic scribes (*see* **The Arts and Culture**, p.56). The library rooms were refurbished between 1732 and 1734, when the main hall acquired its vivacious, stuccoed ceiling fresco, designed by François Cuvilliés.

This set of ecclesiastical buildings is completed by the **Diözesanmuseum** (*Tues–Sun 10–5; adm DM3*). The museum is the largest diocesan museum in Germany, documenting Christian religious art over nine centuries. The 17th-century seminary is an ideal setting for its collection of more than 9000 exhibits from Bavaria, Salzburg and Tyrol, including a stunning Byzantine icon called the *Lukasbild*.

Around the Domberg

The **Altstadt**, below the Domberg, is a pleasant spot where you can stroll about and admire the fine Baroque façades of the beautifully restored canons' houses. Try to visit the **Asamsaal** (*guided tours from tourist office only, April–Oct first Thurs in month*) in the former episcopal lycée at the Marienplatz. In 1707 Hans Georg Asam, father of the famous Asam Brothers, was commissioned to decorate the room with a series of exquisite, allegorical representations of the triumphant progress of science and the divine virtues.

Freising's other prime attraction sprawls out over another gentle hill, southwest of the Altstadt. The former Benedictine monastery of **Weihenstephan** boasts the world's oldest brewery. In 1040 (locals put the date 150 years earlier) the local abbey was granted the privilege of brewing its own beer, which apparently appealed to the monks' temporal senses to the detriment of their spiritual devotion. Nowadays the students of the Faculty of Brewery at Munich's Technical College, present here since 1895, and the **Staatsbrauerei Weihenstephan** (State Brewery) (*Mon–Thurs guided tours on the hour 9–2, except 12 noon; adm DM3 including beer tasting*) make every effort to continue this tradition, possibly even surpassing the skills of their monastic forebears. You can also visit the adjoining *Bierstüberl* (beer tavern) to sample the various traditional brews, including the famed *Stephansquell* and *Weihenstephan*.

Where to Stay and Eating Out

Hotel Bayerischer Hof, Untere Hauptstr. 3, ℰ (08161) 3037 (DM118–170). Warmly elegant, traditional hotel; well-modernized and efficient. The restaurant serves regional specialities. **Freising Penta Hotel**, Alois-Steinecker-Str. 20, ℰ (08161) 9660, ✆ (08161) 966281 (DM260–290). Opened in 1992, along with the airport, this brash modern conference hotel offers service and trappings to the usual high standards. **Dorint Hotel München Airport**, Dr-von-Daller-Str. 3–5, ℰ (08161) 5320, ✆ (08161) 532100 (DM240–300). A touch less upmarket, but even more recent than the Penta, in an older building connected with a modern annexe.

Landshut

'*Landshut, du g'freist mi*' (Landshut, you delight me) a Wittelsbach duke once jotted down at the foot of a letter to his Landshut subjects. The once mighty town of Landshut, straddling the River Isar, still holds much to delight the visitor. Landshut has been the capital of Lower Bavaria since the 13th century, when it ruled over a duchy stretching south as far as Reichenhall and Kitzbühel (now in Austria).

History

Landshut began as a settlement at a bridge over the Isar, first mentioned in 1150. In 1204 Duke Ludwig I founded the town, the present Altstadt, below a new castle known as the Landshut. His son Otto II (the Illustrious) moved his ducal residence here from Kelheim in 1231. In the 14th century the Neustadt and Freyung quarters were laid out, spreading out to the east of the original settlement. The town soon burgeoned under the Landshut branch of the Wittelsbachs, who consistently outshone even their extravagant cousins in Munich. In 1475, at the height of its Golden Age, Landshut played host to the splendid wedding of Duke Georg to Jadwiga, daughter to the king of Poland. The feast became a medieval byword for lavishness (*see* 'Festivals' below for details of the re-enacted wedding). When in the 16th century Ludwig X chose Landshut as his permanent base, he shifted his ducal residence from the incommodious castle to the Stadtresidenz, which he commissioned in 1537 as the first Renaissance-style palazzo north of the Alps. After the 16th century Landshut declined in importance—though from 1800 to 1825 the town nurtured Bavaria's Provincial University before it eventually settled in Munich.

Getting Around

By car: Landshut is 70km northeast of Munich on the A11. This makes it a convenient stopping place if you're *en route* to the Bavarian Forest and Passau.

By train: There are frequent rail connections to Munich (45–60 mins) and Regensburg (60 mins). The Hauptbahnhof is on the northwestern edge of town, a 15-minute ride to the centre by city bus.

The **tourist information office** is in the Rathaus at Altstadt 315, ℗ (0871) 922050.

Festivals

Landshut is most famous as the scene of Germany's largest costume pageant, the **Landshut Wedding**, which is held every four years (next in June/July 1997). For four weeks, mostly at weekends, more than 2000 locals revel in period costume against the backdrop of the historic townscape, re-enacting the splendid marriage festivities of five centuries ago (*see* 'History' above). The celebrations include the wedding procession, tournaments and recitals of medieval music.

The annual **Frühjahrsdult** and **Herbstdult** (Spring Festival and Autumn Festival) in late April and late August are of slightly more modest proportion.

Burg Trausnitz

The massive Burg Trausnitz (*guided tours only, daily 9–12 and 1–5; adm DM1.50*) that broods over the town grew up over four centuries, and is a haphazard mixture of Romanesque, Gothic and Renaissance styles. The Landshut, as the castle was known until the 16th century, was founded in 1204 along with the town that it was to guard, and remained residence of the Wittelsbach dukes until 1543.

Those with sufficient stamina can climb up the steep Burgberg, which connects the Altstadt to the castle complex, in 20 minutes, taking advantage of its sweeping panoramic vistas over the town. (Alternatively take Bus 7 from Altstadt). The Burgberg leads to the outer defences, which include well-preserved sentry walks. Passing through the late Gothic gatehouse you reach the central, arched courtyard, graced by a Renaissance loggia. The Fürstenbau to the west forms the visual centrepiece. Extended in the middle of the 15th century, the building is notable for its lavish Renaissance detail, the product of Prince Wilhelm's attempt to create a suitably elegant residence for his wife Renate of Lorraine. In 1573 he hired a band of Italian artisans to refurbish the interior with a balustraded staircase in an effusive Italianate style. Sadly, most of the grotesque characters that decorated the upper storey were destroyed in a fire in 1961, and the only survivors are the life-size paintings depicting animated groups of playful *commedia dell'arte* buffoons which pop out of the walls of the *Narrentreppe* (Pranksters' Staircase).

Before leaving, have a stroll through the Hofgarten, the castle's expansive gardens that stretch out below its eastern walls with fine views across the town.

The Altstadt

The busy shopping thoroughfare called the Altstadt runs almost the entire length of the town's original medieval core, beginning at the foot of **St. Martin**, a bold Gothic hall church whose unusual brick steeple, shaped like a huge ballistic missile, tapers to a point 133m above the ground, making it the tallest masonry construction of its kind in the world. Unluckily for Master Hans von Burghausen, who started work on the church in 1389, he did not live to see his ambitious project through to completion. Inside the church, the lofty vaulted stonework forms a distant canopy to astonishingly narrow halls, lined by twin rows of slender columns. In the southern aisle is the **Rosenkranz-madonna**, a virtuoso piece of 16th-century woodcarving. This beautifully restored Madonna and Child, by the local sculptor Hans Leinberger anticipates the Baroque style and plays tricks with perspective (try looking at the sculptures from different angles).

If you follow the Altstadt around to the northern edge of the old town centre, you'll become entangled in a lively jumble of brightly coloured façades, impeccably restored houses and romantic alleys of crumbling, very much lived-in old houses, often backing onto colourful, arcaded courtyards. Altstadt 81 is the 15th-century **Pappenbergerhaus**, with stepped gables, all castellated with little merlons and turrets. In Kirchgasse you'll find the **Pfarrhof St. Martin**, which has a splendid wooden staircase leading up to various stuccoed rooms. Nearby, in Obere Ländgasse, is the eye-catching **Palais Etzdorf**, whose Rococo façade was supposedly designed by Johann Baptist Zimmermann.

Still on the Altstadt, opposite the Neo-Gothic **Rathaus**, is the 16th-century **Stadtresidenz** (*guided tours only, daily 9–12 and 1–5, including museums; adm DM1.50*), which supplanted the Trausnitz as the resplendent new seat of the Wittelsbachs, until Bavaria became united under Munich in 1545. Behind a Neoclassical façade (acquired as a result of an 18th-century facelift) is a palace constructed by Italian master builders and modelled on Mantua's *Palazzo del Té*.

A series of Renaissance arcades leads along an Italianate courtyard. A covered staircase from the vaulted western cloister leads up to the state rooms. These begin with the imposing **Italienischer Saal** (Italian Hall), lined with relief portraying the tasks of Hercules and capped by stunning coffer frescoes representing ancient Greek philosophers, heroes and rulers. Then come a series of salons whose names reflect the subjects of their ceiling paintings, such as the Göttersaal (the gods), Sternenzimmer (celestial bodies), Apollozimmer, Venuszimmer and Dianazimmer. Also in the Stadtresidenz is the **Stadt- und Kreismuseum** which contains some fine locally produced ceramics and an interesting collection of medieval armour produced by the town's renowned armourers.

Where to Stay and Eating Out

Romantik-Hotel Fürstenhof, Stethaimer Str. 3, ✆ (0871) 82025, ✉ (0871) 89042 (DM185–210). A stately Jugendstil hotel (completely renovated in 1981) on the outskirts of town, with a genuinely welcoming atmosphere. Soft blue and pink pastel hues, designer curtains and an abundance of floral arrangements add a gentle touch. The *maître d'hôtel* comes from Britain, though delights his guests' palates with new German cuisine in two stylish restaurants.

Pension Sandner, Freyung 627, ✆ (0871) 22379 (DM90). A clean and conveniently situated guesthouse, to the northeast of the Altstadt.

The Hallertau

Fifteen per cent of the world's hops originate from rich agricultural lands of the Hallertau, which line the B13 north of Munich. Undulating fields of crops coat the rolling countryside, punctuated by rectangular patches of tall hop gardens that form delicate pinnacles up and down the hillsides. As each crop comes into season, alternating patches of dark green, yellow-gold and bright green appear, dotted with the white and yellow of a few sleepy villages and scattered farmsteads. Here and there the rhythm is broken by stretches of deciduous and coniferous forest.

Once, swarms of piece-workers used to arrive in the Hallertau to help harvest the overflowing gardens; nowadays machines have replaced all but a sprinkling of manual labourers. The region, however, still maintains its traditional harvest-time festivity, each year choosing a *Hopfenkönigin* (hop queen) amidst much feasting and drinking. The heartiest bash is in **Abensberg** around the beginning of September.

Understandably, the bulk of each year's hop harvest is sucked up by the breweries in and around Bavaria, which fervently observe the *Reinheitsgebot* (*see* p.19). Locally, though, hops have an additional market: in the relatively brief season of mid-March to mid-April succulent, asparagus-like *Hopfensprossen* (hop shoots) appear on the menu of various restaurants of the Hallertau—a culinary experience not to be missed.

Fans of good asparagus should put aside 24 June (St John's Day) to visit the little town of **Schrobenhausen**, in the west of the Hallertau, when the asparagus harvest comes to a festive close. The town also has the **Deutsches Spargelmuseum** (asparagus museum) (*July–Sept Tues–Sun 2–4; adm DM4*), where you can find out everything there is to know about the delicate white shoots.

Ingolstadt

Ingolstadt is perhaps best known for the **Audi** assembly plants mass-producing '*Vorsprung durch Technik*' for world consumption. The story goes that when the Horch motor company moved production from Zwickau in eastern Germany to Ingolstadt after the Second World War, the new management mulled over the need to improve their international image. The old family name of Horch (which in German means 'Listen!') was given a Latin translation, believed to be more appealing to non-German ears. (Those wishing to get to grips with the prestigious Audi road machines should contact the company for details of factory tours, © (0841) 891241).

History

Ingolstadt began as a seigneurial estate of the Franks around AD 800, but was ceded to the Wittelsbachs in the early 13th century. After 1253 Duke Ludwig the Severe fortified the settlement in order to make it his ducal residence. To promote commerce the River Danube was diverted in 1363 to link up with the fledgling town. In the 14th and 15th centuries the town became the ducal capital of the Ingolstadt branch of the Wittelsbachs and was gradually enlarged to an important military stronghold, guarding a vital causeway over the Danube. In 1472 Duke Ludwig the Rich founded the first provincial university in Ingolstadt, which lasted until 1828. The town remained an important military centre until 1945. At times during the 19th-century military personnel stationed in Ingolstadt outnumbered its citizens.

Getting Around

By car: Ingolstadt is on the A9; 60km north of Munich and 90km south of Nuremberg. Most of the Altstadt is pedestrianized, but there is ample parking around the outskirts.

By train: Ingolstadt is on the main Munich–Nuremberg and Ulm–Regensburg lines, and so is served frequently by fast trains (Munich 45mins; Nuremberg 60mins) The Hauptbahnhof is about 2km to the south of the Altstadt. Regular bus services connect both.

Tourist Information

The **tourist information office** in the historic Altes Rathaus, Rathausplatz 2, ℂ (0841) 305417, is the usual cornucopia of advice, maps and information, and offers guided tours and assistance with bookings.

Festivals

July and August are good times to catch Ingolstadt in a celebratory mood. The first weekend in July is the time of the **Bürgerfest**, when the whole town fêtes its civic prowess. At two-year intervals (next in August 1996) Ingolstadt celebrates the **Reines Bierfest** (Real-Beer Festival), commemorating the proclamation of the *Reinheitsgebot* which took place in the town in 1516. Predictably, Bavarian beer drinkers go to great lengths to turn the event into a truly bacchanalian revel.

The Altstadt

Friedhofstraße, approaching the Altstadt from the west, takes you through the **Kreuztor**, the emblem of the city. Built in 1363 as part of new fortifications for an expanding city, the gate stood guard over the western thoroughfare to the old town. It is the only surviving gate out of four—a triumphant and defiant pile, with pixie-capped hanging turrets, all the more impressive for the way that age has weathered its red-brick masonry. A little further down Kreuzstraße, the two brick, asymmetrical, square towers of the **Liebfrauenmünster** appear like equally formidable redoubts. Duke Ludwig the Bearded began this Gothic hall church in 1425 as a suitable place to put his tomb. Inside, most of the church is cast in the usual cathedral gloom, but rows of windows in the central section flood the nave with light, lending a preternatural glow to the side-chapels. Of these, the most impressive are the six on the western side, where double-ribbed vaulting is entwined in a fragile network of branches, at points dangling like slender stalactites from the ceiling. The painting at the superbly restored late Gothic high altar is the *Adoration of the*

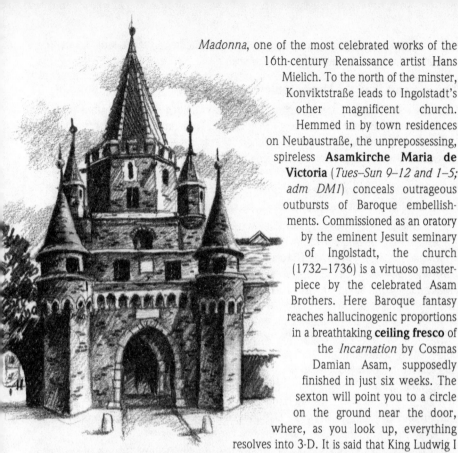

Madonna, one of the most celebrated works of the 16th-century Renaissance artist Hans Mielich. To the north of the minster, Konviktstraße leads to Ingolstadt's other magnificent church. Hemmed in by town residences on Neubaustraße, the unprepossessing, spireless **Asamkirche Maria de Victoria** (*Tues–Sun 9–12 and 1–5; adm DM1*) conceals outrageous outbursts of Baroque embellishments. Commissioned as an oratory by the eminent Jesuit seminary of Ingolstadt, the church (1732–1736) is a virtuoso masterpiece by the celebrated Asam Brothers. Here Baroque fantasy reaches hallucinogenic proportions in a breathtaking **ceiling fresco** of the *Incarnation* by Cosmas Damian Asam, supposedly finished in just six weeks. The sexton will point you to a circle on the ground near the door, where, as you look up, everything resolves into 3-D. It is said that King Ludwig I spent hours lying flat on his back looking at the painting. Another focal point is the **Lepantomonstranz**, in the sacristy. Again, if you ask, someone will open the gates to reveal the sublime gold and silver monstrance, designed by the Augsburg goldsmith Johann Zeckl in 1708 in honour of the Battle of Lepanto (1571), a famous Christian victory over the Ottoman Turks.

A walk back south along Neubaustraße will take you past the **Tillyhaus**, where Johann Tilly, the field marshal of the Catholic armies during the Thirty Years' War, died in 1632. Further down towards the core of the Altstadt, on Ludwigstraße, is the **Ickstatthaus**, a patrician mansion built in 1749 for a local professor and displaying one of the most opulent Rococo façades in town. South of Ludwigstraße is the Rathausplatz and the **Altes Rathaus** with intriguing touches of refashioned Neoclassical achitecture. A few yards to the east of Rathausplatz, is the 13th-century **Herzogskasten** or **Altes Schloß**, which houses the **Spielzeugmuseum** (Toy Museum) (*Mon–Fri 10–1 and 2–6; adm DM2*) with a superb collection of early sheet-metal playthings. Just to the southwest of the Herzogskasten, on the banks of the Danube, an erstwhile barracks has been put to good use: Since 1992 it has housed the **Museum für Konkrete Kunst** (Museum of Concrete Art) (*Tues–Sun 10–1 and 2–6, Thurs 2–8; adm DM3*). In a series of well-fitted-out halls you are given a perspective on avant-garde aspects of contemporary, tangible art forms covering mediums ranging from painting to poetry.

The Ramparts and the Neues Schloß

Since the early 19th century, Ingolstadt has been surrounded by a ring of stone-parapeted fortifications. Between 1828 and 1848 King Ludwig I ordered some 20,000 men to transform Ingolstadt into Bavaria's most formidable fortress town, so that it would live up to its strategically important position on the Danube. The *Schanz* (bulwark), as the massive military fortifications were known, bore the unmistakable stamp of the architect Leo von Klenze (famed for his buildings in Munich), who was eager to demonstrate that military architecture needn't be purely functional, but could also be aesthetically appealing.

The remains of the fortress (large sections were blown up by the Allies in 1945) surround the Alstadt in a polygon, one of the typical forms of 19th-century military architecture. It's worth making your way to the **Glacis**, a broad green belt on a sloping bank around the **Knüttegraben** (town moat) just west of the Altstadt. The Fronte, one of the former bastions now adrift among the fronds and lichen of the park, has been tastefully converted into workshops and a youth centre, while the Kavalier Hepp, designed to bolster the town's western entrance, houses Ingolstadt's **Stadtmuseum** (Town Museum) (*Tues–Sat 9–12 and 1–5, Sun 10–5; adm DM3*), where you can trace the town's architectural development. The contrastingly curved ramparts along the southern bank of the Danube were also subject to a post-war pep up. Here the Neoclassical **Reduit Tilly**, built as a last-ditch stronghold for the Wittelsbach dynasty in time of war, and the whimsical **Turm Triva** have been landscaped into the **Klenzepark**, a large, remarkably peaceful recreation area, laid out and arranged for Bavaria's Garden Show in 1992. The park is an unusual and agreeable contrast to the town, and offers fine views of the Altstadt.

Another blatant expression of former military power is the **Neues Schloß** to the east of the Altstadt, not far from the earlier Herzogskasten. The fortress-like palace dates back to the early 15th century, when the massive structure of 3m-thick walls and three defensive towers were built on the orders of Duke Ludwig the Bearded. Appropriately it is now home to the extensive collection of the **Bayerisches Armeemuseum** (Bavarian Army Museum) (*Tues–Sun 8.45–4.30; adm DM4*), which spans seven centuries of Bavarian military history. Most famous is the splendid booty captured in the 17th-century wars with the Turks, including ornate helmets, horse armour and banners.

Where to Stay and Eating Out

Queens Hotel, Goethestr. 153, © (0841) 5030, ✉ (0841) 5037 (DM155–267). A swish, slickly run, central hotel with views across the Altstadt. Famed for the groaning board at its breakfast buffet.

Hotel Rapensberger, Hardenstr. 3, © (0841) 3140, ✉ (0841) 314200 (DM175–195). Classy hotel combining one of Ingolstadt's historic houses with a newly built annexe.

Donau Hotel, Münchener Str. 10, ✆ (0841) 62055, 🖷 (0841) 68744 (DM140). Well-run little hotel in the town centre. Friendly service and convenient for all the sights. The hotel is attached to a cheery, traditional inn.

Hotel Zum Anker, Tränktorstr. 1, ✆ (0841) 30050, 🖷 (0841) 300580 (DM88–122). A comfortable family-run hotel in the Altstadt, with good restaurant (DM25–45).

Around Ingolstadt

Neuburg and Weltenburg

The small town of **Neuburg** on the River Danube, 26km southwest of Ingolstadt, could have popped up straight out of a Renaissance picture book. Although it dates back to Roman times, Neuburg's glory days started in 1505 when the town became detached from Wittelsbach rule and was governed as capital city of the tiny, newly founded principality of the *Junge Pfalz* (Young Palatinate) by the Prince Electors of the Palatinate in Heidelberg. When fastidious Prince Ottheinrich converted to Protestantism in 1542, he set about the construction of sumptuous palaces. His new subjects, eager to echo their leader's every religious and aesthetic whims, followed suit, and a building boom ensued. The focal point of Neuburg's Renaissance building is the **Schloß** (*Tues–Sun 10–5; adm DM3*) with its massive outer walls lining the tall hill at the town centre. This red sandstone mass appears to arrange itself into towers, domes and graceful arches. But what really catches your eye is the courtyard with arched loggias, asymmetrically grouped around three flanks, its Mediterranean character heightened by the black and white sgraffito paintings of the *Fürstenspiegel* (representations of the princes, harking back to a book on princely conduct by that name) that adorn the inner walls. Successive tiers of images represent favourite Old Testament heroes and hunky Greek deities.

Another example of Protestant fervour in Neuburg is the **Hofkirche St. Maria** on Karlsplatz. This early 17th-century church was designed as a beacon of Protestantism in surrounding Catholic Bavaria, but its intended role was somewhat thwarted when Ottheinrich's successor re-converted to Catholicism in 1614, and instituted rather more stuccoed embellishments to the interior than had been planned in the beginning. Today the church is a colourful pot-pourri of architectural styles ranging from Gothic to Baroque.

Another 19km upstream lies **Kloster Weltenburg**, where you're really spoilt for choice. It's hard to decide whether the abbey or its scenic setting provides the more spectacular sight. At Weltenburg the Danube makes a tight loop and shrinks to just 80m wide, cutting through a gorge of densely forested limestone rocks that have been eroded into truly bizarre shapes. The aptly named **Donaudurchbruch** (Danube's Cleft) forms the perfect scenic backdrop for the monastic complex that sits stolidly on the sandy banks. The best way to take in the whole panorama is to arrive by boat (*see* p.105). The **Klosterkirche** (*daily 7–9pm; adm free*), attached to a Benedictine abbey that is supposedly Bavaria's oldest monastic establishment (*c.* AD 620) is one of the finest examples of Baroque and Rococo architecture along the Danube. A pale building of ochre stone, it maintains a stately serenity despite the hordes of tourists that invade it daily. Inside the church, which was begun by Cosmas Damian Asam in 1716, the *stuccatori* have let loose with Rococo swirls and flourishes. In the hallway before you reach the nave, look out especially for the stuccoed allegories of 'the four last concerns': Death, Last Judgement, Hellfire and Heaven. In his *trompe l'œil* painting of the *Assumption of the Virgin Mary*, over the domed nave, cherubs float up into the sky, past a pyramid of clerics, Old Testament heroes, saints and the Holy Trinity. There's also a finely painted *Last Judgement* by Franz Asam, Cosmas Damian's son, in the porch. Another highlight is the splendid four-columned tableau over the high altar, with a dazzling depiction of a mounted St George slaying the dragon.

Should you find these sheer outbursts of Rococo fantasy somewhat overwhelming, then the beer garden of the adjoining **Klosterschänke** (Abbey Inn) (*daily 9–7pm*) is a good place to stop and recover with a glass of the abbey's own dark beer.

The Altmühl Valley

Like the Bavarian Forest, the Altmühl Valley (German: Altmühltal) has been consistently by-passed by foreign tourists, unaware of what they are missing. The River Altmühl gives its name to a Jurassic valley that winds its way from the heart of the Franconian highlands following a placid, gently rolling course to the resort of Treuchtlingen, then twists through dramatic loops and tight hairpin bends to meet the Danube at Kelheim. Until about 150 million years ago, the valley was the shoreline of a gigantic primordial lake that did a lot to shape the local landscape, leaving large deposits of fossils. Nowadays, by far the most scenic parts are the river's central reaches, where glistening forests and rows of fissured limestone crags drop down to the banks, and shallow rivulets branch out into charming valleys of lush meadowland and juniper-covered heath.

Geological faults that caused individual hills to become detached from the main mass provided the perfect natural defences for feudal overlords, and many are still crowned by castles. But the Altmühl Valley has few major towns and even less in the way of major man-made sights. Some 3000 square kilometres of the valley have been declared Germany's largest **nature park**, harbouring rare specimens of flora and fauna and trees up to 900 years old. The limestone is riddled with caves, some 300 in all, many of which were inhabited during the Stone Age. The surrounding countryside is at its most beguiling in autumn, when the white limestone rocks of the valley are perfectly offset by the golden tones of the trees; but the landscape is remarkable, whatever the time of year. It is a relatively deserted region, popular mainly with Germans on **activity holidays** (*see* below).

Getting Around

By car: A car is the most convenient way to travel around the valley. The A9 traverses the central Altmühl Valley in its Munich–Nuremberg section, while the B2, B13 and the B299 criss-cross the river and take you to dozens of small towns and villages. For a jaunt along the river itself you have to rely on smaller country roads.

Public transport: Chief stations in the valley, on the main rail lines from Munich to Würzburg, are at Eichstätt, Treuchtlingen and Gunzenhausen. There are regular **bus services** centring on Treuchtlingen and Kelheim that can take you to many of the smaller resorts. Ask at the local tourist offices for details.

Hiking: By far the best way to see the Altmühl Valley is on foot. Marked trails give you the option of anything from an afternoon stroll to a fortnight's serious walking. Tourist offices can give you advice on walks and sell maps of the trails. Some travel companies organize long-distance and circular group hikes, and will cart your luggage on ahead of you.

By bicycle: One of the great attractions of the Altmühl Valley is the comprehensive network of cycling routes, often following the hiking trails. There's a famous 160km-long cycling route between Gunzhausen and Kelheim—most of it quite easy going. You can get maps and information on bicycle hire from any of the tourist offices along the way.

Cruises: A sublime way to see the region—if you have the time. A number of companies have joined to form the **Vereinigte Schiffahrtsunternemen** (United Cruise Companies), based at Kelheim. The company offers round-trips and pleasure cruises on the Altmühl and Danube, based at Kelheim. Travelling the full length of the Altmühl involves a cruise on the **Main-Donau-Kanal** from Berching (the furthest limit for cruises) past Beilngries to Kelheim (services operating on most days between May and October; 6 hours; DM30). The Danube offers the most attractive stretch, however, between Kelheim and Kloster Weltenburg; between April and October boats ply the river in and out of the scenic Donaudurchbruch (40 minutes; DM5).

Watersports and rock climbing: With its 200km of gently flowing water, the Altmühl offers the perfect environment for some pleasant and undemanding *Bootswandern* (travelling about by boat) and is particularly suited for novices in canoeing and kayaking. The Altmühlsee (*see* below) near Gunzenhausen and the Kleiner Brombachsee at Absberg are popular lakes for **wind surfers**. **Rock climbers** enjoy the challenge of the cliffs, especially around the Dohlenfelsen near Wellheim-Konstein and around Riedenburg. Again, tourist information offices can help with all sports.

Tourist Information

Altmühl Valley Nature Park: The Information Centre, Notre Dame 1, Eichstätt, ✆ (08421) 6733 (April–Oct Mon–Sat 9–5, Sun 10–5, Nov–Mar Mon–Thurs 9–12 and 2–4, Fri 9–12), will prove a real treasure trove to anyone wanting to explore this wilder sector of the Altmühl Valley. The friendly and efficient staff can help with the region's topography, museums, castles, hotels and farming holidays as well as sports and outdoor activities. A press-button educational display section on the first floor explains the ecology of the varied habitats in the valley.

Weißenburg: Römermuseum, Martin-Luther-Platz 3, ✆ (09141) 907124.

Beilngries: Haus des Gastes, Hauptstr. 14, ℂ (08461) 8435.

Kelheim: Rathaus, Ludwigplatz 14, ℂ (09441) 701234.

Festivals

The main regional bashes around the Altmühl Valley are essentially local affairs though this doesn't mean that strangers aren't welcome. Around **Fasching** (carnival) time (usually in February/March) the inhabitants of Kipfenberg dress outlandishly and parade through the streets, while during their **Limesfest** the menfolk confront each other as Roman legionaries and fierce Germanic warriors. At the end of May, the **Weltumbsegler Niederlandt** (derisory German for the Dutch circumnavigators) is the focal point of revelry in Pappenheim when a group of local gallants whirl about the town in costumes of various periods, making a mockery of the world's major historic events.

From Gunzenhausen to Eichstätt

Just a few kilometres northwest of Gunzenhausen, the waters of the Altmühl and its tributaries have been dammed to create the **Altmühlsee**, a lake that, together with four smaller man-made lakes, spreads over 25 square kilometres and forms a kind of north Bavarian Riviera. There are numerous watersports facilities around the lakeside, and the **Vogelinsel** (Bird Island) to the north of the lake is famous for bird-watching (mostly rare breeds of storks and herons). At **Treuchtlingen**, 20km upstream, where three tributaries join the Altmühl, you can relax in the **Altmühltherme** (*daily 9–8; adm DM7.50*), an indoor leisure centre with various pools, sauna, solariums and its own thermal springs. The town also boasts a 16th-century *Schloß* and the ruins of a 14th-century *Burg*. North of the resort lies the **Fossa Carolina**, an ambitious medieval canal project (*see* below). Beyond Treuchtlingen you can leave the Altmühl for a short detour to **Weißenburg**, a small town that offers a graphic demonstration of Rome's control over the frontier regions of its empire. Just north of the town a 550km-long line of old Roman **Limes** fortifications linked the Rhine and the Danube, preventing Germanic incursions into the province of Raetia after AD 89. Important archaeological monuments of the time have been preserved and reconstructed following a series of 20th-century excavations. The whole northern section of the Altmühl Valley is dotted with the archaeological remains of Roman occupation, notably military forts and farming *villae rusticae*. Two restored and reconstructed Roman military camps, one built in stone and an earlier one protected by palisades, as well as the foundations of **Roman baths** (*April–Dec Tues–Sun 10–12.30 and 2–5; adm DM2*) can be seen around Weißenburg. A visit to the **Römermuseum** (*Mar–Dec Tues–Sun 10–12.30 and 2–5; adm DM3*) in town helps to flesh out the picture of what life in the Roman marches must have been like through a collection of Roman treasure that ranges from silver votive offerings to bronze statues of deities.

Back on the main route, lying on a picturesque bend of the Altmühl 7km beyond Treuchtlingen, is **Pappenheim**. Its charming little cluster of stone and half-timbered buildings rises up towards a skilfully restored 11th-century *Burg* (*Mar-Oct Tues–Sun*

10–5; adm DM3) with an interesting museum containing an assortment of arms and instruments of torture. Next stop, just a few kilometres out of Pappenheim, is **Solnhofen**, which likes to advertise itself as a 'world in stone'. This little resort is a mecca for fossil hunters and hobby geologists who descend each year on the nearby chalk quarries in search of the petrified remains of prehistoric animals. (The local tourist office will even lend you a hammer and chisel.) Solnhofen also prides itself on being the birthplace of the lithography, the art of stone-block printing, and its residents have honoured its 19th-century inventor, Alois Senefelder, with a statue in the middle of town. The impressive **Bürgermeister-Müller-Museum** *(April–Oct daily 9–12 and 1–5, Nov–Mar Sun 1–4; adm DM3)* in Solnhofen's town hall is packed with exhibits illustrating both the history of lithographic printing and the much older imprints of many Ice-Age fossilized creatures, including one of the rare fossils of the archaeopteryx.

After Solnhofen the Altmühl passes through a series of loops to the **Zwölf Apostel** (Twelve Apostles), a wooded range of eerie, fissured boulders, seen at its best from a canoe or kayak. The postcard-pretty hamlet of **Dollnstein** marks the end of the primeval Uraltmühl Valley, in which the river follows the former course of the Danube. Dollnstein is the northern terminus of the scenic **Urdonau-Dampfbahn** *(variable times, summer only)*, a narrow-gauge railway whose antiquated locomotives puff their way through the Wellheimer Valley to Rennertshofen, 21km to the south. On the way you pass the scattered ruins of **Wellheim castle** and the **Dohlenfelsen**, a limestone outcrop whose fissured walls set a rewarding challenge to rock climbers. After Dollnstein the twisting valley opens out between rugged slopes. At one of the tight hairpin bends straddling the river about 11km upstream from Dollnsteinthe lies the town of **Eichstätt**, capital of the Altmühl Valley. This wonky old town has a special link with the English-born missionary saint Willibald, who arrived here in AD 745 and became its first bishop. On the east side houses pass through the Baroque spectrum of white to yellow to cream, propping each other up around the town's two main squares, the Marktplatz and the Domplatz. Standing in their midst is the pale Baroque **Dom**, which shelters the famous **Pappenheimer Altar** *(c. 1490)* with its striking Crucifixion group. Across the river high above the town is the splendid 17th-century **Wilibaldsburg** *(April–Sept daily 9–12 and 1–5, Oct–Mar Tues–Sun 10–12 and 1–4; adm DM4 including museums)*, built as a residence for Eichstätt's prince-bishops. Nowadays the complex houses two museums, the **Historisches Museum** and the **Jura-Museum**, focusing on local history and the palaeontological and geological aspects of the town's environs.

The Main-Donau-Kanal

The idea of a navigable continental waterway to link the Black Sea with the North Sea has existed since the 8th century. In 793 the emperor Charlemagne ordered some 6000 workmen to drive a ditch between the Rivers Rezat and Altmühl, tributaries of the Main and Danube, at a point where they were just 2km apart. But the attempt was thwarted by incessant flooding. Nowadays the remnants of the 'Fossa Carolina' (Latin for Carolingian ditch) form a leafy pond to the north of

Treuchtlingen, celebrated among fishermen. Only in the 19th century did Ludwig I's engineers restart this ambitious canal project. Between Dietfurt and Kelheim the Altmühl was deepened and cleared by dredgers, straightened and canalized to a width of 12m. Eleven locks were built to cope with the changing water levels. After ten years of construction the 'Ludwig-Donau-Main-Kanal' was opened to shipping in 1846, but the venture failed with the advent of steam railways. Today this old canal is like an outdoor museum of industrial archaeology, full of musty bridges, romantic lock-gates, rusty sluices, mossy wharves and diminutive, forlorn lockhouses, many of them designed by none other than the famed Leo von Klenze. An easy way to spot the route of the erstwhile canal is by the fruit trees that line the crumbling towpaths. It is said that the income generated by the trees soon outstripped that of the canal.

In 1992 Charlemagne's vision once again became a reality when the Danube was linked by canal to the Rhine—after 32 years of construction and at a cost of DM5.6 billion—creating a waterway 3500km long. In the process, the Altmühl's lower reaches were transformed beyond recognition by the disproportionate widening of the river and by four massive concrete sluice-gates—ugly and out of place in the enchanting river landscape. At the time, some 850,000 protesters aired their vexation at the wanton destruction of the ecologically sensitive environment, describing the new canal as 'the silliest project since the building of the tower of Babel'. But the Bavarian state government has more plans up its sleeve. Now they want to straighten out the Danube for some 70km between Straubing and Vilshofen, so that the water course will be navigable throughout the year. Conservationists have warned that the new project will precipitate another ecological disaster, and point out that its commercial viability is questionable. It seems that the Danube and the Altmühl Valley must face another period of change and controversy.

From Eichstätt to Kelheim

First stop after Eichstätt is **Pfünz** which greets visitors with life-size bronze statues of two Roman legionaries at the entrance to the town. Pfünz's reconstructed **Roman fort** Vetoniana (*daily; adm free*) neatly complements the Roman encampments of Weißenburg. From Pfünz the river follows some tight turns to **Kipfenberg**, a pretty little village on the southern bank that marks the geographical centre of Bavaria. Surrounded by wooded hills on all sides, Kipfenberg is dominated by its 12th-century **Burg** (*outbuildings only open to the public*), set high on a bluff above the village. On the diminutive Marktplatz you can visit the inspiring **Fasenickl-Museum** (*Wed 3–6 and Sun 2–5; adm DM2*), a colourful and cleverly presented display of costumes and masks pertaining to the village's long carnival tradition. After Kipfenberg the river meanders gently on to **Beilngries**, 14km downstream on the northern side. Here, at the junction with the River Sulz, the walled medieval town nestles in the tranquil surroundings of a little bowl-shaped valley covered largely with a coniferous forest. Out of this rise the two soaring stone towers of **Schloß Hirschberg**. This Baroque residence was built by the prince-bishops of Eichstätt to keep a thumb on the locals, and today houses a Catholic seminary.

The undoubted highpoint of the Sulz Valley is **Berching**, 8km north of Beilngries, which has benefited greatly from the recent completion of the Main-Donau-Kanal, since river boats from Kelheim now moor right alongside the 1100-year-old Altstadt (*see* 'Getting Around' p.105). With its many creaky half-timbered houses, cobbled squares and medieval town walls (complete with nine towers and covered sentry walk), the beautifully preserved town seems stuck somewhere in the 14th century.

Back on the Altmühl, past the town of **Dietfurt**, with its medieval patrician houses, you reach the hamlet of **Altmühlmünster** on the opposite bank. Until the 14th century the local monastery was an important stronghold of the Templars. The town is the starting point for a 14km-long circular footpath through the thickly wooded Brunn Valley to **Schloß Eggersberg**. This 15th-century manor house, brooding in the rural obscurity of the quiet hamlet of Obereggersberg, was built as the hunting lodge of a local aristocratic dynasty and was recently converted into a hotel and restaurant, with sweeping views over the Altmühl (*see* 'Where to Stay and Eating Out' p.110). A small part of the complex houses the **Hofmarkmuseum** (*April–Oct Wed–Sun 2–5; adm DM6*), presenting local history and archaeology. (The Schloß can also be reached by car from Riedenburg.)

The buzzing town of **Riedenburg**, compared to Schloß Eggersberg, seems a world away in spirit, destined to prosper as one of the regional tourist magnets. For this it can thank the Main-Donau-Kanal and the constant influx of day-trippers converging on the town by boat. Completely dominating the townscape are Riedenburg's three castles dating from the 12th and 13th centuries, perched high on the encircling craggy hills. As you explore the town, look out for the **Kristalmuseum** (*April–Oct daily 10–7; adm DM4.50*), where the prize exhibit is the world's largest clump of rock crystals, from Arkansas. Around the next twist of the now canalized river, on the southern bank, you'll find the 11th-century **Schloß Prunn** (*guided tours only, April–Sept daily 9–12 and 1–5, Oct–Mar Tue–Sun 10–12 and 1–4; adm DM2.50*), whose strong stone walls tower precariously over a 70m-high, chalky promontory above the tree-tops. Once the most formidable fortress in the Altmühl Valley, Schloß Prunn is now a well-preserved showcase of a fully appointed medieval castle complex. (It's a long and daunting walk from Nußhausen below to the castle, so try to come by car.)

Following the northern bank of the Altmühl eastwards from Riedenburg will bring you to the tiny village of **Essing**. This was founded by the Celts in 500 BC, but there's nothing exceptional to see, apart from the **wooden footbridges** that span the river's old basin and the new Main-Donau-Kanal. The romantic old Bruck (bridge) and its Bruckturm (gate tower), set against a backdrop of village houses, which rise up the steep limestone crags, are in stark contrast to the swaying, 193m-long, state-of-the-art timbered bridge over the canal (the longest of its kind in Europe). Across the latter you can reach the **Schulerloch stalactite caves** (*guided tours only, Easter–Oct daily 10–4; adm DM4*), about 2km to the east. The caves, with a total length of 400m, were inhabited during the Stone Age. From the Schulerloch caves, you can walk back across the riverfront of the Schellnecker Wand to the vestiges of the 19th-century Ludwig-Main-Donau-Kanal (*see* 'Main-Donau-Kanal' above).

Four kilometres upstream, **Kelheim**, at the confluence of the Altmühl and the Danube, is the most touristy town on the river, its many moored pleasure boats lending a Mediterranean seaside atmosphere. In summer it is a busy, bustling place, thronging with coach parties and day-trippers, but somehow preserving its peaceful, romantic charm. Hemmed in between the river, the Main-Donau-Kanal and the sloping flank of the **Donaudurchbruch** to the west (*see* p.103), it has something of the reckless mood of a holiday island. The Wittelsbach dukes resided in Kelheim until 1231 when, by a tragic quirk of fate, the assassination of Duke Ludwig I on the town's bridge over the Danube caused his successors to steer clear of the place and move to Landshut. There's an Altstadt full of evocative nooks and crannies, a Schloß, dating back to the 12th century, a famous 17th-century *Weißbier* brewery and the three original town gates. From one of these, Mittertor, you start the slow ascent to the imposing **Befreihungshalle** (*April–Sept daily 9–5.30, Oct–Mar daily 10–4; adm DM2*) on a hill of its own just outside of town. The massive, drum-like monument commemorating the Bavarian dead in the wars against Napoleon (surprisingly magnanimous given that Bavarian troops had been an ally of Napoleon for most of the time) was started by King Ludwig I in 1842 and completed by his architect Leo von Klenze five years later. Inspired by ancient Greek architecture, the mostly brick-built, domed rotunda is supported by eighteen marble columns, each topped with an oversize limestone statue representing one of the peoples that rose against Napoleon.

Where to Stay and Eating Out

Gunzenhausen

Hotel zur Post, Bahnhofstr. 7, ✆ (09831) 7061, 📠 (09831) 9285 (DM160–190). No expenses were spared when the former posthouse was refurbished in 1988. The hotel's new wood-panelled day-rooms are especially attractive, as is the restaurant, though the chef is sometimes over-ambitious.

Weißenburg

Hotel Rose, Rosenstr. 6, ✆ (09141) 907123 (DM125–180). Long-established hotel just across from the Rathaus which justifiably prides itself on its antique-furnished rooms, friendly service and solid *gutbürgerliche* cuisine.

Eichstätt

Hotel Adler, Marktplatz 22, ✆ (08421) 6767, 📠 (08421) 8283 (DM160–190). Modernized, 17th-century Baroque mansion on the edge of the Marktplatz. Traditional touches, such as graceful candelabras, remain, but the rooms, though comfortable, are uniformly furnished.

Beilngries

Ringhotel Gams, Hauptstr. 16, ✆ (08461) 256, 📠 (08461) 7475 (DM130–170). Conveniently situated in the town centre, clean and comfortable, despite the rustic touches.

Riedenburg

Schloßhotel Eggersberg, Obereggersberg, ✆ (09442) 1498, 🖷 (09442) 2845 (DM65–195). Occupying a historic hunting lodge with expansive park, this stately country hotel offers varied outdoor pursuits such as horse-riding, angling and cross-country skiing in winter. Here you can live in pampered luxury, among Persian rugs and fine period furniture. The adjoining restaurant is renowned for its ever-so-refined cuisine and hefty bills.

Kelheim

Hotel Aukofer, Alleestr. 27, ✆ (09441) 2020, 🖷 (09441) 21437 (DM98–120). A good hotel with eager management, well-appointed rooms and two conservatories. Close to the Befreihungshalle. Serves its own beer and hearty fare.

East of Munich: Inn-Salzachgau

With some justification, the Inn-Salzachgau, southeast of Munich, styles itself as 'the other Upper Bavaria'. This triangular patch of land, bounded by the converging Rivers Inn and Salzach (marking the Austrian border to the east) is a secluded spot, comprising fertile upland farmland, here and there broken by patches of deciduous woodland. The highlights of the area are thinly spread, but through its scattering of historical sights it constitutes one of the best areas in which to observe the gradual unfolding of the architectural innovations that reached Bavaria via trade routes from beyond the Alps.

Getting Around

By car: Four major *Bundesstraßen* cross the region. Most of the important towns lie along the B12, which runs from Munich (A94 up to Markt-Schwaben) to Altötting (90km) and on to Passau. The B299 runs from Landshut to Altötting (60km), while the B20 connects the latter with Burghausen (15km). The B304 links Munich with Wasserburg (55km). There are two **car ferries** from Mühldorf on the River Inn, one providing a service to Annabrunn, the other to Starkheim.

By train: The main lines serving the region run from Munich to Mühldorf with connections to Altötting (1hr 30mins) and Burghausen (2hrs), and from Munich to Wasserburg (1hr 20mins), where a branch line follows the course of the Inn to Mühldorf.

By bicycle: By far the most pleasurable way of seeing the countryside is by bicycle. Most of the land is fairly flat, and there is a comprehensive network of cycle routes. (Maps and details are available from tourist offices.) You can hire bicycles very cheaply from the parcel counters at most German Rail stations (*see* **Travel**, p.9).

Hiking and boat-trips: Walking is also a good way to get around, but it's essential to get hold of the local *Wanderkarte* (walking map), as it's all-too-easy to get lost. If you have the time for leisurely journeys, converted *Plätten* **salt barges** can take you on a gentle dawdle from Burghausen along some fine stretches of the River Salzach (May–Oct; DM10 per person).

Tourist Information

Wasserburg: Rathaus, ✆ (08071) 10522.

Altötting: Rathaus, Kapellplatz 2a, ✆ (08671) 8068.

Burghausen: Rathaus, Stadtplatz 112–114, ✆ (08677) 2435.

Festivals

The region's main cultural event, the **Musiksommer zwischen Inn und Salzach** (Musical Summer betwixt Inn and Salzach) is shared by several of the region's resorts (Altötting, Burghausen, Kloster Au and others) and attracts top-drawer artists from around Germany. There are two other, contrasting music festivals: the **Week of Church Music** held in Altötting each year in October, and the **International Jazz Week** in March at Burghausen, which includes open-air performances.

Wasserburg

The small town of Wasserburg, which lies just shy of where the River Inn snakes round a narrow tongue of land, is another medieval gem barely touched by the invasion of foreign tourists. The town's prime location on a protruding peninsula first recommended it to a local princely family who made Wasserburg their seat in 1137. From here, they were able to keep tabs on the important salt route from Reichenhall to Munich and could control the waterway trade between the Adriatic Sea and the Danube.

Most of Wasserburg's prime attractions are grouped together on the spacious **Marienplatz**, which looks at its most impressive when approached over the Inn bridge and through the massive 15th-century **Brucktor**. To the east of the square is the **Kernhaus** with its Rococo façade of 1740. Opposite lies the high-steepled, Gothic **Rathaus**. On the far side of the square is the 14th-century **Frauenkirche**, whose interior underwent a Baroque renewal in around 1750. Some of Wasserburg's most evocative streets lie just off the Marienplatz. Follow the narrow, colourful alley marked Schmiedzeile (on the western side of the square) where ancient shops have fancy wrought-iron guild signs. This will lead you to the **Burg**, resting on a gentle elevation on the bank of the Inn. This 12th-century castle was extended in the 16th century and is now an old people's home; the only part accessible to the visitor is the late Gothic chapel in the inner courtyard.

Altötting

Altötting is Bavaria's answer to Lourdes in France or Czestochowa in Poland. By the 15th century, a series of miraculous healings—such as a boy killed by a cart and a drowned child being brought back to life—had elevated this erstwhile Carolingian settlement to a thriving place of pilgrimage. Given the 700,000 or so wayworn devotees who still flock to Altötting each year, particularly around the months of May and October, the town is the one place where you cannot fail to appreciate that the Catholic Church is alive and kicking in Bavaria.

Altötting's adulation of the Virgin Mary centres on the **Gnadenkapelle**, a tiny Gothic brick chapel, built around an even smaller octagonal cell, which you reach from the wide, central **Kapellplatz**, and a bevy of booths selling every conceivable kind of devotional souvenir. Its history goes back to a Carolingian baptistry, in which St Rupert is said to have christened a Bavarian duke as early as the 7th century. Before entering the outwardly unprepossessing chapel, have a look around the **cloisters** that are covered with votive icons and girdled with bundles of the broad wooden crosses that penitents traditionally hump round the chapel. Inside, the gloomy, candle-lit nave is encased in black marble. A myriad colourful rosaries and other *ex votos*, dangling from the soot-blackened walls, usher you to the chapel's centrepoint, the luminous, silver shrine of the **Black Madonna** (c.1300). The Virgin and Child are carved in limewood, swathed in dazzling ceremonial robes and sport glittering coronets. Opposite, an eerie row of urns contain the hearts of 21 Wittelsbach rulers, including that of Ludwig II. Similarly preserved is the heart of Field Marshal Johann Tilly, Catholic hero of the Thirty Years' War and a devout pilgrim to Altötting. His other remains are displayed in a tomb in the vaults of the Stiftspfarkirche (*see* below).

Opposite the south face of the Kapellplatz and completely overshadowing the Gnadenkapelle is the twin-towered **Stiftspfarkirche**, built in the so-called transitional style. It was completed around the same time as the late Gothic nave was added to the Gnadenkapelle, but is more cautiously Romanesque than go-ahead Gothic. The calibre of the pilgrims that came to visit Altöttingen can be appreciated in the adjoining **treasury** (*May–Oct daily 10–12 and 2–4; adm DM1*). It wasn't just the hoi polloi that begged for forgiveness over the centuries. From early on the high and mighty Wittelsbachs and Habsburgs abased themselves before the Black Madonna, repented their sins and showed their gratitude with a welter of votive offerings. Prize of the collection is the magnificent **Goldene Rössl**, a heavily decorated and gilded filigree masterpiece of French origin (*c.* 1400) that depicts the Adulation of the Virgin Mary by King Charles VI of France, with a manservant holding the reins of an enamelled white mare on the base. At the northern end of the Kapellplatz, facing the Gnadenkapelle, lies the **Wallfahrts- und Heimatmuseum** (Pilgrimage and Local History Museum) (*May–Oct Tues–Fri 2–4, Sat 10–12 and 2–4, Sun 10–12 and 1–3; adm DM1*), really only worth a visit if you feel a craving for total immersion in Altöttingen's history of Christian devotion.

Burghausen

'*Voilà la ville souterraine!*' ('Behold the subterranean town!') exclaimed Napoleon as he looked out over Burghausen. His remark seems a fitting reflection on the town's defensive posture in its role as an important military stronghold along the Bavarian-Austrian border. Wedged between the Salzach to the east and a former arm of the river, the Wöhrsee, to the west, Burghausen sprang up under the protective watch of its massive fortress. Today street after street has retained its bright, decorative houses that distinguish the architecture of the Inn-Salzach.

A walk up the steep but straight Burgsteig will bring you to the **Burg**, Germany's longest castle complex with one kilometre of bristling towers and baileys. It was begun in the 13th century and for the next 300 years was the guardian of Burghausen's lucrative salt trade, controlled by the Landshut branch of the Wittelsbachs. The castle fortifications were last extended between 1480 and 1490, in an attempt to ward off an imminent onslaught by the Turks. You enter the Hauptburg through a medieval gateway. Here the main buildings around the inner courtyard date back to the oldest-surviving Gothic origins of the castle complex. Altogether five more baileyed quadrangles spread out to the north, all linked by massive gateways and bridges, progressively marking the transition from Gothic to early Renaissance. These are two interesting museums within the castle precincts, the **Historisches Stadtmuseum** (Historic Town Museum) (*May–Sept daily 9–6.30; adm DM2.50*) in the Hauptburg and the **Fotomuseum** (Photographic museum) (*April–Oct Wed–Sun 10–6; adm DM2.50*) at the northern entry to the Burg.

Down below, the Altstadt hugs the bank of the River Salzach. Space is at a premium on the narrow strip of land, and the old town's generous layout comes as a surprise. Don't be put off by the dull row of riverfront houses: behind them a mesh of gracious burgher houses fans out, a lively jumble of brightly painted façades with many false frontages concealing the high gables. The focal point is the oblong **Stadtplatz**, the main thoroughfare and social hub of Burghausen. At the southern end of the square stands the 15th-century **St. Jakobskirche** with its onion-shaped twin-domes. Across the square is the 14th-century **Rathaus**, and a colourful pot-pourri of stately buildings, including the late Gothic *Wachszieherhaus* (Candle-Maker's House). Ranged around the Stadtplatz are two more 17th- and 18th-century churches, the castellated former **Kurfürstliche Regierungsgebäude** (Administrative Building of the Prince-Elector), now housing the town library and conference rooms, and the splendid Rococo **Taufkirchen Palais**. Not far from where Burghausen's only bridge crosses over the Salzach to Austria, you'll find the mooring from which converted salt barges leave for river jaunts in the summer (*see* 'Getting Around' p.112).

Where to Stay and Eating Out

Wasserburg

Hotel Fletzinger, Fletzingergasse 1, © (08071) 8010, ✉ (08071) 40810 (DM126–159). A historic building in the town centre, newly renovated and well-equipped.

Altötting

Hotel zur Post, Kapellplatz 2, © (08671) 5040, ✉ (08671) 6214 (DM195–270). The grandest hotel in town, part of the Best Western chain. A sleek realm of spacious rooms with a Roman bath and five in-house restaurants.

Hotel Schex, Kapuzinerstr. 13, ✆ (08671) 4021, ✉ (08671) 6974 (DM130–150). A smartly modernized, historic hotel in one of the most atmospheric parts of town. Its restaurant and vaulted inn serves hearty local cuisine.

Burghausen

Ringhotel Glöcklhofer, Ludwigsberg 4, ✆ (08677) 7024, ✉ (08677) 65500 (DM140–160). A comfortable, modern hotel at the entrance to the castle.

Klostergasthof Raitenhaslach, Raitenhaslach 9, ✆ (08677) 706264, ✉ (08677) 66111. (DM130–140). Occupying a tastefully converted wing of a 16th-century monastery, 5km southwest of the town centre. The vaulted dining halls and monastic vestiges make it a rewardingly unconventional guesthouse.

South of Munich

On fine days thousands of Münchners flock out to the southern **lakes** to swim, waterski, windsurf, sunbathe and enjoy all the commercial trappings of German *Freizeit* (leisure time). In just one hour you can be out of the city, breathing bracing Alpine air at the seethingly popular Ammersee or Starnbergersee, or at the smaller Tegernsee or Schliersee. The more distant Chiemsee has the added attraction of King Ludwig II's grandest palace.

Getting Around

Ammersee: 40km southwest of Munich, off Autobahn 96, S-Bahn Line 5 to Herrsching (1hr). **Ferries**, run by Schiffahrt auf dem Ammersee, (✆ (08143) 229) cross the lake to quieter spots.

Starnberger See: 30km southwest of Munich, off Autobahn 95, S-Bahn Line 6 to Starnberg (40min). Bicycles to rent at S-Bahnhof (DM6 per day with S-Bahn ticket, otherwise DM10). **Ferries** ply the shores (DM17.50 round-trip or DM5.50 per stop).

Tegernsee and **Schliersee**: Two lakes 8km apart and 50km south of Munich, off Autobahn 8. Rail connections from Munich Hauptbahnhof (just over 1hr).

Chiemsee: 80km southeast of Munich, on Autobahn 8. There are frequent rail connections from Munich Hauptbahnhof to Prien am Chiemsee (1hr) and ferries will take you across to the islands (Chiemsee Schiffahrt, Seestr. 108, ✉ (08051) 6090; DM8.50 round-trip).

Tourist Information

Ammersee: Rathausplatz 1, Schondorf, ✆ (08192) 226.

Starnbergersee: Kirchplatz 3, Starnberg, ✆ (08151) 13008.

Tegernsee: Kuramt, Rathaus, Tegernsee, ✆ (08022) 180 122.

Schliersee: Kurverwaltung, Schliersee, ✆ (08026) 4069, ✉ (08026) 2325.

Chiemsee: Rathausstr. 11, Prien am Chiemsee, ✆ (08051) 3031.

The Lakes

The **Ammersee** and the **Starnberger See**, just a few kilometres apart, are both large, pretty lakes lined with rich Münchners' holiday villas. In places it is hard to find a stretch of public beach, and when you do it is likely (in good weather) to be packed with fellow pleasure-seekers. Both lakes allow waterskiing (banned on most other Bavarian lakes), and the water is skimmed by power-boats, yachts and windsurfers.

The main resort on the Ammersee is **Herrsching**, which can get very crowded (you can find quieter public beaches by following the path around the lake). From Herrsching you can walk up through the woods (5km, not all easy going) or catch a bus (951 or 956) to **Andechs**, a beautiful 14th-century hill-top monastery. The Gothic church has a fussy Rococo interior and the tomb of the composer Carl Orff, but the Benedictine brothers are more famous for their potent beer (*see* 'Where to Stay and Eating Out' below). Most of the eastern shore of the Starnberger See is private property (though there are public beaches at Berg, Leoni and Ammerland).

Starnberg, right at the top of the lake, is the main resort. From here the cafés, ice-cream stands and windsurfer hire shops spread out down the western shore—a peculiar mixture of Alpine charm and seaside tack. The main beach is at Possenhofen, where King Ludwig II drowned (*see* p.183). Today a small wooden cross (occasionally stolen by devotees) marks the spot where he was found, and there is a chapel to his memory nearby.

Tegernsee, surrounded by forests and lush countryside, against a backdrop of the Alps, is a parade ground for Munich's nouveaux riches and wealthy industrialists from the north. The frantic displays of wealth give the resorts around this beautiful lake an unpleasant edge, and the flood of 'Ruhr roubles' bumps up the prices. The best thing to do is to join the hang-gliders on the peak of the 1722m-high **Wallberg** (*cable car from the southern village of Rottach-Egern; DM18 return*), from where you get a detached and spectacular view. The Benedictine Kloster dates from the early 16th century. Maximilian I turned it into a summer home, and nowadays it is a beer tavern. The tiny **Schliersee**, on the other hand, is far less crowded and uptight, and has a charming country atmosphere. People still wear traditional dress on feast days for their own sakes, and not for tourist photographs. You can mess about in little boats with no fear of being flattened by something fast, and the hang-glider air traffic is not quite so thick. It is also a pleasant place to swim, as the water in summer can reach 25°C, a good 5°C warmer than the larger lakes.

Chiemsee, 40km further west, is a vast lake popular with watersports enthusiasts, but best known as the location of **Schloß Herrenchiemsee** (*daily 9–5; adm DM4*), Ludwig II's final and most ambitious building project. Ludwig idolized the Sun King, Louis XIV of

France, and was determined to build a replica of Versailles in Bavaria. With this in mind he bought **Herreninsel**, an island on the Chiemsee, in 1873. The cornerstone of the new palace was laid five years later. Ludwig's generous patronage of the composer Wagner, and earlier fantasy castles at Linderhof and Neuschwanstein, had all but bankrupted state coffers. This time the king's ministers tried to temper his ambitious plans, but in the end Ludwig got his own way. He sent back plan after plan drawn up by the architect George Dollmann, until finally his proposed palace reached the dimensions of the French original. The garden façade at Herrenchiemsee is an exact replica of the Versailles garden façade, but money ran out in 1885 after only the central part of the palace had been built.

The ferry (*see* 'Getting Around' above) drops you off at a wooden jetty on the northern end of the island. After running the gauntlet of souvenir kiosks, you follow leafy avenues across the meadows, to come somewhat abruptly upon the formal gardens and splendid façade of the *Schloß*. You can only see the interior on a guided tour, but this is well worth it for the sumptuous Parade Chamber (an Audience Hall even more ornate than the one in Versailles); the king's bedroom with its rich, blue, heavily gilded, boat-like bed; the Dining Room with a 'magic table' like the one at Linderhof (*see* p.123) and an exquisitely worked 18-arm Meißen porcelain chandelier; and the stunning Gallery of Mirrors (an exact replica of its Versailles counterpart, with nearly 2000 candles in the chandeliers and candelabras).

Before Ludwig bought Herreninsel, there was a monastery on the island. **Fraueninsel**, a few hundred yards across the water, was (and still is) the site of a Benedictine nunnery. Most visitors head back to the mainland after seeing Herrenchiemsee, so Fraueninsel is left to the relative calm of the nuns, birds, fishermen and a scattering of holiday residents and tourists. The whitewashed church is a quaint mixture of Romanesque, Gothic and Baroque. Next to it is a distinctive 9th-century octagonal bell-tower, topped with a 16th-century onion dome. The **Torhalle** (gatehouse) (*May–Oct daily 11–6; adm free*) has a chapel in the upper storey containing splendid Carolingian frescoes.

Where to Stay and Eating Out

Kloster Andechs, Ammersee. Has a terrace where you can drink strong beer and eat scrumptious food (*see* 'Munich Beer Gardens' p.90).

Bräustüberl, north wing of the Kloster, Tegernsee. A beer-hall popular with thirsty local farmers. Spirited (at times rowdy) alternative to the chic cafés elsewhere on the lake.

Herrenchiemsee Beer Terrace, Herreninsel, near jetty. Shady spot with a fine view over the lake. Despite being in such a tourist trap, the food (schnitzels, sausages and other tourist standards) is well cooked and reasonable (DM15–30).

Kloster Café, Fraueninsel, adjoining the Kloster. Charming café overlooking the lake on the pretty and reposeful nuns' island. You can sip the fiery *Klostergeist* (a liqueur distilled by the nuns themselves) with your coffee or after a meal (DM15–25).

Seehotel Überfahrt, Überfahrtstr. 7, Rottach-Egern, Tegernsee, ✆ (08022) 6690 (DM200). Large, chi-chi lakeside hotel with its own pool and health centre.

Fischerstüberl am See, Seestr. 51, Tegernsee, ✆ (08022) 4672 (DM90–110). Cosy inn with a leafy terrace overlooking the lake. The restaurant serves superb fresh fish.

Haus Huber am See, Seestr. 10, Schliersee (from DM80). Simple, cheery boarding house within a few minutes' walk of the lake.

The Bavarian Alps

The craggy Bavarian Alps stand shoulder to shoulder, just an hour's drive from Munich. At times they plummet abruptly to the edges of icy, sparkling lakes, or stretch out into luscious meadows and rolling forest-land. The air is invigorating, fragrant with wildflowers in the spring, and clear—the hesitant, mournful tune of cowbells carrying for miles across the valleys. The hillsides are dotted with traditional chalets—some with white-washed lower storeys and wooden upper halves, their long balconies cascading with flowers; others entirely of wood with low-pitched roofs and decorative little belfries; yet others with gaudily painted façades.

In winter people in startlingly bright ski-clothes shoot about the snow-covered slopes and crowd into warm *Gaststätten* to drink *Glühwein* or hot chocolate. In summer the Alps become delightfully rural. You can see women in headscarves working in the fields, cowherds leading a handful of prized animals up to mountainside grazing lands, and village-folk resplendent in traditional *Tracht* (costume) for a wedding or feast day. This is a part of Bavaria that will appeal particularly to nature-lovers and winter-sports enthusiasts, though you will also find King Ludwig II's most charming and eccentric castle, and high culture in the form of the famous Oberammergau Passion Play.

Getting Around

By car: The **Deutsche Alpenstraße** (German Mountain Road) is a sign posted tourist route that winds from Lindau on the Bodensee to Berchtesgaden in the east. It is one of the most spectacularly beautiful of all the German Tourist Roads, though it is not quite finished and at times you have to duck into Austria or dip down onto the plains. Even the minor roads are well made, though some passes are steep and twist tortu-ously. In winter it is a good idea to fit snow tyres or carry chains if you are intending to leave the main roads.

By train: The only track that runs the length of the Alps is across the border in Austria (connecting Feldkirch in the west with Innsbruck and Salzburg). However, there are numerous rail routes radiating out of Munich: Mittenwald (1hr 40mins), Oberammergau (1hr 40mins), Berchtesgaden (2½–3hrs), Garmisch-Partenkirchen (1hr 20mins; a *Sonderrückfahrkarte* (special round-trip ticket) almost halves the price: DM28, return or DM70 return including cog-railway and cable car to Zugspitze).

By bus: Private bus companies offer tours from Munich to Alpine resorts. Try **Panorama Tours** (Arnulfstr. 8, © (089) 591 504), who offer a variety of trips including Berchtesgaden (DM65) and Linderhof/Neuschwanstein (DM65).

Walking: Walking is one of the most rewarding and refreshing ways of exploring the region. Local tourist offices can often suggest routes and provide maps. The Bavarian state government has declared six areas of pasture to be common land. Here you can walk about as you please, and will come across mountain cabins offering snacks and fresh milk from the herds. The designated zones are around Garmisch-Partenkirchen, Berchtesgaden, Kreuth (south of the Tegernsee), Schliersee, Aschau (south of the Chiemsee) and Ruhpolding. (Apply to local tourist offices for details.)

Tourist Information

Oberammergau: Eugen-Papst-Str. 9a, ✆ (08822) 1021.

Mittenwald: Dammkarstr. 3. (08823) 33981.

Garmisch-Partenkirchen: Kurverwaltung, Bahnhofstr. 34, ✆ (08821) 1800.

Berchtesgaden: Königseestr. 2 (near Bahnhof), ✆ (08652) 5011.

Festivals

The **Oberammergau Passion Play** began in 1634 after residents of Oberammergau, worried by the first signs of plague in the village the previous year, had vowed that if the pestilence developed no further their descendants would perform the Passion of Jesus every ten years, into eternity. No one in Oberammergau died of the disease, and for generations townsfolk have honoured the pledge—though in 1680 the performance date was altered to coincide with the beginning of each new decade (the next one is in AD 2000). The text has had a chequered history. A rather bawdy original was cleaned up in 1750 and put into high Baroque verse. The 19th century saw the first prose version, and recent modernizations have expunged some rampant anti-Semitism. Nowadays the Passion takes place in a vast open-air theatre which was built in the 1930s. The spectacle lasts the whole day (with a two-hour break for lunch) and nearly half a million people get to see the 100 or so performances between May and September. *Passion Oberammergau* is Village Hall Nativity Play writ enormous. Only locals (1500 of them) may take part, many men cultivating biblical beards for months before the event. Even the props are made by Oberammergau craftspeople alone, and tradition dictates that a local virgin plays Mary. There was outrage in 1990 when not only was the Mother of God portrayed by a mother-of-two, but (even worse in Bavaria) another of the lead actors was a *Protestant*.

As a Roman Catholic stronghold, the Bavarian Alps have a number of **religious festivals**—often involving street processions, dressing up in *Tracht* and feasting. At **Corpus Christi** you'll see the richest collection of local dress, especially around Oberammergau where the men wear knee-breeches, bright waistcoats and heavy leather belts and the women are resplendent in brocaded dresses and otter-fur bonnets. On **Palm Sunday** the rites have intriguing pagan undertones. Churches, streets and homes are decorated with *Palmbosch'n* (silvery willows) festooned with ribbon-like *Geschabertbandl* (dyed woodshavings). Two little cuts are made in the bark to let out witches and druids (not viewed as favourably in Bavaria as they are in Wales). Children carry the branches to church to be blessed, and then out into the fields where they are left to ensure protection for the year ahead.

The autumn **cattle-drive** is the most colourful of all village events. Hardy cowherds (men and women) decorate their animals with elaborate *Faikl*—head-dresses made of ribbons, leaves, feathers and flowers, sometimes up to a metre high—and bring them down from the high Alpine pastures where they have spent the summer. This takes place around *Michaeli* (29 September), though much depends on the weather and it is better to make enquiries locally. In May or June the cowherds and their charges head back for the mountains—but this is done without quite so much display. The cattle drives take place in towns throughout the mountains and foothills. The earliest autumn drive is usually in Garmisch-Partenkirchen (early September), and the last is in Königsee (as late as October), where the cows have to make the last part of their journey by boat. (*See* also pp.130–31).

Oberammergau and its Surrounds

Oberammergau, about 90km southeast of Munich on the B23 (off Autobahn 95), is a small town crushed right up against a sheer granite mountainface and—Passion Play or no—teeming with tourists nearly the whole year through (*see* 'Festivals' for details of the Passion Play.) Most come simply because the town is famous, and are surprised by how pretty it is. You can visit the empty **Passionstheater** (*May–Oct daily 9.30–12.30 and 1.30–5; Nov–April Tues–Sun 10–12.30 and 1.30–4.30; closed Jan*), but despite the exhibition on past Passion Plays in the foyer, this is a dull and rather pointless exercise. A far more rewarding experience is a wander through the streets to look at *Lüftlmalerei*—the bright frescoes that adorn many Alpine homes. These paintings (usually of biblical scenes) became the rage during the Counter-Reformation, when such displays of religious zeal were encouraged. Fresco painting was an expensive business, but Oberammergau was a prosperous town, fat with the takings from Passion Play tourism and woodcarving even in the 18th century. Old *Lüftlmalerei* abounds, and the tradition continues. Some of the best examples are by a local artist, Franz Seraph Zwinck (1749–92). His **Pilatushaus** (in Verlegergasse) is an exquisite work of controlled design and skilful *trompe l'œil* that far surpasses other façades in town—some of which seem wilfully kitsch.

When they aren't donning biblical robes and learning lines, a large proportion of Oberammergauers are chipping away at blocks of wood. The town is renowned for its **woodcarving**, and the streets are lined with shops selling crucifixes, cherubs, nativity scenes and chunky toys. Some shops (such as Holzschnitzerei Josef Albl in Devrientweg, and the Pilatushaus, which is now a crafts centre) have workshops attached where you can watch the craftsfolk chiselling out piece after piece.

Four kilometres down the B23 you come to **Kloster Ettal**, a 14th-century Benedictine monastery that got a massive Baroque facelift during the Counter-Reformation. Ettal pales by comparison with the other Bavarian Baroque churches, but it does have a rather splendid cupola fresco by the Tyrolean artist Johann-Jakob Zeiller.

Ten kilometres to the west is **Schloß Linderhof** (*daily April–Sept 9–12.15 and 12.45–5.30, Oct–Mar 10–12.15 and 12.45–4; adm DM6 including Grotto and Kiosk*), the oddest and most bewitching of King Ludwig II's castles. Ludwig was an absolutist, deeply opposed to his father's namby-pamby ideas of constitutional monarchy. He hero-worshipped the French Bourbons, especially Louis XIV. When he became king in 1864 he wanted to replace Max II's modest hunting lodge at Linderhof with a massive copy of the palace of Versailles, which he planned to call Meicost Ettal (an anagram of Louis XIV's motto *L'état, c'est moi*). He later changed his mind and set his ersatz Versailles on Herreninseln (*see* pp.116–17). Linderhof became a retreat for the dreamy king. Here, in the 1870s, he built a modest 'Royal Villa' (in which the bedroom is by far the biggest room) and set about filling the surrounding parkland with quirky pavilions and life-size stage sets where he could re-enact scenes from Wagner's operas. Like an enchanted prince, Ludwig would descend on Schloß Linderhof in a golden Rococo sleigh, with a retinue of attendants in period livery.

The **Schloß** itself is a modest, rather dumpy Baroque imitation—crispy white and heavily ornamented, like a small over-iced wedding cake. It is periodically upstaged by a 30m spurt of water from the gilded **fountain** (*every hour on the hour 9–5*) which is set at the entrance in the middle of a formal parterre garden. In one corner of the garden, at odds with the strict symmetry, is the old linden tree that gave the castle its name. Inside, the palace is encrusted with gilded stucco and smothered in tapestries, rich fabrics and exotic carpets (one of them made out of ostrich plumes). The high point is the enormous **bedroom** with its 2.7 by 2.1m blue velvet bed, fenced off by a carved and gilded balustrade. In the garden outside, an artificial cascade (built to cool the room in summer) tumbles almost up to the window. In the dining room you can see Ludwig's famous **magic table** which sank through the floor to be loaded up by lackeys in the kitchens below, so that the reclusive king could eat alone, often dressed up as Louis XIV or the Swan Prince. Beyond the formal parterres, a wilder 'English Garden' extends for another 50 hectares, gradually blending into the Alpine countryside. This was the park that Ludwig intended to fill with romantic and fantastic buildings. He didn't realize all his plans, and not everything he built has survived, but his favourite, the **Venus Grotto** (1876), has. This is a 10m-high artificial cavern with a small lake, designed to reproduce the scene in the first act of Wagner's *Tannhäuser*. Garlands of roses hang between sparkling stalagmites and stalactites, all made from canvas, cement and lustrous stones. Hidden lights, some of them underwater, throw streaks of bright, changing colour across the shadows—a spectacular feat of electrical engineering for the time. The gilded shell-shaped boat in which Ludwig loved to be rowed about waits empty on the water.

The **Moorish Kiosk** nearby was built for the 1867 Paris Exhibition and bought by the king in the 1870s. Its stylish minarets look quaintly out of place against a backdrop of the Alps. Inside, the enamelled tail-feathers of the birds on the **Peacock Throne** stand out even against the kaleidoscopic colours of the walls and windows. At the eastern edge of the park is the simple wooden **Hunding's Hut**, based on Wagner's stage directions for the first act of the *Walküre*. It is a recent replica of the original hut (which burnt down in 1945), and isn't really worth the walk unless you're an avid Ludwig- or Wagnerphile.

Garmisch-Partenkirchen and Mittenwald

Garmisch-Partenkirchen, Germany's leading ski resort, lies a few kilometres south of Oberammergau along the main road (B2) at the foot of the lofty Wetterstein range. Two villages, one on each side of the railway line, have merged to form the present town, but retain quite different atmospheres. Garmisch is glitzy, modern and expensive, while Partenkirchen across the track has been more tenacious in holding onto its Alpine village charm and is a little cheaper. Ludwigstraße in Partenkirchen even has some traditional *Luftmalerei*—though not as impressive as in Oberammergau. Most people scuttle out of Garmisch-Partenkirchen as quickly as possible, either to ski, or for the magnificent views from the surrounding mountaintops. The **Zugspitze** (2963m) has the highest peak in Germany. There are two ways of getting to the top by public transport: *Zugspitzbahn* (electric railway) from central Garmisch to Eibsee followed by a dizzy ride on the *Eibseebahn* cable car to the summit; or *Zugspitzbahn* to Eibsee, then rack railway (through a tunnel) to Hotel Schneeferhaus (2645m, good skiing during the winter season) then the *Gipfelbahn* cable car the rest of the way. (*Both methods cost DM50 return (DM30 single) in summer and DM43 (DM29 single) in winter. A 7-day pass costs DM65 (June–Oct) and special ski-passes cost DM112 (3 days) and DM225 (7 days).*) A cheaper option, with nearly as panoramic a view, is **Wank** (1780m), where the cable car from the outskirts of Garmisch costs only DM19 return (DM13 single) and where souvenir kiosk proprietors are bemused by the high turnover of postcards sold to British visitors. **Hikers** might like to tackle the challenging **Alpspitze** (2628m), or to strike out along a path hewn from the rock in the dramatic **Partnachklamm** gorge, southeast of Garmisch.

Mittenwald (20km further southeast, just off the B2) is prettier, less touristy and has a far more authentic atmosphere than Garmisch-Partenkirchen. Chalets with bright frescoes and low overhanging eaves snuggle together in the shadow of jagged peaks, neighbours greet each other brightly in the street, occasionally an ancient tractor chugs through town. The pews in the local church still have family name-plates fixed on the end. In Obermarkt and around Im Gries you'll see some of the richest *Lüftlmalerei* in the district.

In 1683 Mathias Klotz, a local farmer's son who had spent time working in Cremona with the great violin maker Nicolò Amati, returned to teach his craft to local woodcarvers. Today Mittenwald violins, violas and cellos are coveted by musicians around the world. The tiny **Geigenbaumuseum** at Ballenhausgasse 3 (*May–Oct Mon–Fri 10–11.45 and 2–4.45; adm DM3*) displays some of the finest instruments and documents the history of the craft. There is also an open studio where you can watch a violin maker at work.

Mittenwald's pet mountain is **Karwendl** (2385m). The views from the top—over the valley and the Wetterstein range—are even more breathtaking than those from the peaks around Garmisch (*cable car DM23 return, DM14 single*).

Berchtesgadener Land

In the southeast corner of Germany, on the Austrian border, is the **Berchtesgadener Land**, where (local legend goes) dawdling angels who had been commanded to distribute wonders and beauty around the globe were so startled by a divine command to hurry along that they dropped the lot here. Some of the mightiest mountains of the Alps crowd around a slender lake and a lush valley that is now a National Park.

At the beginning of the 12th century some Augustinian monks struggled through the snow from Salzburg, built a priory at Berchtesgaden, and established what was to become one of the smallest states in the Holy Roman Empire. Later, in 1515, the discovery of hugely rich deposits of salt ('white gold') made the prince-archbishops of Berchtesgaden just as wealthy and powerful as their neighbours in Salzburg ('Salt City'). In the 19th century the state was incorporated into Bavaria, and the ruling Wittelsbachs secularized the priory and converted it into a royal residence. But, for many, the name Berchtesgaden has a more sour historical connotation: it was here, in a village just above the town, that statesmen (including Britain's Neville Chamberlain) came to visit Hitler in his rented country retreat, in the vain hope of preventing an invasion of the Sudetenland (*see* p.38). Hitler enjoyed meeting foreign dignitaries in this awe-inspiring mansion, and film footage of the Führer on the grand stairway is indeed impressive (*see* 'Obersalzberg' below).

The hillside town of **Berchtesgaden** teems with tourists. The frantically busy main road that winds through the centre almost puts the kibosh on any Alpine charm, but Berchtesgaden has more to offer than pretty houses and winter sports. In the elegant Renaissance rooms of the Wittelsbach **Schloß** (*May–Sept Sun–Fri 10–1 and 2–5; Oct–April Mon–Fri 10–1 and 2–5; adm DM4.50*), you can see part of the extensive collection of sacred art put together by Crown Prince Ruprecht, son of the last King of Bavaria, who lived here from 1923 to 1955. The German woodcarving (with some fine pieces by the celebrated Tilman Riemenschneider) is especially good, and there is also a good collection of porcelain and Italian furniture. A charming Romanesque cloister and Gothic dormitory survive from the earlier medieval priory.

In the simple **Franziskanerkirche** at the southern end of town you can see a graceful Baroque carving of Christ, and (in the adjoining graveyard) convincing testimony to the healthy mountain air—the tomb of one Anton Adner who lived from 1705 to 1822.

A tour of the disused shafts of a working salt mine, the **Salzbergwerk** (*May 1–Oct 15 daily 8.30–5; Oct 16–April 30 Mon–Fri 12.30–5.30; adm DM12.50; tour 1½hr*) may not sound enticing, but is an experience not to be missed. Men don the traditional thick protective miners' clothing: a felt hat and leather bum-pad. Women get a blue hat and baggy white trousers (it's not a good idea to wear a skirt). Then you huddle together astride a wooden wagon that carries you down a long tunnel deep into the mine. Next you slide down a 30m-long chute (this is the reason for the leather pad) into an enormous vault, glittering with salt crystals. Here you're shown a film and a real miner explains how the equipment works. Then it's off down another long chute to an enormous underground lake where, a little like Ludwig II in his magic grotto, you are borne across the black water on a wooden boat. Finally you're whisked back up to the surface by lift and train.

The **Königsee** (5km south of Berchtesgaden, buses from Hauptbahnhof) is a thin, fjord-like lake that hooks itself around the foot of the **Watzmann** (2713m), Germany's second highest mountain. Crowds flock here whatever the weather; escape them by taking the electric ferry which makes a round trip (DM15) past dramatic mountain scenery.

High in the mountains east of Berchtesgaden is the little village of **Obersalzberg** (cable car DM10 return), the site of Hitler's **Berghof**, his mountain retreat. The house was badly bombed during the war, and reduced to rubble by US troops in 1952—and so it remains, overgrown and unsignposted. A better reason for visiting Obersalzberg is the 'Eagle's Nest', a restaurant at the summit of the **Kehlstein** (1834m) (special buses take you from the village up a magnificent winding road, and then you travel the last 124m in a lift inside the mountain). The Eagle's Nest was built as a teahouse and given by Martin Bormann (Hitler's adviser and private secretary) to his boss as a 50th birthday present, but the Führer seldom used it. Today it is very commercialized, but nothing can detract from the splendour of the view across the Alps—as far as Salzburg in clear weather.

Shopping

For centuries **Oberammergau** dealers have been creaming off the best **woodcarvings** from local family workshops and selling them in town. Most of this carving has a religious theme, and much is churned out for the souvenir market, but there are some fine artists at work. If you pay a bit extra, you can commission a piece from someone whose work takes your fancy. Where you shop will be very much a matter of personal taste, but try Toni Baur (Dorfstr. 27) for really vibrant secular pieces and Josef Albl (Devrientweg 1) for more traditional religious work. There is a craft centre and co-op at the Pilatushaus (in Verleger-Gasse), where prices are a little lower. In **Berchtesgaden** the carvers concentrate more on dolls and toy horse-carriages. The local speciality is *Spanschachteln*, brightly painted wooden boxes. You can get all of these at Schloß Adelsheim (Schroffenbergallee 6). If you have DM10,000 to spend on a **violin**, head for **Mittenwald**, where Anton Maller (Stainergasse 14) sells instruments of world renown. If your budget isn't up to that you can settle for a chocolate or marzipan version, on sale all over town.

Activities

The best **skiing** is in the western part of this region. Garmisch-Partenkirchen hosted the 1936 Winter Olympics and is still a World Cup downhill, super giant slalom and ski jump centre—and it's easier on the pocket than most Swiss resorts. Good and intermediate skiers should head for the Zugspitze and Kreuzeck Hausberg (where there are two classic black pistes); beginners will be happier on the gentler slopes of Wank. Mittenwald and Oberammergau specialize in cross-country skiing. The season is generally from December to April—though in this region it can last a little longer. Further east, around Berchtesgaden, the runs are not as exciting (though they are pretty). However, the town is a vibrant centre for **other winter sports** such as tobogganing, skating, curling and ice-skittles.

Hikers are very well catered for. Alpine refuges are dotted all over the mountains and offer shelter, refreshment and often overnight facilities as well at minimal cost. There are some excellent marked routes, especially around Königsee and in the Berchtesgaden National Park. Maps and details of these are sold at local tourist offices. Local mountaineering schools (such as the Bergersteigerschule Karwendl-Wetterstein, Dekan-Karl-Platz 29, Mittenwald, ℰ (08823) 2341; or the Deutsche Alpen- und Kletterschule, Ettalerstr. 36, Oberammergau, ℰ (08822) 1772) offer climbing courses and individual guides.

Hang-gliding, ballooning, cycling and **white-water rafting** are popular; you can hire equipment and get tuition in most of the main resorts (try Outdoor Club Berchtesgaden, Bahnhofstr. 11, Berchtesgaden, ℰ (08652) 66066; or Heinzelmànn-Reisen, In der Artenreit 13, Schönau am Königsee, ℰ (08652) 2530).

Where to Stay

expensive

Hotel Böld, König-Ludwig-Str. 10, Oberammergau, ℰ (08822) 3021, ℯ 7102 (DM168–246). Smart hotel with a lick of Alpine charm and a herbal sauna, steam bath, solarium and jacuzzi—in fact most of what you need for a hedonistic holiday.

Hotel Geiger, Berchtesgadener Str. 103–105, Stanggaß, Berchtesgaden, ℰ (08652) 5055, ℯ 5058 (DM150–300). Large converted farmhouse in the valley just outside town. Heavy furniture and a solidly respectable atmosphere.

Posthotel Partenkirchen, Ludwigstr. 49, Garmisch-Partenkirchen, ℰ (08821) 51067 (DM150–220). Atmospheric old coaching inn in grand Bavarian style.

moderate

Hotel Wolf, Dorfstr. 1, Oberammergau, ℰ (08822) 3071, ℯ 1096 (DM98–180). Modern Bavarian-style hotel a few minutes' walk from the Passionstheater. Rooms in the top two storeys have wooden balconies, banks of flowers in the window boxes and mountain views.

Hotel Alte Post, Dorfstr. 19, Oberammergau, ℰ (08822) 1091, ℯ 1094 (DM80–138). Rustic Bavarian hotel braving a busy junction in the middle of town.

Die Alpenrose, Obermarkt 1, Mittenwald, ℰ (08823) 5055 (DM120–150). A 13th-century merchant's house with painted ceilings, panelled nooks and individual flourishes of carving in the bedrooms—right in the centre of one of the prettiest towns in the region.

Post Hotel, Obermarkt, Mittenwald, ℰ (08823) 1094 (DM140–190). Considers itself a dash above the Alpenrose up the road. It is more upmarket, but not as cosy.

Hotel Vier Jahreszeiten, Maximilianstr. 20, Berchtesgaden, ℰ (08652) 5026, ℯ 5029 (DM140–180). Sleepy old hotel that has sprouted an angular modern extension. Ask for one of the rooms with a balcony and mountain view.

Hotel Krone, Am Rad 5, Berchtesgaden, ✆ (08652) 62051 (DM90–150). Quiet, family-run hotel with fine views, away from the bustle of town. Done up with local painted furniture, and with a sunny terrace for summer breakfasts.

inexpensive

Haus Alpenruh, Schillerweg 2, Mittenwald, ✆ (08823) 1375 (DM60–80). Charming little *Pension* at the edge of the village.

Pension Almrose, Purschlingweg 3a, Oberammergau, ✆ (08822) 4369 (DM42–56 without private bath). Clean and friendly, with an Alp at the bottom of its garden.

Pension Haus am Berg, Am Brandholz 9, Berchtesgaden, ✆ (08652) 5059 (DM68–96). Good-value *Pension* perched on the hillside overlooking the town. Most rooms have their own balcony.

Ohlsenhof, Von-Brug-Str. 18, Garmisch-Partenkirchen, ✆ (08821) 2168 (DM60–80). Friendly, well-run guesthouse popular with younger travellers.

Youth Hostels: Mahlensteinweg 10, Oberammergau, ✆ (08822) 4114; Jochstr. 10, Garmisch-Partenkirchen, ✆ (08821) 2980; Buckelwiesen 7, Mittenwald, ✆ (08823) 1701.

Private rooms in local houses go for DM20–30 per person (including breakfast). Look out for *Fremdenzimmer* signs or ask at the tourist office. You will have most luck in Oberammergau, or nearby Unterammergau, an authentic little farming village with a whiff of dung in the air.

Eating and Drinking

Oberammergau

Zauberstuberl, Eugene-Papst-Str. 3a (DM10–30). Cosy spot for lunch, especially in winter when the chef comes up with five or six different thick, warming soups.

Berggasthof Kolben-Alm, take Kolben-Alm cable car, ✆ (08822) 6364 (DM20–35). Small hillside guesthouse that serves great cold-meat platters and steamy noodle-rich Bavarian food. You might catch a *Hüttenabend*, when locals and hikers get together for a festive sing-song.

Café Hochenleitner, Faistemantelgasse 7, ✆ (08822) 1312. The best place to head for if you want to sample Bavarian country baking—there is good coffee and a tempting array of *Torte*.

Gasthof Gries, Im Gries 41 (DM25–35). Sausages, noodles and hunks of meat swimming in thick gravies—all hearty local fare.

Zur Brücke, Innsbrucker Str. 38, ✆ (08823) 1388 (DM25–50). The place to go if you like good beer, zither music and yodelling with your meal.

Arnspitze, Innsbrucker Str. 68, ✆ (08823) 2425 (DM30–50). Mountain views and mother's own cooking.

Berchtesgaden

Vierjahrszeiten, Hotel Vierjahrszeiten, Maximilianstr. 20, ✆ (08652) 5026 (DM30–50). Popular restaurant that serves excellent fish dishes (such as perch cooked in foil with shrimps and mushrooms).

Garmisch-Partenkirchen

Alpenhof, Bahnhofstr. 74, ✆ (08821) 59055 (DM20–70). Wide variety of local cuisine—from sausage snacks to finely cooked fish—served up in defeatingly generous portions.

The Allgäu

Legend has it that it was in the Allgäu that the Devil tempted Christ. The offer must have been hard to refuse: the Allgäu (literally: Alp settlement area) offers an alluring mixture of lush pre-Alpine pastures and towering mountains. This archetypally Bavarian countryside did, in fact, belong to neighbouring Swabia, and locals still have a reputation for a distinctly Swabian staidness. As you get closer to Augsburg, the countryside opens up a little and sightseeing takes a backseat to healthy outdoor fun. Although the health resorts and magnificent Baroque and Rococo mountain churches are popular with the Germans themselves, foreigners tend to whizz by on their way to better-known Alpine resorts. This is, by the way, cheese country, and no visit is complete without sampling some of the local fare.

Getting Around

By train: There are regular rail connections between Augsburg and Füssen and Bad Wörishofen; and between Augsburg and Oberstdorf (change here for Lindau and Pfronten).

By car: By far the best way to see the Allgäu Alps is using your own transport. The 120km stretch from Füssen to Lindau broadly follows the **Deutsche Alpenstraße** (*see* p.120). The B308, which takes in most of the scenic road, links up at Sonthofen with the B19 to Oberstdorf.

By bus: Regional bus services are run by German Rail with main lines operating between Füssen and Oberstdorf; Füssen and Pfronten; Sonthofen and Oberstdorf, and between Oberstaufen and Lindau. There are local services between Oberstdorf and the Kleinwalsertal.

Hiking: To appreciate both the scenery and the rural life you really need to get out and walk along the many footpaths in the Allgäu Alps. Hiking is made easier and more enjoyable by the profusion of well-signposted trails. The four- to six-hour hikes wind among regional towering peaks, including the **Heilbronner Weg** near Oberstdorf and the less demanding **Hörnertour** near Fischen. Tourist offices can give you advice on **guided walks**, and sell maps of the trails.

Cable cars: Less energetic visitors can take advantage of several cable car services that offer pain-free ascent to many peaks and panoramic viewpoints. Thus the Untere Breitenberg (10mins), the Nebelhorn (20mins), the Felhorn (15mins), the

Kanzelwand (20mins), the Walmendiger Horn (15mins) and the Hochgrat (20mins) are accessible by gondola.

Tourist Information
Füssen: Kaiser-Maximilian-Platz 1, ✆ (08362) 7077 or 7078.
Oberstdorf: Marktplatz 7, ✆ (08322) 7000.
Lindau: Am Hauptbahnhof, ✆ (08382) 26000.

The Allgäu Alps from Füssen to Lindau

The Allgäu Alps, hemmed in by the Upper Bavarian Alps to the east and the Austrian border to the south, gradually peter out towards the west, just before the shores of the Bodensee. Romantic foothills build up to a somewhat more rugged landscape strung with trim highland villages. Admittedly, the peaks of this 150-km-long mountain range don't rise as high as in the Upper Bavarian Alps (none is above the 2600m mark), but nonetheless, belvederes dotted about the area offer vast panoramas of classic picture-book scenery.

Füssen is a popular starting point for visits to the famous royal castles of Neuschwanstein and Hohenschwangau (*see* pp.183–4) and the southernmost town of the Romantic Road. The busy health resort itself isn't a very auspicious beginning to this well-trodden tourist route since, despite its old age and pretty setting on the Lech river, there is not much of interest to see except an odd 17th-century Dance of Death fresco-painting in the **St. Anna-Kapelle** attached to the parish church of St Mang.

Skirting the **Weißensee** lake and a plateau area offering wonderful views of Füssen against the Säuling (2041m), the road takes you to **Pfronten**, the name given to a federation of 13 villages that lie in the Pfrontener Tal and date back to a medieval 'farmers' republic' which had its own constitution. Nowadays the 'sun terrace' on the Breitenberg (1838m) and the Falkenstein (1277m), as well as the Hochalpe skiing area (1500m), offer hiking and winter sports facilities, while the villagers get on with their cattle farming.

To the northwest of Pfronten, on the B309, lies **Nesselwang**. Just before you reach this health and winter sports resort, turn left and continue to the **Wallfahrskirchlein Maria Trost** at the foothill of the Alpspitze (1575m). The little Baroque pilgrimage church, built between 1662 and 1725 and draped with Rococo frescoes, is considered among the finest small churches in the Bavarian Alps.

Continuing down on the B310 from **Oy-Mittelberg**, past the picturesque **Grüntensee**, you come to **Wertach**. Both towns have been health resorts since the beginning of the 20th century, frequented by thousands of health-seekers for their peaceful, recuperative atmosphere. It's then just a few kilometres' drive to **Jungholz**, an Austrian enclave that is only accessible from the German side. For just under 700 years this resort has been Austrian (it was sold to a landowner from Tyrol and subsequently assumed Austrian sovereignty) and enjoys the same economic status as the nearby Kleinwalsertal (*see* below).

The Viehscheid

The clanking of cowbells could be said to be the Allgäu's theme tune. Nowhere else does agricultural life makes itself felt more splendidly than in the pastoral tradition

of the Viehscheid. The autumn events that take place in villages all around the Allgäu Alps (usually in the second or third week of September) are among the bucolic highlights of the Bavarian calendar.

At the end of summer grazing, herds of cattle are driven down from pastures high in the alps. Before reaching the villages, the herds of cows are decked out in colourful finery: the lead cows (only one in every herd) wear large ornamental head-dresses made by the farmers' wives, and often huge ceremonial cowbells. The rest of the cows are decorated with smaller bunches of brightly coloured flowers. The herds are then driven into the villages, where the inhabitants offer up thanks for their safe return.

So many people, tourists and locals alike, come to see these events each year that the accompanying beer tents are often larger than the pastures that the cows have come from. Some villages don't even advertise their Viehscheid festivals any more in the hope that they won't get overwhelmed by outside visitors. On one level the festivals can seem very touristy, but they are usually a serious matter for the villagers. The thanksgiving is a solemn tribute to the animals they depend on for their livelihood. If a cow is killed in an accident in the high summer pastures, there is usually no Viehscheid in the village that year.

A few kilometres from where the B310 runs into the B308, the **Jochstraße** winds up to the **Kanzel**, a popular vantage point overlooking the magnificent Ostrach valley (famous for its wild flowers in spring and summer), and further on to the high mountain-village of **Oberjoch**, before turning into the valley to **Hindelang**. Together with its neighbouring village of **Bad Oberdorf**, the town is one of the most important holiday health resorts in the Allgäu Alps. Its most intriguing sight is the **St. Jodok-Kirche**, a fairly ordinary little church that contains the **Hindelanger Altar**, a beautiful 16th-century altarpiece by Jörg Lederer, one of the region's most celebrated artists. For keen hikers, the area offers numerous beautiful trails through uninhabited forests and along the jagged limestone heights of the surrounding mountains. It is possible to reach the summits of three peaks from here: the Daumen (2280m), the Geißhorn (2249m) and the Hochvogel (2593m).

Beyond Hindelang, in an area that stretches out below the Grünten (1738m), you come to **Sonthofen**, the site of the chilling Ordensburg, built in 1935 as a training centre for Hitler's military élite and still a military barracks. Sadly, this resulted in severe war damage to the old winter sports resort, though the most important monuments have been carefully restored. The Gothic **Pfarrkirche St. Michael** is particularly interesting. Rebuilt in the Baroque style, the church contains some wooden altar-figures that were carved by Anton Sturm in 1748 and resemble closely those he made for the better-known Wieskirche (*see* pp.178–9).

From Sonthofen you can either head due west or allow for a much more rewarding detour that cuts deep through the most spectacular mountain valleys and peaks of the **Upper Allgäu**, eventually ducking into the Tyrolean Alps. Skiing in the area is second only to that is the Bavarian Alps. As usual, there's an excellent network of marked hiking trails. The upland plateaus are covered with coniferous forests of pine and fir, while the months from May to July see the Alpine countryside awash with cyclamen, rhododendron, anemones, gentian and—still further up—the edelweiss.

First stop along the B19 is the picturesque resort of **Fischen**. Just beyond it lies **Oberstdorf**, the southernmost village in Germany. The resort itself is now a popular winter sports centre for all kinds of outdoor pursuits such as skiing, ice-skating and ski-jumping. However, the quaintness of the place is preserved as it has never outgrown the characteristics of a cosy mountain village. Oberstdorf forms the end of the Iller valley and the slowly rising, rocky mountainsides that surround the place make hill-walking much the best way to explore the area. One of the most spectacular hikes takes you eastwards along the peaks and gorges of no fewer than ten 2000m-high mountains until it reaches the Oy valley. Here the scenery is at its most luxuriant in spring and summer, brimming with wild flowers and foliage. The **Breitachklamm** offers the spectacle of a deep, impressively curling riverine gorge, very narrow in places, with the gushing white-water of the Breitach shooting over mossy rocks and lined by ancient forests. Until the turn of the 19th century this amazing gorge was known under the name of *Zwing* and was allegedly haunted by gruesome spectres called *Zwinggeister*.

As you near the Austrian border the road takes you to the **Kleinwalsertal** on the Austrian side, which shouldn't be missed.

The Kleinwalsertal

 The Kleinwalsertal, jutting into the Allgäu Alps from Austria, is something of an oddity. When in the 13th century the Walser—German emigrants from the Upper Valais (now in Switzerland)—populated this uninhabited valley of the Breitach river, they soon found themselves subjects of the dukes of Tyrol.

However, through the centuries, the Walsers' economic survival as highland farmers proved barely tenable as, especially in winter, they felt cut off from Austria by the Allgäu Alps. In 1891 the situation was reversed when this isolated valley was granted the special status of a *Zollausschlußgebiet* (customs-free zone). The result is a curious mix of Austrian sovereignty and German economic administration, which may have lessons for a united Europe. Today the hamlets of **Riezlern**, **Hirschegg**, **Mittelberg** and **Baad** that make up the Kleinwalsertal have Austrian police under

Austrian law (passport not required), German customs, a German postal service but Austrian stamps, and the only legal tender is the Deutschmark. (The Austrian phoneboxes take only German coins!). Look out for the unusual costume of the female Walsers, consisting of loose-fitting black dresses and brown fur hats.

Back on the B308, past **Immenstadt**, is the **Großer Alpsee**, a high mountain lake that bends around the foot of a set of craggy heights. The shoreline has an agreeably empty feel to it, a world apart from the hectic lakes of Upper Bavaria. There's a small marina in the village of Bühl at the eastern tip where boats and windsurfs boards are available for hire. From Bühl you can get a great view of the blue-green lake and the surrounding peaks by ascending on foot to the hilly **Immenstädter Horn** (1489m). Afterwards, try a quiet but cold swim from the lake's large public beach.

A few kilometres down the road, along the beautiful **Konstanzer Tal**, you come to the health and spa resort of **Oberstaufen**, at the foot of the Hochgrat massif (1834m). Until 1947 the resort was a sleepy village known for its particularly pure air. This changed when a refugee physician from Silesia settled in the neighbourhood and established a clinic modelled on the unique Schroth dietetics. The treatment is based on the gradual purge of the body which is achieved through special dietary rules, towel-packs and drinking cures. Oberstaufen remains the only approved Schroth health resort in Germany and has more than 80 clinics, sanatoriums and special health hotels. Particularly worth seeking out is the **Bauernhofmuseum** (Farming Museum) (*May–Oct Wed 2–5, Sun 10–12; adm DM2*) a little way back at Knechtenhofen. It has an original Alpine farmhouse on site and offers fascinating insights into the rural culture of the Allgäu as it was—and, to some extent, still is.

Continuing westwards on the B308, you find yourself atop the **Paradies** (908m), a high horseshoe bend in the road that winds its way along a steep gradient down into the Weißach valley. Do take time to stop at the atmospheric **Café Paradies** on this road, as it affords stunning vistas over some fine forested hills of the Bregenzer mountains—as far as the distant Alpenzell Alps in Switzerland on a clear day.

Northwest of the village of **Oberreute**, the small town of **Lindenberg** makes its well-preserved appearance. Nowadays it is chiefly known for the quality of the Allgäu cheese that comes from its dairies (*see* below). Before leaving, however, have a look at the **Hutmuseum** (Hat Museum) (*Wed 3–5.30, Sun 10–12; adm DM1*), on the Hirschstraße. In the 18th century local horse dealers adopted the art of straw-weaving from Italy and developed a thriving hat factory. The museum contains specimens of hats from around 1850 to the present, and includes live demonstrations showing how straw hats are made.

Before arriving at **Lindau** the road weaves down from the eastern foothills of the Pfänder (1064m), running close to the Austrian border. This final stretch commands amazing panoramic views of the **Bodensee** (Lake Constance).

The Allgäu Cheese Industry

The Allgäu is renowned for the quality of its cheese and is glibly referred to as Germany's *Käsküche* (cheese kitchen). Today, half a million Allgäu cows produce more than 2

billion litres of milk every year. Two thirds of this output is made into cheese, accounting for 25 per cent of the German market.

With its rich, undulating pastures, the Allgäu has long been a dairy farming area, but cheese is a relatively recent product of local experimentation. Carl Hirnbein, a hill farmer from the village of Grünten brought in Dutch and Swiss cheese makers in the mid-19th century. Within 50 years, brands such as Allgäuer Limburger, Emmentaler, Romadur and Bergkäse won nationwide recognition. And within a further two decades the cheese maker Josef Kramer from nearby Wertach added the Weißlacker cheese to the list. Experts are still not quite sure whether the distinctive nature of Allgäu cheeses was developed intentionally or accidentally as a result of the failure to imitate other cheeses. But whatever the case, whether scientific discovery or happy accident, the cheeses are full of flavour and well worth sampling.

Lindau

Tourists flock (by car and by foot) across the causeway to the island resort of Lindau, but here they are swallowed up by the bustling, colourful, rather Mediterranian town. Lindau is an architectural bouillabaisse, with little bits of everything from 13th-century fortification towers to the spanking new Inselhalle recreation centre. The entrance to the tiny harbour is guarded by a weatherbeaten lighthouse and a haughty Bavarian lion. In town (on Reichsplatz, near the harbour) look out for the delightfully eccentric 15th-century **Altes Rathaus** with its curly gables, witty *trompe l'œil* and gaudy assortment of frescoes. On Marktplatz, to the north, is the **Haus zum Gavazzen**, a Baroque patrician palace with rather more muted murals. This houses the **Stadtmuseum** (Town Museum) (*April–Oct Tues–Sun 10–12 and 2–5; adm DM2*), an ideal museum for a rainy day. There's nothing very spectacular here, but lots to keep you entertained. Downstairs there are *Totentafeln*, wooden fold-out tables from the 17th century, used to depict a dead notable's life and achievements. On the first floor are some fine period rooms, and further up into the rafters you'll find old clocks, dolls' houses and traditional painted furniture—and get occasional glimpses out across the red roofs of Lindau. The collection of mechanical musical instruments (*guided tours only, 30mins, 2–5pm*) is a good place to round off your visit.

Across on the other side of town, beneath the multi-turreted **Diebsturm** (Thief's Tower, built in 1350) is the earthy little 11th-century **St. Peter-Kirche**, which houses a superb *Passion Cycle* by Holbein the Elder—his only surviving frescoes. The church is now a very simple war memorial.

Where to Stay and Eating Out

Pfronten

Hotel Bavaria, Kienbergstr. 62, ✆ (08363) 5004, ✉ (08363) 6515 (DM266–370). Modern, chalet-style hotel, with traditional Alpine flair and cuisine, located in the village of Pfronten-Dorf.

Oberstdorf

Pension Wiese, Stillachstr. 4a, ✆ (08322) 3030 (DM170–200). Although the Wiese family originate from Hamburg, they have managed to fill each room with an authentically local and charming ambiance. No restaurant.

Oberstaufen

Kurhotel zum Löwen, Kirchplatz 8, ✆ (08386) 4940, ✉ (08386) 494222 (DM260–310). A centrally located spa hotel in one of the resort's most beautiful houses (with fancy flower frescoes adorning its façade). The gourmet restaurant excels in salmon dishes and delicious salads.

Lindau

Hotel Reutemann, Seepromenade, ✆ (08382) 5055, ✉ (08382) 505 5202 (from DM210). Large, efficiently run hotel set slightly back from the throngs on the promenade.

Hotel Stift, Stiftsplatz 1, ✆ (08382) 4038, ✉ (08382) 5586 (DM140–162). A relaxed, friendly hotel in the Altstadt.

Zum Sünfzen, Maximilianstr. 1, ✆ (08382) 5865 (DM30–45). Converted 14th-century house in the Altstadt that serves good, plain meals.

North of the Allgäu Alps

This is a gentler, less spectacular journey than the one that leads through the Allgäu Alps (*see* above), but its course through the alpine foothills of central Allgäu is nonetheless full of seductive charm. Both Memmingen and Kempten, the main towns at the north and south points of the itinerary, are attractive and richly historic. Between them, and in the broad spread of countryside to the east of the road that connects them, lie several towns and villages—some of them of outstanding beauty—which in the modern era have become famous as spa resorts.

Getting Around

By train: There are connections between Memmingen and Augsburg and Memmingen and Ulm. Kempten can be reached from Munich, Ulm and Augsburg via Kaufbeuren.

By car: Memmingen is 35km from Kempten on the A7. The best way to visit the small towns and villages along the way, though, is to depart from the *Autobahn* and to use the criss-crossing main roads in the region.

By bus: Main *Regionalbus* lines offer services from Kempten to Kaufbeuren: from Kempten to Füssen, from Memmingen to Ottobeuren and from Memmingen to Buxheim.

Memmingen: The office is in the Baroque **Parishaus** at Ulmer Straße 9, ✆ (08331) 850172.

Kaufbeuren: Kaiser-Max-Str. 1, ✆ (08341) 40405.

Kempten: Rathausplatz 29, ✆ (0831) 2525237.

Festivals

Memmingen celebrates its famous annual **Fischertag** in July. For centuries, this festive event has taken the form of a spectacular fish hunt in the *Stadtbach*, the town's largest canalized pond. More than 800 amateur fishermen from Memmingen, armed only with landing nets, vie with each other to catch the largest trout in the muddy waters and thus hope to become the *Fischerkönig* (Fishermen's King). The locals assure you that the tradition has a practical background as, in the old days, each year the pond was drained, and the fishermen's enthusiastic competitiveness provided a convenient way of emptying it of fish—together with most of the mud. The **Wallensteinfest**, also at Memmingen, is held at four-year intervals (next in July 1996). This costumed festivity commemorates the town's occupation in 1630 during the Thirty Years' War, when the Imperial army's headquarters under the fearsome Albrecht von Wallenstein set up camp here.

Elsewhere, rural festivals—sometimes consisting of bizarre folk rituals—fill the calendar. Every five years (next in 1995) the **Wilder-Männdle-Tanz** takes place in the Oybele hall in Oberstdorf; 14 local men wearing lichen skirts and headdresses made of forest leaves, pound out their wild, rhythmical dance in 17 curious scenes, wielding clubs and large wooden tankards in an attempt to exorcise the evil spirits of the mountain forests. **Fasnet** comes to Lindau in late February or early March. This festival is an offshoot of the Swabian carnival season and features processions of colourfully dressed characters wearing outlandish wooden masks.

The end of July brings the **Tänzelfest** to Kaufbeuren, when the whole town comes together in a celebration centring on its schoolchildren. Emperor Maximilian I of Austria used to stay in his 'beloved' Kaufbeuren whenever he could and in 1497, it is said, he initiated the festivities. Nowadays some 1600 local youngsters in colourful processions bring to life scenes from the town's 1000-year-old history, including those played out by the emperor and his jester Kunz von der Rosen, plus historic guild dances and a crossbow contest.

Memmingen

You don't need to go on a guided walk to get to know Memmingen. The clear arrangement of the historic townscape with its tiny crisscrossing ducts, immediately sets the tone of this unhurried provincial market town southwest of Augsburg. Add to this highly original townscape a rich history and a tradition of agreeable festivals, and you have what deserves to be considered one of the most enticing small towns in the Allgäu.

For centuries Memmingen was a Free Imperial City and jealously guarded its municipal wealth behind the medieval **Stadtmauer**, of which several sections, including five impressive 15th-century gateways, survive. An indication of the importance of commerce to Memmingen (merchants from the town were the first in Germany to establish trade posts in the New World) is the fact that the self-conscious symbol of civic pride, the 16th-century **Rathaus**, is overshadowed by several patrician mansions in the old town centre. By far the most impressive is the **Siebendächerhaus** on Gerberplatz, a timbered building with seven gabled roofs (hence its name), that once housed the headquarters of the tanners' guild.

Grouped around the **Marktplatz**, another ensemble of municipal buildings includes the cheerful late 15th-century **Steuerhaus**. It later underwent a Rococo transformation which tattooed the walls above its ground-level arcades with exuberant green and rich russet frescoes. Also marking the town's era of prosperity here is the richly Baroque **Großzunft**, the town's early 18th-century guild hall, its façade enlivened by a graceful balcony.

Memmingen is at its most animated during its annual **Fischertag** (*see* 'Festivals' above).

A few miles northeast of Memmingen lies **Buxheim** whose former **Carthusian monastery** (*April–Oct Mon–Fri 10–12 and 2–4; Sat and Sun 2–4; adm DM4*) tells an extraordinary story. In 1691 Ignaz Waibel, a local sculptor from Memmingen, carved an extravagantly elaborate set of 31 early Baroque choir stalls for the *Klosterkirche*. The monastery was secularized in 1803. These magnificent pieces of furniture were sold by auction to an overseas buyer in 1886 and, by some circuitous route, found their way to the Bank of England. They were subsequently given to an Anglican convent in 1891. When some 70 years later the convent moved from London to Hythe in Kent, a new Mother Superior pleaded for the return of the stalls to Germany. Only in 1979, though, did the Bavarian authorities succeed in bringing back these lost pieces of virtuoso woodwork which, after painstaking repair work, were eventually restored to the Carthusian church in Buxheim in July 1994.

Around Memmingen: Kneipp Country

The area between Memmingen to Kempten is known as Kneipp country, as each year thousands of *Kneippianer* throng to a belt of spa towns to seek health and rejuvenation.

The Kneipp Story

 Kneipp treatment holds a very special place among Germany's spa cures. This health-care programme, devised by the Catholic parson Sebastian Kneipp (1821–1897) at the end of the 19th century, is based on natural healing powers. Kneipp drew on the bountiful natural resources at his disposal—water, sunshine and pure mountain air—and combined them into a health régime for his parishioners' benefit. In 1889 he wrote about his observations of the remedies in his *So sollt ihr leben* (This is the way you ought to live), which has since become a reference work for hydrotherapists. Anyone who has felt the tingling effect of natural therapies will gladly confirm the end result. The Rothschilds in Paris, Pope Leo XIII and Theodore Roosevelt all

consulted Kneipp for the restitution of their flagging health. Today, water-treading in specially devised exercise pools has become synonymous with Kneipp's proven methods, but, with more than 60 special Kneipp spas in Germany, the cures now encompass a wider synthesis of hydrotherapy, herbal therapy, nutritional therapy, physiotherapy and biorhythmic balance.

Down the A7 from Memmingen lies **Grönenbach**, a quaint little resort that works hard to maintain its high standards as a health spa. Just to the northwest lies the village of **Kronburg**, with its mighty Renaissance castle perched above the town. However, by far the most intriguing place to visit is the **Schwäbisches Bauernhofmuseum** (*Tues–Sun 9–6; adm DM5 including guided tours*), which is laid out at the western end of the town at Illerbeuren. The open-air museum brings together some 20 original buildings from the rural Allgäu foothills including farmsteads and workshops of diverse traditional crafts.

Along serene country roads that weave back across the A7, you come to the Benedictine abbey at **Ottobeuren**. Its present Baroque architecture is mainly the work of Johann Michael Fischer and was completed between 1737 and 1766. Johann Joseph Christian, one of the leading sculptors of the day, and the Augsburg artist Johann Michael Feichtmeyer were the driving force behind the interiors. You enter through a deliberately dimmed porch into a vast, exhilaratingly bright hall. There are pulpits way above your head, abundant flocks of putti, and licks and curls of stucco and gold. Behind all this joyous abandon, however, you sense a strong controlling hand. Especially worth seeking out are the richly carved choir stalls and the reliquaries in the side altars. Entire human skeletons recline on two of the tombs, decked out in gauze, velvet and gold. The three organs, built by the master Karl Joseph Riepp, rank with the most beautiful church organs in the world.

In the adjoining **museum** (*Mon–Sat 10–12 and 2–5; Sun 10–12 and 1–5; adm DM2*) you can see more religious carving and painting, and some exquisite 18th-century inlaid furniture, and visit the small **Baroque theatre** and elegant **library**.

If you are in search of some therapeutic treatment, try a relaxing break in the adjacent health resort by the same name. Health-seekers can also follow a number of Kneipp exercise trails along the Günz valley. The outlying village of **Stephansried** to the north of the resort is the birthplace of Sebastian Kneipp. Some 25km on the B18 to the northeast of Ottobeuren lies **Mindelheim**, which has a graceful Baroque **Liebfrauenkirche** and a 14th-century bastion, the **Mindelburg**. Tucked away in the Baroque **Silvesterkirche** is the **Schwäbisches Turmuhrenmuseum** (Swabian Tower Clock Museum) (*Wed 14–16, last Sun in month 10–12 and 2–4; DM3*), where you can delve into the history and technical aspects of the clocks that once graced several churches and townhalls of the region. Over the centuries Mindelheim has retained a very special relationship with the British Isles. In 1704 the town, together with the Mindelburg, became the personal possession of John Churchill, the Duke of Marlborough, following his success at the Battle of Blenheim, and for the next ten years remained an isolated outpost of Britain in the Allgäu.

Back on the B18, the road takes you to **Bad Wörishofen**, the undisputed centre of natural cure therapies in the region. The village rose to fame after Kneipp made it his base in

1855. Ultra-modern spa facilities now form a large part of its overall appearance. The hub of the spa quarter is the **Sebastianeum**, founded by Kneipp himself and now housing sanatoriums and overnight facilities for some 7000 visitors.

In Bad Wörishofen look out for the **Dominikanerinnenkloster** with its Baroque **Marienkirche**, ornately decorated by the fresco-painting brothers Dominicus and Johann Baptist Zimmermann. The abbey also houses the **Kneippmuseum** (*Wed–Fri 3–6; Sun 10–12; adm DM2*) with artefacts and printed material relating to the life and work of the Allgäu 'water healer'.

Turning south at Buchloe, follow the B12 to **Kaufbeuren**, a town widely underrated when compared to the much better-known medieval counterparts of the nearby Romantic Road. The town's intact medieval centre with 15th-century walled defences reveals an array of splendid Gothic and Renaissance buildings. The **Fünfknopfturm** (Five-Button-Tower) is the town's landmark and, together with the round **Blasiusturm** of the fortified Gothic **Blasiuskapelle**, forms an impressive part of its medieval military architecture.

In the gently rolling countryside along the Iller valley, on the B12, lies the town of **Kempten** in the heart of the Allgäu.

Kempten

The designation 'capital of the Allgäu' seems a superfluous marketing ploy. This medium-sized town on the banks of the Iller river is a real visual treat, with an impressive array of monuments as testament to its varied history. The site has been inhabited since Celtic times. Romans, Alemannic kings and Benedictine prince-abbots were all subsequent rulers, and the town received the privileges of a Free Imperial City in 1361. Modern-day Kempten in fact represents a merger between two separate towns. When in 1527 the more progressive free burghers adopted the Reformation, the people from the part of town around the abbey remained staunchly loyal to the Catholic prince-abbots. This caused a deep divide, and both towns alternately found themselves at the receiving end of the ravages of the Thirty Years' War.

Architectually, the erstwhile religious division is still detectable and the **Freitreppe**, a popular step ascent built in the 19th century to disguise the visible signs of the split, serves to mark the borderline between the two. On one side the domed **Stiftskirche St. Lorenz** rises over the maze of Catholic Kempten. This abbey church, built between 1652 and 1666, is part of an extensive complex of ecclesiastical buildings and adjoins the **Residenz**, the former palace to the prince-abbots. This ensemble is one of the earliest examples of Baroque architecture in Bavaria.

Imperiously boasting Protestant control of the burgher part of town, the more economical late-Gothic **St. Mang-Kirche** on the other side honours the 8th-century patron saint to the Allgäu. The burgher church provides fitting company for the nearby **Rathaus**, a step-gabled Renaissance construction with Rococo exteriors, and the **Ponikauhaus**, a 16th-century merchant's residence.

Should the idea of exploring ancient Roman Kempten (Cambodunum) appeal to you, go to the **Archäologischer Park Cambodunum** (*Tues–Sun 10–4.30; adm DM4*), to the east of the River Iller. In 1885 the town's Roman remains were discovered nearby and carefully unearthed, revealing a forum, basilica, temple and thermal baths. To give a graphic idea of the excavation site, an archaeological park was designed and a full-size Gallo-Roman temple precinct was reconstructed on its original stone foundations. (Reconstructed thermal baths are due to open in mid-1995.) The result is somewhat conjectural and may upset the archaeological purist, but to the uninitiated visitor this glimpse of ancient culture may well come as a revelation.

More Roman artefacts of the conventional kind can be found in the patrician **Zumsteinhaus** on Residenzplatz; this houses the **Römisches Museum** (Roman Museum) (*Tues–Sun 10–4; adm DM4*).

Where to Stay and Eating Out

Memmingen

Gasthaus Weißes Lamm, Hallhof 9, ✆ (08331) 2102 (DM36–68). A small, good-value guesthouse in the town centre.

Kaufbeuren

Hotel Neue Post, Füssenerstr. 17, ✆ (08341) 93750, ✆ (08341) 937532 (DM79–180). Located in **Biessenhofen**, 7km south of Kaufbeuren. King Ludwig II used to stay in this former coaching station when travelling to Neuschwanstein Castle. Despite its dejected, yolk-yellow façade the hotel offers good service and lots of sport activities (angling, para-gliding, ice-skating, horse-riding, etc). The restaurant has gourmet standards and serves excellent fish dishes and Swabian cuisine.

Hotel Goldener Hirsch, Kaiser-Max-Str. 39-41, ✆ (08341) 43030, ✆ (08341) 430369 (DM140–185). A centrally located, smartly modernized, historic hotel. Owner-chef Ginther's local cuisine is a real treat.

Kempten

Hotel Fürstenhof, Rathausplatz 8, ✆ (0831) 25360, ✆ (0831) 2536120 (DM190–450). An attractive conversion of a 17th-century patrician residence. Several Hohenstaufen and Habsburg emperors and princes have stayed here.

Akzent-Hotel Bayerischer Hof, Füssener Str. 96, ✆ (0831) 73420, ✆ (0831) 73708 (DM152–180). Newly converted from stately mansion, this is a friendly, imaginatively decorated hotel in the town centre. Has a small Chinese restaurant.

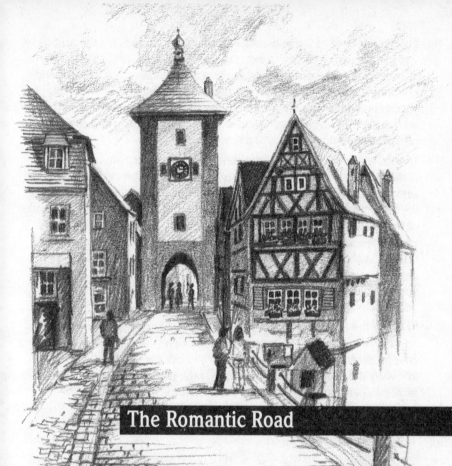

The Romantic Road

The prominence of the Romantic movement in German art, literature and music might lead you to expect that Germany's oldest tourist route is in some way associated with Wagner's powerful operas or Caspar David Friedrich's dramatic paintings, but the Romantische Straße is, in fact, 'romantic' with a small 'r'—more in the style of *Love Story* than *Wuthering Heights*; of cosy firesides and soft focus grassy meadows, rather than surging passions and dramatic scenery.

The route sets off from the university town of Würzburg and meanders through vineyards and rolling countryside, past the showy medieval gems of Rothenburg and Dinkelsbühl. Then it marches on south through the Fugger family stronghold of Augsburg. From here you follow the path of the Via Claudia Augusta—the ancient road that connected Augsburg and Rome—and end with a flourish in Füssen, in the Alpine foothills, a total of 343km altogether. Your progress is punctuated by stops in Baroque palaces, grand churches and cute *Fachwerk* villages, and as you near the mountains you find Neuschwanstein and Hohenschwangau—two of Ludwig II's whimsical castles.

Not only the Romans trod this road. So also did rampaging emperors, crusaders and pilgrims to various churches along the route. Nowadays your fellow travellers are most likely to be busloads of tourists, devoutly following the route signs and alighting at the marked sights. But even the smallest deviation from the very well-beaten track can take you to forgotten corners, ignored by the throngs pounding by.

Getting Around

This really is motoring country. The route is well signposted (in both directions) and for visiting some of the sights and doing your own exploring a car is essential. A determined driver could cover the full 343km in a day, but there would be little point. Most of the delights of the Romantic Road are architectural, and it takes time to savour them. Simply trundling through the pretty but uneventful countryside would be monotonous. Allow five days to a week for a reasonably unhurried tour.

It is possible, though time-consuming and tedious, to attempt the journey by a combination of rail and local buses. A far better idea, if you are relying on public transport, is to take the **Romantic Road Bus** (Eurobus Line 190 A; information and advance booking: Deutsche Touring GmbH, Am Römerhof 17, 6000 Frankfurt/Main 90; ✆ (069) 790 3256; ✉ (069) 70 4714). It is a festive coach, popular with backpackers and trippers from around the world. The bus runs daily from May to October, stopping at all the main sights. Often stops are only long enough for a quick look around, but you can also stay overnight and catch the next bus through. A ticket for the full 10-hour journey costs DM85, but the company also accepts German rail passes.

You can of course also travel the Romantic Road from south to north (the bus runs both ways), but the route builds up in a more logical crescendo if you start in the vineyards of the north and end up in Ludwig's castles in the Alps.

Würzburg

Würzburg is wine, water and light. To the west the brawny Marienberg fortress swaggers above the town; to the east the Baroque Residenz rests gracefully in its gardens; through the middle flows the Main—'like a child between father and mother', remarked the writer Heinrich von Kleist in 1800. Vineyards slope right into the centre of the town. On sunny days the sharp light reflects off the Main and throws everything into vivid relief.

Around AD 500 the Franks systematically began to wipe out local tribes, and by AD 650 had established a Duchy at 'Virteburch'. A few decades later the wandering Irish bishop, Kilian, came to preach Christianity and was killed for his troubles (thus ensuring canonization). But Kilian had done his work well: by AD 742 Würzburg was a bishopric, and in the 12th century it got its own cathedral. In 1397 King Wenzel the Lazy promised to make Würzburg a free Imperial city—but he never got round to doing so. It wasn't until the late 17th century, with the arrival of the powerful Schönborn family as prince-bishops, that Würzburg really came into its own.

This early Würzburg—a dreamy town of Baroque palaces, *Fachwerk* houses, narrow alleys and shady corners—was flattened in 20 minutes by Allied bombers on 16 March 1945. Of the 108,000 inhabitants, barely 5000 crawled out of the ruins, and Würzburg became known as the *Grab am Main* (grave on the Main). Much of the new city is modern, but the monuments have been carefully restored, and you can still find quiet old courtyards, madonnas in niches on the streets, elaborate Baroque fountains and poky, gas-lit alleys.

The best time to visit Würzburg is in the autumn, when the grapes are being harvested, and you can huddle in Weinstuben, at the end of long 'golden days', sipping freshly fermented wine. The city is popular with Germans for short-break holidays. In season it becomes crowded over weekends, but is much quieter during the week and outside August and October.

Getting Around

By car: Würzburg is on the A3, 110km from Frankfurt and 130km from Nuremberg.

Car hire: Europcar, Am Hauptbahnhof, © (0931) 12060; Hertz Höchberger Str. 10, © (0931) 41 5221.

Mitfahrzentrale: Bahnhofsvorplatz-Ost, © (0931) 12904.

By train: Würzburg is on the main ICE **rail** route from Hamburg to Munich. Connections to other cities in Germany are fast and frequent, and there's an hourly train to **Frankfurt Airport** (1hr 20 mins away). For ticket and timetable information, © 1 94 19. Once in town, all the tourist sights are within walking distance.

Public transport: If you do find you need to use public transport, you could invest in a 24-hour pass (DM5, DM4 over weekends). The main bus station is just outside the Hauptbahnhof.

Taxi: ✆ (0931) 19 410.

Tourist Information

Tourist information offices: Hauptbahnhof, ✆ (0931) 3 74 36 (Mon–Sat 8am–8pm); Haus zum Falken, Market Square, ✆ (0931) 3 73 98 (Mon–Fri 9–6, Sat 9–2).

Post office: Bahnhofsplatz 2 (open until 8pm, even on Sundays and also runs a **bureau de change**).

Emergency numbers: Police ✆ 110; doctors and dentists ✆ (0931) 1 92 22.

Festivals

Würzburg holds a world-renowned **Mozart Festival** annually in June. Concerts are held in the Residenz—with the highlight being the *Kleine Nachtmusik* concert (first and last Saturdays) performed by lamplight in the gardens. There is also a **Bach Festival** towards the end of November. On the first Saturday in July Würzburg erupts with the **Kiliani**, a procession followed by a fortnight of partying to celebrate St Kilian's Day. In the last weeks of September there is a huge **wine festival** beside the Friedensbrücke, where all the local producers present their wares, but a more intimate alternative is the **Burgerspital Wine Festival**, held towards the end of June in the Burgerspital courtyard.

The Residenz

Situated to the east of the city (follow Kaiserstraße and Theaterstraße from the Hauptbahnhof) the prince-bishops' **Residenz** (*April–Sept Tues–Sun 9–5, Oct–Mar 10–4; adm DM4.50*) is its pearl, and a good place to start your visit. In 1720 the new Prince-Bishop Johann Philipp von Schönborn decided he wanted to build a palace that was altogether grander and more modern than the draughty old Marienberg fortress that had housed his predecessors. The problem of how to finance his vision was handily solved when he was obliged to confiscate the 600,000-florin fortune of a disloyal chamberlain. Johann Philipp's uncle—Elector of Mainz and Prince-Bishop of Bamberg—wryly suggested that a monument dedicated to the hapless official should be erected in front of the palace.

The Schönborns were an influential family (spawning at least a dozen bishops), infected with the *Bauwurm* (literally: building worm—the lust to build) and graced with good taste. Johann Philipp showed remarkable foresight in choosing as his chief architect a young bell-founder and cannon-maker who had showed some flair as an amateur draughtsman (having designed his own house and come up with a city plan for Würzburg). Balthasar Neumann went on to become one of the greatest German architects of the age, and through him the prince-bishop realized his dream of building a *Schloß über*

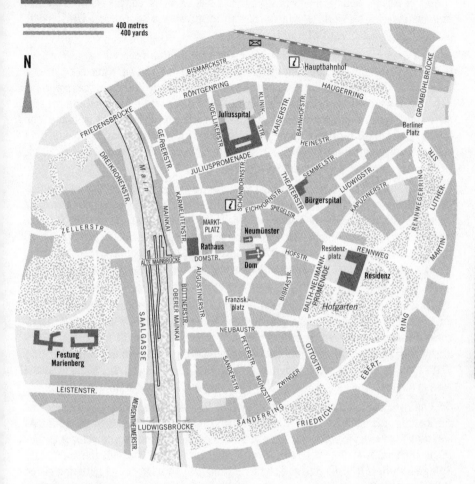

die *Schlösse* (castle to beat all castles)—a massive, U-shaped Baroque sandstone pile that stands resplendent in its own square. After its completion, the Residenz became the talk of the civilized world. Half a century later it still impressed Napoleon, who quipped that it was 'the loveliest parsonage in Europe'.

The **Vestibule** (entrance hall—big enough for a coach-and-six to do a comfortable U-turn in) has a low ceiling with a rather half-hearted *trompe l'œil* dome and a few licks of restrained classical decoration. Neumann's original design was even plainer—perhaps to intensify by contrast the surprises he had up his sleeve.

Guests stepped out of their carriages right on to Neumann's magnificent **staircase**. Here the low vaulting of the vestibule seems to break open to reveal the blue sky and wispy clouds of a ceiling **fresco** high above. The painting (by the celebrated Venetian artist

Giovanni Battista Tiepolo) depicts allegories of the four known continents paying tribute to the prince-bishop. Neumann himself sits astride a cannon on the cornice below his patron, proudly surveying his work. (Neumann, plus staircase, can also be seen on a DM50 note).

At 18m by 32m, the fresco is the biggest in the world, yet it arches over the staircase without the support of a single pillar. Neumann carried off this spectacular feat of engineering by having the ceiling built out of feather-light pumice stone. Nobody believed it would work. A rival architect threatened to hang himself by the neck from the roof, confident that it would collapse under his weight before he could be strangled. An irritated Neumann suggested that the prince-bishop have a battery of artillery fired off in the stairwell to prove the strength of his design. Neither test was carried out, but Neumann's confidence was vindicated in 1945, when Allied bombs destroyed most of the rest of the Residenz, but not the stairway or its vaulting.

Each step is only a few centimetres high (designed to prevent shocking flashes of ladies' ankles), and they are perfectly spaced, inducing an exhilarating Hollywood glide as you sail up and down. At the top of the stairs, you come to the **Weißer Saal** (White Hall). Here the renowned stucco artist Antonio Bossi, who was already on the brink of madness, was given free rein and he let loose a feverish blaze of stucco work, before completely succumbing to his psychosis. The room is painted entirely white (now a little grey), to give full prominence to the stucco, but also to rest the eyes before the onslaught of the State Rooms.

The first of these, the oval **Kaisersaal** (Imperial Hall—the German Emperor used the Residenz whenever he was in the area) was also decorated by Tiepolo and Bossi. The frescoes, showing scenes from Franconian history, rank with Tiepolo's finest work. They bristle with life and play delightful tricks, at times even popping out into 3-D relief. The vast supporting cast of classical deities get just the same meticulous treatment as the leading players. (One amorous couple has even been featured in *Playboy* magazine.)

To 70m right and left of the Kaisersaal stretch the Imperial Apartments. This is the part of the Residenz that suffered most from Allied bombing, but it has been lovingly rebuilt. As you walk from room to room, you get a sense of the restorers' growing confidence as they refine their skills at the old crafts. Two rooms shouldn't be missed: the sumptuous **Spiegelkabinett** (Mirror Cabinet), with its hand-painted mirrors and glittering gilded stucco, and the **Grünes Zimmer** (Green Cabinet) with exquisite Rococo lacquer work.

Back downstairs, off the eastern end of the vestibule is the **Gartensaal** (Garden Hall). Gardens offered an escape from the strictures of formal 18th-century courtly behaviour. Beyond the palace walls you could let your hair down a little. (Courtiers often got into the spirit of things by dressing up as carefree peasants.) The Garden Hall, which opens out directly into the grounds, was a sort of buffer zone used for serving up food and as a setting for musicians. In his stucco work Bossi has hidden mirrors that flicker with a magical, mysterious light when the chandeliers are lit. The fresco (by Johann Zick) explores the contrast between stiff courtly formality and happy abandon. Smaller pictures of putti wickedly send-up the more serious treatment of a 'Banquet of the Gods' in the main painting.

There are more cheeky putti on the bastions in the garden behind the Residenz, carved by the court sculptor Peter Wagner. Things take a more disturbing turn south of the building, where rape is the theme, with two heavy statues, the 'Rape of Proserpine' and the 'Rape of Europe'. Before leaving, have a look at the Court Chapel (in the southern wing of the building), another Neumann triumph, with spiralling columns, curving balconies and graceful arches.

Around Town

The town centre, bounded by gardens which follow the line of the old city wall, is nick-named the *Bischofs Hoed* (Bishop's Mitre) by the locals, because of its shape. Würzburg is not a museumpiece, but in amongst the everyday bustle you will suddenly come across quiet pockets that belong to another age, or will turn a corner to a surprise view, past the glass and concrete to the river or mountains and vineyards beyond.

The Dom

A walk from the Residenz down Hofstraße will bring you to the **Dom**. The 12th-century church seemed to have survived the 1945 air raid relatively intact (though the heat from surrounding fires melted the bells), but one year later the roof of the nave collapsed, and the cathedral had to be substantially rebuilt. It is worth a visit mainly for the vast array of Franconian sculpture—seven centuries' worth of bishops' effigies. By far the most impressive is the portrait of the 92-year-old Rudolf von Scherenberg (1499), carved with an almost discomfiting realism by Germany's most eminent late-Gothic sculptor, **Tilman Riemenschneider** (1460–1531). Riemenschneider arrived in Würzburg in 1483, and as well as being a prolific sculptor twice managed to become *Bürgermeister*. He was imprisoned in 1525 for persuading the city council to join the Peasants' Revolt (1524–5). Some say he was tortured, and his hands were left crippled; others say it was his spirit that was broken—but after his release he never carved anything of note again.

Look out also for the intricately carved lectern (possibly also by Riemenschneider) and a 13th-century Epiphany group where the kings' robes are patterned with the heraldic eagle, rose and *fleur-de-lis* to represent Germany, Britain and France, then the world's leading nations.

The Neumünster

After the timeless hush of the Dom the city centre seems hectic. To the right, on Küschnerhof, you'll find the **Neumünster**, built in the 11th century to house the remains of St Kilian and his fellow missionaries, but now largely dramatic, sweeping Baroque. Beyond the northern exit of the church is the peaceful **Lusam Garden**, where you can see one remaining wing of the original 12th-century cloisters—a dainty row of carved Romanesque pillars and arches. In one corner, the minstrel Walther von der Vogelweide (d.1230), Germany's equivalent of Chaucer, lies buried. There are little shallow water-bowls on each corner of the memorial, in answer to the poet's last wish that birds should always have a reason to visit his grave. He was wildly popular in his time and, 750 years on, locals still make sure that the grave is never without flowers.

The Marktplatz

West of the Neumünster you can cut through intriguing alleys of shops to the **Marktplatz**. On the northern side of the square is the pretty **Haus zum Falken**, built as a priest's house in the 14th century, but given a dextrous Rococo stucco façade when it became an inn in 1751. Next door is the Gothic **Marienkapelle**, most interesting for its exterior carvings. On the tympanum above the north portal is a rather odd Annunciation. God communicates with the Virgin through a speaking tube, down which the baby Jesus can be seen surfing earthwards. Riemenschneider's lithe, erotic Adam and Eve on the south portal caused a scandal when they were first seen, mainly because a beardless Adam was thought disrespectful. The statues you see are 19th-century copies; the originals are in the Mainfränkisches Museum (*see* below), safe from corroding fumes. Balthasar Neumann (*see* p.48) is buried in the church (which was only called a 'chapel' because it was built by burghers, and the stuffy bishop refused to grant it the status of a parish church).

There was a constant and hard-fought battle between townsfolk and clergy of Würzburg, where one in five of the population was a priest. The **Rathaus** on the western side of the square was bought by the burghers in 1316, and continually enlarged to cock a snook at the bishops—but it remains very much in the shadow of Würzburg's ecclesiastical buildings. Inside is the fine Romanesque **Wenzel Hall**, where in 1397 the burghers set out to to wine, dine and woo King Wenzel into granting the city free imperial status—a brave but fruitless attempt to snatch power from the bishop. (The hall is visitable during office hours, when not in use.)

Along Juliuspromenade

Halfway along Theaterstraße, east of the Marktplatz, you come to the **Bürgerspital**— almshouses, founded in the 14th century, that derive their income from large, excellent vineyards. A narrow arch leads you to the quiet courtyard, where sturdily shod grannies sit happily on benches along the walls. A possible explanation for their contented smiles is that the Bürgerspital administration traditionally grants residents a glass of wine a day, and a bottle over weekends.

Around the corner on the Juliuspromenade is another worthy institution, the **Juliusspital**, founded by the prince-bishop in 1576 and now used as a hospital. Pop in for a look at the Baroque **Fürstenbau** (erstwhile residence of the prince-bishop) and wander through to the peaceful gardens at the back. At harvest-time this little park buzzes with activity as grapes are carted in to the Juliusspital's winery.

Further down the Juliuspromenade you come to the River Main, and a twin-armed 18th-century **crane** built by one of Balthasar Neumann's sons. From here it is a pleasant walk south along the river to the **Alte Mainbrücke**, a beautiful old bridge dating largely from the 17th century, and decorated with 12 enormous statues of saints.

Festung Marienberg

Across the bridge, on the hill, is **Festung Marienberg**, a hotch-potch of fortifications, some dating back to the 13th century, that formed the prince-bishops' palace prior to the building of the Residenz. The buildings are all carefully restored, but devastation by the Swedes during the Thirty Years' War, the Prussians in the 19th century and Allied bombs during the Second World War have left little of the original interiors intact. You can, however, visit the dinky 8th-century **Marienkirche** (one of Germany's oldest) and an impressive 105m-deep **well**, chipped out through solid rock in 1200 to ensure a water supply when the fortress was under siege. The **Zeughaus** (arsenal) now houses the **Mainfränkisches Museum** (*April–Oct Tues–Sun 10–5, Nov–Mar closes 4; adm DM3*) which has a superb collection of Riemenschneider sculpture and a wine museum.

On top of the next hill is the **Käppele**, a compact pilgrimage church (the devout climb the hill on their knees) built by Neumann in the 1740s. However you've managed your passage to the top, you'll find the view back across town exhilarating.

Würzburg ✆ (0931–) **Where to Stay**

Hotels in Würzburg are not particularly cheap. In the summer and early autumn booking at least a fortnight ahead is advisable.

moderate

Hotel Würzburger Hof, Barbarossaplatz 2, ✆ 5 38 14, ✉ 5 83 24 (DM160–230). Has been run by the same family for nearly a century and is getting gradually grander all the time. It is centrally situated, and double-glazed against traffic noise.

Hotel Zur Stadt Mainz, Semmelstr. 39, ✆ 5 31 55, ✉ 5 85 10 (DM180–200). An old inn, recently renovated and fitted out with comfortable old furniture. All rooms have TV and double glazing.

Hotel Alter Kranen, Kärrnergasse 11, ✆ 5 00 39, ✉ 5 00 10 (DM130). The best bargain in town. It is a central, cosy hotel, with friendly management. Front rooms overlook the Main with views up to the Marienberg and the vineyards.

inexpensive

Hotel Am Klein-Nizza Park, Friedrich-Ebert-Ring 20, ✆ 7 28 93 (from DM90 without private bath). A simple hotel which overlooks a park behind the Residenz. About the cheapest conveniently situated hotel.

Youth Hostel: Burkarder Str. 44, ✆ 4 25 90.

Eating and Drinking

Local wines are renowned as among the best in Germany (*see* below). If you come to Würzburg at harvest time, try a glass of *Federweißer* (known locally also as *Bremser*)—a cloudy, fermenting grape-must that tastes like fruit juice, looks like scrumpy cider, and has you under the table within minutes. A slow glass with a slice of home-made *Zwiebelkuchen* (a sort of onion quiche) is a fine way to end an autumn day.

Moszuppe, a rich wine and cream soup, makes a tasty starter. Committed gourmands can follow this up with one of the heartier Franconian dishes, such as *Schmeckerli* (stomach of veal). Alternatively, you could nibble on a *Blooz* (a plate-sized salty cracker) or a couple of *Blaue Zipfel* (sausages poached in spicy vinegar). These go an odd blue colour when cooked, but taste delicious. Würzburgers love fish and cook it well. Carp comes baked or served up '*Sud*' (poached in heavily spiced wine and vinegar). *Meefischli* is whitebait from the Main. Locals say the fish should never be longer than the little finger of St Kilian's statue on the bridge, and that they should swim three times—in water, fat and wine.

Restaurants and Taverns

expensive

Haus des Frankenweins, Mainpromenade, next to the old crane, ✆ 1 20 93 (DM100). As well as being a vortex for oenophiles, the restaurant lures gourmets to its fresh carp, exotic roulades and upmarket versions of an old Franconian *Brotzeit*.

moderate

Bürgerspital, Theaterstr. 19, ✆ 13861 (DM20–45). Cellar restaurant of famous local wine producer which offers the complete range of in-house wines (the dry Kerner is particularly good) and tasty Franconian dishes.

Juliusspital-Weinstuben, Juliuspromenade 19, ✆ 54 080 (DM20–40). Atmospheric, though cavernous. Their wines are world-renowned and they serve a good harvest-time *Federweißer*. The Franconian cooking is good too.

Fischbäuerin, Katzengasse 7, ✆ 42487 (DM25–55). The best place to try *Meefischli* and other seasonal fish dishes.

Hotel zur Stadt Mainz Restaurant, Semmelstr. 39, ✆ 5 31 55 (DM25–55). Run by the sort of cook who can turn the simplest ingredients—like oxtail and brown sauce—into a heavenly experience, but on some nights it seems that every visitor to Würzburg has heard about her.

inexpensive

Weinhaus Schnabel, through a plain door at Haugerpfarrgasse 10, ✆ 53 314 (DM15–25). A good no-nonsense establishment with stolid waitresses, bright lights and inexpensive servings of many Franconian specialities.

Bars and Cafés

Locals call their cafés *Bäcken*. In the summer there is a jovial temporary beer-garden on the east bank of the Main, in front of the Haus des Frankenweins. Sitting on the wall with your legs dangling over the water, looking up across the old bridge to the Marienberg, you can sip your drink in one of the best spots Würzburg has to offer.

Zum Stachel, Gressengasse 1. Was the headquarters for local farmers during the Peasants' Revolt, and gets its name (the Spike) from a mace hanging outside the door. The tiny courtyard is a jigsaw of balconies, loggias and stairways, draped with creepers—rather like a tightly designed set for a Shakespeare play.

Sternbäck, Domstraße. A welcoming bar squeezed into an old house, though in the summer people sit outside under the trees.

Brückebäck, Alte Marienbrücke. Across the Alte Mainbrücke from the centre. A trendy bar where students and the youthful smart set line up against the plate-glass windows, and look out across the river.

Franconian Wine

'Dagegen sende mir noch einige Würzburger; denn kein anderer Wein will mir schmecken und ich bin verdrüßlich wenn mir mein gewohnter Lieblingstrank abgeht.' (Send me some more Würzburger, for no other wine is so much to my taste, and I get grumpy without my favourite drink).

Goethe in a letter to Christiane Vulpius; 1806

Goethe put his money where his mouth was: he ordered 900 litres of Franconian wine (Frankenwein) in 1821 alone. The superb wines from the vineyards around Würzburg are one of Germany's best kept secrets. Most of the vines are tucked away between stretches of forest and pasture (wherever they can best escape the crippling frosts), so you hardly notice that they are there. Yields are small, which means that when the wines do make it past the voracious locals to the outside world, they are expensive, and hence often ignored. Yet it was a Franconian wine that was chosen to represent Germany's viticulture at Queen Elizabeth II's coronation banquet, and for the Pope to tipple when he visited Germany in the 1980s.

The wines come in dumpy, flat, round-shouldered flasks known as *Bocksbeutel*. These were supposedly invented by grape-growing monks who wanted to smuggle wine out into the fields—and so were around long before Mateus Rosé was even a gleam in a publicist's eye. Almost exclusively white, the wines are mostly dry, pithy, flavoursome—often similar to burgundies—and heartily alcoholic. At one time most Franconian wines were made from the Silvaner grape—a bit of a non-starter in other regions, but here producing rich, honeyed wines. Sadly, Silvaner has been supplanted by the ubiquitous Müller-Thurgau, the wine-drinkers' equivalent of easy listening. Yet even this usually wimpish grape manages to pack a few beefier punches in Franconian wines. Heavy frosts and short summers mean that growers have something of a struggle getting Riesling grapes to ripen, but when they do (in hot years like 1976) the results are extraordinary.

In Würzburg, Riesling and Silvaner grapes bake away on the heat-retaining limestone slopes below the Marienberg fortress and in the famous Stein vineyard south of the city. These supply three of Germany's greatest wine producers: the **Bürgerspital**, Theater-straße/Semmelstraße (*cellars open Mon–Thurs 7.30–12 and 1–4.45, Fri 7.30–12; shop* *open Mon–Fri 9–6 and Sat 9–12*); the **Juliusspital** (*bulk purchases from Klinilkstr. 5, open Mon–Thurs 8–12 and 12.30–4.15, Fri 8–12; smaller quantities from Koellikerstr. 1–2, Mon–Fri 9–6, Sat 9–1*); and the **Hofkeller**, Residenzplatz (*Mon–Fri 8.30–5.30, Sat 8.30–12*). Each offers wine-tastings, but if you'd prefer a more general introduction to local wines visit the **Haus des Frankenweins** on the Main next to the old crane (*open Mon–Fri 10–6 and Sat 10–1*), which offers a wide selection from all over the region and can give helpful guidance and advice. You should certainly sample some Rieslings and Silvaners from the Stein vineyards, but some of the newer wine varieties can be just as exciting. Kerner, in particular (a blend of red Trollinger and Riesling) can produce a strong, fruity, dry white wine.

A Wine Tour around Würzburg

A drive out of town south along the B13 will take you to **Randersacker**, where the Pfülben vineyards produce good Rieslings. There's a growers' co-operative at Maingasse 33 (*open Mon–Fri 8–12 and 2–6, Sat 8–12*), and a good private estate is Weingut Gebrüder König, Herrngasse 29 (*open daily 8–6*). The village of **Sommerhausen**, a few kilometres on, is an enchanting cluster of grey stone houses, with vines and geraniums bursting out of cracks in the walls. There's a 16th-century Rathaus with pinnacled gables, and a Renaissance castle in the high street. In autumn the whole village bustles with the urgencies of harvest, and you catch fragrant whiffs of ripe pears and the musty odour of crushed grapes. A colony of artists works here, and sometimes contributes to the small **Christmas Market** during Advent—the best (and most kitsch-free) in the area. There is also a minuscule theatre above the old tower gate, which attracts audiences from as far away as Würzburg. **Weingut Konrad Schwarz**, Schleifweg 13 (✆ (09333) 221 for appointment) uses grapes from the excellent Ölspiel vineyards to make velvety Spätburgunder reds.

If you turn eastwards, past the villages of Ochsenfurt and Marktbreit (both with typically Franconian red and grey half-timbered houses), you come to **Kitzingen**. Here, walk past the Rathaus and into a yard behind the Landratsamt and you'll come to the cellars of the **Alte Kitzinger Klosterkeller**, part of an 8th-century Benedictine nunnery. Hadeloga—the stalwart sister of the Frankish King Pippin the Short—got over the shock of seeing her paramour dancing in the local market with another woman by founding (rather than running off to) a nunnery. As Mother Superior she set her noble nuns to work in the fields, and soon they were producing excellent wines.

Today you can visit their cellars (the oldest in Germany) and sit among the huge old vats sampling wines. Here you could try one of the more recent grape varieties—such as the fruity, rather flowery Bacchus. Tastings are conducted under the deft guidance of erstwhile German Wine Queen, Karin Rickel, ✆ (09321) 700589 (*shop open Wed, Thurs and Fri 9–12 and 1–6, Sat 10–1*). Kitzingen also has the official German carnival museum, the **Deutsches Fastnachtsmuseum**, at Im Falterturm (*April–Nov Sat and Sun 2–5; adm DM2*), with costumes, masks and other bits and bobs from the pre-Lenten revels.

From Kitzingen, you can follow the B8 south to **Iphofen**, where the fertile red marly soils produce delicious, mouth-filling wines. Here even Müller-Thurgau grapes manage a heady, aromatic bouquet, and it is a good place to try some of the newer hybrids (such as Scheurebe or Perle).

The town itself seems dreamily lost in time. Much of the old town wall is intact. The quaint 13th-century *Fachwerk* **Rödelseer Tor**, with its jumble of different roofs, seems to prop itself up by leaning in all directions at once. A sumptuous Baroque Rathaus comes as a surprise after narrow streets of half-timbered houses, and in the late-Gothic St Veit's church, you can see some fine Riemenschneider carving. Rieslings from the Julius-Echterberg and Kronsberg vineyards are superb. (These were the wines chosen for Queen Elizabeth and the Pope.) **Weinbau Hans Dorsch**, Rödelseer 8, ✆ (09323) 13 75 (*Mon–Sat 8–6, Sun 9–12*) makes good wines from these vines, and also from the superior Kalb slopes.

North of Iphofen, off the B286, you come to **Volkach**, a busy little wine town propelled by its ebullient *Ratsherr* (councillor) and 'Wine Ambassador', Waldemar Sperling. When he isn't dolled up in medieval garb for a wine-tasting or festival, he runs the tourist office, or whizzes around town making sure that everyone is organized and contented. There's a 16th-century Rathaus and some romantically crumbly bits of old city wall. Down a side-street off the Marktplatz is the **Schelfenhaus**, a Baroque residence (now converted for public functions) where you can see some fine stucco work by a Bamberg artist named Vogel (bird), who used to sculpt a bird somewhere into his work as a trademark. On a hill above the town, in the little church of Maria im Weingarten, is one of Riemenschneider's most exquisite works, the *Madonna im Rosenkranz* (Madonna in a Wreath of Roses; 1524). It shot to international fame when it was 'art-napped' and held for a ransom in 1962. The poor parish couldn't come up with the money, so the editor of *Stern* offered DM100,000 for its return. The original was easily picked out from the numbers of fakes that sprouted up in response to the reward, because (unbeknown to most) it had a hollow back.

At **Weinbau Max Müller I**, Hauptstr. 46, ✆ (09381) 12 18 (*open Sat and Sun*), you can taste some Rieslaner wines—a new hybrid fast becoming a local speciality. Near Volkach, at the top of the **Vogelsburg**, you can admire the fine view while sipping spicy Traminer wines made by local Augustinian nuns. The village of **Escherndorf**, back down the hill, is famed for a vineyard called Lump, which produces some of the region's best wines.

Tourist Information

Randersacker: Markt Randersacker, Maingasse 9, ✆ (0931) 70 82 82.

Sommerhausen: Rathaus, ✆ (09333) 216.

Kitzingen: Schrannenstr. 1, ✆ (09321) 2 02 05.

Iphofen: Marktplatz 27, ✆ (09323) 30 95.

Volkach: Rathaus, ✆ (09381) 4 01 12.

Wine-growing towns have the best festivals of all—less raucous than beer festivals, but with more style and an infectious conviviality. The townsfolk will often elect a Wine Queen (as much for her knowledge of wine as good looks and personality) and there is much eating, dancing and drinking of local wines. As well as the Würzburg wine events (*see* above), there are well over 100 smaller village festivals held between May and November. Rather like traditional British fêtes, many of these are organized by local associations such as Voluntary Fire Brigades or sports clubs. Look out for wayside signs advertising a **Weinfest** in the early summer and autumn, especially in the villages around Volkach.

Where to Stay

It is possible to base yourself in Würzburg and visit the wine villages on a day trip. The most idyllic of the villages for a longer stay is **Sommerhausen**. The **Pension am Schloß**, Hauptstraße, ℰ (09333) 13 04 (DM110) is right at the heart of things. All rooms have television, and guests can hire bicycles for jaunts into the vineyards. Private rooms in Sommerhausen cost around DM30 per person. (Try Frau Brand, Zwischenweg 7, ℰ (09333) 14 58—or enquire through the tourist office.)

In **Iphofen** you'll find the charming **Gästehaus Fröhlich**, Geräthengasse 13, ℰ (09323) 3030 (DM70–90), run by German-Canadian Ruth Perry. All the rooms are warmly and individually decorated with old furniture, and there is a café downstairs that serves delicious homemade cakes.

For something grander, head for **Volkach** and the **Hotel Vier Jahrezeiten**, Hauptstr. 31, ℰ (09381) 37 77, ℰ (09381) 47 73 (from DM120), built in 1605 as a residence for the prince-bishop. The rooms are sumptuously decked out with antiques and cabinets of Bohemian glass.

Zur Schwane, across the road at Hauptstr. 12, ℰ (09381) 515 (DM110–170), is a family-run hotel with its own vineyard and schnapps distillery, and a breakfast buffet that even locals try to get in on.

Eating and Drinking

expensive

Restaurant von Dungern, Hauptstr. 12, **Sommerach**, ℰ (09333) 1406 (around DM70). People travel out from Würzburg to sample Franconian cuisine, here elevated to gourmet heights with local mushrooms, wines, guinea fowl and rabbits all helping in the ascent.

Hotel Zur Schwane Restaurant, Volkach (*see* above) (around DM100). Deserves its place in the list of the top 444 restaurants in Germany, with adventurous concoctions such as venison in a red cabbage and walnut sauce.

moderate

Gasthof Goldener Stern, Maxstr. 22, Iphofen, ✆ (09323) 3315 (DM25–45). Looks fairly ordinary from outside, but serves scrumptious food. The owner, Rainer Steinruck, forages around local markets and comes up with simple but inspired dishes-of-the-day (such as turkey fillets with wild mushrooms in a wine and cream sauce) to supplement his usual menu. Iphofen is renowned for its asparagus, and in season this gets on to the menu in a variety of guises.

Weinstube Torbäct, Hauptstraße, Volkach (DM20–45). A good place for a hearty board of sausages, breads and cheeses (or homemade *Zwiebelkuchen*) to knock back with your harvest-time *Federweißer*.

Schloß Hallburg, between Volkach and Sommerach, ✆ (09381) 2340. Converted *Schloß*, most popular on Sunday mornings when you can have a delicious brunch (with some Franconian wine or *Sekt*) to the accompaniment of a live jazz band, and then wander around the romantic gardens. Lunch menus include such treats as local trout with brown sauce.

West of Würzburg: The Spessart and Odenwald

Between Würzburg and Frankfurt, stretching over a distance of more than 100km, is some of Germany's most extensive forestland. Through it the River Main cuts a deep, winding valley into the northwesternmost corner of Bavaria. North of the river, spreading across the Bavarian border into Hesse, is the **Spessart**. South of the river is the **Odenwald**, which reaches into Hesse in the west and Baden-Württemberg to the south. The passion of the prince-bishops of Mainz for game-hunting saved the acres of beech and oak from the axe in past centuries, and strict legislation protects them now.

Both the Spessart and Odenwald are quiet regions of gently rolling hills, forests and small villages which have long been known to local weekend trippers for their lonely walks, but remain relatively undiscovered by outsiders. By far the most popular long-distance hike on the Bavarian side of the Spessart is the 111km long **Esselsweg** (Mule's Path), following the old salt route through acres of woodland and across expansive meadow-lands from Bad Orb to Miltenberg. **Weibersbrunn**, a small resort some 13km southeast of Aschaffenburg, is also a walkers' hotspot. The deciduous forest around here is unusually dense and becomes quite dramatic under lowering skies. The village itself is attractive, with an unassuming **parish church** whose Crucifixion, dated 1470, is a perfectly preserved example of a rustic depiction. The neighbouring hamlet of Rohrbrunn was the site of the notorious **Wirtshaus im Spessart** (Spessart Inn), which was immortalized by the writer, Wilhelm Hauff (1802–27) in his tale about the highwaymen of the Spessart. Sadly, the robbers' hideout was recently flattened by a motorway. Several footpaths converge at Rohrbrunn. Among these is a walk which trails past the **Forsthaus Echterspfahl** (a converted forester's house that dishes up delicious meals), then meanders the fine hilltops to **Schloß Mespelbrunn** (*mid-Mar to mid-Nov Mon–Sat 9–12 and 1-5; Sun 9–5; adm DM2*), a dreamy, moated Renaissance palace with exhibits of some fine suits of armour and weaponry.

Getting Around

By car: One major motorway crosses the region. The A3 (one of Germany's main north-south arteries) runs from Frankfurt to Aschaffenburg (40km), through Aschaffenburg to Würzburg (97km), and on to Nuremberg. Most of the important towns of the Odenwald lie along the B469, which dips south from Aschaffenburg to Miltenberg (37km) and Amorbach (42km).

By train: Major rail routes criss-cross the region, with Aschaffenburg the hub of the rail lines to Frankfurt (30mins) and to Würzburg (40mins). There are regular rail connections between Aschaffenburg and Miltenberg (45mins) and between Aschaffenburg and Amorbach (1hr 15mins via Miltenberg).

Tourist Information

Aschaffenburg: Dalbergstr. 6, ℂ (06021) 395800.

Miltenberg: Rathaus, ℂ (09371) 400119.

Amorbach: Altes Rathaus, ℂ (09373) 20940.

Festivals

For bell-ringers, travelling to Aschaffenburg is nothing short of a pilgrimage. Every summer at the beginning of August enthusiastic campanologists head for Schloß Johannisburg for the **Carillonfest**. Aschaffenburg's favourite folk festival is the ten-day **Volksfest** in mid-June, with feasting and fireworks in the Altstadt. Hundreds of people from far and near pour into Miltenberg for its **Michaelis-Messe**, a nine-day funfair in the last week of August. In October and November Miltenberg hosts the **Kulturwochen im Herbst**, a weekly sequence of concerts and exhibitions. In Amorbach each year, especially around Easter and Pentecost, there is a cycle of excellent **organ concerts** in the Abteikirche. Details of the annual programme are available from the local tourist office.

Aschaffenburg

Approaching from Würzburg on the A3, the first city of note you come to is Aschaffenburg, 'giving the Bavarian lion the wag in its tail', as one Bavarian poet described it. Since the Second World War much of this wagging has been done by American GIs, and thousands of US troops are still stationed here. In stark contrast to the surrounding countryside, Aschaffenburg raises a line of massive stone façades along the River Main. The largest and most imposing of these is square-built **Schloß Johannisburg** (*April–Oct Tues–Sun 9–12 and 1–5; Nov–Mar Tues–Sun 10–12 and 1–4; adm DM3.50*), testament to the immense secular power of Mainz's prince-bishops, who called the tune here from the 10th to the early 19th century. The Renaissance palace was commissioned by arch-bishop Johann Schweickard von Kronberg as a second residence and was built between 1604 and 1614 on the site of an earlier castle destroyed by the margrave of Kulmbach. The prince-bishop was a child of his time, fired with aspirations to the grandeur that befitted his status as Elector of the Holy Roman Empire. Appropriately, the palace grew into a massive red-sandstone pile, consuming the equivalent of 45 million Deutschmarks on the way. It was carefully restored after extensive damage during the Second World War. Inside you'll find a branch of the **Bavarian State Gallery** (*same times*), with fine paintings by Lucas Cranach and other Franconian artists. Each year in August hundreds of visitors come to the *Schloß* to hear virtuoso bell-ringing performances (*see* 'Festivals' above). If you want relief from the tourist throngs, and the dings and the dongs, head for the **Pompejanum**, the folly of a Roman villa that King Ludwig I had constructed on a hill north of the *Schloß*. Or to set quite another peal ringing visit the **Schloßwein-stube** (Palace Wine Tavern), where there is a tantalizing selection of Franconian wines.

The Altstadt, southeast of Schloß Johannisburg, centres on the Stiftsplatz, which is domi-nated by the late Romanesque basilica of the **Stiftskirche** (with an interesting medieval crucifix depicting the *Mourning of Christ*). The **Neues Rathaus** combines a Neoclassical façade with a more modern building, put up after the Second World War. Nearby, in Wermbachstraße, is the Schönbormer Hof, a fine Baroque mansion which is now home to the **Naturwissenschaftliches Museum** (Science Museum) (*Thurs–Tues 9–12 and 1–4; adm free*), with displays on the zoology, mineralogy and geology of the Spessart. To the east of the Altstadt is the **Schöntal**, a landscaped garden with Mediterranean magnolia groves and a pheasantry that complement neatly the wild, romantic layout of **Schönbusch** on the western side of the River Main, one of the first English-style gardens in Germany. Set around a diminutive 18th-century **Baroque palace**, the **Pavillon** (*April–Sept Tues–Sun 9.30–12.30 and 2–4.30; adm DM3*), are wild flowers, open meadows and a whimsical series of pint-size follies including man-made ponds, islets, canals and temples.

A little way out of the city centre, but a must—even for those usually bored by the achievements and foibles of motoring—is the **Rosso Bianco Collection** (*April–Oct Tues–Sun 10–6; Nov–Mar Sun 10–6; adm DM10*). This contains the world's largest array of sports cars—some 200 in all—including streamlined racers such as the Blitzen-Benz which clocked up 228kph (140mph) in 1909, or Porsche's 356 Roadster of 1948.

Miltenberg

Emerging absolutely unscathed from the Second World War, Miltenberg is by far the most romantic town in the region. Street after street of decorated half-timbered houses—around 150 buildings in all spanning four centuries—stretch out along the River Main below an old hill-top castle.

The best place to begin a walk around is the triangular **Schnatterloch**, the town's historic market square. Across both ends of the square are uninterrupted cascades of step-gabled façades that prickle with decorated portals and corner oriels. Much the most imposing street, however, is **Hauptstraße**, the pedestrianized main shopping thoroughfare leading east from the Schnatterloch. The bright row of half-timbered burgher and municipal houses are mostly built on ground-floor walls of warm red sandstone, using the simple, square-framed **Ständerbau** technique. Today the wooden beams are painted ochre or grey, but originally they were daubed with ox blood, in striking contrast to the white walls. The street leads past the 15th-century **Altes Rathaus** down to the five-storeyed **Riese**, Miltenberg's best-known pile of *Fachwerk* architecture. It has been a guesthouse since at least 1504 and is the cosiest and most atmospheric of the hotels in town (*see* 'Where to Stay' below). The present building was put up in 1590 as a hostelry to be 'worthy of a prince', and vies with the *Bären* in Freiburg in the Black Forest for the title of Germany's oldest guesthouse.

A walk back uphill from the market square will bring you to the **Mildenburg**, which rises up over the town. First mentioned in 1226, the castle was strengthened by the arch-bishops of Mainz as a check to their rivals at Würzburg, and to keep better watch over the trading stations on the River Main. Star attraction in the courtyard (*open daily except Mon; adm free*) is the **Toutonenstein**, a puzzling 5m-high monolith which was discov-ered nearby in the 19th century—with a cryptic set of initials (CAHF). The stone would seem to date from Roman times but so far no one has come up with an explanation for the letters, though there have been some amusing attempts. One local wag suggested '*Cerevisiam Amant Hassi Fortiter*' (Beer is not at all to the liking of the Hessian people).

Amorbach

Amorbach's gets its name from the Benedictine Abbot Amor of Aquitaine, who, after working among local tribes as a missionary for some 20 years, founded a monastery here in AD 734. Benedictine monks continued to live here up until secularization in 1803. The good abbot's relics, kept in the abbey, were held to be particularly useful to childless couples praying for fertility.

Nowadays the small town, which is brimming with handsome half-timbered buildings, stands in the shadow of the **Abteikirche**, once the abbey's church, built between 1742 and 1744. The refreshingly plain Baroque interior is considered to be architect Maximilian von Welsch's masterpiece. White stucco predominates, with the ceiling frescoes and side altars adding discreet touches of colour. The best view of the interior is from just in front of the filigree wrought-iron rood screen. From here you'll also have a fine view of the **organ**, the church's greatest treasure. The 18th-century instrument is an astonishing piece of workmanship consisting of more than 5000 pipes and 30 bells, with 63 stops. Understandably, the Abteikirche is the venue for a number of prestigious annual organ recitals (*see* 'Festivals' above).

Abutting the southern side of the church is the rambling 18th-century monastic **Residenz** (*guided tours; Mon–Sat 9–12 and 1–5, Sun 12–5; adm DM2.50*). Inside, all trace of the original design is lost under layers of redecoration commissioned by the Princes of Leinigen when they acquired the building in the 19th century. The Neoclassical **Grüner Saal** (Green Hall) is grandly done up in white and green and the **library** has an energetic ceiling fresco, glorifying the Virtues, Wisdom and Science.

Aschaffenburg

Aschaffenburger Hof, Frohsinnstr. 11, ✆ (06021) 21441, @ (06021) 27298 (DM178–196). Aschaffenburg's classiest address attracts conference organizers with its modern-style appearance and spacious rooms—but scores badly when it comes to atmosphere. Good, inexpensive restaurant (DM25–44).

Ringhotel Wilder Mann, Lüherstr. 51, ✆ (06021) 21555, @ (06021) 22893 (DM165–195). Modernized 16th-century building on the edge of the Altstadt. Quiet, folksy hotel—but a touch stuffy.

Miltenberg

Hotel Riesen, Hauptstr. 98, ✆ (09371) 3644 (DM108–178). Reputedly Germany's oldest guesthouse. Converted personally by the owner in the 1970s, the hotel has upmarket service in an understated way. Individual rooms are named after former aristocratic guests of the hotel. You can sleep surrounded by heavy antique furniture in the room where Emperor Frederick or Empress Maria once spent the night. There is a snug little restaurant on the ground floor where you can eat good, hearty dishes.

Amorbach

Relais et Châteaux Hotel Der Schafhof, Schafhof 1, ✆ (09373) 8088, @ (09373) 4120 (DM190–260). Romantic old building on the very edge of town (3km west of centre), once an 18th-century Benedictine monastery. Now a comfortable modern hotel with rooms furnished in Baroque style. The restaurant uses products from its own garden.

Rothenburg ob der Tauber

Sixty kilometres south of Würzburg, along the route of the Romantic Road, lies Rothenburg ob der Tauber. A prosperous town until the 17th century, Rothenburg never really recovered from an exhausting sequence of occupations during the Thirty Years' War. No new building took place for centuries. Although it was badly bombed in the Second World War, Rothenburg was painstakingly rebuilt, and today survives almost perfectly intact as a medieval museum piece. It takes half an hour to skirt the town on the **sentry walk** atop the old city wall. Steep roofs crush right up against the ramparts, and you get a splendid view of the *Fachwerk* alleys, pointy gables, turrets, spires and decorated façades that draw coachloads of tourists all year. It is all very pretty: 'gingerbread architecture', sniff some people contemptuously—and, like gingerbread, a little of Rothenburg goes a long way.

The **tourist office** on the Marktplatz, ✆ (09861) 4 04 92 (Mon–Fri 9–12 and 2–6, Sat 9–12) can give you a small map marked with suggested walks, as well as plentiful information on the town.

On Whit Monday locals in the appropriate garb act out Burgermeister Nusch's drinking feat, though no one really attempts to match it (see below); and one Sunday each month in spring and summer you can see the jolly *Schäfertanz* (Shepherd's Dance) in front of the Rathaus (the dance supposedly began as a celebration of Rothenburg's deliverance from the Plague). Vast crowds turn out to watch both events. The Advent Christmas Market has a long-established reputation as one of the best in Germany.

The best time to see the town is very early in the morning, before the hordes hit the streets. As the mist drains out of the alleys down to the River Tauber in the valley far below, you might quite expect to see someone in tights and a floppy hat trundle past in a heavy wooden cart. Even when the streets (and side-streets) fill up with tourists, Rothenburg doesn't entirely lose its medieval atmosphere. In the **market square** farmers rub shoulders with trinket-sellers. In the autumn there are stalls selling *Federweißer* wine direct from the barrel, and during Advent a Christmas Market clusters around the side of the Rathaus, up against St Jakobskirche.

In the gable of the **Ratsherrntrinkstube** overlooking the square, little figures in the windows near the clocks act out Rothenburg's most historic moment (*on the hour from 11am to 3pm and also at 9pm and 10pm*). In 1631, during the Thirty Years' War, the formidable General Tilly captured the town, but agreed to spare it if one of the councillors could down the contents of a *Meistertrunk* (a 3-litre tankard of wine) in one go. Georg Nusch, a former *Bürgermeister*, took up the challenge. He saved Rothenburg in ten minutes, but needed three days to sleep off the effects.

On the western side of the square is the **Rathaus**. The front part of the building is Renaissance, but behind that an earlier Gothic hall pokes up a slender, 61m-high tower. Inside you can see the bare Imperial Hall (*daily 8–6; adm free*), and descend to the gloomy dungeons. Just behind the Rathaus is Rothenburg's famous **Christkindlmarkt**, a shop which sells all the traditional trappings of a German Christmas the whole year round.

Impressive old mansions line the **Herrngasse** (which extends westwards past the Rathaus), though the city's grandest home is the **Baumeisterhaus** in Schmiedgasse. Statues of the Seven Virtues grace the first floor, while the Seven Deadly Sins frolic on the floor above. (Nowadays the Baumeisterhaus is a restaurant—*see* below). North of the market looms the Gothic **St Jakobskirche**, where you can see the superb *Heiligblut-Altar* (1504), carved in limewood by Tilman Riemenschneider.

If miserable weather makes wandering the streets uncomfortable, then you could head for one of the small museums. The best are an originally furnished **Handwerkhaus**

(Craftsman's House) at Alter Stadtgraben 26 (*Easter–Oct daily 9–6 and 8pm–9pm; adm DM3*) and the **Kriminalmuseum** at Burggasse 3 (*April–Oct 9.30–6, Nov–Feb 2–4; adm DM3.50*) with its collection of medieval punishment and torture instruments. The **Puppen und Spielzeugmuseum** (Doll and Toy Museum), Hofbronngasse 13 (*daily 9.30–6, Jan and Feb 11–5; adm DM3.50*) has a vast selection of dolls from all over the world, and some exquisite dolls' houses; and the **Reichstadtmuseum**, Klosterhof (*April–Oct daily 10–5, Nov–Mar 1–4; adm DM2.50*), housed in a former Dominican convent, preserves many of the old fittings and equipment, as well as relics, of Rothenburg's 13th-century Jewish community.

Rothenburg ob der Tauber © *(09861–)* **Where to Stay**

Most of the visitors that pour into Rothenburg are day-trippers. An overnight stay is not as expensive as you might expect in such a tourist trap, and it does mean that you can see the town at its quietest.

moderate

Hotel Reichs-Küchenmeister, Kirchplatz 8, © 20 46, ⊗ 8 69 65 (DM120–180). Attractive modern conversion of a 16th-century patrician house, with its own sauna, steamroom and jacuzzi.

Hotel Roter Hahn, Obere Schmiedgasse 21, © 50 88, ⊗ 51 40 (DM125–180 DM). A cosy, family-run hotel in a 14th-century building that was once an inn run by relatives of the *Meistertrunk*-downing *Bürgermeister*.

inexpensive

Hotel Hornburg, Hornburgweg 28, © 84 80 (DM90). A capacious old Franconian villa—some of the rooms are enormous. Just outside the town wall. The staff are friendly, and happy to lend books and bicycles to guests. No restaurant. **Private rooms** in the Altstadt work out at around DM50 for a double. Try Herr Hess (Spitalgasse 18, © 61 30), or Herr Schneider (Alte Stadtgraben 11, © 32 11)—or enquire at the tourist office.

Eating and Drinking

Baumeisterhaus, Obere Schmidgasse 3, © 34 04 (DM30–65). One of the most atmospheric places to eat in Rothenburg—albeit popular with tourists. You can sit in heavy-beamed dining rooms, or the medieval courtyard draped with creepers. There is a café where you can munch on *Apfelgebäck*, and a restaurant serving fine Franconian food (try carp dipped in egg and breadcrumbs, then fried until it shines).

Rothenburger Bierstube, Klingengasse 38 (DM25–35). More off the beaten track, nestling up against the city wall in a quieter part of town. Good beer and *gutbürgerliche* cooking.

Glöcke, Am Plönlein 1 (DM25–35). Popular with locals for tasty, simple cuisine.

Feuchtwangen

At first glance, there seems little to merit a stop at the small town of Feuchtwangen about 30km south of Rothenburg along the Romantic Road. However, the **Stiftskirche** that dominates the colourful **Marktplatz** is worth a quick stop. This collegiate church was built in the 13th and 14th centuries and has a high altar dating from 1484, featuring side panels painted by Albrecht Dürer's teacher, Michael Wohlgemut. Abutting the church to the south are the Romanesque **cloisters**, a popular venue for annual open-air concerts between June and August. Little craft workshops crowd into the cloisters' half-timbered upper storey, where you can find a pewter worker, pastry-cook, potter, cobbler, weaver and dyer, exercising their skills before curious onlookers (*guided tours mid-Aug–Oct and Easter to mid-May Sat and Sun 10–12, 2–4; adm DM2.50*). To round off your visit, gen up on local history at the **Heimatmuseum** (*April–Oct Tues–Sun 10–12, 2–6, Mar, Nov and Dec Tues–Sun 10–12, 2–5; adm DM4*) which focuses on the furnishings and trappings of Feuchtwangen homes over the centuries.

Where to Stay and Eating Out

Romantik Hotel Greifen-Post, Marktplatz 5, ✆ (09852) 2002, ✉ (09852) 4841 (DM165–225). Conveniently situated in the town centre, and perfectly clean and comfortable with classy antique furniture. The *pièce de résistance* is the swimming pool in the former Renaissance courtyard. The restaurant serves good, hearty Franconian food.

Dinkelsbühl

Dinkelsbühl (40km south of Rothenburg) covetously vies with Rothenburg for top position in the league of most romantic towns in Germany, but is more compact and has less of a touristy atmosphere. Dinkelsbühl claims to be the older of the two, dating back to the 7th century AD. By the end of the 13th century trade was flourishing, and the town has become an influential member of the Swabian League, nestling within a ring of impressive protective defences. Nowadays Dinkelsbühl is a town that invites aimless wandering. Side streets lure this way and that into inviting alleys of overhanging houses, past a mish-mash of *Fachwerk*, Gothic and Renaissance architecture. Even the tourist strips seem jolly rather than tacky.

Tourist Information

The **tourist office** on the Marktplatz, ✆ (09851) 90240, can supply an outstanding collection of maps and information, including details of walks in the company of the town's night watchman.

For ten days in the middle of July, the sounds of merriment reverberate around Dinkelsbühl's Altstadt in celebration of the **Kinderzeche**, a series of plays, parades, dances and fireworks commemorating a memorable event of the town's history during the Thirty Years' War. In 1632, the story goes, the weeping of a contingent of local children under the leadership of one of the guard's daughters mollified the Swedish commander, who had besieged the town and threatened its destruction. The main event of the festival, the re-enactment of the crucial meeting, takes place in the Schranne in the town's centre. Open-air concerts by the renowned *Knabenkapelle* (boys' choir), dressed in 18th-century uniforms, are a celebrated feature of the festival.

Usually the second Sunday of September sees the **Stadtfest** in Dinkelsbühl, and with it more pageants and bacchanalian revels.

Dinkelsbühl's medieval core is neatly protected by the **Stadtmauer**, which is guarded by 17 towers and pierced by four massive gateways. To enter the **Altstadt** use the east gate, the 13th-century **Wörnitz Tor**. This approach offers by far the most picturesque view of the River Wörnitz and the tamer waters of the moat against a backdrop of the ancient wall, dotted with towers of all shapes and sizes. Sadly, the stone walls have lost their parapets along most of the circuit and you must rely on the town's **Alte and Neue Promenade** outside the western defences to get a good idea of the appearance of Dinkelsbühl's walls in the Middle Ages.

The Altrathausplatz leads past the old Rathaus building onto an even larger square, the **Marktplatz**, fenced off at its eastern end by the **Münster St. Georg**, the town's symbol. The church was built between 1448 and 1499 and is one of the finest examples of a late Gothic *Hallenkirche* in Germany. From the ouside the Münster looks fairly ordinary, but the interior is startling, surrounded by soaring spear-shaped windows, delicately placed so as to let in floods of light. As if not to intrude, the delicate stonework rises between the windows, then fans out into the vaults in slender, graceful lines. The **high altar** seems enormously distant; on it a late Gothic Crucifixion panel—supposedly painted by the Nürnberg artist, Michael Wohlgemut—glows mysteriously.

A few yards to the northwest across the Weinmarkt towards the **Rothenburger Tor**, is the 16th-century **Deutsches Haus**, once the home of a wealthy burgher family, now converted to the leading hotel in town (*see* below). Its richly decorated façade makes it one of the finest examples of Renaissance half-timbering in Germany. Look out for the beautifully carved corbels of miniature figurines sprouting from the vertical beams. Separated by a small alleyway is the 17th-century **Schranne**. This brick structure with dainty Renaissance gables used to be a granary and nowadays serves as festival hall, where the annual *Kinderzeche* is performed (*see* 'Festivals' above).

Nördlinger Straße, with its neatly curved, closely packed arrangement of half-timbered façades, leads to the **Nördlinger Tor**. Just outside the protective shield of the wall and gate, stands the 15th-century **Stadtmühle**, one of the most unusual buildings in

Dinkelsbühl. Although a mill, it was fortified with barbicans, gun loopholes and a protective strip of water. Inside, the **Museum 3. Dimension** (*April–Oct daily 10–6 Nov–Mar, Sat and Sun 11–4; adm DM10*) features an array of state-of-the-art displays that revolve around the world of optical, three-dimensional imagery.

Where the Night Watchman Still Calls

Dinkelsbühl has preserved an age-old traditon, once a common feature of towns across Europe: the night watchman. He begins his round from the Marktplatz every night at 9pm (9.30pm in summer), from April till October and at Christmas. Quaintly dressed in buckskin breeches, grey cloak and black felt hat and equipped with a halberd, horn and lantern, he sets off on his walk through the streets and narrow alleys, and blows his horn and sings out loudly at more than 20 fixed stops along the way: '*Hört Ihr Leut und laßt Euch sagen ... !*' (Listen well, you burghers, to what I've to tell you ... !). Until 1889 the town had four night watchmen who served as sergeants-at-arms and imposed the night's curfew, kept watch for fires and checked the gates and sentries. Today the night watchmen have become more of a tourist attraction and many visitors follow their footsteps through Dinkelbühl's history.

Where to Stay and Eating Out

Hotel Deutsches Haus, Weinmarkt 3, ✆ (09851) 6058 and 6059, ✉ (09851) 7911 (DM160–210). Only a few hotels in Germany can claim to occupy a more spectacular medieval residence. Original pieces of period furniture grace the entrance hall and the décor of most rooms harmonizes well with the historic exterior. Its elegant restaurant is celebrated for sumptuous meals and wines.

Minotel Goldene Kanne, Segringer Str. 8, ✆ (09851) 6011 and 6012 (DM110–220). Not for nothing has this dainty hotel in the Altstadt won an award from the Bavarian state government. If you can afford it, try to stay in one of the two suites overlooking the town centre.

Hotel Eisenkrug, Dr.-Martin-Luther-Str. 1, ✆ (09851) 6017, ✉ (09851) 6020 (DM90–150). A dinky hotel in the shadow of the Weinmarkt—with pink façade and lots of individual touches. Good, solid restaurant and a wine bar in vaulted cellar.

Gasthof Goldener Anker, Untere Schmiedegasse 22, ✆ (09851) 57800, ✉ (09851) 578080 (DM75–140). A small, traditional, family-run guesthouse with timber-panelled rooms on the ground floor.

Nördlingen im Ries

The area to the south of Dinkelsbühl is known as the **Ries**—a fertile basin about 25km in diameter and surrounded by a range of hills rising up to 100m. For a long time scientists believed that the Ries basin was the result of some pre-historic volcanic activity. However, deep-earth rock samples, extracted through a series of boreholes between 1961 and 1974, prompted geologists to come up with a new explanation for the odd landscape. They established that, some 15 million years ago, a giant asteroid of around 1200m in diameter, travelling at a speed of 30 to 50km per second, must have hit the earth's surface here, making a crater 1500m deep. Nowadays the lush loess soil in the Ries provides the region with the fitting epithet of 'Bavaria's Bread Basket', yet it was thought to be close enough to a lunar terrain for NASA to send their Apollo 14 and 17 astronauts here as part of their field training.

In its midst of the basin lies Nördlingen, with its old town walls oddly echoing the almost perfect circle of the surrounding crater hills. Nördlingen is probably the most modernized of the Romantic Road trio of walled medieval towns.

Tourist Information

The **tourist office** is conveniently located in the historic Leihaus on Marktplatz and can supply you with maps, ideas for a tour of the town and for walks in the surrounding countryside.

Festivals

Nördlingen's residents like to live it up, and will apparently use any historical occasion as an excuse to do so. Locals mark the arrival of spring with a 16th-century festival for children called **Stabenfest**, held in mid-May. The central feature is the procession of sumptuously dressed boys and girls from the Weinmarkt to the Kaiserwiese outside the town walls, where in good Bavarian fashion the event erupts into general merrymaking. At this point the proceedings are punctuated with *Stabenlieder*, witty bardic lyrics, often with caustic references to the town's history.

Mid-June brings the 14-day **Nördlinger Pfingstmesse** to the Kaiserwiese—folk festival with funfair and lots of beer-quaffing which represents the unbroken tradition of Nördlingen's formidable medieval Whitsun fairs.

The **Scharlachrennen**, held at two-year intervals (next in 1995), sees a spirited rendition of a celebrated horse race, first held in 1438, when the winning jockey received a bale of handsome scarlet cloth (hence its name). Since then, the event has expanded to include not only the traditional flat racing, but foot-races for the youngsters of Nördlingen.

The medieval pageant known as the **Historisches Stadtmauerfest** is performed every three years (next in September 1996). The burghers of Nördlingen dress up in period costumes and frolic through a series of lively medieval processions. There are also displays of traditional crafts.

There has been an Alemannic settlement here since the 6th century AD. The town's golden age, though, came between the 14th and 16th centuries when its busy *Pfingstmesse* (Whitsun fair) attracted traders from all over Germany. By 1327 the town had outgrown its old circular defensive moat, prompting the building of the present **Stadtmauer** with eleven towers, five gateways and two bastions. The wall is the most complete in Germany with 3km of its length intact; you can walk around the entire parapet in an hour (the **Reimlinger Tor**, the town's oldest gateway, provides a convenient access point). The wall, like most of the buildings in Nördlingen, was made out of the local moonrock-like deposits.

After the ramparts, head straight for the **Georgskirche**, the mighty parish church in the middle of the town which provides the best starting point from which to explore the **Altstadt**. This 15th-century late-Gothic hall church is Nördlingen's pride and joy. The highlight of the interior is the soaring Baroque **high altar**, resplendent with an ornate Crucifixion group believed to be the work of the celebrated sculptor Nikolaus Gerhaert van Leyden. The building's focal point, however, is the 89.5m-high **Daniel**, a steeple named after the illustrious Israelite leader of the Old Testament. You can climb up the 365 steps (*daily 9–dusk; adm DM2.50*) for a fine view of the town and the outlying villages of the Ries.

On the north side of the Georgskirche is the **Marktplatz**, where several municipal buildings compete with each other in gaudy brilliance. The 14th-century **Rathaus** wins by a long chalk, thanks largely to its magnificent exterior stone stairway with its four fluted columns of Gothic and Renaissance origin. Diagonally opposite, you'll find the 16th-century **Leihaus**, which houses the local tourist office. To the west is the three-storeyed, timber-framed **Brot- und Tanzhaus**, a former trading hall. On Baldinger Straße, which runs northwards from the Marktplatz past the **Gerberviertel** (Tanners' Quarter), is the former **Spital zum Heiligen Geist**. Established and richly endowed in the 13th century as the town's hospital and almshouse, with its own church, the complex now houses the **Stadtmuseum** (*closed till spring of 1995*) with an astonishingly fresh set of reredos panels that were originally crafted as the altarpiece for the Georgskirche by the local artist, Friedrich Herlin, and an interesting diorama of the Battle of Nördlingen of 1634 (*see* below). From here you can amble down along the semicircular **Herrengasse**, atop part of the razed town defences, to reach the Weinmarkt and the adjoining **Hallgebäude**, an old salt and wine storehouse of the 16th century. On its southeast edge the Weinmarkt blends into the Neubaugasse where you'll find one of the most attractive houses in town. The mellow reddish tones in the restored timber-framed façade of the 17th-century **Wintersche Haus** look magnificent when seen from a distance. Come closer, and you will marvel at the beautifully carved front door with Baroque arabesque embellishments.

If the idea of retracing the extraordinary geological history of the region appeals to you, the **Rieskrater-Museum** (*Tues–Sat 10–12, 1.30–4.30; adm DM5*) presents some fascinating insights. The museum occupies a 16th-century barn—in sharp contrast to its innovative displays. The staff can arrange geological tours of the Ries for interested groups.

Nördlingen's Türmer

Nördlingen has had its fair share of close shaves in several military conflicts. Twice during the Thirty Years' War, in 1634 and in 1645, the town was besieged by rival armies,

and twice these events culminated in fierce battles just outside the town. Not surprisingly, the burghers set great store by their walled defences and the guards who manned all five gates, and by the Daniel, which served admirably as the town's tallest watchtower. According to local lore, though, it was an alert woman of Nördlingen who saved the town from a raid by the Count of Oettingen in 1440. She apparently noticed a pig rubbing against one of the town's wooden gates, and, it being unlocked, the gate opened. Uttering the words *'So G'sell so!'*, she drove the animal off and was able to bolt the gate just in time. After that the woman's words became the password for Nördlingen's sentries. Nowadays the *Türmer* stand in for their erstwhile colleagues as night watchmen, taking it in turns to occupy the lookout post near the top of the Daniel. Every night, at half-hour intervals between 10pm and midnight, the traditional 'All's well!' rings out across the roofs of the slumbering town.

Where to Stay and Eating Out

Flamberg Hotel Klösterle, Beim Klösterle 1, ✆ (09081) 88054, ✉ (09081) 22740 (DM170–210). Opened in 1991, this stylish hotel combines two of the town's historic buildings, the eponymous former abbey building (1243) and the half-timbered *Pflug* (1420). The hotel is an intriguing example of medieval architecture blended with top-class hospitality. The restaurant, in the former abbey church, serves regional specialities.

Gasthof Zum Engel, Wembinger Str. 4, ✆ (09081) 3167 (from DM80). Pleasant converted brewery near the town walls. Meals DM20–30.

Around Nördlingen

Neresheim and Kaisheim

Two vivacious outbursts of Baroque architecture lie close to Nördlingen. At **Neresheim**, 19km to the southwest, the **Abteikirche St. Ulrich und Afra** was the final accomplishment of the Baroque architect Baltasar Neumann, who started rebuilding the abbey church of the Benedictine monastery in 1747. After his death in 1753, master masons from nearby Donauwörth concluded his work. The unusually airy and spacious interior, with domed ceilings and energetic ceiling frescoes by Martin Steinach, remains its main attraction. Six kilometres from Donauwörth lies the former Cistercian **abbey church** of **Kaisheim**. Smarting under the austerity of their monastic restrictions, the Cistercian monks put their all into just a small number of furnishings. There's a graceful Baroque high altar (1673) and some fine choir stalls. The wistful decoration that covers the organ parapet with cherubs, putti and drapery, makes a rare spot of near-opulence in the church.

Harburg

Harburg, 15km southeast of Nördlingen, is a pretty little town with creaky half-timbered houses on the River Wörnitz. What really draws the crowds to Harburg, however, is the imposing **Schloß** (*guided tours Tues–Sun 9–11.30, 1.30–5.30; adm DM8*), crowning a knob above the town. First mentioned in 1093, the Staufian castle was given to the loyal Counts of Oettingen in 1295, a privilege that became hereditary in 1407 (it is still owned by their descendants). Nowadays the rambling castle is one of the best preserved complexes of its kind in southern Germany—an architectural pot-pourri spanning seven centuries. The main courtyard is reached via a series of medieval defensive structures and is surrounded by some interesting functional buildings, such as the **Kastenhaus** dating from 1594, once a granary, later turned into stables and an armoury; and the **Burgtvogtei**, the 16th-century castle manor, that has been converted to an inn and small hotel. The 12th-century western keep, known as **Diebsturm** (Thieves' Tower), adjoins the courtyard and is the castle's oldest surviving structure. For many, the highlight is the treasures held in the **Fürstenbau** (*guided tour adm DM8*). This 16-century building contains the lavish art collection of past and present burgraves, including spectacularly carved masterpieces by Tilman Riemenschneider.

Höchstädt and the Battle of Blenheim

Leaving the main route of the Romantic Road at **Donauwörth**, the B16 takes you 30km southwest to Höchststadt, on the northern bank of the Danube. From the outside, there's little to suggest that there's anything remarkable about the town. However, the town is indelibly associated with the Churchills. On 13 August 1704, in a decisive battle of the War of the Spanish Succession, an Allied army under John Churchill, the Duke of Marlborough, combined with Habsburg troops under Prince Eugene of Savoy to defeat a Franco-Bavarian army. The actual site of the **Battle of Blenheim**, as it became known in the English-speaking world (hence Blenheim Palace in Oxfordshire), lies close to the village of **Blindheim** and is easily accessible from all sides. Nowadays a sombre **sword-shaped monument** not far from where the B16 leaves Höchstsadt towards Blindheim, as well as a small memorial stone in the village and a plaque on the walls of its cemetery, commemorate those who died in the battle. The **Heimatmuseum** (*first Sun in month 2–5; adm free*) in the former Rathaus of Höchstädt makes an essential supplement to a visit, as it includes two interesting dioramas and artefacts collected from the battlefield.

Dillingen

Ten kilometres further southwest along the B16, the restful town of Dillingen stretches gracefully along the Danube. The town dates from the 13th century, but soon developed as the ancestral residence of the prince-bishops of Augsburg. When in 1564 the town's university, founded as a college of Catholic theology 15 years earlier, was handed over to the Jesuit order, it soon became a centre of the Counter-Reformation in southern Germany.

Dillingen is dominated by Baroque Jesuit architecture, although the earlier structures of other monastic orders are in evidence as well. All the main buildings of interest are conveniently concentrated in a narrow quadrangle in the **Altstadt**, between Konviktstraße, Kardinal-von-Waldburg-Straße and Königstraße. Start your walk at the small square in front of the early Baroque basilica of the **Stadtpfarkirche St. Peter**. Pan the square and immediately your eye is caught by the 18th-century blue-gold column of the **Immaculata-Säule**, backed by the mellow russet portal of the early 18th-century **Franziskanerinnen-kirche Mariä Himmelfahrt**. Continue your stroll past the **Rathaus**, an amalgam of the original 15th-century town hall and a 17th-century patrician residence, and past the one-time **Dominikanerinnenkloster St. Ulrich** (now housing a school for girls), to the extensive complex of the **Jesuitenkolleg** and the 17th-century **Universität**. Following the suppression of the order of Jesuit priests in 1773 and the subsequent secularization of all church property in 1803, the Catholic university buildings nowadays serve as both a seminary for the Catholic church and a modern teacher-training college. Especially impressive is the **Goldener Saal** (*May–Oct Sat and Sun 10–4; adm DM1*), the erstwhile auditorium with resplendent Rococo interior, including the vivacious ceiling frescoes by the 18th-century artist Johann Anwander, visual hymns of praise to the Virgin Mary. Towards the end of the central faculty buildings, you'll reach the **Studienkirche**, whose converted Rococo furnishings came to be an inspiration to many churches in southern Germany simply because cohorts of Catholic priests went through the stringent seminary at Dillingen. Both the Studienkirche and the Goldener Saal have recently undergone painstaking restoration programmes.

Augsburg

Augsburg has been hoarding treasure for over 2000 years. Its Romanesque cathedral is outshone by the Gothic St Ulrich's, and both are eclipsed by the Renaissance Rathaus. Garlands of Baroque gables hang between Rococo palaces. The streets are so wide, that some look more like squares. A 17th-century Italian visitor enthused that the roads were wide enough to fit 10 wagons abreast. The host of luminaries connected with the city includes the Roman Emperor Augustus (after whom it was named), Hans Holbein the Elder and Younger, Martin Luther, Mozart (whose father was born here, and who often returned to give recitals) and the 20th-century engineers Rudolf Diesel and Willi Messerschmidt. Augsburg doesn't commemorate Messerschmidt because of his Nazi sympathies; and for a long time they also ignored another famous son, the left-wing playwright Bertolt Brecht, who dismissed his home-town as a bourgeois *Scheißstadt*.

Augsburg was founded by Tiberius (step-son of the Emperor Augustus) in 15 BC, and soon became a prosperous trading city on the Via Claudia Augusta, the road to Rome. By the 13th century it was a Free Imperial City, and reached its zenith in the 15th century with the rise to power of two local merchant families, the Fuggers and the Welsers. Despite being constantly locked in battles of one-upmanship with each other, they amassed fabulous amounts of money, and wielded the most extraordinary international influence. Between them they came to own entire countries in South America, propped up the financially ailing royal houses of Europe and made Augsburg the financial centre of the world. Their wealth put the Medicis' fortunes in the shade.

Yet as well as this grand heritage, Augsburg also has the world's first social housing complex (built by the Fuggers in 1514), charming alleys and crumbly stone houses. It is a university town with a warm café life that takes the hard gloss off its stately façade.

By car: Augsburg is on the A8, 60km northwest of Munich and 160km southeast of Stuttgart.

Car hire: Avis, Klinkerberg 31, ✆ (0821) 3 82 41.

By train: Augsburg is a busy rail junction. Over 90 trains a day can take you to and from all parts of Germany (Munich, ½hr ICE; Würzburg, 2hrs ICE; Frankfurt, 3 hrs). The **Hauptbahnhof** lands you west of the centre amidst unpromising modern buildings, but it is only a 15-minute walk to the Altstadt, past the tourist office and local bus station.

Public transport: A day ticket for the trams and buses costs DM5, though you are unlikely to need it unless you are staying in the suburbs.

Taxis: ✆ (0821) 35 025.

The main **tourist information office** is near the Railway Station, Bahnhofstr. 7, ✆ (0821) 50 20 70 (Mon–Fri 9–6, Sat 9–1). Its staff can supply you with maps and information, offer city tours and guided city walks in English and can book your accommodation. There is a smaller information office on Rathausplatz (open Mon–Wed 7.30–4, Thurs 7.30–5.30 and Fri 7.30–12).

Post office: Viktoriastr. 3 (near the main station).

Medical emergencies: ✆ 1 92 22.

Police: ✆ 110.

There are two big **folk festivals**—one at Easter, and the other at the beginning of September. Both have accompanying street markets in the Jakobviertel. The **Christkindlmarkt** during Advent is one of the best Christmas markets in Germany (after Nuremberg and Munich), and is especially renowned for the quality of its live music, and for its 'alternative' Christmas stalls selling environmentally sound and politically correct products.

The Rathausplatz

The city's elegant **Rathaus** is a good place to start your tour. Augsburg's 17th-century Master Builder, Elias Holl (1573–1646), was one of the most important architects of the German Renaissance. In 1614 Holl returned from a trip to Italy brimming with new ideas. His rhetoric was as skilful as his draughtsmanship. Within weeks he had persuaded the city council to rip down the old Gothic Rathaus, and commission him to build a more majestic expression of their might. Holl's monumental building, with its simple, clean proportions and twin onion-domed towers is a gem of civic architecture. Inside you'll find

Augsburg

400 metres
400 yards

N

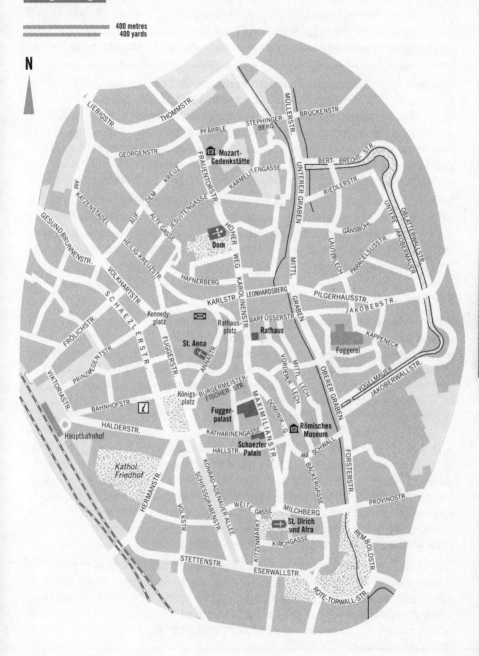

LIEBIGSTR.
THOMMSTR.
PFÄRRLE
STEPHINGER BERG
MÜLLERSTR.
BRÜCKENSTR.
GEORGENSTR.
Mozart-Gedenkstätte
FRAUENTORSTR.
KARMELITENGASSE
UNTERER GRABEN
BERT- BRECHT- STR.
RIEDLERSTR.
AM KATZENSTADEL
AUF DEM KREUZ
ALTE GASSE
JESUITENGASSE
HOHER WEG
GÄNSBÜHL
UNTERE JAKOBERMAUER
OBLATTERNWALLSTR.
GESUNDBRUNNENSTR.
HEILIG-KREUZSTR.
Dom
HAFNERBERG
LAUTERLECH
PARACELSUSSTR.
VOLKHARTSTR.
KARLSTR.
KAROLINENSTR.
LEONHARDSBERG
PILGERHAUSSTR.
JAKOBERSTR.
S C H A E Z L E R S T R.
Kennedy-platz
Rathaus-platz
BARFÜSSERSTR.
MITTL. GRABEN
KAPPENECK
FRÖLICHSTR.
St. Anna
ANNASTR.
Rathaus
Fuggerei
VORDERER LECH
MITTL. LECH
VOGELMAUER
JAKOBERWALLSTR.
PRINZREGENTENSTR.
FUGGERSTR.
Königs-platz
BÜRGERMEISTER-FISCHER- STR.
MAXIMILIANSTR.
DOMINIK.-G.
OBERER GRABEN
FORSTERSTR.
VIKTORIASTR.
BAHNHOFSTR.
Fugger-palast
Römisches Museum
HALDERSTR.
KATHARINENGASSE
AM SCHWALL
PROVINOSTR.
Hauptbahnhof
Schaezler Palais
HALLSTR.
Kathol. Friedhof
KONRAD-ADENAUER-ALLEE
SCHIESSGRABENSTR.
BÄCKERGASSE
HERMANSTR.
VOLKSTR.
WEITE GASSE
MILCHBERG
REMBOLDSTR.
St. Ulrich und Afra
KITZENMARKT
KIRCHGASSE
STETTENSTR.
ESERWALLSTR.
ROTE-TORWALL-STR.

the magnificent **Goldener Saal** (*free access during office hours*). Burnt out during an air raid in 1944, it was finally restored (to a somewhat over-pristine state) only in the 1980s. Every crinkle, twirl or protruding finial of the carved wooden ceiling has been lavishly gilded. Set among all this nutwood, limewood and gold, 14m above your head, are panels of richly coloured paintings depicting personal and civic virtues. Thankfully, grisaille wall frescoes and a gentle pastel-coloured marble floor help subdue the riot.

Next door to the Rathaus is the 70m-high **Perlachturm**. The foundations date from the 11th century, but most of the rest was built 200 years later to serve as a watchtower. Then in 1615 Elias Holl rounded it off with a dome to complement those on his Rathaus, and to house the bells from the old city hall. The word 'Perlach' comes from the Old German for 'bear dancing', and was probably the name of a Roman amphitheatre on the site. Today the bruins could jig to merry Mozart tunes played (*at 11am, 12 noon, 5pm and 6pm*) on a carillon installed in 1985 to celebrate Augsburg's 2000th anniversary.

In the middle of Rathausplatz stands the ornate **Augustusbrunnen**, a fountain built in 1594 to honour Augustus Caesar, the city's founder. In the summer, this vast square is packed with tables, benches and umbrellas, and becomes one enormous *Bierstube*, while on the far side of the square, in hushed, carpeted cafés, spruce pensioners keep each other company over *Kaffee und Kuchen*.

The Dom

A short walk northwards up Hoher Weg, brings you to the **Dom** (begun 1060)—a hotch-potch of different architectural styles. Shadows of the original Romanesque arches can be seen above later Gothic windows; the twin spires date back to the 11th century; the high altar was installed in 1962; and there is a bright and sugary Rococo chapel (a favourite for weddings) off the north aisle. The cathedral's art treasures should not be missed. The series of **Prophet Windows** (1140) is the oldest cycle of stained glass in the world. Five prophets are depicted in bold colours and simple designs. All (except David, who is crowned) wear the peculiar pointed hats that medieval Jews were required to wear. There is an outstanding **bronze portal**—most of it dating back to the 12th century—and an eloquent cycle of paintings by **Holbein the Elder**, showing scenes from the life of the Virgin. In the crypt you can pay your respects to past Bishops of Augsburg, who were being buried on this spot a century before work on the Dom was even begun. In the court-yard outside the Dom, are the ruins of the foundations of the ancient church of St John the Baptist (*c.* 960), which include a full-immersion font that was probably part of a secret Christian baptistry in the cellars of a 6th-century Roman house.

Just beyond the Dom, you'll find the **Mozart-Gedenkstätte** (Mozart House) at Frauentorstr. 30 (*Mon, Wed and Thurs 10–12 and 2–5, Fri and Sun 10–12; adm free*) which mainly documents the life of Mozart Senior, who was born in Augsburg but soon upped sticks for Salzburg and Vienna. Young Wolfgang frequently gave concerts in his father's home town, his recitals on one occasion coinciding with a heady 15-day romance with his cousin Bäsle.

Luther and the Fuggers

A wander back down Annastraße brings you to **St Anna's**, built as a Carmelite monastery in 1321. You would be forgiven for thinking that this church was the wrong way around, for a memorial chapel built in 1509 by Jakob Fugger and his brothers fills the *whole* of the west chancel and completely upstages the rest of the simple basilica. This **Fuggerkapelle**, with superb marble carving by Hans Daucher, became the touchstone for Renaissance design in Germany.

In the east cloister, a flight of simple wooden stairs (the **Lutherstiege**) leads up to a set of rooms housing an exhibition on the life of Luther. Unfortunately, most of the exhibits are textual, and commentary is in German only.

 In 1518 Luther was summoned to a court of the inqusition in Rome. His patron, Johann Friedrich of Saxony, fearing for the priest's life, persuaded the Pope to hold the hearing in Augsburg. The pretext was that an ailing Luther couldn't make the journey to Rome (though he did manage to walk the full 500km from Wittenberg to Augsburg, where he stayed at St Anna's). He was interrogated by Cardinal Cajetan at the home of Jakob Fugger between 12 and 14 October, but they couldn't reach an agreement. On 20 October, under threat of arrest, Luther slipped out of town.

At the next Diet, in 1530, the Augsburg Confession laid out the basic tenets of the Lutheran faith, but it wasn't until 1555, with the signing of the Peace of Augsburg that the struggle between the two churches in the Holy Roman Empire was resolved (*see* p.35). Later, St Anna's became a Lutheran church. Jakob Fugger, a fervent Roman Catholic who imported bands of Jesuits to try and tip the balance in Augsburg, must be turning in his monumental grave.

From here make your way across to Maximilianstraße, which leads south from Rathausplatz. Until 1957 Maximilianstraße was named after King Maximilian I Joseph of Bavaria. Then it was decided to rename the street after Emperor Maximilian I (1459–1519), a great lover of Augsburg. This odd gesture in effect changed nothing at all. Two very stylish 16th-century fountains grace the street—the first topped with a statue of Mercury, the second with a robust Hercules. They were designed by Dutch sculptor Adrian de Vries to symbolize Augsburg's merchants and master craftsmen respectively. Just before the Hercules fountain, at Maximilianstr. 36–38, is the conglomeration of three houses that formed the 16th-century **Fuggerpalast**. The building is still home to Fugger descendants, but you can nip around the back for a look at the **Damenhof**, a pretty little Italianate courtyard with arcades of Etruscan pillars, a musicians' balcony and traces of the original frescoes.

 The Fugger family fortune was largely established by Jakob Fugger the Rich (1459–1525). The youngest son of a *nouveau-riche* merchant family, he wanted to become a priest but at the age of 19, following the deaths of his father and older brothers, he was hauled back out of the monastery to run the family firm. He went off to Venice

for business training, and was so fired by the Italian way of life that on his return he almost single-handedly introduced the Renaissance to Germany. (The buildings he commissioned became models for the movement throughout the country.) He also brought with him double-entry book-keeping, took risks in buying up some flooded mines and ended up with monopolies over Hungarian copper, Austrian silver and Spanish quicksilver. Soon he had amassed a fortune that historians estimate was the equivalent of the combined assets of today's top ten multinational companies. The rulers of Europe came to him to borrow money to pay their armies, and for the bribes needed to put a new emperor on the throne. (The election of Emperor Charles V in 1519 was financially secured through 543,585 florins from the Fuggers and 143,333 florins from their arch-rivals the Welsers.) In return Jakob Fugger extracted concessions and favours that increased his wealth and power even more.

In his late forties he married a woman half his age. For 20 years he showered her with gifts and they entertained lavishly—but had no children. Jakob died in 1525, leaving his fortune to his nephew Anton. His wife remarried three weeks later—to some scandal, but very little surprise.

Anton ran the firm well, but lost his nerve a little over the dangerous trade with the Americas and the West Indies. (Charles V had given the Welsers control over Venezuela; the Fuggers were offered Chile and Peru, but declined as Anton felt that pirates and conquistadors made the venture too risky.) The family fortune gradually crumbled. Today's Fuggers own a bank and some property, but are not nearly as well off as their predecessors.

Further down Maximilianstraße (just opposite the Hercules Fountain) is the **Schaezler Palais** (*Tues–Sun 10am–5pm, Oct–April to 4pm; adm free*), built in 1770 for a wealthy silversmith. Inside is a compact Rococo ballroom, almost in its original resplendent shape with deep mirrors, glittering crystal chandeliers and a ceiling painting showing Europe as the centre of the world. Marie-Antoinette (who was on her bridal procession from Austria to France) popped in for three minuets during the grand opening ball, and the room at once became the social hub of Augsburg. Today the candles on the rows of chandeliers are lit only for an occasional Mozart concert.

Much of the Schaezler Palais is given over to a mediocre collection of Baroque art, but at the back it connects up with a 16th-century convent, now the **Staatsgalerie** (*times as above*). Here you can see a striking portrait of Jakob Fugger in his favourite Venetian brocade cap by Albrecht Dürer (1518), and a series of paintings of Roman basilicas (1499–1504) by Holbein the Elder and local artist Hans Burgkmair (1473–1531).

Maximilianstraße runs up to the church of **St. Ulrich und Afra**—a lofty Gothic structure with a Bavarian onion spire added in the 16th century. Shrines to Ulrich and Afra are inside, and three golden altars (1607) packed with saints and cherubim tower up above the choir. The adjacent **Ulrich Lutheran Church** used to be a sort of clerical souvenir shop, selling trinkets and indulgences, but after the 1555 Peace of Augsburg was given to the Lutherans as a gesture showing that they could live in happy harmony with the Catholics right next door.

The Jakobviertel and Fuggerei

If you duck east off Maximilianstraße, you come to the **Jakobviertel**, once the poorer part of town. Now, among the clutter of restored medieval houses and narrow streets, you find galleries, craftshops and museums. The **Römisches Museum** (Roman Museum) at Dominikanergasse 15 (*Tues–Sun 10–5, Oct–April to 4pm; adm free*) is housed in an old Gothic hall church. The highlight of the collection is an AD 2 bronze horse's head, probably part of an equestrian statue. The **Holbein Haus** at Vordere Lech 20 (*Tues–Sun 10–5*) commemorates its famous resident with a few documents, but is mainly used for contemporary art exhibitions.

Still smarting from the insults Brecht heaped upon them, the citizens of Augsburg only recently swallowed their pride and opened the **Brecht Haus**, Auf dem Rain 7 (*Tues–Sun 10–5, Oct–April to 4pm; adm free*). The playwright was born here in 1898, the son of a paper factory owner, and went off to study medicine in Munich in 1919, where he first tried his hand at theatre. The exhibition centres mainly on Brecht's life in Augsburg—which isn't the most enthralling part of his career.

Jakob Fugger wanted to be sure that he would go to heaven. Reliable sources had it that this was a difficult feat for a rich man—but that a good stock of prayers on the right side of the Doomsday Book could ease the passage. So in 1523 Fugger built a housing estate for Catholics who had been made poor 'through no fault of their own', setting the rent at one Rhenish guilder per annum—and one 'Our Father', one 'Hail Mary' and one 'Creed' daily, in his favour. Today the **Fuggerei** in Jakoberstraße is still financed and run by the Fugger family; residents pay DM1.72 rent a year (the equivalent of a Rhenish guilder) and still offer up the prescribed prayers for their benefactors.

The estate, designed by Thomas Krebs, is a model of social housing, way ahead of its time. Houses are separated by wide lanes; there are trees, fountains and individual gardens. The houses are divided into two parts, each with separate entrances: one tenant has the attic, the other the garden. Every bell pull is different to give front doors a little individuality.

Mozart's great-grandfather lived at No.14. He had been ostracized and reduced to poverty after burying the corpse of an executioner. Next door, at No.13, you can visit a house in its original state (*Mar–Oct 9–6; adm DM1*) to marvel at the ingenuity of the design. The bright front room (used as a workroom) has windows onto the street, and back into the kitchen. A special handle allows you to open the front door to customers without leaving the work bench. The stove that heats the workroom is loaded from behind the wall in the kitchen (to reduce the fire risk).

Upstairs in the bedrooms there are niches for candles (also to prevent fires). The cottages are cosy and compact, and modern residents look blissfully content—even though they have to put up with streams of staring tourists and pay a 50-Pfennig fine to the night watchman if they come home after 10pm.

expensive

Drei Mohren Hotel, Maximilianstr. 40, ✆ 51 00 31, ✉ 15 78 64 (DM274–340). Mozart, Goethe and any number of archdukes and princes have stayed here before you. This is the poshest address in town, though bland modernization has all but destroyed the old atmosphere.

moderate

Hotel Ost, Fuggerstr. 4–6, ✆ 3 30 88, ✉ 3 55 19 (DM160–185). A quiet hotel near the centre, with friendly management. The Bahnhof is a five-minute walk away, and there's a parking garage nearby. No restaurant.

Hotel Post, Fuggerstr. 5–7, ✆ 3 60 44 (DM130–150). Just across the road from the Hotel Ost, with décor that veers from the spartan to the impressively kitsch. The owner, Frau Weiss, is popular with the local American military for her motherly care and hearty cuisine.

inexpensive

Pension Georgrast, Georgenstr. 31, ✆ 5 02 61 (DM72–96). Very good value. It is central, quietly situated and even offers special deals on Chinese massage and health cures. No restaurant.

Bayerischer Löwe, Linke Brandstr. 2, ✆ 70 28 70 (from DM62). Among the cheapest and most cheerful of the group of *Pensions* in the northeastern suburb of Lechhausen. No restaurant.

Youth Hostel: Beim Pfaffenkeller 3, ✆ 3 39 09.

Eating and Drinking

Though it is technically in Bavaria, Augsburg is really the easternmost outpost of Swabia, and the cooking is appropriately refined. You'll find *Spätzle* (shredded noodles) with nearly everything. They are delicious straight from the pot, covered with brown butter and breadcrumbs or cheese and fried onions. *Zwetschgendatschi* is a local speciality so popular that it has earned Augsburgers their nickname ('*Datschiburgers*'). It is a yeasty lump of pastry smothered with plums and cinnamon sugar, and you'll find it in cafés all over town.

Restaurants and Taverns

expensive

Bistro 34, Hunoldsgraben 34, ✆ 3 92 94 (DM50). Crammed with junkshop furniture and draped with pearls and feather boas. It serves whatever inspires the Italian, Greek and Swabian chefs (the fillets of pork in Armagnac are delicious).

Welser Küche, Maximilianstr. 83, ✆ 3 39 30 (DM70). Hosts a nightly banquet where meals from Philippine Welser's original 16th-century cookbook are served.

moderate

7-Schwaben-Stuben, Burgermeister-Fischer-Str. 12, ✆ 31 45 63 (DM25–45). Popular tavern serving Swabian cuisine. While you are looking through the menu nibble on some of the delicious dark bread with *Griebenschmalz* (lard with chopped onion and apple).

Fuggerei-Stube, Jakobstr. 26 (DM25–45). At the Fuggerei, and one of the best places in town for Swabian food. Try *Krautspatzen* (noodles with bacon and sauer-kraut—surprisingly delicate, and far tastier than it sounds).

inexpensive

Bücher Pastet, Korneliusstraße. Restaurant in the cellar of a bookshop. For around DM7 you'll get the dish of the day (usually something delectably Swabian)—and can refill as many times as you like. They also serve a spicy home-brewed beer.

Bars and Cafés

Kreßlesmühle, Barfüßerstr. 4, ✆ 3 71 70. An arts centre in an old mill. *The* place to be if you're a student, school truant or jazz fan. There's a café (with a popular beer garden), live music (anything from blues singers to wandering Sephardic balladeers), and also good theatre and film.

Kahnfort, Riedlerstr. 11. A wooden chicken-run of a bar right on the river's edge. On summer's afternoons (for a small fee) you can make off in one of the boats bobbing underneath the windows.

Perlach Bar, tucked into the wall of the church at the Perlachturm, and over-looked by nearly everyone. A cupboard-sized-bar where you can sip a *Schnapps* on a freezing winter's afternoon.

Zeughaus, Zeugplatz. The beergarden is popular with thirty-somethings who are reluctant to shake off their student years. A restaurant inside serves good, inexpensive meals.

Café Eber, Rathausplatz. The best place to join the Datschiburgers at their favourite culinary pastime.

Landsberg

The town of Landsberg dates from a 12th-century castle of Henry the Lion which was built here to control the lucrative salt trade on the old road from Salzburg to Memmingen. The castle has long gone and what is left is a small town (40km from Augsburg on the Romantic Road), which rises steeply from the gushing water of the River Lech. The town is another beautifully preserved medieval site that seems stuck in the days of yore, with timber-framed houses. In this century, though, Landsberg has become indelibly associated with Adolf Hitler, as he spent nine months in the local prison following his unsuccessful *Putsch* of 1923—time that he put to use in writing *Mein Kampf.*

Tourist Information

The **tourist office** is in the Baroque **Rathaus**. Its free town map outlines the somewhat circuitous *Stadtrundgang.*

The **Rathaus** on the central Hauptplatz makes a good jumping-off point for a walk round the town. The floridly stuccoed Rococo façade of the town hall (home to the local tourist office) was designed and realized by Dominikus Zimmermann, architect of the Wieskirche (*see* below). Zimmermann settled in Landsberg from 1716 and was bürgermeister between 1749 and 1754. He was also in charge of building the **Johanneskirche** (1750–52) situated to the south of the Hauptplatz and modelled on his more famous pilgrimage church.

The signposted **Stadtrundgang**, a walk through the city devised by the tourist office, takes in the best of the sights, weaving down crooked alleys and beneath arches, and climbing upwards to the fortified wall, of which a stretch of around 300m, with a series of barbicans, survives intact. From the top of the wall you get views of red-tiled roofs huddled by the River Lech. Brightly coloured, roughcast shops and houses pop out of it like barnacles, and it has grown a few eccentric gateways—odd patchworks of different period styles. The most striking of these is the 15th-century Gothic **Bayertor** (*May–Oct 10–12, 2–5; adm DM1*), the town's heraldic emblem and one of best preserved of its kind in southern Germany.

Where to Stay

Hotel Goggle, Herkomer Str. 19–20, ℂ (08191) 3240, (08191) 324100 (DM140–250). Built on the base walls of an older hotel from 1670, it successfully captures the rich tradition of its predecessor.

Ludwig's Castles and the Wieskirche

Soon after Augsburg, the faint smudge on the horizon begins to resolve itself into the peaks and shadows of the Alps. As you travel nearer, the atmosphere seems to sharpen, there's a growing chill in the air and the countryside begins to erupt in rocky outcrops.

In the middle of the rolling fields that lead up to the foothills, you'll find the **Wieskirche** (which tourist brochures rather alarmingly refer to as 'The Church of our Flagellated Lord in the Meadow'). This is a pilgrimage church. The object of veneration is a wooden statue of Christ, which was rejected (as being too ugly) from the local Good Friday procession. Later it was found that, if you prayed hard enough, the figure shed real tears. Pilgrims flocked from afar, and in 1746 Abbot Marianus II decided to build a grand church to accommodate them. The result was one of the finest examples of Rococo architecture in Germany. The architect, Dominikus Zimmerman (*see* p.49), was so pleased with it that he came to live in nearby Landsberg for the rest of his life. Light streams in through the windows, reflects off the brilliant white walls and pillars and picks out the curls and licks of gilded stucco. Cherubs and angels peek out from behind garlands of foliage, and in the middle of an effervescent ceiling fresco (by J. B. Zimmerman), the resurrected Christ sits resplendent on a rainbow.

Sadly, despite its isolated setting, the Wieskirche swarms with tourists. There are clusters of coaches and souvenir kiosks all the way up to the door. You even have to endure piped music. When the church was finished in 1754, Abbot Marianus used his diamond ring to scratch into the window of the prelates' chamber the words: 'At this place abides happiness, here the heart finds peace'. He must be turning in his grave.

Just as you get to the Alpine foothills you come to Neuschwanstein and Hohenschwangau, two castles which once belonged to the dreamy, eccentric King Ludwig II of Bavaria (1845–86).

King Ludwig II of Bavaria

In the 19th century Bavaria was ruled by a fairytale King. He had piercing blue eyes and carefully curled dark locks. He built fantastical castles in the mountains and was so excited by German legends that he used to dress up and act them out with his friends. The official story has it that he was quite mad, and drowned himself in the Starnberger See—but exactly what happened in the last days of his life is obscured by half-truth and deceit on the part of his scheming ministers.

In Bavaria King Ludwig II has cult status. Perhaps his hopeless, self-destructive romanticism appeals to the national psyche. To foreigners he is known mainly as the builder of Neuschwanstein, the white castle made famous by the film *Chitty Chitty Bang Bang* and featured in countless German tourist leaflets. But Ludwig's real contribution to the world is a far more significant one. He appreciated and championed the operas of the composer Richard Wagner at a time when that alone would have been enough to have him certified. Without the king's sustained, enthusiastic and generous support it is doubtful that Wagner would ever have had the opportunity to produce the work he did.

Ludwig was born on 25 August 1845. Three years later his grandfather, King Ludwig I, was forced to abdicate following a scandalous affair with the 'Spanish' dancer Lola Montez (alias Mrs Eliza Gilbert, a British housewife who later ran off with, and bigamously married, an Old Etonian guardsman). The infant Ludwig's father became Maximilian II of Bavaria, but reigned for just 16 years, so it was at the tender age of 19 that the pretty young prince assumed the throne. He was fastidious about his appearance ('If I didn't have my hair curled every day, I couldn't enjoy my food,' he said) and enjoyed the costumes that came with his new role (though he sometimes paraded under a parasol with his helmet under his arm, so as not to spoil his coiffure). Mundane affairs of state, however, held little appeal, and the young king soon antagonized his cabinet.

Even as a toddler Ludwig had begun to reveal the proclivities that were later to seal his fate. His mother, Queen Marie, noted in her diary that the infant Ludwig loved art, would build churches and monasteries with his toy bricks, enjoyed dressing up (usually as a nun) and was always giving away his toys and money. As he grew older Ludwig came to revere the Bourbons of France, especially Louis XIV, the 17th-century 'Sun King'. The splendours of Versailles (which Ludwig visited in 1867) and the rich romance of German legends such as that of Lohengrin, the Swan Prince, inspired him to build three dream castles: Neuschwanstein (1869, *see* p.183), a shrine to Lohengrin, Tannhäuser and other medieval German heroes; Herrenchiemsee (begun 1878, *see* p.116), a mock Versailles; and Linderhof (1879, *see* p.123) with its magical grotto. All in all, these three castles cost around 31 million Marks. This was approximately the amount of the indemnity paid, without a peep of protest, to Prussia after the Seven Weeks' War—but Ludwig's frittering such money away on beautiful buildings put his ministers in a flap.

Another cause for ministerial complaint was the king's infatuation with Richard Wagner. Ludwig heard his first Wagner opera (*Lohengrin*) in 1861. In the words of an attendant courtier the music had 'an almost demoniacal' effect on the young prince, who became so convulsed with excitement that he seemed in danger of having an epileptic fit. At that time Wagner's music was considered by many to be cranky, ugly and even dangerous. Ten years later Mark Twain was to write (also of *Lohengrin*): 'The banging and slamming and booming and crashing were something beyond belief. The racking and pitiless pain of it remains stored up in my memory alongside the memory of the time I had my teeth fixed...the recollection of that long, dragging, relentless season of suffering is indestructible.' (He did admit that the now famous Wedding Chorus was 'one brief little season of heaven and heaven's sweet ecstasy and peace during all this long and diligent and acrimonious reproduction of the other place'.) Today Twain's opinion might still find some sympathizers. Certainly in the 1860s Ludwig's conviction that no one could 'possibly remain unmoved by this magical fairytale, by this heavenly music' was not a common one—though it also hints that the monarch (whose lack of musical ability had driven at least one teacher to despair) was captivated less by Wagner's music than by the world of fantasy the operas evoked.

As soon as he became king, Ludwig set about tracking down his hero. Wagner had gone into hiding. *Der Ring der Nibelungen* and *Die Meistersinger* were unfinished, all the leading opera houses had declared *Tristan* impossible to stage, and the extravagant composer had run up enormous debts. Cabinet Secretary Pfistermeister spent three weeks in pursuit of the elusive Wagner, who was certain that powerful creditors were on his tail. The hapless secretary travelled from Vienna through Switzerland and finally unearthed his quarry in Stuttgart. Wagner was whisked back to Munich for an emotional meeting with the king. An intense and passionate friendship developed between the two—amounting to far more than straightforward royal patronage: Ludwig worshipped the composer. Wagner wrote of Ludwig that 'he knows and understands everything about me—understands me like my own soul,' and later: 'He is like a god! If I am Wotan, then he is my Siegfried.' He wrote (to others) of the tremendous inspiration he derived from Ludwig, and the two kept up a relentless and gushing correspondence, even when they were seeing each other almost daily.

The king paid off Wagner's debts, set him up in a villa in Munich, granted him a stipend that exceeded that of a senior minister and promised him an enormous sum on completion of the *Ring*. Although the money that Ludwig lavished on Wagner was from his personal fortune, not state coffers, the cabinet became increasingly alarmed at the influence the composer wielded. Cabinet Secretary Pfistermeister and Minister-President von Pfordten (nicknamed Pfi and Pfo) connived to get rid of Wagner, and in the end they succeeded. In December 1865 Ludwig, convinced by Pfi and Pfo that his behaviour was alienating his subjects, asked Wagner to leave Munich, but the friendship continued at a distance, and the king continued to pour money into Wagner's projects, including the establishment of the Bayreuth Festival.

Ludwig's relationship with Wagner was almost certainly platonic. The king *was* a homosexual but, when he wasn't agonizing over what he considered to be a mortal sin and swearing himself to months of celibacy, he was in love with a succession of grooms, handsome cousins, and attentive *aides-de-camp*. In 1867 Ludwig had proposed to his cousin Sophie, the daughter of Duke Max in Bayern, but after postponing the wedding date a number of times he finally admitted that he couldn't go through with it and broke off the engagement. The only woman he had any real time for was Sophie's sister, the Empress Elizabeth of Austria (*see* pp.70–71). He loathed his mother, saying that her 'prose' destroyed his 'poetry'. He avoided her as much as possible and referred to her alternately as 'that old goose', 'the widow of my predecessor', or by an honorary title—'the Colonel of the Third Artillery Regiment'. Ludwig and Elizabeth, however, adored each other. They had been friends from childhood—she 'the dove', and he 'the eagle'—and they remained deeply attached until his death. Apart from Elizabeth, Wagner and a few long-lasting loves (notably his equerry Richard Hornig), Ludwig had few close friends. He was a shy and solitary figure who slept most of the day, and went for long, lonely rides in the dead of night. At Linderhof there was even a device which lowered his entire dining table into the kitchens, where it could be replenished with food so that the king could be quite alone when he ate.

More and more Ludwig began to inhabit his dream-world, increasingly neglecting affairs of state. He ran up huge debts building and decorating his castles, and had to borrow millions of Marks from the Bavarian State Bank. By 1884 there seemed a real possibility that Linderhof and Herrenchiemsee would be repossessed by creditors—but nothing could dissuade Ludwig from his mission. Finally, the cabinet decided that the king had to go. As Ludwig's brother, Otto, was insane, his mild-mannered uncle Prince Luitpold had to be persuaded to act as regent. The easiest way to ensure Luitpold's backing was to have Ludwig declared insane too.

There was a history of madness in the family. Apart from brother Otto (who had suffered from convulsions since childhood) there was a string of odd, bewildered souls on his mother's side, and also the Princess Alexandra—a highly strung aunt who was convinced that she had swallowed a grand piano made of glass. Ludwig's own bizarre behaviour was a rich source of evidence for a case to be made against him. Early in 1886 the Minister-President Freiherr von Lutz and some cabinet colleagues set about having Ludwig certified. A thick wad of 'evidence' was put together—much of it gossip from servants, many of whom had been dismissed and had a grudge against the king. The prominent alienist Dr Bernhard von Gudden certified Ludwig on the basis of this report, without having once examined his patient.

Certainly Ludwig was subject to violent outbursts of frenzied temper and was obsessively shy of the public; at banquets he would hide behind banks of flowers and have the band play so loudly that conversation was impossible. His admiration for the Bourbons gave him a taste for absolute monarchy: he once spoke of selling Bavaria and using the money to buy a kingdom which he could rule with supreme power. He occasionally demanded that he be dressed in full regalia (which had to be fetched from a strongroom in Munich) for his midnight rides; after reading a book on the Chinese court he went through a phase of demanding that servants prostrate themselves before him; he would mete out extraordinary medieval punishments ('Pluck out his eyes') to those who had offended him, though courtiers took these with a pinch of salt, and only pretended to carry them out. His nocturnal lifestyle, solitary habits and theatricality make him seem very odd indeed, but there is little hard evidence of true madness. Rather, Ludwig was a dreamy eccentric with the power, money and position to pamper his whims and make his fantasy world real. Naturally, he cast himself as king of this world, and demanded the deference that this implied. He could, and did, commission private performances of operas he loved, and have scenes he particularly enjoyed repeated again and again; build grottos, gardens and entire castles which made fairytales come to life; dress up and live for a while the life of one of his legendary heroes. But (much though he loathed his administrative role) he had an astute understanding of international affairs and was capable of rational, intelligent political argument, even at the height of his so-called 'madness'. He could also be disarmingly down-to-earth, and was adored by local peasants as the tall and handsome king who would suddenly appear from nowhere, plonk himself down next to some woodcutters and share their lunch, or chat knowledgeably about cattle with a cowherd.

The night that Dr Gudden and a deputation from the cabinet came to apprehend Ludwig was cold and rainy. The party arrived at Hohenschwangau around midnight, planning to cross the valley to neighbouring Neuschwanstein, where the King was staying, the next morning—but a loyal coachman cottoned on to what was happening and warned the king. When the officials (who had been feasting sumptuously) noticed that the coachman was missing, they suspected that the secret of their mission was out, and set off at 3am, in formal dress and somewhat the worse for wear, for Neuschwanstein. Here they found their paths blocked by the police, the fire-brigade and crowds of loyal locals who had come to protect their king.

The members of the commission were arrested, but the machinery of Ludwig's downfall was already in motion. Ludwig failed to heed advice either to flee to the Tyrol, or to appear in public in Munich in order to show that he was not mad, and on 12 June 1886 a second commission arrived to take him to the castle at Berg, on the Starnberger See. Ludwig was devastated, drinking heavily and threatening suicide. The next evening, though, he seemed calm enough to go for a walk in the grounds with Dr Gudden, unaccompanied by warders. The two never returned. Later that night both of their bodies were fished out of shallow water at the edge of the lake. Exactly what happened remains a mystery. Perhaps Ludwig attempted suicide, and Gudden drowned while trying to save him—or maybe Ludwig vengefully murdered Gudden, but suffered a heart attack while doing so. (He *was* overweight, but also a good swimmer—so it is hard to believe that he could drown in just a few feet of water.) Whatever the explanation, Ludwig's death was tragic and pointless. The Empress Elizabeth, who perhaps understood him better than anyone, burst out when she heard the news: 'The king was not mad; he was just an eccentric living in a dream-world. They might have treated him more gently...'

Towards the end of his life, Ludwig became preoccupied with building grand, theatrical castles (*see* also pp.116 and 123). The king himself drew up plans for **Neuschwanstein** (*April–Sept 8.30–5.30, Oct–Mar 10–4; adm DM8*), with the help of a stage designer rather than an architect. Work was begun in 1869 and went on right up to Ludwig's deposition in 1886. The sparkling white Schloß, with its sprinkling of spires and turrets, became a prototype for Walt Disney fairytale castles. Neuschwanstein opened as a museum three weeks after Ludwig's apparent suicide, and has been a tourist trap ever since. Notices command you to obey all members of staff, not to stray from your tour group and warn that you are not guaranteed a tour in the language of your choice. You are churned through the castle in groups of 60, as guides mechanically reel off their spiel in 35 minutes flat (probably about half as long as you waited in the queue for a ticket). Then it's off down the hill and up the other side to Hohenschwangau to start all over again.

For all that, Neuschwanstein is well worth the battle. The castle is ingeniously situated. From one side you look out across flat grassland to the shimmering Alpsee; other windows open straight onto an Alpine gorge with bounding cascades. You slip giddily from stagy Byzantine halls into heavily carved wooden dens. (Fourteen woodcarvers toiled for nearly five years just to finish the king's bedroom.) Corners, windows and doorways are draped in rich brocades (usually in Ludwig's favourite blue) and the walls are painted with scenes from the legends that inspired Wagner's operas.

Hohenschwangau (*same times and prices*) is not as impressive. King Maximilian II (Ludwig's father) rebuilt it from the ruins of a 12th-century castle in the 1830s. It was here that Ludwig grew up and spent much of his reign. (He only ever stayed in the fantasy castle across the valley for six months.) Lohengrin, the Swan-King, is supposed to have lived in the original Schloß. Ludwig was obsessed with swans, and with the legend (*see* p.180). He loved to dress up as Lohengrin, and often got Prince Paul von Thurn und Taxis (a young favourite) to act out the story in a swan-shaped boat on the Alpsee, while a band played appropriate snippets from Wagner's opera.

For the most part, the rooms in Hohenschwangau are tame, rather homely Neo-Gothic. When Ludwig became king he changed the ceiling fresco in the Royal Bedroom from a day to a night sky—with an artificial moon and twinkling stars lit by lanterns from behind. This bedroom was the scene of a fracas between a young Ludwig and the seasoned actress Lila von Bulyowsky. Afterwards, *she* claimed that she had been shocked by the nude women in the murals and, besides, would never dream of seducing a mere boy. *He* claimed that she had chased him around the room. They both said that they spent most of the evening sitting on the bed reciting *Egmont*—up to the scene of the kiss.

Where to Stay and Eating Out

Of the three *Gaststätten* that have been built next to the Wieskirche, the **Moser** is the best value. Like the others, it serves up Bavarian tourist favourites, with lots of cheese and beef from the ubiquitous Allgäu cows.

The comfortable **Schloßhotel Lisl**, Hohenschwangau, © (08362) 8 10 06, ② (08362) 8 11 07 (DM100–240) is in the valley between Ludwig's castles, and has good views of both. It sets itself high standards, despite being in such a popular location, and staff are attentive and courteous. The hotel has a beer garden, and two restaurants serving good Bavarian food. In the nearby village of Schwangau, the cosy **Pension Neuschwanstein**, Schwangau, © (08362) 82 09 (DM90) has a perfect view across to Neuschwanstein and the Alps. It is in the style of a traditional Bavarian Alpine chalet, so all rooms have a small wooden balcony (though not every one has a view). The café downstairs serves tasty home-made cakes.

Eastern Bavaria

From a natural fountain in a palace garden near the Black Forest, the River Danube flows swiftly eastwards across Germany on its route to the Black Sea. One of the most captivating stretches is in eastern Bavaria, just before the river crosses the border into Austria. It wends its way through fertile meadows, glides under medieval bridges, past castles and monasteries and through the wealthy merchants' city of Regensburg. Then it flows past the Bavarian Forest—the largest natural wilderness in Europe—before slipping by the Italianate town of Passau and out of Germany.

During the Cold War this eastern corner of Bavaria, wedged between the Alps and Czechoslovakia, was all but ignored by the Germans themselves, let alone foreign visitors. Today it is still removed from mainstream tourism and offers intriguingly different architecture, unrivalled natural beauty and glimpses of a way of life that has barely changed this century. Folk traditions and festivals thrive here as nowhere else in Germany, and people participate for their own enjoyment rather than as a performance for tourists.

Regensburg

Regensburg is a mosaic of romantically crumbly plasterwork in yellow ochre, pale green, faded pink and terracotta, with the odd sooty bump of Roman wall and flounce of medieval stonework. Despite an august history as an important trading and administrative centre, it is an intimate, lived-in old slipper of a town—its fabric patched, darned and lovingly restored, but never charmlessly pristine.

Modern Regensburgers prefer to inhabit old buildings, rather than simply revere them. As you trundle your trolley through the supermarket, you may have to manoeuvre around Romanesque pillars; a dress shop changing-room might be wedged under a Gothic arch; the deli across the road was probably once a chapel. In the early evenings, as the lights come on in first-floor apartments, you can glimpse vaulted ceilings, rich Gothic carving and dark panelled walls.

A university town with first-rate breweries, Regensburg brims with good cheer. Visitors from Charlemagne to Mozart and Goethe have been struck by its felicitous position on the Danube. Some choice museums and the angelic Domspatzen (literally: cathedral sparrows; a world-famous boys' choir) add to the attraction.

History

The French call Regensburg *Ratisbonne*, from the old name of Radasbona, which suggests early Celtic origins. But the first known settlement at this point on the Danube was **Castra Regina**, a Roman fortress established by Emperor Marcus Aurelius in AD 179. Despite hostility between the Romans and surrounding Celtic and Teutonic peoples, there

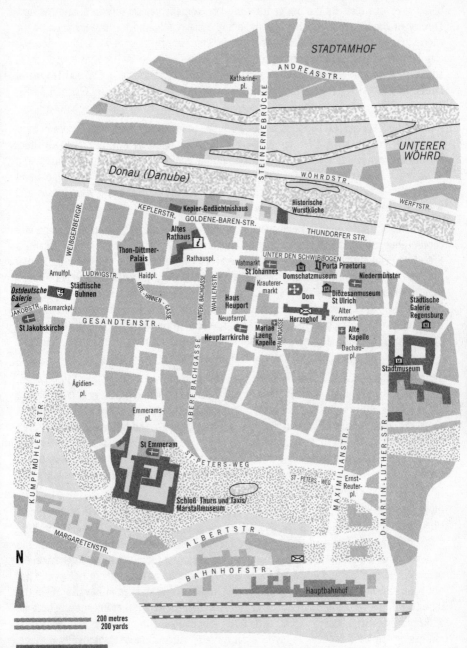

STADTAMHOF

ANDREASSTR.

Katharine-
pl.

UNTERER
WÖHRD

Donau (Danube)

WÖHRDSTR.

WERFTSTR.

KEPLERSTR.

Kepler-Gedächtnishaus

Historische
Wurstküche

GOLDENE-BAREN-STR.

THUNDORFER STR.

Altes
Rathaus

WEIBGERBERGR.

Thon-Dittmer-
Palais

Rathauspl.

Watmarkt

UNTER DEN SCHWIBBOGEN

Porta Praetoria

Arnulfpl.

LUDWIGSTR.

Haidpl.

St Johannes

Domschatzmuseum

Niedermünster

Ostdeutsche
Galerie

Städtische
Buhnen

Krauterer-
markt

Dom

Diözesanmuseum
St Ulrich

JAKOBSTR.

Bismarckpl.

Haus
Heuport

Herzoghof

Alter
Kornmarkt

Städtische
Galerie
Regensburg

St Jakobskirche

GESANDTENSTR.

Neupfarrpl.

Mariae
Laeng
Kapelle

Alte
Kapelle

Neupfarrkirche

Stadtmuseum

Dachau-
pl.

Ägidien-
pl.

Emmerams-
pl.

St Emmeram

ST-PETERS-WEG

ST-PETERS-WEG

Ernst-
Reuter-
pl.

Schloß Thurn und Taxis/
Marstallmuseum

MARGARETENSTR.

ALBERTSTR.

N

BAHNHOFSTR.

Hauptbahnhof

200 metres
200 yards

KUMPFMÜHLER STR.

OBERE BACHGASSE

UNTERE BACHGASSE

WAHLENSTR.

ROTE-HAHNEN-GASSE

PFAUENGASSE

MAXIMILIANSTR.

D-MARTIN-LUTHER-STR.

Regensburg

must also have been some fraternizing, for soon a mixed-race tribe, the Baiuvarii, outnumbered everyone else. By the 6th century the last Romans had disappeared, and the new **Duchy of Bavaria** was ruled by the Agilolfing dynasty—Frankish rulers installed by the Merovingian kings. The Agilolfingers made Regensburg their seat, and under the Carolingian king **Charlemagne** (who resided here from 791 to 793) it remained a city of administrative and ecclesiastical importance, playing host to the occasional **Imperial Diets**. When the Diets became permanent in 1663—in effect the first German parliament—the Regensburg Rathaus was chosen as their venue, and remained so until 1803.

Meanwhile, because of its position on the Danube (an important east–west European thoroughfare) and near the Brenner Pass over the Alps to Italy, Regensburg flourished. Medieval Regensburger coins have been found from Venice to the Scandinavian coast, and as far away as Kiev. Arbeo of Freising, an 8th-century monk, marvelled at the 'gold and silver, purple cloths, iron, wine, honey and salt' that filled the city's warehouses and weighed down the boats on the Danube.

 Later a brisk trade in slaves and weapons further swelled local coffers to make 13th-century Regensburg the largest and richest city in south Germany. By the time it became a **Free Imperial City** in 1245 Regensburg was also a centre of culture and learning. Two of the first epic poems in German, the *Kaiserchronik* and the *Rolandslied*, originated here. Generations of wealthy merchants built show-piece townhouses—first cosy Romanesque, then more swanky Gothic. Fortified mansions with high towers, inspired by Italian city villas, rose up all over town. At the peak of Regensburg's prosperity there were over 60 of them, and around 20 still survive. (Apart from a battering at the hands of Napoleon, the city has been relatively unscathed by war.)

The Wittelsbachs succeeded to the duchy in 1180, and moved the capital first to Kelheim, and then to Landshut and Munich. New trade routes bypassed Regensburg and by the end of the 14th century the town had been overtaken as a trading centre by Nuremburg and Augsburg. Regensburg has never forgiven the Wittelsbachs. The bitterness became even more intense in the 19th century when the rulers plundered Regensburg's monasteries and churches for art treasures to add to their private collections and to top up state funds. Locals speak of 'the largest art-robbery of the 19th century': 'They would have taken the cathedral if they could have moved it.'

In 1853 the relatively poor town scraped together what money it could to build a Royal Villa, in an attempt to lure the Wittelsbach monarchs for at least an occasional visit. King Ludwig III treated this gesture of apparent reconciliation with contempt, dismissing the little palace as 'an aviary' and finally carting off its furniture too. Even today Regensburgers bristle at the fact that the Royal Villa is neglected and used as government offices and has not been restored as a museum (like other Wittelsbach residences in Bavaria). One the other hand, they counter brightly, the centuries of neglect meant that Regensburg became a 'Sleeping Beauty', unable to replace its historic buildings with new ones and ignored by rampaging armies. So today the town remains pretty much in its original medieval shape, although the establishment of the university in 1967, new BMW, Toshiba and Siemens factories and a blossoming tourist industry have provided an awakening kiss.

By car: Regensburg is about 120km from Munich (on Autobahn 9 and 93) and 100km from Nuremberg (on Autobahn 3).

Car hire: Sixt Budget, Im Gewerbepark 6, Gebäude A1, ☎ (0941) 401 035.

Mitfahrzentrale: Jakobstr. 12, ☎ (0941) 57400.

By train: Trains run frequently to Munich (1½hrs) and Nuremberg (1hr), and seven times daily to Cologne (5¾hrs) and to Vienna (4¼hrs). The **Hauptbahnhof** (information ☎ (0941) 19419) is about 15 minutes' walk from the centre of town (straight down Maximilianstraße).

Boat trips: Gebrüder Klinger (Steinerne Brücke, ☎ (0941) 55359) offer excursions and round trips on the Danube (a trip to Walhalla and back takes about two hours, a one-way cruise to Passau takes most of the day). You can also go on short city cruises to see Regensburg's skyline, and brave the whirlpools under the Steinerne Brücke (DM7.50). City trips leave from near the Historische Wurstküche and most Danube cruises leave from Werfstraße on the island of Untere Wöhrd. Short trips through the Donaudurchbruch gorge leave from Kelheim (20km southwest of Regensburg off the B16, or rail to Saal then DB bus). Boats run daily from mid-May to early September (9.15am, 10am then every 30 minutes until 5pm; DM7 return).

Public transport: Regensburg is compact, so everything you're likely to want to see is within easy walking distance. If you do find that you need buses you can pick up a route plan from the information office at Ernst-Reuter-Platz 2 (near the station).

Taxis: ☎ 57000.

Tourist office: Altes Rathaus, ☎ (0941) 507 2141 (Mon–Fri 8.30–6, Sat 9–4, Sun 9–12).

Post office: Main post offices are on Domplatz and next to the Hauptbahnhof.

Police: ☎ 110.

Medical emergencies: ☎ 19222 or 73073.

Market days: Fruit and vegetable market, Alter Kornmarkt and Neupfarrplatz (Mon–Fri 6–12). Flower market, Altdorferplatz (Mon–Sat 6–12).

The biggest bash of the lot is the **Altstadt Festival** (held in the summer) with jugglers and street theatre, a morality play about Emperor Charles V and Barbara Blomberg (*see* below), folk music and loads of food and drink.

There are also two big **beer festivals**, the *Frühjahrsdult* (two weeks in May) and *Herbstdult* (two weeks in Aug/Sept). Of the many annual music festivals the **Bach-Woche** (Bach week, June or July) is the most renowned, and the **Bayerisches Jazz-Weekend** (July) is the jolliest, with up to 50 amateur jazz bands blasting away in bars, squares and normally secluded courtyards. As well as the usual **Christmas Market** (on Neupfarrplatz), there is a special **Crafts Christmas Market** on Haidplatz, where you can buy local carving, weaving and all types of hand-made gifts. The **Domspatzen** (cathedral choir) perform right through the year, with special concerts at the Christian festivals.

Around the Cathedral

Regensburg's giant **cathedral**—the finest Gothic church in south Germany—looms over the town's low red rooftops, looking rather as if it had been dropped there by accident. Construction began soon after 1260 on the site of an earlier Romanesque building but, as with so many German Gothic churches, it was only completely finished when the twin towers went up in the 19th century.

In the cathedral's back courtyard is the **Eselsturm** (Donkey Tower), a remnant of the original Romanesque church, called after the donkeys who used to wind their way up the ramps inside carrying building material. The architect of this church made a bet with the builder of the Steinerne Brücke that he would finish first (*see* 'Along the River' below). He lost rather dismally: the bridge was finished in 11 years, long before the cathedral. If you look up on to the roof of the Eselsturm, you can see a little statue of the hapless architect. He threw himself off the tower when he lost the bet.

Work on the present cathedral came to a complete halt for 100 years during the Reformation, when the Protestant city fathers wouldn't grant the bishops any money. When work resumed in the 17th century, the interior was decorated according to the new Baroque fashion—which meant that all the medieval stained-glass windows were replaced with clear glass. Recent restoration work has tried to recapture the old Gothic mood, and all that remains from the Baroque period is a splendid gold and silver altar. One set of 14th-century windows was left (in the south transept), containing parts of windows (exquisitely made with fingernail-sized pieces of glass) from the original Romanesque church. Across in the north transept is a modern window in a bold, rather ethnic design. This caused a local rumpus when it went up in 1986—people said it looked like a totem pole. Other highlights of the church include 13th-century statues of the Annunciation, with a beaming Gabriel and suitably stunned Mary, both wrapped in swathes of perfectly carved cloth; and two niches at the western nave entrance containing grotesque little figures of the Devil and his grandmother.

To see the **cloisters** you must go on a guided tour (*May–Oct Mon–Sat 10am, 11am and 2pm, Sun 12 and 2; Nov–April Mon–Sat 11, Sun 12; adm DM2.50*). This is worth it for a look at the **Allerheiligenkapelle**, a graceful Romanesque chapel with traces of original 12th-century frescoes, and the 11th-century **Stephanskapelle** which still has its original altar (with openings at the base where the faithful would pop in notes with requests to their saint, whose relics lay inside). On the north side of the cathedral, the **Domschatzmuseum** (Cathedral Treasures Museum) (*April–Oct Tues–Sat 10–5, Sun 11.45–5; Dec–Mar Fri and Sat 10–4, Sun 11.45–4; adm DM2*), housed in a former bishop's palace, has richly embroidered vestments dating back to the 11th century and rooms of sacramental treasures—including some fine Jugendstil pieces. The **Diözesanmuseum St. Ulrich** (*April–Oct Tues–Sun 10–5; adm DM2, DM3 for joint ticket*), around the back of the cathedral, is worth a visit for the building itself, a 12th-century court chapel. The supremely elegant arches inside are covered in ornamental frescoes from the 16th to 17th centuries. Most notable of the collection of paintings and sculptures to be seen here is the aptly named *Beautiful Madonna* by the great Regensburg painter Albrecht Altdorfer (1480–1538).

Altdorfer's Madonna once hung in the tiny Gothic church of **St. Johannes**, just at the entrance to the cathedral and formerly its baptistry. Early in 1992 the priest in charge of St. Johannes decided that its tower needed a clock and, much to the consternation of the purists, he raised the money and put one up—a rather elegant timepiece complete with musical bells. Across the square, directly opposite the cathedral, is a former patrician palace, the **Haus Heuport**. In the porch you can see the 14th-century carvings of a wicked seducer (with a snake crawling out of his back) luring a virgin with an apple. The maid has just spilt her cup of oil. The exact history of the statues isn't known, but love letters (written in Latin), found buried under the stairs just a few months before this guide went to print, might throw some light on the matter.

A few strides south brings you to Neupfarrplatz. Stranded on a concrete island in the middle of this expanse of tarmac and paving is the **Neupfarrkirche**, a rather plain church built on the site of a synagogue which had been destroyed in 1519. Just before the church was finished the city council adopted the Reformation, so this became Regensburg's first Protestant church. Nearby, on Pfauengasse (just off the south side of Domplatz) through an unassuming little door, is Regensburg's smallest chapel, the **Mariae Laeng Kapelle**. In the 17th century the notion arose that if you wrote out your prayer on a piece of paper as long as Mary, your request would be granted. The Church didn't approve, but the belief proved tenacious and the chapel is still cluttered with flapping notes and framed messages of thanks.

A walk back eastwards across the Domplatz brings you to the Alter Kornmarkt, where you'll find the **Herzoghof** (Ducal Court), a 13th-century mansion with a stone tower, probably the site of the first Agilolfinger residence (nowadays it belongs to the Post Office). On the south side of the Alter Kornmarkt is the **Alte Kapelle**, a sober church from the outside, but a Rococo riot within; while off the northern end of the square is the **Niedermünster**, a Romanesque basilica, now the cathedral parish church. Recent excavations have uncovered Merovingian, Carolingian and even Roman predecessors (these can be viewed by appointment only, © 560 200). Down towards the river, on Unter den Schibbögen, you can see the heavy stone blocks of **Porta Praetoria**, once the northern gate of the Roman fort. Part of the tower and one of the arches are still preserved.

Along the River

After the cathedral, Regensburg's most prominent landmark is the **Steinerne Brücke**, a stone bridge of 16 graceful arches that spans the Danube. It was built between 1135 and 1146 in preparation for a crusade (the wooden bridge it replaced would have collapsed under the massed ranks of a departing army). The builder supposedly made a pact with the Devil. If the Devil helped him to win his bet with the cathedral's architect by finishing the bridge first, then the first soul that crossed it would be despatched immediately to Hell. The wily builder won his bet, and foxed Satan too: first to cross the bridge was a donkey. As the only strong and defendable river-crossing along the entire length of the Danube at the time, the Steinerne Brücke contributed greatly to Regensburg's success as a trading town. Two of the three **gates** on the bridge were blown up by Napoleon, but you can see the third—which he left intact as a fitting frame for his triumphal entry into the city. The bridge still rests on its original foundations—sturdy piles of stone that have never had to be repaired and that confuse the powerful Danube into a series of whirlpools. Legend had it that only a virgin could sail across these rapids and survive. Undaunted by this, local companies offer boat trips across them.

Alongside the gate is the **Salzstadel** (City Salt Store, now a restaurant), built between 1616 and 1620. Boats carried the precious 'white gold' along a canal that went right into the building. Inside you can see the lift shaft up which the salt was hauled to safe storage. If you look carefully at the old wooden beams in the ceiling, you'll see that they are still encrusted with white crystals. Next door is the **Historische Wurstküche** (*see* 'Eating and Drinking' below), a sausage kitchen probably built as the bridge workers' canteen. Mozart munched the delicious Regensburger *Wurst* here, and lodged across the way in the **Zum Weissen Lamm** (as did Goethe some years later).

A short walk west along the river brings you to Keplerstraße, named after Johannes Kepler (1571–1630) whose work on planetary motion ranks him with Copernicus as a founder of modern astronomy. He lived on and off in Regensburg throughout his life, and died in the house at No.5, now the **Kepler-Gedächtnishaus** (*guided tours Tues–Sat 10am, 11am, 2pm and 3pm, Sun 10 and 11; adm DM2.50*), which contains a less than riveting collection of period furniture and instruments, and displays on Kepler's life and works. Also on Keplerstraße, however, is the **Runtinger Haus**, one of the best preserved Regensburg patrician palaces. It was built for the Runtinger family around 1400. Matteus Runtinger joined together two older houses by building a grand banqueting hall, seating nearly 120 (it is still hired out for grand parties) and had his architect copy features of Italian villas he had seen on his travels. Unfortunately, you can't visit the house, which is now the offices of the Bavarian Monuments Bureau. Rich merchants such as Runtinger, bringing back these new architectural ideas from Italy, sparked off a fashion for **fortified mansions** with solid castle-like towers. The towers were (like the number of horses you had) merely a status symbol: most were completely empty, save for a chapel at ground level. The houses were built around courtyards, which were entered through an arch large enough to drive a coach through, and closed off by a heavy wooden door. All around town you can glimpse these courtyards—often with Italianate first-floor loggias.

The Merchant Quarter

The **Altes Rathaus**, on Rathausplatz just west of the cathedral, was the centre of medieval Regensburg. The oldest section was built in the mid-13th century. A banqueting hall was incorporated in about 1360, and a Baroque eastern wing was added in the early 18th century. From the outside the Rathaus is an unassuming building with just one flourish—a decorative Gothic balcony from which the Holy Roman Emperor would wave to a respectful populace. The square itself was the scene of much imperial pomp. When Ferdinand III was crowned in the 16th century, the streets as far as the cathedral were covered in red, white and yellow cloth, coins were thrown to the crowd and a fountain gushed red and white wine.

To see the magnificent **interior** of the Rathaus you need to go on a guided tour (*May–Sept Mon–Sat 3.15pm in English; Mon–Sat 9.30, 10.30, 11.30, 2, 3, 4 and Sun 10, 11, 12 in German; adm DM3, tickets from the tourist office—ask for* Reichstagmuseum Führung). The highlight of the tour is a visit to the **Imperial Hall** (once the banqueting chamber) where the Perpetual Imperial Diet of the Holy Roman Empire sat from 1663 to 1806. It is a small, but sumptuously decorated room with an impressive free suspended wooden ceiling, and is laid out just as it was when nobles from around the empire came to wrangle about imperial policy. There is a simple canopied chair for the emperor, and punishingly hard, colour-coded benches (green for princes, red for electors) for the rest. The tour also includes a well-equipped **Torture Chamber** (torture was only abolished in 1806).

The streets around the Rathaus still follow Roman and medieval lines. **Wahlenstraße**, south of Rathausplatz, and the surrounding alleys, such as Untere-Bachgasse, Obere-Bachgasse and Kramgasse are the most rewarding spots for looking at historic city architecture. Wahlenstraße is the city's oldest street. Here you will find the **Goldener Turm**, the highest remaining patrician tower (now with a wine bar at the top). Obere-Bachgasse 7 was the painter **Albrecht Altdorfer's house**, and at No.15 are the remains of one of the **private chapels** that used to grace the merchants' towers.

Obere-Bachgasse, at its northern end, becomes Untere-Bachgasse. From here, if you duck down the quaint little medieval alley of Hinter der Grieb, then along Rote-Hahnen-Gasse, you come to **Haidpaltz**. This vast square was once a jousting arena and the scene of a bloody battle in the 10th century between one Krako the Hun and a local hero called Dollinger. Dollinger won, and earned himself (as well as the usual purse of gold) immortality in the form of the Dollinger Ballad, still recited today. These days Haidplatz is the stomping ground of scruffs with ghettoblasters.

On the northern end of the square is the former inn **Zum Golden Kreuz**, which from the 16th to the 19th century was the grand lodging place of princes visiting the town to attend the Diet. The 46-year-old **Emperor Charles V** caused tongues to wag when he used the hotel as a trysting place during his affair with the local teenage beauty **Barbara Blomberg**. One of the results of the liaison was a son, Juan de Austria, who was born here in 1547. He banished his mother to a nunnery (she had continued her errant ways long after Charles V died) and went on to become an heroic soldier and Governor of the Netherlands. Further along the square is the big Neoclassical **Thon-Dittmer Palace**, which unites several earlier Gothic houses and is now an arts centre with an elegant wood-panelled concert hall. The large courtyard is surrounded by graceful Renaissance galleries and is used in the summer for outdoor performances.

A few minutes' walk west of Haidplatz (along Ludwigstraße, then down Drei-Mohren-Straße and across Bismarckplatz) is the mysterious old **St. Jakobskirche**. It is also known as the *Schottenkirche* (Scots' Church) after the Irish monks who founded it in 1090. (The Irish were at that time referred to as *Schotte*—ironically the monastery became a Scottish one in the 16th century, and remained so until its dissolution 300 years later.) The Romanesque portal is covered in puzzling pagan-like designs. The whores and hangmen that crowd together with mermaids, monsters and more conventional Christian iconography defy modern attempts at interpretation. The two most feasible theories are that the carvings depict a scene from the Last Judgement, or tell the story of the original Irish monks' voyage across the seas in answer to Charlemagne's call. The dim interior, with its low arches and oddly carved pillars, evokes an early Christianity, rich with ancient rites and rituals. In the Byzantine apse is a carved 12th-century crucifixion group with a dramatically miserable Virgin and Mary Magdalene.

Further west at Dr.-Johann-Maier-Str. 5, but worth the extra 10 minutes' walk, is the **Ostdeutsche Galerie** (East German Gallery) (*April–Sept Tues–Sat 10–1 and 2–5, Sun 10–1; Oct–Mar Tues–Sat 10–1 and 2–4, Sun 10–1; adm DM2.50; Bus 11 or 6*), an interesting collection of 19th- and 20th-century paintings, graphics and sculpture by artists who lived or worked in the former East Germany. As well as pieces by such notables as Otto Dix, Lovis Corinth and the expressionist Karl Schmidt-Rottluff, there is some odd, rather kitschy surrealist work from the 1960s and 1970s. There is also a good collection of early 20th-century sculpture, which includes Käthe Kollwitz's poignant *Soldatenfrauen* (1937).

South of the Centre

Obere-Bachgasse leads south to Emmeramsplatz, which is dominated by the church of the **St. Emmeram** monastery, founded in the 8th century on the site of an old Roman church, and for centuries one of the most important centres of learning in Europe. In the 19th century the monastery was secularized. Its new owners, the Princes von Thurn und Taxis (*see* below) kitted it out with such new-fangled inventions as flushing toilets, hot and cold running water and electric lights. The church itself, however, remains in use. Part of the interior was splendidly reworked in 1730 by those famous Baroque designers, the Asam brothers—though the older parts of the church (most notably the 12th-century vestibule) have more charm and mystique. Around the right-hand side of the main altar you can see fragments of a wall that dates back to Carolingian times, and in the crypt there are remnants of 8th-century wall-paintings.

The **Schloß Thurn und Taxis** is immediately behind the church. The fortune made in pioneering a European mail service in the 16th century (and cornering the monopoly well into the 19th) has made the 'T und T's' probably the richest family in Germany. They own 17 per cent of Regensburg, vast tracts of forestland in Germany and Canada, and the largest private Bavarian brewery (locals nickname the beer *Tod und Teufel*—Death and the Devil). The present Fürst (prince) is still a boy, but his mother, Gloria, (who was some 30 years her late husband's junior) cuts a dash on the Munich social scene. In Regensburg she is known as 'the punk princess', and at the Café Princess in town you can buy succulent chocolates called *Kese Gloria* (saucy Gloria). Her Regensburg home boasts more rooms than Buckingham Palace, and some of the finest furniture in the land. The family sold up castles in the west of Germany just before the Second World War, and removed the contents to Regensburg, which escaped bombing.

If the family is not at home, you are allowed in for a glimpse of the breathtaking **interiors** (*guided tours only, Mon–Fri 2pm and 3.15pm, Sun 10 and 11.15; adm DM3, information © (0941) 504 8181*). The tour includes the beautiful former **cloisters** which exhibit the range of Gothic style from the 12th to the 14th centuries. There is also a **Marstallmuseum** (Museum of the Palace Mews) (*guided tours, Mon and Wed–Sat 2 and 3.15, Sun 10 and 11.15; adm DM3*), a glittering collection of carriages, sleds and sedan chairs.

East of the Centre

Two more museums are a short walk east of the Alter Kornmarkt. The **Stadtmuseum** at Dachauplatz 2–4 (*Tues–Sat 10–4, Sun 10–1; adm DM2.50*), housed in an old Minorite monastery, ploughs through 2000 years of Regensburg history. Its 100 rooms of exhibits make viewing quite a task, but displays are well laid out. There is an interesting cutaway model of a Roman house, and another of the Steinerne Brücke with all three gates intact. Regensburg's most famous artist, Albrecht Altdorfer (1480–1538), has a room to himself. He was a painter of the **Danube School**, who were known for the elaborate landscapes they used as backgrounds to their work—lush Austrian and Bavarian scenery that often completely overwhelmed the main subject of the painting. Altdorfer's art made him rich, and he became a town councillor and official city architect.

The **Städlische Galerie Regensburg** (Municipal Gallery) (*Tues–Sat 10–4, Sun 10–1; adm DM2.50*) is in a converted 15th-century house known, aptly, as the *Leerer Beutel* (empty purse). Here you'll find a rather thin collection of 19th- and 20th-century German art.

Regensburg © (0941–)   **Where to Stay**

expensive

Altstadthotel Arch, Haidplatz 4, © 502 060, ● 502 0668 (DM164–280). The connoisseur's address. A grand old patrician palace which has been stylishly converted. The nickname ('Ark') comes from its odd, bulging boat shape. Most rooms are spacious and all are tastefully decorated.

Bischofshof, Krauterermarkt 3, ✆ 59086, ✉ 53508 (DM175–200). A richly fitted-out inn that was once the bishop's palace. The rooms are elegant and comfortable and the service impeccable. These days the hotel is the meeting place for everyone who is anyone in Regensburg local politics.

moderate

Münchner Hof, Tändlergasse 9, ✆ 582 6265, ✉ 561 709 (DM120–140). Smart, newly renovated hotel. The rooms are small, but often have quaint features such as a Gothic wall-niche or old wooden beams. Service is brisk and friendly.

Kaiserhof am Dom, Kramgasse 10–12, ✆ 54027, ✉ 54025 (DM120–125). Old, family-run hotel in the shadow of the cathedral. Convenient but a bit spartan.

Hotel Rote Hahn, Rote Hahnengasse 10, ✆ 560 907 (DM110). A simple but atmospheric hotel in a 16th-century building in the Merchant Quarter. Some of the rooms are rather small, but still good value and you will find the staff friendly and attentive.

inexpensive

Spitalgarten, St Katharineplatz 1, ✆ 84774 (DM60 without private bath). Romantic old building with the Danube and a beer garden right outside.

Stadlerbräu, Stadtamthof 15, ✆ 85682 (DM54). Fairly basic, but clean and comfortable guesthouse situated across the Danube in a lively student quarter.

Eating and Drinking

On a fine evening in Regensburg you can have great fun wandering about the medieval alleys and nosing out a restaurant, an old courtyard café or beer garden hidden behind high stone walls. First just the clinking of glasses gives them away, then a shaft of light leads you through an arch or up a passage to a drink and good cheer. Here are a few tips to start you off.

Restaurants and Taverns

Historiches Eck, Watmarkt 6, ✆ (0941) 58920 (DM50–80). Coolly decorated establishment with suave service and a well-prepared, imaginative menu. You can have simple, succulent venison steaks, or delicate fare such as perch with an asparagus sauce, served with onion confit and wild mushrooms.

Zum Krebs, Krebsgasse 6, ✆ (0941) 55803 (DM50–70). Upmarket restaurant in a medieval house. Tasty Franco-German cuisine.

Hotel Bischofshof am Dom, Krautermarkt 3, ✆ (0941) 59086 (DM40–70). The chef worked for the T und T's for over a decade. Now he runs this smart hotel and makes sure the restaurant is one of the best in town. Delicious variations on traditional German dishes.

David im Goliathaus, Watmarkt 5, ℗ (0941) 561 858 (DM40–60). Attractive restaurant with a roof-garden where you can eat such well-tried perennials as prawn cocktail and duckling with orange.

Bräuerei Kneitinger, Arnulfpaltz 3, ℗ (0941) 52455 (DM15–25). Good, inexpensive Bavarian food in an old tavern atmosphere. Try the pancake soup or the baked carp.

Historische Wurstküche, An der Steinerne Brücke, ℗ (0941) 59098 (DM10). The medieval McDonald's. For 850 years the little hut on the Danube has dished out Regensburger pork sausages—grilled over beechwood fires and served with sweet mustard and sauerkraut. The same family has owned the *Wurstküche* for the past 200 years. In the summer you sit at long tables beside the river. In winter you crowd into the minuscule, smoke-filled restaurant-cum-kitchen.

Dampfnudel-Uli, Watmarkt 4, ℗ (0941) 53297 (DM5–15). Cluttered and eccentric little restaurant that occupies what was once a private chapel in the base of the medieval Bamburger tower. Uli and Vroni Deutzer serve sweet Bavarian dumplings smothered in a variety of sauces—ranging from simple vanilla to concoctions of fruit, beer and wine.

Bars and Cafés

Hemingway's American Bar, Obere Bachgasse 3–5, ℗ (0941) 561 506 (DM20–40). Fashion victims, dynamic young things with designer spectacles, and the occasional Bogart *manqué* eye each other up as they drink cocktails or eat salads out of huge glass bowls. Homesick Americans will find comfort in the menu.

Café Kominski, Hinter der Grieb 6. Another place to see and be seen as you sip your *Feierabend* drink.

Café Orphée, Untere Bachgasse 8, ℗ (0941) 52977. Wood-panelled French-style café and crêperie. Around the back there is a pretty little garden with a fountain.

Altstadt Café, Hinter der Grieb 8, ℗ (0941) 52646. Traditional café with attractive courtyard garden—popular with locals for long breakfasts.

Türmchen, Wahlenstr. 14. Cosy wine bar at the top of a high fortified tower.

Café Prinzeß, Rathausplatz 2, ℗ (0941) 57671. The oldest *Konditorei* in Germany. It opened in 1686 to serve pralines to the French delegates at the Imperial Diet, and still produces mouthwatering chocolates and cakes.

Beer Gardens

Bischofshof, Am Dom, ℗ (0941) 59080. Beautifully situated right at the foot of the cathedral in what used to be the bishop's palace garden. The beer garden is still owned by the Bishop of Regensburg, and everyone drinks here—from tourists to the mayor. You can get a delicious *Brotzeit* (meat and cheese snacks, DM6–10) to go with your beer.

Spitalgarten, Katharineplatz 1, ℗ (0941) 84774. Right on the Danube, tucked in between the Steinerne Brücke and an old hospital. Popular with laid-back locals.

Kneitinger Keller, Galgenburgerstr. 18. Rip-roaring 1200-seater beer garden within staggering distance of the University.

Zum Gravenreuther, Hinter der Grieb 10, ℗ (0941) 53348. Old inn with a charming little courtyard garden. Work up an appetite first for the hearty Bavarian fare, such as liver dumplings or roast pork with caraway seeds.

Entertainment and Nightlife

There is a thriving **classical music** scene in Regensburg, with concerts taking place in a variety of atmospheric old halls and churches. The tourist office publishes a **Monatsprogramm** (Monthly Programme) of what's on, and also offers a **ticket reservation service**. The city's main theatre, the **Städtische Bühnen**, Bismarckplatz 7, ℗ (0941) 59156, stages mainly opera and dance. The most vibrant venue in town is the **Thon-Dittmer-Palais**, Haidplatz 8, ℗ (0941) 507 2432, offering a varied fare of jazz, classical music and theatre. In summer it holds performances outdoors in its graceful Renaissance courtyard. The **Turmtheater im Goliathhaus**, Watmarkt 5, ℗ (0941) 562 233, sparkles with cabaret and small-scale musicals. Children enjoy the **marionettes** at the **Figurentheater**, Dr.-Johann-Maier-Str. 3, ℗ (0941) 28328 (performances Sept–May, Sat and Sun 3pm).

Nightlife in Regensburg centres mainly on cafés and beer gardens (*see* below), but, if you feel like dancing, head for the Sudhaus in Unterebachgasse. The town's noisy and frustrated youth frequent cafés and discos (such as Scala) in the Pustet Passage, off Gesandtenweg near Haidplatz.

Around Regensburg

Shining white on a hill above the Danube, 11km east of Regensburg, stands **Walhalla** (*April–Sept daily 9–6; Oct 9–5; Nov–Mar 10–12 and 1–4; adm DM1.50*), a pompous monument modelled on the Parthenon. It was put up by King Ludwig I in 1842 to honour Germany's heroes, though some have slipped in with dubious qualifications. Featured among the 200 or so plaques and busts of soldiers, artists, philosophers and other notables, you'll find the Dutch humanist Erasmus, Copernicus (a Pole) and scatterings of Austrians and Swiss. It is not a very enthralling site to visit, but the views over the Danube are pretty, and the surrounding park is good picnic territory. You can get to Walhalla by car (take the road along the north bank of the Danube, through Donaustauf), though it is more interesting to go by boat (*see* 'Getting Around' above).

An even more attractive boat trip follows the section of the Danube to the Donaudurchbruch and Klosterweltenburg, for which you board at **Kelheim**, 20km southwest of Regensburg (*see* p.110).

Passau

All over Europe towns with a few canals or more than one river flowing through them are flattered with Venetian epithets. Passau, the 'Bavarian Venice', is one of the few that comes anywhere near deserving the hype. Napoleon felt it was quite the most beautiful town he had overrun in all Germany. The 18th/19th-century traveller and naturalist, Alexander von Humboldt, ranked Passau among the seven most beautifully situated cities in the world. If you stand on the high battlements of the Veste Oberhaus fortress and look out over the Altstadt, you might be inclined to agree.

Most of Passau is packed onto a peninsula at the confluence of the rivers Danube, Ilz and Inn. Light reflecting off the water blanches the pastel shades of square Italianate buildings, giving Passau the air of a sunny Mediterranean town. Only when you look closer, and notice how the outdoor tables with their bright umbrellas have been ranged in strict orderly rows, are you reminded that the *piazza* is a *Platz*.

Few foreigners know about this little town at the eastern edge of Germany. Yet in the 14th century Passau was a flourishing trading centre, with turnover on the three rivers more than double that on the Rhine. For centuries the burghers battled with the powerful prince-bishops who owned the town. The wealthy merchants hoped for independence, like their neighbours in Regensburg. But the bishops, ensconced in one of the most impenetrable fortresses in the land, always won. Passau craftsmen did, however, succeed in developing the finest sword blades in Europe, and a 13th-century Bishop of Passau spent his quieter moments writing down the *Nibelungenlied*, Germany's most popular epic poem.

In 1662 a fire reduced the medieval town to rubble, and the present Baroque town was built by fashionable Italian architects. But, as with Regensburg, Passau's fortunes were already on the wane and the city's only recent claims to fame are that Wagner almost chose it over Bayreuth as the site for his music temple, and that a local photographer invented the picture postcard. Today Passau is a university town with a small student population and a reputation for unpleasant right-wing politics.

Getting Around

By car: Passau is just off Autobahn 3, 90km from Linz in Austria, 170km from Munich, 100km from Regensburg and 225km from Nuremberg. If you are travelling from Nuremberg or Regensburg, then the regional road B8, which follows the Danube, is a more **scenic route**. Most **parking garages** are to be found along the southern bank of the Danube.

Car hire: Europcar, Hauptbahnhof, ✆ (0851) 54235.

By train: The **Hauptbahnhof** (information ✆ (0851) 55001) is 10 minutes' walk west of the Altstadt. There are frequent connections to Linz (1hr 10mins), to Vienna (3hrs), Munich (2hrs), and to Regensburg (1hr 10mins).

Boat trips: Passau is one town really worth viewing from the water. The leading shipping company on this stretch of the Danube is **Wurm & Köck** (Höllgasse 26, ✆ (0851) 929 292). They offer a 45-minute **Dreiflüsse Rundfahrt** (Three Rivers Cruise, DM7) as well as longer trips as far as Linz (DM30 return). The **Donau-Dampfschiffahrts-Gesellschaft** (DDSG, Im Ort 14a, Dreiflußeck, ✆ (0851) 33035) can take you to Vienna. Most boats leave from the Luitpold-Hängebrücke.

Taxis: ✆ 57373.

Tourist Information

The **tourist information office** at the Neues Rathaus, Rathausplatz (Mon–Fri 8.30–6, Sat and Sun 10–2; Nov–Mar Mon–Fri 8.30–5) can help out with maps and leaflets about Passau. The **Infostelle** (Mon–Fri 9–5, Sat and Sun 9–1), alongside the Hauptbahnhof can also give you information on the region—including Austria and the Bavarian Forest.

Police: ✆ 110.

Medical emergencies: ✆ 1 92 22.

Post office: Next to the Hauptbahnhof (Mon–Fri 8.30–12.30, 2–5.30, Sat 8–12).

Market days: Fruit and vegetable market, Tues and Fri mornings on Domplatz.

Festivals

During the **Maidult** in May, the whole town seems to become one large, bright market, and its citizens give themselves over to almost continuous beer-drinking. For the **Burgerfest** at the end of June the formula is enriched by dance, music and sports such as bungee-jumping. At the other end of the scale, the long-established **European Weeks** (EW) from June to August attract to Passau some astonishing European names from the worlds of opera, ballet and classical music.

The Altstadt

Even at close quarters, Passau's Altstadt—with its arcaded streets, narrow alleys, archways, covered stairways and wrought-iron gates—seems more Italian than German. That said, once you've wandered about and soaked in the general atmosphere, there is not very much to see. **St Stephan's Cathedral** is the best place to begin a walkabout. The church is at the highest point in the Altstadt, largely because it rests on the heaped-up ruins of numerous predecessors and of the original Roman Fort Batavis. Today's Baroque church was built in the 17th century to replace a Gothic one all but destroyed by the town fire. The interior is heavily laden with white stucco, but has an impressive gilded canopied pulpit, crawling with cherubs and angels. The **organ** is the largest in the world. With 231 stops and 17,388 pipes it is roughly twice the size of the one in London's Royal Albert Hall. If you come at 12.30pm on weekdays (during summer) or on Thursdays at 7pm, you can hear a recital (*adm DM3 lunchtimes, DM6 evenings*).

Residenzplatz, behind the cathedral, is a small cobbled square lined with patrician mansions. From here you get the best view of the controlled and rather elegant late-Gothic east end of St Stephan's. Alongside is the grand 18th-century **episcopal palace**. A walk down Schrottgasse brings you to the Gothic **Rathaus**, which defiantly faces the bishops' fortress across the river. The building was the home of the wealthy Haller family, who for generations led citizens' rebellions, and as early as 1298 had given up some rooms for use as a town hall. Lovers of rich décor can pop inside for a look at the **Großer Saal** (*Easter–Oct Mon–Fri 10–12 and 1.30–4, Sat and Sun 10–4; adm DM1*), a weighty conglomeration of Baroque marble, 15th-century stained glass and enormous 19th-century wall paintings.

On the other side of the Rathausplatz in the Hotel Wilde Mann is the **Passauer Glas-museum** (*daily 10–4; adm DM3*), a vast and excellent collection of glassware, well worth a visit even if you're not a connoisseur. Exhibits range from the exquisite to the wacky— room after room resplendent with painted glass, clear glass, garish colours and curious shapes. The Jugendstil and Art Deco pieces are particularly good, and there is some finely painted 19th-century work. East of the Rathaus, on Bräugasse, you'll find the **Stiftung Wörlen** (Wörlen Foundation museum of modern art) (*Tues–Sun 10–6; adm DM5*). There is no permanent collection, but visiting exhibitions are of a high standard and the building, with its pretty arcaded courtyard, makes an attractive setting whatever is on show.

Veste Oberhaus

The medieval bishops' fortress of Veste Oberhaus looms over the town from the top of a rocky outcrop across the Danube. It is easy to see how the building became the focus of the citizens' anger, and also why it proved hopelessly unassailable over the centuries. Today the fortress has been converted into a warren of **museums** (*Tues–Sun 9–5, closed Feb; general adm DM3*). You can reach Veste Oberhaus by crossing the Luitpoldbrücke, then walking up a precipitous flight of stairs cut into the rock. If that seems a little daunting, you can catch a bus from the Rathausplatz (*April–Oct, half hourly from 11.30 to 5*). Once there you can wander through the old rooms and courtyards and see early Passau picture-post-cards and maps of Bavaria in the **Lithograph Museum**; some nondescript contemporary art in the **20th-Century Gallery**; Gothic painting and sculpture in the **Diocesan Museum**; a collection of craftsmen's tools, and sculpture by the city's most famous artist, Hans Wimmer, in the **City Museum**; and some rickety old wagons in the **Fire Brigade Museum**. But by far the best reason for visiting the fortress is for the magnificent views over Passau and the three rivers. The pale Danube, the muddy Inn and the Ilz, turned a deep green-black by the marshy soils of the Bavarian Forest, swirl together in marble colours, before continuing eastwards. Interestingly, although the Inn is deeper, broader and has travelled further to get here than the Danube, it is still regarded as a tributary.

expensive

Hotel Wilder Mann, Am Rathausplatz, ✆ 35071, 📠 31712 (DM130–230). A converted 11th-century palace on the Danube, and one of the best hotels in the region. The rooms are sumptuously decorated—mostly with antiques (the best ones are at the back, with balconies overlooking a quiet garden). The service is relaxed and friendly, there's a Michelin-starred restaurant, a swimming pool in the Gothic vault, and even an in-house museum (*see* above).

moderate

Hotel König, Untere Donaulände 1, ✆ 35028, 📠 31784 (DM 140–150). Modernized hotel with comfortable rooms looking out across the river to the Veste Oberhaus. The new architects managed to slip a sauna and solarium into the design.

Altstadt Hotel, Braügasse 23–29, ✆ 3370, 📠 337 100 (DM120–160). Smart, modernized hotel with a terrace-restaurant overlooking the point where the three rivers meet. The hotel has its own underground garage.

inexpensive

Pension Rößner, Braügasse 19, ✆ 2035, 📠 36247 (DM80–90). Family-run *Pension* right on the Danube. The rooms are small, but cosy.

Pension Weißes Lamm, Theresienstr. 10, ✆ 2219 (DM47–50). Clean pension in the modern, pedestrianized shopping precinct, but within easy walking distance of all the Altstadt sights.

Eating and Drinking: Restaurants and Taverns

Heilig-Geist-Stiftschenke, Heilig-Geist-Gasse 4, ✆ 2607 (DM25–35). A *Weinstube* that dates back to 1358. Heavy wooden tables under low arches, bread in baskets and good wine thumped down in ceramic jugs. The food is mouthwatering—with fish from their private waters and a lengthy pancake menu (the wild mushroom fillings are delicious).

Zum Jodlerwirt, Schrottgasse 12, ✆ 2422 (DM25–45). The venue for *Weißbier* aficionados, with yodelling and jolly folk music on Saturdays and hearty Bavarian cuisine, such as venison ragout and potato dumplings.

Ristorante Zi'Teresa, Theresienstr. 26, ✆ 2138 (DM15–40). Homemade pizzas and pasta in a popular restaurant with a small garden. **Drei Linden**, Steinweg 6 (DM20–30). Cosy *Gasthof* near the cathedral. Good local and Austrian dishes—especially fish and game.

Theresiencafé, Theresienstr. 14. Tranquil daytime café with a small courtyard garden. Ideal for late breakfasts and lunches.

Café Kowalski, Obersand 1. Away from the tourist crush, but crammed with local trendies and students. The tiny balcony overlooking the Inn is popular at sundown.

Café Duft, Theresienstr. 22. Central café with a neighbourhood atmosphere—the honeypot of local gossip. You can also get a bite to eat.

Café Aquarium, Unteresandstr. 2. Aptly named chrome and glass box where people go to be seen.

Goldenes Schiff, Unteresandstr. 8. Popular student drinking tavern with a tiny garden round the back. Serves good cheap grub too.

The Bavarian Forest and the Upper Palatinate

The **Bavarian Forest** (German: *Bayerische Wald*), which gives its name to the eastern-most strip of Bavaria, is one of the last wild areas in Europe. It spreads way into Bohemia across the Czech border, and merges in the north with the **Upper Palatinate** (German: *Oberpfalz*). This confusing echo with the Rhineland region arises because the area was ruled by the powerful Electors Palatine of the Rhine, a senior branch of the Bavarian Wittelsbachs.

This is an idyllic land of meadows and wildflowers, forests in unimagined shades of green, hidden lakes and fast, chuckling streams. When the mists come down the woods seem secret and isolated—but more often than not the sun is shining, the air seems honey-scented and is filled with the warbles and chirrups of birdsong. This is one of the few places where the roadsign showing a leaping deer can be taken literally.

City Germans scoffingly refer to this out-of-the-way part of their country as the 'Bavarian Congo', yet this gives you the clue to its charm. Here you will find that life goes on in much the same way as it has done for centuries. There are story-book farmyards, colourful local festivals and hardly any foreign tourists at all. The food is excellent, and accommodation encouragingly cheap.

Despite the lush appearance of the countryside, the soil is rocky and hard to farm—but it does contain large silica deposits. This, and the abundance of firewood for furnaces, led the medieval woodsmen to take the cue from their Bohemian neighbours and begin blowing glass. (Town names that end in '-hütt' or '-reuth' derive from the old German word for a glassworks.) Today **glass-blowing** is still more an individual craft than a large industrial affair. Most larger factories use traditional methods, and dotted around the forest towns are workshops where you can watch craftspeople puffing and sweating beside glowing furnaces.

By car: A car is essential if you really want to get about the area easily and explore remoter corners. Roads are all well made. The most scenic routes are along and around the B85 and the B22.

By train: If you are coming by train, head for Grafenau or Furth im Wald, both of which are handy bases for exploring the countryside. Trains leave from Regensburg and Passau, but you will have to change two or three times, and the journey will take up to three hours.

Hiking: As always in Germany this is well organized, with marked routes around the forests, and mountain huts where you can sleep the night. Tourist offices and bookshops can supply you with detailed maps. The most determined hikers could try the 180km *Nördliche Hauptwanderlinie* (Furth im Wald to Dreisesselberg, 7–10 days). The *Südliche Hauptwanderlinie* (105km, Rattenberg–Kalteneck, 5–7 days) in the rolling hills near the Danube valley is easier on the legs. An even softer option is the route through the middle of the forest from Kötzing (near Cham) to Bayerisch Eisenstein (on the Czech border; 50km, 2 days).

By bicycle: Perhaps the ideal way to see the area—you can get about at a civilized speed, stop where you like, and really appreciate the countryside. You'll need a bike with gears, though, as some parts of the Forest can be quite hilly. Again, there are all sorts of marked routes ranging from those you can knock off in a few hours to some that take days.

The Bavarian Tourist Office (Landesfremdenverkehrs-verband Bayern e.V., Prinzregentstr. 18, D–80535 München 22, ℰ (089) 212 3970) brings out a detailed brochure (available from tourist offices throughout the area) which grades cycle routes according to difficulty and also suggests those which are suitable for children.

Tourist Information

Bavarian Forest National Park: The Visitor Centre, Hans-Eisenmann Haus, Böhmstr. 35, Neuschönau (near Grafenau), ℰ (08558) 1300 (*Mon–Sat 9–5*) runs slide-shows about the Park and the *Waldsterben* (forest death, *see* below). They also offer tours of the park, sell maps, and can give hiking suggestions.

Cham: Cordonhaus, Propsteistr. 46, ℰ (09971) 4933.

Furth im Wald: Schloßplatz 1, ℰ (09973) 3813.

Grafenau: Rathausgasse 1, ℰ (08552) 42743.

Kötzing: Herrenstr. 10, ℰ (09941) 602 150.

Waldsassen: Town Administration, Johannisplatz 11, ℰ (09632) 8828.

Roman Catholic farmers find lots of excuses to celebrate, and the towns around the Bavarian Forest are alive with colourful religious parades, seasonal festivals with ancient pagan roots, and busy fairs. Festivities take many forms—from costume parades requiring months of preparation, to a village bash in a beer tent, accompanied by a man on an electric accordian. Early spring and summer, Easter and Corpus Christi are the most rewarding times of the year to catch the local revels.

The most famous festival in the region, and one of Germany's largest, is the **Drachenstich** in Furth im Wald on the second and third Sundays in August. There is a fair, lots of food and beer and an opening procession with 200 horses and many hundreds more people in *Tracht*. The highlight is a re-enactment of St George's battle with the dragon (a spectacle which goes back over 900 years, making it the oldest piece of folk theatre in Germany). A local lad dons armour and slays an 18m luminous green (and these days mechanized) monster, which dies dramatically, spurting blood all over the delighted onlookers. The performance lasts 75 minutes and is repeated at intervals throughout the festival. Tickets cost from DM5 (standing) to DM30 and can be booked through the *Drachenstich-festausschuß* (Stadtplatz 4, ✆ (09973) 9254).

The **Pfingstritt** is an impressive procession of decorated horses and men in *Tracht* that makes its way, on Whit Monday, from Kötzing (near Cham) to the pilgrimage church at Steinbühl, 7km away (starts 8am). There a couple are symbolically married, and the whole show returns to Kötzing for a knees-up in the town square.

From Passau to Zwiesel

The first stop out of Passau, 20km up the B85, is **Tittling**, where you'll find the **Museumsdorf Bayerischer Wald** (*daily 9–5.30; adm DM5*), an impressive outdoor museum of some 50 reconstructed farmhouses dating from the 15th to the 19th centuries. A little further along the B85, a side-road ducks off to Grafenau, Spielgau and Frauenau, three towns that border the vast National Park. The towns, while not in themselves particularly attractive, are full of *pensions* and rooms to let and make convenient bases for ventures into the forest.

Grafenau is the most touristy, with a railway station and intermittent invasions of coach parties. At **Frauenau** you can visit the **Freiherr von Poschinger Kristallfabrik**, Moosauhütte, ✆ (09926) 703 (*guided tours Mon–Sat 9.45–11.30 and 12.45–1.30; adm DM1.50*), a glassworks which has been in the same family for 14 generations and which won worldwide fame for its Jugendstil pieces. Although the company now employs over 200 workers, they still use traditional glass-blowing methods. **Glashütte Valentin Eisch**, Am Steg 7, ✆ (09926) 279, also admits visitors and has a reputation for zanier, more avant-garde work. The **Glasmuseum**, Am Museumpark (*daily 9–5; adm DM3*) has a collection of glass from ancient Egyptian to modern times (though not as impressive as the one in Passau) and gives you a thorough technical introduction to glassmaking in the area. The nearby village of **Zwiesel** is a centre for many of the individual glassblowers and smaller firms—most of whom welcome casual visitors.

The **National Park** itself is 13,000 hectares of rolling moorland, lush forest and mountains. It is dotted with inns and private guesthouses, and in some places there are reserves for animals (such as bears, lynx and buffalo) that used to roam freely. The air here is as unpolluted as in the centre of an ocean, but sadly the forests are succumbing to *Waldsterben*, the fatal disease that has affected nearly 80 per cent of Germany's trees. Many blame acid rain caused by pollution from British factories, but recent research points the finger at exhaust fumes from the millions of cars that shoot about the German *Autobahns*. Despite the alarming statistics, the forests appear healthy enough.

From Zwiesel to Waldsassen

Country roads winding north of Zwiesel bring you to **Bodenmais**, a bustling resort that seems made up entirely of glassware shops and *pensions*. It is, however, a good base for visiting the **Arbersee**, a dark lake squeezed between forested slopes at the foot of the region's highest mountain—**Grosser Arber** (1456m). The summit of the mountain, and a panoramic view, can be reached by chair lift. You can also hike along the river Arber, which drops in a series of falls and cascades through the **Risslochschlucht** gorge.

A few kilometres further on you come to the towns of **Kötzing** and **Furth im Wald** (*see* 'Festivals' above). The fearsome *Drachenstich* dragon can be seen all year round in a lair near the Furth im Wald tourist office. There is also a display on the history of the pageant. Nearby is the small walled town of Cham, a hub of local transport and famous for its beers. The local Hofmark brewery produces the malty *Würzig-Mild* and tasty, somewhat bitter *Würzig-Herb*. Here the countryside opens out, and the B22 takes you north through a lonely landscape dotted with copses, isolated farms and the odd ruined castle. The town of **Waldsassen**, 130km up the road from Cham, is, however, very much worth the journey for its impressive Baroque **Stift** (collegiate church) and **Stiftsbibliothek** (library) (*summer Tues–Sun 10–11.30 and 2–5, winter 10–11 and 2–4*). The library is a rich mixture of old volumes and elaborate woodcarving. Its upper gallery is supported by a series of figures carved to represent everyone connected with books. At times the connections become a little strained (such as the figure of the shepherd: the skins of his flock were used as bookbinding). From Waldsassen it is only a short journey west to Bayreuth or Nuremberg.

Where to Stay

Accommodation in the Bavarian Forest is plentiful and cheap. You can get private rooms from as little as DM16 per person. Many of these are in farmhouses or in cottages in the woods, and are often a much better bet than hotels. Look out for the *Fremdenzimmer* or *Zimmer zu vermieten* signs. Small villages such as the romantic **Klingenbrunn** (5km from Spiegelau, on the edge of the National Park) are better alternatives to the towns, and will almost always have empty rooms.

Grafenau

Steigenberger Hotel Sonnenhof, Sonnenstr. 12, ✆ (08552) 4480, ✆ 4680 (from DM200). A smart modern hotel designed to pamper your every whim. All the rooms have balconies, and in-house facilities include tennis courts, a steam bath, sauna, swimming pool, jacuzzi and hunky ski instructors.

Säumerhof, Steinberg 32, ✆ (08552) 2401 (DM120–180). Comfortable, tastefully decorated rooms, and personal attention from the owner—who also cooks superb meals.

Hohenau

Die Bierhütte, Bierhütte 10, Hohenau, ✆ (08558) 315, ✆ 2387 (DM150–170). Cosy hotel between Grafenau and Freyung, set beside a small lake. The romantic old building was once a glassworks and brewery, and is these days run with tender loving care by the Störzer family.

Bodenmais

Bayerwaldhotel Hofbräuhaus, 8373 Bodenmais, ✆ (09924) 7021, ✆ (09924) 7210 (from DM90). Traditional Bavarian hotel, owned by the same family for over 100 years. It is friendly, *gemütlich* and also offers a Fitness Centre and indoor pool.

Furth im Wald

Hotel zur Post, Stadtplatz 12, ✆ (09973) 1506 (DM60–90). Comfortable hotel in the middle of town.

Hotel Gasthof Himmelreich, Himmelreich 7, ✆ (09973) 1840 (DM70–80). Quiet pension, set a little back from the busy High Street.

Hohenbogen, Bahnhofstr. 25, ✆ (09973) 1509 (DM60–80). Cheery, down-to-earth *Pension* with spotless rooms. Also serves good meals (DM20–40).

Eating and Drinking

Dotted all over the forest are inns and small villages with guesthouses where you can have a good meal for under DM20 a head. The following suggestions might start you on your way.

Brauerei-Gasthof Eck, Eck 1, Böbrach, ✆ (09923) 685. Picture-book hillside inn with an in-house brewery. Excellent cuisine and good beer.

Brauereigasthof Kamm, Bräugasse 1, Zenting, ✆ (09907) 315. House brewery serving some fairly hearty Bavarian dishes such as venison ragout and wild mushroom pancakes.

Säumerhof, Steinberg 32, ✆ (08552) 2401, Grafenau (DM35–50). Superb, imaginative cuisine using local produce and game, and a relaxed friendly atmosphere.

If you would like to spend some time on a **farm**, or learn how to make traditional Bavarian Sunday roast pork and dumplings, some local farmers take in guests between May and October, and are happy to show you around their farms and farm kitchens. Prices vary according to the length of your stay, but work out at around DM160 per person per week, including breakfast. The following are renowned for their scrumptious Sunday roasts: Marile Geier, Emminger Str. 23, Schöllnach, ✆ (09903) 347; Hannelore Koller, Alberting 35, Grafling, ✆ (0991) 25326; Anni Weiherer, Eidsberg 36, Grafling, ✆ (0991) 25756.

Franconia

Franconia was a patchwork of secular and ecclesiastically ruled states until the 18th century, when it was drawn into union with Bavaria (*see* **History** p.36). But even after union with Bavaria, Franconians resolutely retained their own dialect and cultural identity. The Cold War division of Germany was strongly felt here. Many communities suddenly found themself cut off from the ancient cultural and trade links with Thuringia and Saxony. Now once again in the geographical centre of Germany, the region is becoming a popular tourist destination, with great stretches of land designated as nature reserves. Almost equally enticing are the numbers of towns which are virtually period pieces of differing epochs.

See also **The Romantic Road, pp.143–69.**

Nuremberg (Nürnberg)

Nuremberg is Bavaria's second largest city and the capital of Franconia. It is a 'city with a past', most recently remembered as the scene of vast Nazi rallies and the 1945–9 war crimes trials. Before Allied bombers flattened 90 per cent of the Altstadt in a single air-raid on 2 January 1945, Nuremberg had been considered one of the most beautiful towns in Germany. It was a centre of art, science, trade and craft; home to Albrecht Dürer, Germany's most famous painter, to Hans Sachs (the original *Meistersinger* of Nuremberg), and to the inventors of the first world globe, the pocket watch and the lead pencil. Luther wrote that 'Nuremberg shines throughout Germany, like a sun among the moon and stars'. Pope Pius II praised the town's dazzling splendour and wryly remarked that 'the Kings of Scotland would be glad to be housed so luxuriously as the ordinary citizens of Nuremberg'. Adalbert Stifter, a 19th-century poet, enthused that the entire city was a work of art whose 'gracefulness, serenity and purity' of line filled him with irrepressibly gratifying feelings.

These days you would be forgiven for not getting quite so excited about Nuremberg. It is an odd mixture of dull modern architecture and painstakingly restored old buildings. No longer a vortex for art and industry, it is, however, an attractive and lively town, justifiably famous for its Christmas Market, scrumptious sausages and chewy gingerbread. There is some first-rate art to be seen, and the German National Museum, based here since 1852, has one of the most varied and impressive collections in the country.

History

Nuremberg's zenith was in the Middle Ages. It had been declared a Free Imperial City by Frederick II in 1219 and was at a nexus of the western world's main trade routes: from the Balkans to Antwerp, from Hamburg to Venice and from Paris to Prague. The city was also famed for its bell-founders, candlestick-makers, woodcarvers, glass-painters and, above all, for producing precision scientific instruments. By the 16th-century Nuremberg had become equally celebrated for its painting and sculpture, and was beginning to achieve an almost mythical status in the eyes of many Germans. That is why, even after

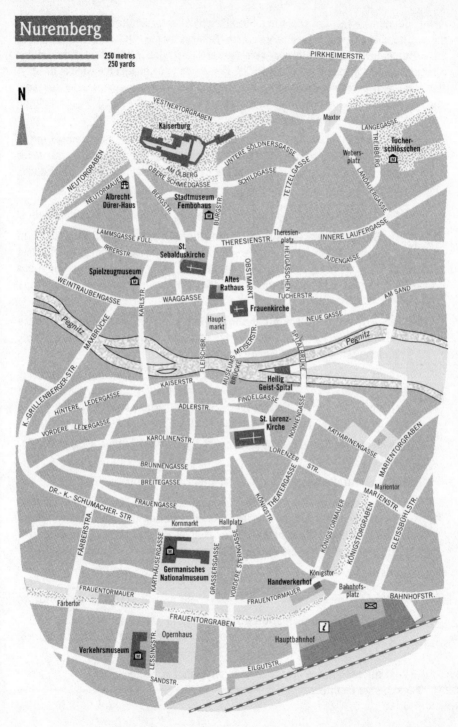

Nuremberg

250 metres
250 yards

N

PIRKHEIMERSTR.

VESTNERTORGRABEN

Kaiserburg

Maxtor

LANGEGASSE

TREIBBERG

Tucher-
schlösschen

UNTERE SÖLDNERSGASSE

Webers-
platz

NEUTORGRABEN

AM ÖLBERG

OBERE SCHMIEDGASSE

SCHILDGASSE

TETZELGASSE

LANDAUERGASSE

NEUTORMAUER

Albrecht-
Dürer-Haus

BERGSTR.

Stadtmuseum
Fembohaus

BURGSTR.

LAMMSGASSE FÜLL

THERESIENSTR.

Theresien-
platz

INNERE LAUFERGASSE

IRRERSTR.

St.
Sebalduskirche

HEUGÄSSCHEN

JUDENGASSE

Spielzeugmuseum

WEINTRAUBENGASSE

WAAGGASSE

Altes
Rathaus

OBSTMARKT

TUCHERSTR.

AM SAND

KARLSTR.

Frauenkirche

NEUE GASSE

Pegnitz

MAXBRÜCKE

Hauptmarkt

FLEISCHBR.

MEISERSTR.

SPITALBRÜCKE

Pegnitz

KAISERSTR.

MUSEUMS-
BRÜCKE

Heilig
Geist-Spital

K. GRILLENBERGER STR.

HINTERE LEDERGASSE

ADLERSTR.

FINDELGASSE

St. Lorenz-
Kirche

NONNENGASSE

KATHARINENGASSE

MARIENTORGRABEN

VORDERE LEDERGASSE

KAROLINENSTR.

LORENZER STR.

BRUNNENGASSE

BREITEGASSE

Marientor

MARIENSTR.

GLEISSBÜHLSTR.

DR.- K.- SCHUMACHER- STR.

FRAUENGASSE

THEATERGASSE

KÖNIGSTR.

KÖNIGSTORMAUER

KÖNIGSTORGRABEN

FÄRBERSTR.

Kornmarkt

Hallplatz

KARTHÄUSERGASSE

GRASSERGASSE

VORDERE STERNGASSE

Königstor

Bahnhofs-
platz

BAHNHOFSTR.

Germanisches
Nationalmuseum

Handwerkerhof

FRAUENTORMAUER

FRAUENTORMAUER

Färbertor

FRAUENTORGRABEN

LESSINGSTR.

Opernhaus

Hauptbahnhof

Verkehrsmuseum

EILGUTSTR.

SANDSTR.

new trade routes to the Americas had robbed the city of its wealth (by diverting trade with the east from land to sea), Nuremberg became the focus for the Pan-German movement in the 19th century. Later the Nazis were to warp this symbolism even further. Hitler commissioned huge monuments to his 1000-year Reich to be built at the edge of the city, and Nuremberg became the scene of rousing Nazi rallies. The Allies, too, seemed to recognize this symbolic importance when they chose Nuremberg as the venue for bringing the surviving Nazi leaders to trial after the war.

Today Nuremberg still produces pencils and scientific instruments, and is noted in the industrial world as a leading manufacturer of children's toys. But, though it is a mecca for street entertainers in the summer, Nuremberg has lost any claim to being the cultural centre of Germany.

Getting Around

By air: Nuremberg **airport** (information ℗ (0911) 350 6200) is just 7km north of the centre. There are frequent flights to local German airports, and also connections to London, Amsterdam, Paris, Milan and Brussels. A bus shuttle service will run you to the Hauptbahnhof in 20 minutes (every 30mins, 5am–11.30pm).

By train: The **Hauptbahnhof** is south of the Altstadt, just outside the old city wall. Intercity trains run hourly, with connections to Hamburg (4hrs), Frankfurt (2¾hrs) and Munich (1½hrs).

By car: Nuremberg cowers in the middle of one of Europe's biggest motorway junctions: *Autobahns* connect you to every major city in Germany. One word of warning—since reunification the A9 to Berlin has become treacherously busy, and in some places isn't quite up to the load—traffic is heavy, and sometimes jams fast.

Car hire: Avis, Nuremberg airport, ℗ (0911) 528 966; Europa, Fürther Str. 31, ℗ (0911) 260 308.

Mitfahrzentrale: Allersberger Str. 31a, ℗ (0911) 446 9666.

Public transport: The Altstadt is quite small enough to get about on foot. However, should you need it there is a comprehensive network of buses, trams and U-Bahn lines. The same tickets are valid on all three. Prices depend on how many zones you cross, and can be bought at most stops.

Taxis: ℗ 20555.

Tourist Information

The main **tourist information office** is opposite the Hauptbahnhof, ℗ (0911) 233 632 (Mon–Sat 9–8). There's a branch in the Altstadt at Hauptmarkt 18, ℗ (0911) 233 634 (Mon–Sat 9–1 and 2–6, Sun 9–1 and 2–4).

Post office: Located next to the Hauptbahnhof at Bahnhofplatz 1. It also offers **exchange facilities**.

Police: ✆ 110.

Medical emergencies: ✆ 533 771.

Market days: There is a good weekday fruit and vegetable market on the Marktplatz. At the beginning of the asparagus season in May, this becomes a market devoted to asparagus.

Festivals

Nuremberg has the largest and most famous **Christkindelsmarkt** (Christmas market, literally: Christ-child's market) in Germany. At the beginning of the 17th century it became the fashion to give children presents at Christmas rather than at New Year, which had previously been the custom. The market that grew up in Nuremberg to meet the demand for carved toys and tasty goodies became the prototype for similar fairs now held in nearly every town in the country.

From the Friday before Advent until Christmas Eve the Market Square is transformed into an enchanted land of wooden stalls and bright bunting, smothered in pine leaves and lit by lanterns. Despite the market's enormous popularity, you'll find little kitsch or tatty commercialism. Vendors pile their stalls with hand-carved wooden toys, traditional decorations and all kinds of craftwork. Aromas of *Glühwein*, grilling sausages and freshly baked ginger *Lebkuchen* soften the sharp winter air.

You can buy the *Rauschgoldengel* (gold foil angels), *Zwetschgenmännle* (odd figures made from crêpe paper and prunes) and the kind of straw wreaths that have decorated Nuremberg homes at yuletide for centuries. At dusk on the first day a 'Christ-child' ringingly recites a prologue from the balcony above the entrance to the Frauenkirche, and little terrestrial angels peal out carols down below. A few days later, together with strings of school-chums all bearing home-made lanterns, they wind in procession up the hill from the Market Square to the castle.

The **Altstadtfest** in late September is ostensibly a celebration of Franconian folk culture, but it is really a rollicking knees-up, with mounds of food from all over the world and beer flowing freely. The **Toy Fair** (the largest of its kind in the world) held every February is peopled mainly by mums, dads and business folk walking between the stacks of teddies and playing the latest computer games. Big boys' toys whizz about during the **Norisring car races** in late June. Roads to the southeast of the city are closed off to make a long racetrack, traffic piles up, and you are deafened by car and helicopter engines for days on end.

Cultural events tend to cluster around the summer months. At the end of May you can catch **Musica Franconia**, a week of concerts of ancient music played on period instruments. Then the **Kulturzirkus**, an international theatre festival of increasing renown, is held in June—as is Europe's oldest sacred music festival, the **Orgelwoche** (literally: organ week). Buskers and street entertainers descend on the city's streets for a fortnight in July/August for the **Bardentreffen** (Bards' Meet). They're joined by more established names who also give open-air concerts. In October the **Ost-West Jazzfestival** hosts bands playing anything from Dixie to free jazz.

The Kaiserburg

The Kaiserburg (*daily April–Sept 9–12 and 12.45–5, Oct–Mar 9.30–12 and 12.45–4; adm DM3, guided tours only*), lording it on a rock over the northern edge of the Altstadt, gives Nuremberg its unmistakable skyline of odd stone blocks and quirky towers. The view back down over the jumble of red-peaked roofs transports you back to medieval times, and gives you a good idea of the layout of the town.

The eccentric cluster of buildings that makes up the Kaiserburg grew up over centuries, and is, in fact, two castles merged into one. On the **eastern spur** of the rock is the **Burgrave's (Count's) Castle**. From the 11th until the end of the 12th century this was a fortress belonging first to the Salian kings (an ancient Frankish line) and then to the local Burgraves of Nuremberg. When the last of the line of the original Burgraves died in 1190, he was succeeded by his son-in-law, Frederic I of Zollern, founder of the Hohenzollern dynasty. During the 13th and 14th centuries the castle was the Hohenzollern's chief seat in Western Franconia, but the burghers of Nuremberg didn't take too kindly to their rule. After a number of hostile clashes the Hohenzollerns were finally defeated, and they sold the castle to the city in 1414.

The **Imperial Castle** on the **western spur** was a seat of the powerful Hohenstaufen line in the 12th century. The Hohenstaufens provided Holy Roman Emperors from 1138 to 1254. Even after the family's decline the castle continued to play an important role in empire politics. In 1356, in a decree known as the **Golden Bull**, Emperor Charles IV had commanded that the first Diet summoned by any newly elected German king had to be held at the castle. This held true for two centuries (until the Diet moved permanently to Regensburg), making Nuremberg one of the political centres of the empire. In 1427 the western spur too was taken over by the town and incorporated into the city defences, but it remained the property of the Holy Roman Empire.

The oldest part of the Kaiserburg is the gloomy **Fünfeckturm** (Pentagonal Tower, *c.* 1040), the only part of the original Salian building to survive. It now shares the eastern spur with the solid **Luginslandturm**, a tower put up in one go during the 14th century by burghers keen to keep a watchful eye on what was happening in the Burgrave's castle. Once they had ousted the Hohenzollerns, the citizens joined the two towers with a Gothic **Kaiserstallung** (Imperial Stables, built 1494, now a Youth Hostel).

The main body of the castle is on the western spur. The late-Gothic **Palas** was the Hohenstaufen family living-quarters. Only the east wall of the original Romanesque building remains, the rest was built by Emperor Frederick III in the 15th century. The guided tour takes you through rather bare state rooms and suites. Most of the Kaiserburg had to be rebuilt after the Second World War. The outside of the castle is impressive, but interiors tend to be empty and devoid of any atmosphere. One building that did survive the Allied bombs is the **Kaiserkapelle**, a *Doppelkapelle* ('double chapel', *see* p.42) with an airy upper tier for the emperor and his family, and a squat, dim lower storey for humbler beings. There is a crucifix in the Upper Chapel said to be by the renowned local carver, Veit Stoss. The Nuremberg *Doppelkapelle* is the only one known to have an additional west gallery and choir tower—the solid **Heidenturm** (Heathens' Tower). Out in the forecourt you can see the **Tiefer Brunnen**, a well probably as old as the castle itself and so deep that it takes 6 seconds for a stone dropped from the top to hit the water.

The Northern Altstadt

Just below the Kaiserburg is the **Tiergärtner Tor**, one of four gates in the wall which still surrounds the medieval Altstadt. The area around the Tiergärtner Tor is one of the most attractive parts of the Altstadt. Lanes of half-timbered houses open out onto a cobbled Platz that, especially in the summer, is a hive of buskers, back-packers and other merry youth. Just outside the city wall (west along Johannisstraße) is the **Johannisfriedhof** (*April–Sept 7–7, Oct–Mar 8–5*), one of Germany's oldest and best-known cemeteries. Elaborate 16th- and 17th-century tombstones depict the scenes from the lives of the deceased. Among locals buried here are the *Meistersinger* Hans Sachs (*see* p.58), the sculptor Veit Stoss (*see* p.45), and the artist and polymath Albrecht Dürer (*see* pp.46–7).

The **Albrecht-Dürer-Haus** (*Mar–Oct and during Christkindelsmarket Tues–Sun 10–5, Wed 10–9; Nov–Feb Tues–Fri 1–5, Wed 1–9, Sat and Sun 10–5; adm DM3*), where Germany's most complete Renaissance Man lived from 1509–28, is just across the square from the Tiergärtener Tor. The house is worth a visit for its cosy atmosphere and authentic medieval interiors, though you won't find any original Dürer paintings. There are, however, a few engravings and first editions of his treatises. Modern artists have also contributed some rather odd homages to the great man.

Down Bergstraße (also just across from the Tor), in the **Altstadthof** (a 16th-century courtyard), you'll find the **Hausbrauerei** (*hourly guided tours Mon–Fri 2–7, Sat and Sun 11–7; adm DM4.50*), a working antique brewery, with cellars deep under the Kaiserburg. After your visit you can taste the murky beer in an adjoining pub. Further south, down Albrecht-Dürer-Straße and across Weinmarkt, you come to **Weißgerbergasse**—the most attractive lane of half-timbered houses in the city, now mainly given over to restaurants and cafés. Down Karlstrasse, which also leads off Weinmarkt, is the **Spielzeugmuseum** (Toy Museum) (*Tues–Sun 10–5, Wed 10–9; adm adults DM5, children DM2.50*). At the time of writing the museum was closed for renovations, but if it has been re-opened it should be worth a visit for its vast collection of mainly 18th–20th-century toys. Germany was Europe's main manufacturer of toys—notably mechanical and tin toys—in the 19th century. Back eastwards along Schustergasse you come to the twin-towered **St Sebalduskirche** (1225–1379), Nuremberg's oldest parish church. Inside, resting on 12 bronze snails, is the richly decorated brass **Shrine of St Sebald**. Cast by Peter Vischer in 1391–7, it is generally considered to be the highpoint of German Renaissance metal work. There is a moving **crucifixion scene** by Veit Stoss on the pillar behind the Shrine.

On a pillar in the nave is a charming, delicately coloured early 15th-century carving of **Mary with a halo**.

Around the corner on Burgstraße is the **Stadtmuseum Fembohaus** (*Mar–Oct and during Christkindelsmarket Tues–Sun 10–5, Wed 10–9; Nov–Feb Tues–Fri 1–5, Wed 1–9, Sat and Sun 10–5; adm DM3*), really only worth a visit for a look at the heavy stucco ceilings and wood-panelled rooms transferred here from other patrician mansions around town. A more rewarding museum is the intimate **Tucherschlößchen** at Hirschelgasse 9 (*guided tours Mon–Thurs 2, 3, 4pm, Fri 9, 10, 11am, Sun 10 and 11am; adm DM1.50*), a few minutes' walk up towards the university in the northeastern corner of the Altstadt. This was the Renaissance mansion of the Tucher family, who made their fortune manufacturing astronomical instruments, and later importing textiles and brewing beer. The house was destroyed during the war, but completely restored by the family themselves. There is a loving, personal touch to the displays of fine furniture and painting. The highlight of the tour is the **Tucherbuch** (1590–6), a family chronicle with stunningly beautiful illustrations. Tours are in German only, but you can ask for a printed English translation.

Around the Hauptmarkt

The **Hauptmarkt** is the centre of town, and scene of a bustling, countrified daily **market** of stalls laden with fruit, fresh herbs and homemade cakes and breads. Across the northern end of the square is an exuberant Renaissance **Altes Rathaus**, built in the style of a Venetian *palazzo*. Here you can visit the **Lochgefängnisse** (*April–Sept Mon–Fri 10–4, Sat and Sun 10–1; adm DM3*), medieval prison cells complete with a fully equipped torture chamber. Outside, on the western side of the square, is a replica of the completely over-the-top **Schöner Brunnen** (Beautiful Fountain), a filigreed Gothic spire, gaudily painted and crowded with figures of electors, prophets and other church heroes. The trickles of water that spout from the base seem quite gratuitous.

The pretty step-gabled **Frauenkirche**, erected by Emperor Charles IV in 1355, is just across the square. Although the church was badly bombed, the intricately carved **tympanum** above the entrance porch survived intact. In the 16th century a pretty oriel and clock were added to the façade. Above is a gold and blue ball that shows the current phase of the moon. Below is a Glockenspiel (nicknamed the **Männleinlaufen**) that commemorates Charles IV's 'Golden Bull' (*see* above). At noon the carillon rings out merrily and figures of the seven electors circle three times around a statue of the emperor. Above the main altar in the church is the painting called the **Tucher Altar** (1445), a lively composition by the best artist working in Nuremberg prior to Dürer, an unknown painter now named the 'Master of the Tucher Altar'.

West of the Hauptmarkt (along Augustinerstraße, then down towards the River Pegnitz) is the big, half-timbered **Weinstadel**, a medieval wine store. Willows on the river banks and the covered wooden **Henkersteg** (Hangman's Bridge) make a picture-postcard scene. South of the Hauptmarkt you can cross the river over the Museumbrücke. From here you can see the sprawling stone buildings of the **Heilig-Geist-Spital** (a medieval hospital) on the left, and the neat **Fleischbrücke** (modelled on Venice's Rialto Bridge) on the right.

The Southern Altstadt

By crossing the Museumsbrücke, and following Königstraße (a brash, modern shopping precinct), you come to the **St Lorenz-Kirche** (1250–1477). From the outside St Lorenz looks almost identical to St Sebalds, begun some 25 years earlier: the communities on either side of the river were in fierce competition with each other at the time. The parishioners of St Lorenz did eventually show a little more imagination. Instead of merely imitating their rivals' building, they turned to models in France. The interior of the church is spectacular High Gothic, with a glittering **rose window**, and a prickly 20m-high **tabernacle**, by the local mason Adam Kraft. Above the high altar you can also see more fine carving by Veit Stoss—his polychrome **Annunciation**.

Outside the church is an eye-catching fountain, the **Tugendbrunnen**. The Seven Virtues look a little nonplussed as water squirts from their breasts, and from the up-raised trumpets of supporting cherubs. Across the square is the oldest house in the city, the 13th-century **Nassauer Haus**, which has a turreted upper storey and a prettily carved oriel window.

Huddling around the **Königstor** (at the end of Königstraße, in the south-eastern corner of the Altstadt) is the **Handwerkerhof** (Artisans' Courtyard) (*Mon–Sat 10–6.30*). Here candlemakers, tinworkers, dollmakers and others ply their crafts in a twee medieval atmosphere while tourists look on and buy, and also consume vast quantities of *Bratwurst* and *Lebkuchen.*

The Germanisches Nationalmuseum

The imposing Germanisches Nationalmuseum (*Tues–Sun 10–5, Thurs 10–1; adm DM5*) is on the Kornmarkt (just off Königstraße, across Hallplatz). Its enormous collection of German art and artefacts—gathered from earliest times to the 20th century—is housed in the **Karthaus**, a 14th-century Carthusian monastery. Modern buildings have been integrated into the old Gothic fabric: plate glass and sharp angles contrast quite startlingly with gentler lines and worn stone. Floor plans are available at the entrance, but this museum is fun to explore at random. You can wander through cloisters resplendent with fine carvings, duck through low doors into dim little rooms stuffed with old furniture, climb up narrow stairs to see cabinets of seemingly forgotten cultural ephemera. You can be diverted for hours, and can get quite enjoyably lost.

The **ground floor** is devoted to medieval art, prehistoric artefacts and collections of musical instruments and hunting equipment. The pick of the painting and sculpture is in rooms 8–14. There is work by famous Würzburg woodcarver **Tilman Riemenschneider** (*see* p.44), as well as notable pieces by the local artist and villain **Veit Stoss**. In his exquisite *Raphael and Tobias* (1516) the swirls and billows of the angel's cloak seem to float in the wind. He finished the carving soon after he had been convicted of forging promissory notes, branded on both cheeks, imprisoned and stripped of his status as a Master Craftsman. Two paintings are especially worth seeking out. The gentle, touchingly intimate *Madonna of the Sweet Pea* (1410) by the **Master of St Veronica** is one of the finest examples of the 'soft style' of the Cologne School (*see* p.45). This stands in contrast to the powerful, naturalistic 'hard style' of painters such as **Konrad Witz**. His *Annunciation* (1444) shows an attempt to portray perspective and a treatment of light that was revolutionary for the time.

In the southwest wing of the ground floor you'll find the magically named **Golden Cone of Ezelsdorf-Buch** (1100 BC). The cone, stamped with intricate patterns, is over 88cm high and made from a single piece of paper-thin gold (crushed up, it would fit easily into a matchbox). The southeast wing contains a superbly displayed collection of musical instruments. There is a 12-minute slide show introducing the collection, and headphones dotted around the hall give you a chance to hear recordings of the instruments you're looking at.

The upper floor is haven to a variety of traditional costumes, toys and domestic objects, sculpture and painting from the Renaissance onwards, arts and crafts of the 20th century and the first ever world globe (designed by Martin Behaim in 1491). The **Behaim Globe** has pride of place in Room 35. Nicknamed the *Erdapfel* (Earth Apple), it is, apart from the absence of Australia and the Americas (both then unknown to the Western world) and the odd bit of distorted coastline, remarkably accurate. Behaim based his globe on the latest charts supplied by Portuguese navigators, as well as Ptolemy's map of the 2nd century AD— information which led Columbus to believe that he had reached the Far East when he came across the Americas (and so called its people Indians).

Renaissance and Baroque paintings are hung in Rooms 33–64. Here you can see an extensive collection of works by **Dürer**, such as the eloquent portrait of his bright-eyed octogenarian teacher, *The Painter Michael Wolgemut* (1516). There is also fine work by **Lucas Cranach the Elder**. Look out for the wryly detailed *Venus with Cupid Stealing Honey* (1530). **Hans Baldung** (nicknamed 'Grien' because of his preference for green clothes) is also well represented. In his **Sebastian Altar** (1507), the artist himself (in a dashing red hat and the inevitable green cloak) stands next to the martyred saint, and confidently eyes the viewer.

Most impressive of all are the objects and instruments from Nuremberg's Renaissance heyday as a centre of crafts (Rooms 65–74). The artistry of the **Schlüsselfelder Ship**, a gilded silver tablepiece made around 1503, is breathtaking. A mermaid supports a three-masted ship which is finished in meticulous detail. The rudder can move and the deck and rigging swarm with 74 minute, individually cast sailors.

The 20th-century art in the museum is less exciting. However, in Room G (in the northernmost wing) you can see **Ernst Kirchner's** rather wretched *Self-portrait as a Drunkard* (1915), one of this Expressionist's best works.

South of the City Wall

Just outside the Altstadt boundaries (in Lessingstraße, off Frauentorgraben) is the **Verkehrsmuseum** (Transport Museum) (*daily 9.30–5; adm DM4*). Here, among the old post coaches and model trains you'll find 'Adler', the **first German railway locomotive**. It ran on a track which opened in 1835 between Nuremberg and nearby Fürth.

The grey, looming, half-finished piles built by Hitler as monuments to his Third Reich are to be found in **Luitpoldhain** (*Tram 12*), a park in the southeastern suburbs. This is the setting for the images we are familiar with through old newsreels: from the podium draped with swastikas Hitler made his ranting speeches to the vast stadium filled with a roaring sea of spectators all raising their hands in the *Sieg Heil* salute. Today the buildings are supposedly a memorial to the Nazis' victims, but there seems something distasteful in the fact that they are still used as sports halls and decked out in bunting for fairs and pop concerts.

At the northern entrance to the park is the **Luitpoldarena**, scene of SS parades. Behind that is the **Kongresshalle** (modelled on the Colosseum in Rome, but never completed). Across an artificial lake is the **Zeppelin Tribüne**, designed by star Nazi architect Albert Speer for the massive September rallies. The torches and colonnades have been stripped off the podium, but the massive stadium (holding 70,000) remains. It is windswept and overgrown, but still used by the US Army as a sports ground and during the Norisring motor races (*see* 'Festivals' above).

Shopping

For pewter, stained-glass, pottery, jewellery and handmade knick-knacks, head for the Craftsmen's Courtyard (*see* 'Southern Altstadt' above). Much of the centre of Nuremberg is taken up by the usual pedestrianized shopping zone. In Königstraße, Karolinenstraße and Kaiserstraße you'll find all the major department stores and a few swish boutiques. Schmidt's bakery on the Hauptmarkt sells *Lebkuchen* cooked to a recipe that has been a family secret for centuries.

Entertainment and Nightlife

The local **listings magazine** is *Plärrer* (DM3.50 from news stands). The tourist office brings out a monthly *Monats Magazin* (DM2) and **Sommer in Nürnberg**, a free guide to summer events.

The best music, theatre and opera in Nuremberg happens during the summer arts festivals (*see* 'Festivals' above). At other times the city tends to be outshone by Munich. The local **Opernhaus** and **Schauspielhaus** on Richard Wagnerplatz (south of the Altstadt just outside the city wall; box office ✆ 231 3808) keep up a reasonably high standard. The local **orchestra**, the Nürnberger Symphoniker, plays at the Meistersingerhalle in Luitpoldhain (Tram 12, box office ✆ 492 011). You can also pre-book tickets at a booth on the second floor of the Karstadt department store, opposite the Lorenzkirche.

The Roxy (J. Lossmannstr. 116, ✆ 48840, Tram 8) has a wide-ranging, frequently changing programme of **films** in the original language. The trendiest **disco** in town (often with live music) is **Mach 1** (Kaiserstr. 1–9), hotly followed by Tanztempel One (Rothenburger Str. 29). The **Green Goose** (Vordere Sterngasse 25) has a friendly crowd, and plays New Wave and rock. Das Boot (Hafenstr. 500, Bus 67) offers standard chart music in a converted ship. Over weekends it will cost you around DM10 to get into a disco or nightclub, though this sometimes entitles you to a free drink.

Big time **pop stars** perform at the Serenadenhof (Bayernstr. 100, ✆ 55554). Dixieland is the sole fare at Schmelztiegel (Bergstr. 21), a small **jazz** cellar near the Tiergartenertor. There's a less hearty atmosphere, but better music, at Steps (Johannisstr. 83, Bus 34).

Nürnberg ✆ (*0911–*)

Where to Stay

expensive

Atrium Hotel, Münchener Str. 25, ✆ 47480, ☎ 474 8420 (DM234–398). Classy, glassy modern hotel in the Luitpoldhain Park, with its own pool, sauna, gym and sun terrace.

moderate

Merian-Hotel, Unschlittplatz 7, ✆ 204 194, ☎ 221 274 (DM165). Stylish, well-run hotel in a pretty area of the Altstadt. It has comfortable, tastefully decorated rooms—some look out over a shady square with a fountain—and impeccable standards of service.

Burghotel, Lammgasse 3, ✆ 204 414, ☎ 223 458 (DM160). Folksy hotel at the foot of the Burg. Facilities are smart and modern, and it has a swimming pool.

Hotel Elch, Irrerstr. 9, ✆ 209 544, ☎ 241 9304 (DM150–185). Lovely medieval half-timbered inn in the Altstadt. Rooms can be a bit on the small side, but the atmosphere and friendly, personal service make up for it.

Hotel Marienbad, Eilgutstr. 5, ✆ 203 147, ☎ 204 260 (DM138–170). One of the best of a bunch of nondescript hotels around the Hauptbahnhof. It is clean, efficiently run and there to fall back on if everywhere else is full.

inexpensive

Alt-Nürnberg, Breite Gasse 40, ✆ 224 129 (DM50–60 without private bathroom). Comfortable, centrally situated guesthouse.

Fischer, Brunnengasse 11, ✆ 226 189 (DM67 without private bathroom). Cheap, clean and cheerful.

Vater Jahn, Jahnstr. 13, ✆ 444 507 (DM65–85). Good value, relaxed *pension* near the Hauptbahnhof.

Eating and Drinking

Nuremberg has two culinary claims to fame: ***Nürnberger Bratwurst*** (sausages the size of your little finger) and ***Lebkuchen***, a spicy gingerbread made with honey and nuts. Traditionally *Lebkuchen* are sold only at Christmas, but nowadays you can eat them all year round. *Nürnberger Bratwurst* should be made entirely of pork. The sausages are served on pewter plates, with sauerkraut, potato salad or hot white radish. Six is the minimum order, 'real men' knock back a dozen at a time and if you order more than ten you get them on a heart-shaped plate. Snack stalls sell them '*Zwaa in an Weckla*' (two in a roll). Usually *Bratwurst* are grilled over wood fires, but you can also get them *Nackerte* ('naked'—raw, peeled, mixed with onions, pepper and paprika and spread on black bread), or as *Blaue Zipfel* (marinated in spiced vinegar—reputedly a good hangover cure). *Bauernseufzer* are long, smoked *Bratwurst* which can be eaten raw or boiled.

Restaurants and Taverns

expensive

Entenstub'n, Günthersbühler Str. 145, ℂ 598 0413 (DM80–100). Elegant Michelin-starred restaurant with a shady garden terrace. Famed for its asparagus mousse and fine fish dishes.

Heilig Geist Spital, Spitalgasse 16, ℂ 221 761 (DM45–60). The 15th-century eating hall of the old hospital, extending right out over the River Pegnitz. Excellent, wide-ranging menu with good game and veal dishes.

Goldenes Posthorn, An der Sebalduskirche, ℂ 225 153 (DM45–60). Romantic old inn. Dürer's local, founded in 1498 and still serving up good Franconian meals. There's a delicious potato soup, and tasty asparagus dishes in season.

moderate

Der Nassauer Keller, Karolinenstr. 2–4, ℂ 225 967 (DM35–50). Low ceilings, low lights and strategically placed suits of armour in the cellar of Nuremberg's oldest house. Renowned for their saddle of lamb and old Franconian cookery.

Böhms Herrenkeller, Theatergasse 19, ℂ 224 465 (DM35–50). Traditional tavern with a good wine list and hearty Franconian dishes. Try the *Schweine-braten* (roast pork with potato dumplings) or the *Krautwickala* (stuffed cabbage leaves).

Irrer Elch, Irrerstr. 9, ℂ 209 544 (DM25–50). Cosy medieval tavern with good home-cooking. Game and carp dishes are a speciality.

inexpensive

Prison St Michel, Irrerstr. 2 (DM20–35). Popular French restaurant that serves everything from scrumptious galettes (wholemeal pancakes) to standards such as duckling with orange.

Bratwurst-Häusle, Rathausplatz 1, ℂ 227 695 (DM15–25). The huge chimney puffs out grilled-sausage aroma right across the square. Locals and tourists pack inside for the best *Bratwurst* in town.

Bratwurst-Glöcklein, Im Handwerkerhof, ℂ 227 625 (DM15–25). In the Craftsmen's Courtyard and very touristy, but serves up good *Bratwurst*.

Café Sebald, Weinmarkt 14, ✆ 225 225. Lively, trendy café in the midst of a cluster of half-timbered houses. Also serves good salads and light meals.

Ruhestorung, Tetzelgasse 31, ✆ 221 921. Busy bar in the northern Altstadt, popular with students.

Weinkruger, Wespennest 6–8, ✆ 232 895. Popular wine tavern in the cellar of an old monastery. In the summer it spills out onto a riverside terrace. There's a large wine list, and also good meals.

Tücherbrau am Opernhaus, Frauentorgraben. Busy and attractive beer garden along the city wall, opposite the Opera House.

Café Kröll, Hauptstr. 6–8, ✆ 227 511. Traditional café on the Hauptmarkt. Good coffee and mouth-watering cakes.

Bayreuth

Before the border with the old DDR came down, Bayreuth was a sleepy little town, forgotten in an isolated pocket of West Germany and brought out into the light just once a year for the famous Wagner Festival. The inhabitants were prosperous and conservative, and seemed to begrudge the appearance of the new Bayreuth University in the late 1970s, belittling it with the diminutive *Universitäla*.

The hordes that poured in a decade later—stuffed five to a Trabant, rubbing holes in the steamed-up windscreens and peering out at the wealthy West—were almost too much to bear. Bayreuth is still reeling from the shock. It is now a bustling town on the main Berlin/Munich axis of Germany. The burgeoning numbers of students are asserting their presence and give the town a little life and flair. This, and some fine 18th-century architecture, make Bayreuth worth a visit in its own right.

The Baroque and Rococo buildings are mostly the legacy of the Margravine Wilhelmina, sister of Frederick the Great. In 1731 the cultured, intelligent and passionate Wilhelmina was married to the Margrave of Bayreuth. Had it not been for her father's inept, bungled matchmaking, she could probably have been Queen of England. Instead she was lumped with a provincial Margrave with a reputation as a crushing bore. Not to be defeated by this, Wilhelmina set about transforming Bayreuth into a glittering centre of the arts, and employed some of Europe's top architects to give the town a face-lift.

A century later the composer Richard Wagner chose Bayreuth as the centre for staging his operas. He came to live here with his wife Cosima and her father Franz Liszt, built a theatre and laid the foundations for the annual festival. However, Wagner's nationalism and anti-Semitism appealed to the Nazis and the Bayreuth Festival, as Germany's cultural mecca, became tainted with a fanaticism that it is only just beginning to shake off. Many blame Wagner's English daughter-in-law, Winifred, for cultivating Hitler's patronage, and having him to stay as a house guest when he came to Bayreuth for festivals during the 1930s.

Getting Around

By car: Bayreuth is 85km north of Nuremberg on Autobahn 9, the main route between Berlin and Munich (230km away). Much of the centre of town is pedestrianized. The main parking lots are northeast of the centre off the Wittelsbachring.

   Car hire: Avis, Marktgrafenallee 6, ℭ (0921) 26151; Hertz, Erlanger Str. 43, ℭ (0921) 51155.

By train: The **Hauptbahnhof** is 10 minutes' walk north of the city centre. There are hourly trains to Nuremberg (1hr).

Tourist Information

The **tourist information office**, Luitpoldplatz 9, ℭ (0921) 88588, can help with booking accommodation and offers good walking tours around the town.
Police: ℭ 69182.
Medical Emergencies: ℭ 22222.

Festivals

Every year, for the five weeks from July to the end of August, around 60,000 people cram into Bayreuth for the **Wagner Festival**, the biggest and most important celebration of the composer's work in the world. The festival was founded by Wagner himself. After much bitter wrangling with the Bavarian finance ministry, but with the ardent patronage of King Ludwig II, the Maestro set about designing a theatre and creating a temple to his own art. The first festival (which opened with the *Nibelungen* in 1876) was a complete flop. Wagner even had to sell the costumes to try and recoup costs. It was his second wife, Cosima, who really established the event. She reigned over the festival until 1908, when she handed over to her son Siegfried. Administration remains very much a family affair. Today the show is run by the composer's grandson Wolfgang. Performances take place in the original red-brick Festspielhaus (guided tours Tues–Sun 10–11am, 1.30–3, closed Oct; adm DM3) on a hill north of the centre (past the Bahnhof, along Bürrgerreuther Straße). An imposing, but not particularly beautiful building, it has punishingly hard seats and brilliant acoustics. Official ticket prices range from DM30 to DM230, and tickets go on sale from mid-November. How they are meted out remains a mystery to outsiders (even to the Bayreuth tourist office, who will not be able to help you at all). Agencies around the world get batches—but with no regularity or apparent reason behind the allocation. Individuals have to apply in writing the year before they hope to attend (to Kartenbüro, Festspielleitung, Postfach 10062, D-95445 Bayreuth). The pattern here seems to be that you will strike lucky every fifth or seventh year.

The townspeople's answer to these shenanigans is the **Frankische Festwoche** (Franconian Festival), which usually occurs concurrently with the **Bayreuther**

Volkfest (Folk Festival) for a week in May/June. Here, as well as top-rate cultural fare from the likes of the Bavarian State Opera, you'll find beer tents, a funfair and much jolly merrymaking.

The City Centre

Margravine Wilhelmina's most impressive contribution to Bayreuth architecture is the **Markgräfliches Opernhaus** (*guided tours Tues–Sun 9–11.30 and 1.30–4.30; adm DM2.50*) on Opernstraße, just east of the tourist office. The Margravine commissioned the great Bolognese theatre builder Giuseppe Galli Bibiena and his son Carlo to design the Opera House. From the street it is a plain, rather insignificant building. Even the simple grey foyer with wooden cut-out balustrades doesn't lead you to expect much, but beyond the auditorium doors lies one of the most beautiful and atmospheric theatres in the land. The entire Rococo interior is made of wood—carved, gilded, marbled and painted in deep, subdued greens. There's a tasteful scattering of garlands and putti, and some rich ceiling paintings. The wood gives the theatre intimacy and warmth (as well as excellent acoustics), and also an odd sense of artifice. The theatre itself seems to have all the magic of a stage set. The bell-shaped stage is 27m deep—the largest in Germany until 1871. Its size and good acoustics helped lure Wagner to Bayreuth, but he later decided that even the Opernhaus couldn't cope with the grand productions he had in mind, and built the even bigger Festspielhaus on the hill. Margravine Wilhelmina was an accomplished painter, writer, actress and composer: on the tour of the theatre you get a chance to sit down, soak in the atmosphere, and listen to a recording of one of her works.

Running west from Opernstraße is the town's main shopping street, **Maximilianstraße**. At No.57 you can see the high triangular gable of the 400-year-old sandstone pharmacy, the **Mohren Apotheke**. The northern side of the street is dominated by one of Bayreuth's landmarks, the Baroque **Altes Schloß**, now a tax office. The *Schloß* has twice had to be completely rebuilt: once in recent history, after Allied bombing in 1945, and once in 1753 after it had burnt down. (Some say the Margrave started the fire deliberately, as he wanted a new palace and his wife's extravagance had already drained and alienated the Treasury.) An elegant 16th-century octagonal stone tower juts up behind the *Schloß*. A ramp inside allowed the Margraves to ride their horses right to the top, but today you can climb up for a splendid view of Bayreuth only if you go on the official City Tour.

In Kanzleistraße, which runs south off Maximilianstraße, is the **Stadtmuseum** (*July and Aug Mon–Fri 10–5, Sept–June Tues–Fri 10–5; adm DM2*), a run-of-the-mill museum enlivened by the model ships and miniature cannons used at the beginning of the 18th century by Margrave Georg Wilhelm for the spectacular naval battles he used to stage on the artificial lake behind his palace.

Further on is the **Stadtkirche**, with a quaint stone bridge connecting the tops of its delicate towers. The church is the only building in town which predates the Renaissance. At the back of the church is the diminutive **Schwindsuchtshäschen**, the town's smallest house, which is barely as wide as a car. Kanzleistraße leads into **Friedrichstraße**. Here Margrave Friedrich gave away land cheaply and donated building materials to anyone who would build acccording to plans approved by his architects (who were firmly under the control of Wilhelmina). The result is a sustained and grandiose stretch of Baroque architecture.

Off the northern end of Maximilianstraße (across the Wittelsbachring, at Kulmbachstr. 40) is the **Brauerei- & Büttnerei-Museum** (Brewery and Cooper's Museum) (*guided tours Mon–Thurs 10am*). The half-hour-long tour takes you through the fully functional 19th-century steam brewery, and ends up with free samples in a 1920s-style beer bar.

The Neues Schloß and Villa Wahnfried

If you follow Ludwigstaße, south of Opernstraße, you soon come to the sumptuous **Neues Schloß** (*guided tours Tues–Sun 10–11.30 and 1.30–4.30; adm DM3*), built when the Altes Schloß burned down. Wilhelmina herself had a hand in much of the interior design. The showpiece of the castle is the **Zedernsaal** (Cedar Chamber), a warm, wood-panelled dining hall. In the curious **Spiegelzimmer** (Mirror Room), Wilhelmina intended the irregular fragments of mirror that line the walls to be a comment on the vanity of an age that was overly concerned with appearances.

A shady **Hofgarten** extends behind the *Schloß*. At the eastern end of the garden you come to **Villa Wahnfried**, once Wagner's home and now the **Richard-Wagner-Museum** (*daily 9–5; adm DM2.50, DM3.50 in July and August*). Wagner designed the house himself, and lived here from 1874 to 1883 with his second wife Cosima (whom he had stolen from his leading conductor Hans von Bülow. The house is built around a large central reception hall, where the best musicians of the day gave recitals, and the Wagners held soirées with royals, intellectuals, musicians and artists dancing attendance. The museum houses an interesting collection of Wagner memorabilia, and costumes and photographs of past productions. In the cellar is an intriguing collection of set-designers' models. Wagner and Cosima lie buried in a simple grave behind the house.

The Eremitage

Set amidst wheatfields and woodland on the eastern borders of town (along Königsallee—Bus 2 from Marktplatz) is the romantic **Eremitage** (*guided tours Tues–Sun 9–11.30 and 1–4.30; adm DM2*). Originally built by Margrave Georg Wilhelm (Friedrich's predecessor) as an ascetic retreat (hermitage) from his reputedly voluptuous court, the Eremitage and its park were later given to Margravine Wilhelmina as a present. The frustrated Margravine gave vent to the passionless tedium of her marriage by turning the spartan retreat into a glamorous country seat. She escaped here with her talented friends, and poured her heart out in emotional memoirs which caused a scandal when they were published decades after her death. The palace itself is a mildly interesting Rococo building: the real attraction of the Eremitage lies in the gardens. They include extravagant **fountains** and a **water grotto**, an **artificial ruin** used as an open-air theatre where Wilhelmina herself played Racine's *Bajazet* with Voltaire, and the **Sonnentempel** (Sun Temple). This dumpy dome, to one side of the main palace, is covered with a sort of 18th-century pebbledash of blue and green stones that sparkle in the sunlight. On top is a gilded statue of Apollo driving a chariot pulled by three rearing horses.

Standard prices are given below. Expect an increase of *at least* 20 per cent during the Wagner Festival. Rooms over this period are booked out months in advance.

expensive

Bayerischer Hof, Bahnhofstr. 14, ✆ 22081, @ 22085 (DM150–250). Plush modern hotel close to the station and convenient for the Festspielhaus. The rooms are well-appointed, the staff unobtrusively attentive and the hotel has its own swimming pool and loads of parking space.

moderate

Hotel Goldener Anker, Opernstr. 6, ✆ 65051, @ 65500 (DM140–200). Old-style hotel with smallish but comfortable rooms. Right near the old Opernhaus, and convenient for all the city sights.

Gasthof zum Edeln Hirschen, Richard-Wagner-Str. 77, ✆ 64141, @ 52115 (DM90–110). Well-run family guesthouse with simple, comfortable rooms.

Fränkischer Hof, Rathenaustr. 28, ✆ 64214 (DM95–120). Small, central hotel with friendly management.

Gasthof Goldener Löwe, Kulmbacher Str. 30, ✆ 41046, @ 47777 (DM96–110). Charming, countrified brewery-cum-guesthouse in a quiet spot still quite close to the centre of town.

inexpensive

Gasthof Zum Herzog, Herzog 2, Kulmbacher Str., ✆ 41334 (DM78–86, some rooms without private bathroom). Clean, comfortable and good value.

Youth Hostel: Universitätsstr. 28, ✆ 25262 (Bus 4).

Eating and Drinking: Restaurants and Taverns

Annecy, Gabelsbergerstr. 11, ✆ 26279 (DM40–60). Relaxed atmosphere and good, unpretentious French cuisine—scrumptious casseroles and poultry dishes.

Wölfel, Kirchgasse 12, ✆ 68499 (DM25–50). Cosy tavern, ideal for a meal after a drink at the Eule. Serves excellent Franconian cuisine. You can get delicious baked carp, or ham cooked in a doughy pastry.

Brauereischänke am Markt, Maximilianstr. 56, ✆ 64919 (DM20–40). A little touristy, but with a jolly atmosphere and hearty Franconian fare: good sausages and pork with raw dumplings.

Bars and Cafés

Rosenau, Badstr. 29, ✆ 65136. Good beerhall which has a beer garden and a friendly atmosphere.

Herzogkeller, Hindenburgstraße, ✆ 43419. Vast beer garden which is popular with students.

Eule, Kirchgasse 8, ✆ 57554. Known as Bayreuth's *Künstlerkneipe* (artists' pub). Musicians and singers used to gather here after festival performances. The walls are covered with photographs that span decades of Wagnerian stars. It's the nearest the town comes to a Festival Museum, and worth a visit (even though today's celebrities tend to stay outside Bayreuth and socialize in their private apartments).

Café Florian, Dammallee 12a, ✆ 56757. Festival or no, the watering-hole for Bayreuth's 'in' crowd.

Operncafé, Opernstr. 16, ✆ 65720. Elegant café next to the old Opernhaus. A good place for coffee and gooey cakes.

North of Bayreuth

The B2/B303 from Bayreuth leads to the heart of the Fichtelgebirge (about 35km), passing through **Bad Berneck**, a health resort whose ultra-modern clinics intrude on a picturesque setting, complete with a 15th-century fortified chapel and the ruins of a 12th-century castle, perched on a hill above the town. East of Bad Berneck, thick blankets of conifers shroud the granite hills of the **Fichtelgebirge** (Spruce Mountains). The range is shaped like a horseshoe opening up onto the foothills of the Bohemian Forest in the Czech Republic. Although the mountains are really no more than chunky hills, they do include the **Schneeberg** (1051m) and the **Ochsenkopf** (1024m), two of the highest peaks in Franconia. The landscape is less dramatic than further southwest in Franconian Switzerland, so the area has escaped the full impact of tourism and remains a sleepy backwater of farms and villages, with the odd dilapidated castle.

Rich deposits of tin, lead, silver and gold in the Fichtelgebirge gave medieval Franconia its economic clout. In later centuries, as the minerals began to run out, the locals turned to textile-production, glass-blowing and porcelain manufacture, the last of which still plays a significant role in the region's economy. Fichtelgebirge ceramics can be found in classy shops throughout Europe. The tourist office has cashed in on the industry by designating a **porcelain road** along the B15, linking the towns of Marktredwitz, Thierstein and Selb. In **Selb**, near the Czech border, the whole town revolves round china. Here are the Rosenthal and Hutschenreuther porcelain factories, and an obviously prosperous community. There is a **porcelain fountain** standing imperiously in Selb's swish pedestrian precinct, and you'll even find yourself walking on **porcelain cobblestones**. The **Museum der Deutschen Porzellanindustrie** (Museum of the German Porcelain Industry) (*Tues–Sun 9–17; adm DM2*) in neighbouring **Hohenberg** gives a very comprehensive account of the history of porcelain production, with examples of different period styles.

An alternative route to the northwest of Bad Berneck on the B303 whisks you to the Franconian Forest (about 50km). First stop is **Wirsberg**, a creaky half-timbered cluster of houses surrounded almost completely by forest. The village styles itself as the 'Verdant Wedding Village', a kind of Bavarian Gretna Green. Provided that you have all the correct paperwork (this is, after all, Germany), the local *Bürgermeister* promises to marry you at any time of the day. Beyond Wirsberg, the B289 leads to Kulmbach, a mecca for all serious beer-drinking folk in Bavaria.

Kulmbach

If Bayreuth caters to loftier cultural aspirations, Kulmbach takes care of the more mundane things in life. In a *Land* that boasts some 800 breweries—about half of all those in Germany's—Kulmbach has the distinction of not only brewing more beer than anywhere else in Bavaria, but also drinking the largest share *per capita*. Beer-brewing has a long tradition in Kulmbach—up to the beginning of the 15th century each citizen was entitled to brew his own beer.

Today the four big breweries in town pride themselves on their attention to detail, in choosing their strain of barley, specifying how it should be kilned in the maltings, selecting hop varieties, finding the spring water of the requisite softness and breeding yeasts that confer subtle and complex background flavours. You can sample local brews on a pub-crawl of brewery-owned *Gaststätten*, or go on one of the rewarding guided tours offered by the three leading breweries in town (*see* 'Tourist Information' below). The cold and extremely powerful *Eisbock* is Reichelbräu's star product, but still considered small beer next to EKU's ominously named *Kulminator 28*, at 22 per cent proof said to be the world's strongest brew.

However, Kulmbach is not all beer and skittles. In the **Unterstadt**, fine old burgher houses are grouped around a spacious **Marktplatz**. From here you can walk up through the older **Oberstadt** to Kulmbach's other attraction, the **Plassenburg**, from where you'll get panoramic views over the town and surrounding countryside. The castle dates from the 12th century, but most of what you see today was built 400 years later. Inside the walls a number of residential buildings are crammed together round an impressively ornate Renaissance courtyard. The castle itself houses the **Deutsches Zinnfiguren-museum** (National Museum of Tin Figurines) (*April–Sept Tues–Sun 10–5; Oct–Mar Tues–Sun 10–3; adm DM3*), where a series of over 200 dioramas, with around 300,000 figurines, take you from the Middle Ages to modern times. Also on the Plassenburg is the **Staatliche Sammlungen** (Bavarian State Collection) (*same times; adm DM3*), displaying a good stock of hunting weapons and an Iron Age amphora containing sediments of beer brewed more than 2500 years ago.

Tourist Information

The **tourist information office** is in the modern Stadthalle, Sutte 2, ℂ (09221) 95880. Generally, Kulmbach's **breweries** can be toured by groups only. You can make a booking by phoning: Kulmbacher Reichelbräu AG ℂ (09221) 705225, Erste Kulmbacher Actienbrauerei ℂ (09221) 882283; Mönchshof-Bräu GmbH ℂ (09221) 80519. Individuals can, however, join a guided tour of the Mönchshof brewery Tues–Thurs at 1pm and Fri at 11am; adm DM11, including beer-tasting and snack).

Kulmbach has its fair share of festivals. The main one is the bacchanal nine-day-long **Beer Week**, which takes place in a gargantuan tent between July and August. Less strenuous is the **Zinnfigurenbörse** (Tin Figurines Exchange), a collectors' fair in early August of alternate years (next in 1995).

The Beer-and-Castle Road

The B85 past Kulmbach is yet another theme road, the **Bier- und Burgenstraße** (Beer-and-Castle Road) that stretches far into Thuringia past parades of fortresses and towns with traditional breweries. Working your way up the route, you come to Kronach, another medieval gem of the Franconian heights.

Kronach

'*In Kronach schmeckt der Dreck wie Honig*' ('In Kronach even the dirt tastes like honey') goes a local saying. It is indeed a charmed town, which has preserved many of its half-timbered buildings. The hometown of Lucas Cranach the Elder, the quirky Renaissance painter (*see* p.47), also has a bold Renaissance **Rathaus** and a **hall church** that represents a high point in Franconian Gothic. The town lies in the shadow of the **Veste Rosenberg**, a fortress complex, dating back to the Staufian epoch, but much altered in the 16th and 17th centuries. Nowadays the impressive ring of pentagonal bastions has lost its menace, and the keep and the buildings round the inner courtyard house two interesting museums: the **Frankenwaldmuseum** (Museum of the Franconian Forest; *Tues–Sun 2–5; adm DM2*), and the **Fränkische Gallerie** (Franconian Gallery; *April–Dec 10–5; adm DM3*), which has some fine works of Lucas Cranach the Elder and Younger.

The **tourist information office** is on Marktplatz 5, near the Rathaus, ✆ (09261) 97236.

The Franconian Forest

Back on the B85, which now closely follows the path of the River Haßlach, the road winds through the **Franconian Forest** (German: *Frankenwald*), on past Ludwigstadt to **Burg Lauenstein** (*April–Sept Tues–Sun 9–11.30 and 1–4.30; Oct–Mar Tues–Sun 10–11.30 and 1–3; adm DM2*), high on a promontory overlooking the woods. Stretching south from the Thuringian Forest, the Franconian plateaux rise to a height of 600m. A sparsely populated, heavily wooded stretch of countryside (most of it is a **nature park**), the Franconian Forest is dotted with half-forgotten villages, whose residents once lived by processing timber. The web of rivers that cut through the attractive wooded hillsides proved ideal for timber rafting as well as the source of power for numerous watermills.

The Franconian Forest is popular with walkers, though a novel way of seeing some of the more unspoilt parts is on a reconstructed **log-raft**, floating down the River Wilde Rodach.

The rafts depart from Wallenfels, northeast of Kronach, usually at weekends (*May–Sept*). The **Flößermuseum** (Rafters' Museum) (*Tues–Fri 9–11 and 2–4; Sat, Sun 2–4; adm DM2*) in nearby Marktrodach vividly depicts the harsh lives that the rafting folk once led.

The best walks in the area are in the glades around the Rivers Rodach and Tetau. Following the Rodach gorge you pass a series of historic timbered **saw-mills**, then cross the river at Steinwiesen before heading north through the Leitsch Valley to the slate-roofed village of Tschirn. The **Rennsteig**, one of the region's oldest and finest long-distance wilderness footpaths, cuts through the northern Franconian Forest (on the western side of the B85), from Tetau all the way to Steinbach am Wald.

Tourist Information

Kronach: Frankenwald, Amtsgerichtsstr. 21, ✆ (09261) 60150.

Where to Stay and Eating Out

Bad Berneck

Kurhotel Zur Mühle, Kolonnadenweg 1, ✆ (09273) 6133, ✉ (09273) 1489 (DM150–180). A quiet, well-equipped spa hotel with pool and views over the Kurpark.

Kronach

Bauer's Hotel, Kulmbacher Str. 7, ✆ (09261) 94058, ✉ (09261) 52298 (DM134–145). This charming little hotel also has the best restaurant in town. The delicious home-cooked food includes local dishes and imaginative specials.

Kulmbach

Best-Western Parkhotel, Luitpoldstr. 2, ✆ (09221) 6030, ✉ (09221) 03100 (DM154–196). The town's most upmarket hotel. Attentive care and comfort, but little flair and situated on a busy traffic junction.

Hotel Kronprinz, Fischergasse 4-6, ✆ (09221) 84031, ✉ (09221) 1585 (DM130–160). Right in the historic Unterstadt, beneath the Plassenburg. Traditional décor, though some rooms are on the small side.

Bamberg

> Das ist eine Stadt, die steckt voller Raritäten, wie die Kommode einer alten Großmama, die viel zusammenscharrte. (*This is a city stuffed with more curiosities than an old, hoarding granny's chest of drawers.*)
>
> Karl Immerman (19th-century traveller).

Bamberg is a vibrant university town, just west of Bayreuth, built on seven hills along the River Regnitz. It is a hot contender for the title of the most beautiful town in Germany, yet is inexplicably ignored by most foreign tourists. The Thirty Years' War and the Second

World War—which together caused the ruin of so many German cities—left Bamberg relatively unscathed. It has managed to salvage at least one good example of every European architectural style from Romanesque onwards. Without losing its medieval structure or charm, the town enjoyed a Baroque building boom when some of the era's greatest architects slipped decorous mansions in between the wonky half-timbered houses that prop each other up along Bamberg's steep, winding alleys.

Bamberg also has a splendid cathedral, boisterous student life, a symphony orchestra of world repute, and ten excellent local breweries—just the sort of mixed bag that can make a small German town a delight.

Getting Around

By car: Bamberg is just off Autobahn 70, which links it to Würzburg (100km) and Bayreuth (70km), and Autobahn 73, which runs south to Nuremberg (60km). The biggest and most convenient undercover parking garage in the city is beneath Maximilianplatz, near the Rathaus.

By train: The Bahnhof (information ✆ (0951) 19419) is 15 minutes' walk from the centre. (To get to the Rathaus walk down Luitpoldstraße, turn right into Obere Königstraße and then cross the Kettenbrücke.) There are hourly connections to Würzberg (1hr) and frequent trains to Nuremberg (¾hr) and Munich (2½hrs).

Taxis: ✆ 15015.

River cruises: You get superb views of Bamberg from the river, especially in the early morning. Tickets for boat trips can be bought from Bamberger Veranstaltungstdienst (Langestr. 24).

Tourist Information

The **tourist information office**, Geyerswörthstr. 3, ✆ (0951) 871 161, is on an island in the Regnitz (April–Sept Mon–Fri 9–7, Sat 9–5; Oct–Mar Mon–Fri 9–6, Sat 9–2).

Post office: Ludwigstr. 25, near Bahnhof (Mon–Fri 7–7, Sat 7–2, Sun 11–1).

Banks: Branches of most German banks are situated along Hauptwachstraße/ Grüner Markt.

Police: ✆ 110.

Medical emergencies: ✆ 19222.

Festivals

Roman Catholic Bamberg's main festival is **Corpus Christi** (May/June) when there is a church procession with many people dressed in Tracht. There is more traditional dress and dancing, as well as water-jousting during the **Sandfest** in August.

The Lower City

The lower part of the city is the scene of Bamberg's day-to-day commercial life. The hub of all the activity is **Maxplatz**, where there is a busy weekday fruit and vegetable market. On the northern side of the square stands the ponderous, imposing **Rathaus** (originally a seminary) designed by the great Baroque architect, Balthasar Neumann. Grünermarkt, a wide boulevard of Baroque buildings, leads south off Maxplatz. The most impressive façade belongs to **St Martin**, a stately Jesuit church built in 1686–83 by the Dietzenhofer brothers (who designed many of Bamberg's best Baroque buildings). Inside there is a rather clever *trompe l'œil* dome.

Grüner Markt leads on to the Obere Brücke, a bridge over the River Regnitz. Linking the Obere Brücke and the Untere Brücke, a few yards downstream, is the **Altes Rathaus**, certainly the oddest town hall in Germany. The Rathaus completely covers an island in the middle of the river, so it seems to float like a rather gaudy boat tethered to the two bridges. The basic structure is Gothic, though this was given a Rococo boost in the late 18th century. A soaring stone gateway arches over Obere Brücke. On one side of the arch stretches a wing emblazoned with bright murals, on the other side a little half-timbered addendum hangs out over the water.

From the Untere Brücke you can see **Klein-Venedig**, a cluster of half-timbered fishermen's houses that come right up to the water's edge. On the other side of the river the hills bristle with a variety of church spires. To the east of the bridges, in streets lined with faded ochre buildings reminiscent of Italy, you'll find two of the most ostentatious Baroque mansions in the city. The **Böttingerhaus** (Judengasse 14) has an opulent portal and courtyard, bulging with stucco work by the local artist Vogel. The house was built by the Franconian *chargé d'affaires* in 1707–13. Later he built himself a summer river-palace almost next door. The **Concordia** (at the end of Concordiastraße) is, however, best viewed from across the water. This you can do by ducking down an alleyway at the bottom of Concordiastraße and over the bridge onto the Geyersworth island.

The Nonnenbrücke takes you from the island across to Schillerplatz back on the northern river bank. Here you will find the **E.T.A. Hoffmann-Haus** (*May–Oct Tues–Fri 4–6, Sat and Sun 10–12; adm DM1*). E.T.A. Hoffmann (1776–1822) was a Romantic painter, composer and writer who is today most remembered for his bizarre short stories. Two of his tales inspired Romantic ballets—Delibes' *Coppelia* and Tchaikovsky's *The Nutcracker*. Hoffmann himself (who had an eccentric, even schizophrenic personality) is the subject of Offenbach's opera *The Tales of Hoffmann*. For most of his life Hoffmann was a civil servant, but while he lived in Bamberg (1808–13) he tried to make a career of his various artistic talents. The museum contains a large collection of memorabilia, but is really only worth a visit if you are a Hoffmann fan.

The Domstadt

In the 11th century Emperor Henry II first established the Bishopric of Bamberg in the hope that the city would become the capital of the Holy Roman Empire and rival Rome in importance. His dreams weren't realized, but Bamberg did become a famous centre of learning in the Middle Ages, and the prince-bishopric he created was to last until Napoleon's secularization. The cathedral and ecclesiastical palaces that crown Bamberg's main hill are known as the Domstadt (Cathedral City), in contrast to the commercial town down below. From the Altes Rathaus you wind through narrow alleys and up precipitous stairways to the large, sloping **Domplatz**. This square presents a magnificent spectrum of European architecture from Romanesque beginnings in the cathedral to Gothic, Renaissance and Baroque in the surrounding buildings.

The Cathedral

The first **cathedral**, commissioned by Emperor Henry II, burnt down twice. Construction of the present one began around 1215 and lasted until 1237—two decades that saw the flowering of Gothic architecture. The east chancel of the cathedral is earthy, rounded Romanesque; the west chancel flighty, pointed Gothic. Between them the nave is a perfect illustration of the Transitional style. The four towers mirror each other with just a slight distortion that reflects the changes that those two important decades produced: the spires on the western end are a touch lighter, sharper and more delicate than their solid Romanesque counterparts.

The **Fürstenportal** (Prince's Portal, 1228) on the north side of the nave is a supreme feat of Romanesque carving. Apostles and Old Testament prophets line arches that recede towards a heavy wooden door. On the tympanum, Christ presides authoritatively over the Last Judgement. Inside, gathered around the east choir, are more fine early **13th-century sculptures**. A youthful, pregnant Virgin, swathed in superbly worked folds of cloth, is flanked by an aged Elizabeth (also known as 'The Bamberg Sibyl'). Two much simpler female figures, *Synagogue* and *Ecclesia*, represent the Old and New Testaments. Synagogue is blindfolded, skinny and wears a thin, seemingly transparent shift. Ecclesia has a crown, fuller garments and a smug smile. Most famous of all is the statue of the **Bamberger Reiter** (Bamberger Rider *c.* 1235). No one knows who the horseman is— possibly Constantine the Great, maybe one of the Magi. He sits proud on his steed, reins in check, staring far into the distance. The whole statue quivers with energy, but holds unfortunate memories for many. Hitler saw it as a pinnacle of German artistic perfection, and during the Third Reich reproductions adorned public buildings everywhere. The **Imperial Tomb** in the centre of the nave contains the remains of the saintly 11th-century ruler Emperor Henry II and his consort Kunigunde. The top and sides are covered in carvings depicting events from their lives by the famous medieval sculptor Tilman Riemenschneider (*see* p.44). To the left of the west chancel you can see the deeply burnished, though sadly unfinished, **Weinachtsaltar** (Nativity Altar, 1520–3), one of the last works of the Nuremberg sculptor Veit Stoss.

The **Diözesanmuseum** (Diocesan Museum) (*Easter–Oct Tues–Sun 10–5.30; adm DM2*) is across the cloisters in the chapterhouse (another Balthasar Neumann building). Here you'll find some richly woven ecclesiastical vestments, including robes belonging to Henry II and Kunigunde and the papal vestments of Pope Clement II—the only pope to be buried in Germany. He died in 1047, and his tomb is in the western choir, but is not accessible to the public.

The Alte Hofhaltung

Alongside the cathedral is the Alte Hofhaltung, a motley complex which comprises the former imperial and episcopal palace and old imperial Diet Hall. The **Ratstube**, a graceful Renaissance building on the corner nearest the cathedral, now houses the **Historisches Museum** (*May–Oct Tues–Sun 9–5; adm DM2*), a missable collection of bits and bobs relating to the city's history. Next to this is a grand Renaissance stone gateway, the **Reiche Tor** (Imperial Gate). It is flanked by allegorical figures of the Pegnitz and Main rivers and shows Henry and Kunigunde carrying a remarkably accurate model of the cathedral. Through the arch you come to the big, uneven cobbled **inner court**. All around the edges are striking, four-storey, 15th-century half-timbered buildings with wooden galleries and heavy, drooping eaves.

The Neue Residenz

The rest of the Domplatz is taken up by a later palace, the huge L-shaped Neue Residenz (*April–Sept daily 9–12 and 1.30–5, Oct–Mar 9–12 and 1.30–4; adm DM3*). The palace is yet another product of the powerful Schönborn family (*see* pp.144–5), whose mutual one-upmanship resulted in a scattering of grand buildings across Germany. The Baroque Residenz was commissioned by Prince-Bishop Lothar Franz von Schönborn (who was also Archbishop and Elector of Mainz), and built by Leonhard Dientzenhofer in 1697–1703. The **interior** is worth a visit for a look at the bright frescoes in **Kaisersaal**, and also a finely painted **Chinesische Kabinett**. The building also houses the small **Staatsgalerie**, a not particularly notable collection which includes works by Cranach the Elder and Hans Baldung Grien. Around the back of the palace is a **rose garden**, a fragrant retreat with serene statues, a Rococo summerhouse (now a café) and a magnificent view over Bamberg.

Michaelsberg and Altenburg

A footpath leads up from Aufseß-Straße (behind the Residenz), through orchards to the top of Michaelsberg, another of Bamberg's seven hills. The Benedictine **abbey** of St Michael on top of the hill is now an old people's home, but you can visit its Baroque church which has delicate paintings of over 600 medicinal herbs on the ceiling. The abbey cellars house the **Fränkisches Brauereimuseum** (*Tues–Fri 1–4.30, Sat and Sun 1.30–4; adm DM3*), a small museum of beer and brewing history. Outside, a spacious terrace looks out over Bamberg and the surrounding countryside, and there is a small café under the trees.

Retracing steps down Michaelsberg and continuing along Maternstraße, you reach the **Karmelitenkloster**. The church is another Dientzenhofer Baroque showpiece, but the **cloisters** (*daily 8–11 and 2–5.30*) are serenely Romanesque. Nearby, on Unterkaul, is Bamberg's finest Gothic church, the **Obere Pfarrkirche**, while uphill (along Altenburger Straße) is the **Altenburg** (1109), a ruined castle complete with moat and bear pit.

Where to Stay
expensive

St. Nepomunk, Obere Mühlbrücke 9, ✆ 25183, 📠 26651 (DM190–240). Stylish hotel that teeters over the Regnitz on stilts. The rooms are sumptuously decorated and the service is impeccable.

moderate

Hotel Alt Ringlein, Domanikanerstr. 9, ✆ 54098, 📠 52230 (DM130–180). Spruce, newly modernized hotel, part of which has been an inn since 1545. It nestles in the shadow of the cathedral, and is run by a capable and attentive family.

Barock-Hotel am Dom, Vorderer Bach 4, ✆ 54031, 📠 54021 (DM125–145). A beautiful old Baroque building in a quiet, shady street behind the cathedral. The rooms aren't very imaginatively furnished, but they're comfortable enough and the management is helpful and friendly.

Weierich, Lugbank 5, ✆ 54004, 📠 55800 (DM95–120). Rustic, cosy inn, centrally situated.

inexpensive

Spezial, Obere Königstr. 10, ✆ 24304 (DM80). Comfortable tavern run by a local brewery, a few minutes' walk from the lower city.

Fässla, Obere Königstr. 21 (DM90). Also owned by a local brewery, but a little more upmarket with TV in the rooms and a hearty breakfast buffet.

Youth Hostel: Wolfsschlucht, Obere Leinritt 70, ✆ 56002.

Eating and Drinking

Bamberg is most famous for its beer. There are ten local breweries, which together produce around 30 different kinds. Locals rate highly the *Rauchbier* (smoky beer) made from smoked malt following a 16th-century recipe. The taverns owned by the breweries are also often recommendable places for tasty good-value meals.

Zum Schenkerla, Domanikanerstr. 6, ✆ 56060 (DM25–35). Lively 17th-century tavern. Good beer and light meals.

Spezial, Sternartstraße (DM25–35). Beer cellar with garden, popular with locals and serving well-prepared food.

Dom-Terrassen, Unterer Kaulberg 36 (DM25–45). Unassuming *Gaststätte* near the Karmelitenkloster. Splendid terrace with views over the Domplatz.

Michaelsburg. There's a small café for *Kaffee und Küche*, as well as a larger *Gaststätte* (meals DM25–55) on the Michaelsburg. Both have terraces overlooking the town.

Café Domherrenshof, Karolinerstr. 24. Big basket chairs, high Baroque ceilings and a terrace with a view up to the Neue Residenz. Good place for breakfast or a lunchtime snack.

Entertainment and Nightlife

The **Bamberger Symphoniker**, once the *Deutsches Orchester* of Prague, skipped the border as the Iron Curtain was falling. They give concerts all over town, but one of the most enchanting ways to hear them is at the regular candlelit performances in the Kaisersaal of the Neue Residenz. Members of the *Symphoniker* also form the **Bamberg Baroque Ensemble**, which plays chamber music, and there are various other groups of high quality performing around town. **Tickets** for all concerts can be obtained from Bamberger Veranstaltungsdienst, Lange Str. 24, ✆ 25255. Nearby is **Downstairs** (Lange Str. 16), the **nightclub** most popular with Bamberg's trendies.

North of Bamberg

Just northeast of Bamberg, at Memmeldorf, lies **Schloß Seehof**, one of the two palatial residences that the prince-bishops of Bamberg commissioned in the 17th and 18th centuries (the other is Schloß Weißenstein at Pommersfelden). Built at the turn of the 17th century, the square building was given the full early Baroque treatment, with the addition of four stout octagonal towers. Nowadays the Schloß is the home of Franconia's office for the preservation of historic monuments. They have brought new life to the adjoining landscaped gardens, which had become overgrown and uncared for since the estate's secularization in 1803.

Continuing a few miles further on along the B173, you come to **Staffelstein**, a charming little string of Franconian half-timbered buildings, laced between a dolomite bluff and the River Main. On the diminutive Marktplatz you can see the town's pride and joy, the picture-postcard Baroque **Rathaus** (1687). At the **Städtisches Museum** (Town Museum) (*April–SeptTues–Fri 10-12 and 2–4 Sat, Sun 2–4; 19 Dec–9 Jan Sat, Sun 2–4; adm DM2*), you can find out all about **Adam Riese**, the mathematical wizard who was born locally in 1492, and whose name has long been the byword for arithmetic accuracy to every German schoolchild.

Beyond Staffelstein, in an area of rugged little hills, two more cheerful Baroque buildings appear on either side of the B173. Standing alone, high above the woods to the west is **Kloster Banz**. Founded in 1069 by the Benedictine order, the monastery received a complete Baroque facelift after 1695. The princely dimensions of the estate enticed the Wittelsbachs into buying it in 1814, with a view to turning it into a palace. Today it is home to a training and conference centre of the Bavarian Christian Social Party. The **church** at the far southwest corner is the most eye-catching building in the complex, and the interior of the church is considered one of architect Johann Diezenhofer's master-pieces: crimson, grey and golden tones suffuse the oval-shaped nave, with the delicate Franconian woodcarving of the **choir stalls** adding a touch of class. Crowning a slope on the opposite side of the main road, the **Vierzehnheiligen** counterbalances Kloster Banz. This pilgrimage church was built on the spot where, in 1519, a shepherd had seen three successive apparitions of fourteen of Franconia's favourite patron saints. A chapel was built here as early as 1525, but the present Baroque church is based on designs by Balthasar Neumann. The church is a brilliant example of the spatial illusionism that was to become a Neumann speciality: the interior, based on a series of ovals, appears to be much larger than is actually the case. The marble and the gold-leaf stucco combine to produce some dazzling effects, but even finer are the masterly, highly theatrical *trompe l'œil* ceiling frescoes by Giuseppe Appiani, with a foreshortened Annunciation above the choir and a central cycle illustrating the 14 saints who gave the church its name. The same saints adorn the **Gnadenaltar**, a free-standing altar with an ostentatiously ornamented baldacchino. This central altar is on a par with the outrageously tinselly Rococo **high altar** at the east end, creating an equally inviting, joyful atmosphere.

From Vierzehnheiligen it is just 25km on the B289 and B4 past the town of **Lichtenfels**, famed for its wicker work, to Coburg.

Coburg

Standing magisterially on a leafy hill above the town is one of the most outstanding sights of northern Franconia, the awesome **Veste Coburg**. From far away the castle's towers and gabled buildings poke up like the points of a crown, from behind a mighty ring wall.

The Veste can look back on more than 750 years of history. From 1353 it was linked with the Wettin rulers of Saxony and Thuringia, becoming one of their chief residences in the 16th century. The descendants of the Wettins, the **Saxe-Coburg-Gotha** family, provided spouses for royal families all over Europe, including Queen Victoria's consort, Prince Albert. The complex was almost completely rebuilt in the 16th and 17th centuries, and is now a **museum** (*April–Oct Tues–Sun 9.30–1 and 2–5; Nov-Mar Tues-Sun 2-5; adm*

DM2.50) with a vast and important collection of engravings and other work by Rembrandt, Cranach, Dürer *et al*, and a captivating cross-section of over four centuries of period interiors in the timber-framed Fürstenbau.

Coburg's **Altstadt** is laid out in a series of twisting streets between the castle hill and the River Itz. In the middle is the **Stadtplatz**, dominated by the late 16th-century **Rathaus** and the Stadthaus (*c.* 1600), the former ducal chancellery. In both, the dying flickers of the Renaissance are fused with the new spirit of early Baroque. Close to the central square you'll find two prime examples of half-timbered architecture: the **Münzmeisterhaus** (1348), generally regarded as one of the most beautiful examples of Franconian *Fachwerk*, and the **Hofapotheke** (*c.* 1400), a former apothecary with a late Gothic oriel projection.

Proof that the new dynastic ties with (among others) the courts at St Petersburg, London, Lisbon and Stockholm did, in fact, pay off for the Saxe-Coburg-Gothas is the 16th-century **Schloß Ehrenburg** (*guided tours Tues–Sun 10, 11, 1.30, 2.30 and 3.30: adm DM2.50*). This sumptuous Renaissance palace in the middle of the town was given a neo-Gothic going-over in the 19th century. One of the curiosities on display is Germany's first operating water-closet installed for none other than Queen Victoria, who didn't want to do without the amenity which had grown so dear to her.

For those who like to people their living rooms with porcelain figurines, the **Hummel porcelain works** in the small town of **Rödental**, just to the northeast of Coburg, afford an insight into the painstaking manufacturing techniques that go into the perky characters which the Franciscan nun Maria Innocentia (1909–46) designed on paper during the 1930s, and which have since been successfully marketed the world over.

Tourist Information

The **tourist information office** is at Herrengasse 4, ℸ (09561) 95071.

Where to Stay and Eating Out

Coburg

Hotel Festungshof, Festungsberg 1, ℸ (09561) 75077, ℻ (09561) 94372 (DM140–210). A newly renovated and well-equipped small hotel on the foot of the hill that leads up to the Veste.

Hotel Goldener Anker, Rosengasse 14, ℸ (09561) 95027 (DM90). A central Hotel with good management and a respected restaurant (DM35–45).

Staffelstein

Kurhotel, Oberauer Str. 2, ℸ (09573) 3330, ℻ (09573) 333299 (DM105–148). A hotel on the outskirts of the town, with its own sauna, solarium, massage and easy access to the **Obermain-Therme**, Bavaria's latest and hottest thermal springs. Generally full of middle-aged Germans taking the *Kur*.

Franconia's Cuisine

 Back in the 14th century monastic scribes in Würzburg started to record their views on a healthy, balanced diet. They have provided us with the oldest-known collection of recipes in the German language. Franconian cooking has come a long way since. To the visitor it may all too often boil down to sausages and sauerkraut, but Franconia has a great deal more to offer, and views its gastronomy almost as an art form. Fertile land and a temperate climate fill the kitchens with an abundance of natural produce, and Franconia is famous for its potatoes, tomatoes, spinach, onions and asparagus. The land north of Nuremberg is known as the *Knoblauchsland* (garlic country).

If you want to stick to sausages, you'll find as many versions as there are towns. Supreme among them all is the original *Nürnberger Bratwurst*, which is no longer than a little finger and is eaten in multiples of half a dozen. In Coburg sausages are traditionally prepared over a charcoal fire of fir or pine-cones, while the *Blaue Zipfel* (Blue Tail-Ends), first made in Bamberg, are simmered in vinegar (which gives them their bluish tinge) together with tarragon, onions, carrots, parsley, mustard and pepper. *Blaue Zipfel* are traditionally served with sauerkraut and a horseradish sauce, or with potato salad.

Potatoes rarely appear *au naturel*, but come dressed up as *Knödel* (dumplings). The classic potato dumpling in Franconia is made of about two-thirds raw potatoes and one-third boiled ones, sometimes blended with flour, maize-meal or toasted bread-crumbs. There are many variations on this theme, such as liver, bacon and bread dumplings. The latter must be soft and fluffy enough to be broken open with a fork.

Thrift has also traditionally been an important feature of the Franconian cuisine. A meal must be satisfying, but not cost too much; a good example of this is the tasty cheese dish *Gerupfter* (a favourite accompaniment for *Federweißer*), made with Camembert and butter seasoned with paprika, rolled into a ball with egg yolk and finely chopped onions. Sometimes a little beer or wine is added for good measure. This rule of simplicity has also inspired housekeepers to produce desserts from inexpensive ingredients, and there is a wide variety of cooked puddings. *Ausgezogene*, tiny slabs of filled pastry, are probably the most popular creation. The dish's name (literally: something drawn out) describes how the sweetened dough was once rolled between the housewife's knees so as to shape the pastry.

Between Bamberg and Bayreuth: Franconian Switzerland

Franconian Switzerland (German: *Fränkische Schweiz*) is the name that is gushingly given to the triangular area between Bamberg, Bayreuth and Nuremberg by the 19th-century German Romantics. In fact the landscsape is far from Alpine, although it does have some surprisingly deep valleys, lush meadows, blankets of cherry and apple groves, and sudden outcrops of dolomite rock, some with stalactite caves and topped by gaunt castle ruins. Franconian Switzerland has long been a popular holiday destination and is a good spot for hiking.

Getting Around

Local buses are erratic and train routes tend to follow a circular course around the edges of the region, so the best way to get around is **by car**. Bamberg, Bayreuth and Nuremberg are equally convenient starting points. The B2, B470 and B22 cut across the area, but in order to see the more remote scenery it's best to resort to local roads.

The main **train lines** serving the region run from Forchheim to Ebermannstadt, with a connection to Behringermühle; from Nuremberg to Gräfenberg and from Nuremberg to Neunkirchen, with a connection to Simmelsdorf-Hüttenbach.

Franconian Switzerland is very much an area to explore **on foot** or **by bicycle**. On 4000km of signposted walking trails, you can follow in the footsteps of the Romantic literati who first trudged this unspoilt beauty spot. The region is also well laid out with cycle paths, and you can hire bicycles from the train stations at Bamberg and Forchheim.

Tourist Information

Ebermannstadt: Tourismus-Zentrale Fränkische Schweiz, Oberes Tor 1, ✆ (09194) 8101.

Forchheim: Rathaus, ✆ (09191) 84338.

Pottenstein: Gästezentrum am Rathaus, ✆ (09243) 70841.

Festivals

Nearly every village and small town in Franconian Switzerland has festivals to mark a religious holiday or the arrival of spring and autumn. Many locals dress up in *Tracht*, and the bigger festivals often include folk-dancing competitions. One of the most spectacular events is in Forchheim at the end of July, when the traditional **Annafest** is celebrated with a ten-day funfair. Muggendorf holds an annual **Kürbisfest** (Pumpkin Festival) in late September, and nearby Pottenstein observes Epiphany (6 January) with a **Lichterfest** (Festival of Lights), an evening parade of locals bearing candles and torches.

From Bamberg to Pottenstein

Pommersfelden, 20km south of Bamberg along the B505, is the site of **Schloß Weißenstein** (*guided tours April–Oct 9–12 and 2–5; adm DM5*). Set amidst the forests and vines of the **Steigerwald**, the splendid Baroque palace was built by Prince-Bishop Lothar von Schönborn at the turn of the 18th century, at about the same time as the

Würzburg Residenz and the Neue Residenz in Bamberg. Much of the original architecture survives intact, including the grand three-storeyed **flight of steps** in the main building, and an eye-catching fricassee of marble and stucco at the entrance to the **Marmorsaal** (Marble Hall). Avid wearers of Levi's 501s might like to head out to the village of **Buttenheim**, 17km northeast of Pommersfelden, the birthplace of Levi Strauss, a Jewish pedlar's son who emigrated to the United States in 1847 to become one of the most prolific producers of blue jeans.

If you continue a few kilometres southeast, you will come to **Forchheim**, a half-timbered town that lies in forest land along the River Pegnitz, halfway between Bamberg and Nuremberg. Those with a taste for regional costumes should look in at the pretty village of **Effeltrich**, 8km south of Forchheim. Here, at most weekends, rosy-cheeked villagers step out with a swish of frilly *Trachten* (traditional dress). From Forchheim, you can either potter about Franconian Switzerland, or follow the B470, which closely hugs the path of the River Wiesent. The road takes you to the cherry-growing village of **Pretzfeld** and its 16th-century castle. Just to the south, the gently undulating **Trubach Valley** stretches out along the course of this tributary of the Wiesent. At one time, the valley was crammed with well over 200 **water-mills**, used to process rich local deposits of iron ore. Today just eight remain, preserved under a protection order.

Working your way back on the road to Pretzfeld, **Ebermannstadt**, another sleepy town with a cluster of Franconian half-timbered buildings, lies a few kilometres northeast. If you turn off the B470 at Ebermannstadt, you reach—down a series of narrow country roads and past the small town of **Aufseß**—the beautiful **Thurnauer Land**. This northern part of Franconian Switzerland has a similarly wild beauty of stubby hills, burbling streams, drifts of wild flowers, and energetic bands of hikers. Yet further north, at **Zwernitz Castle** near Hollfeld, you will find **Sanspareil** (*daily; adm free*), a rugged, romantic garden laid out around the crag-top ruin of the castle, and including fanciful grotto landscapes. Wilhelmine von Bayreuth modelled the garden on the one created at her brother's palace of Sanssouci in Potsdam in the late 18th century.

Back on the B470, the countryside opens up a little as you get closer to **Muggendorf**, a town of richly coloured houses, idling beneath a ruined castle. This is the oldest resort in Franconian Switzerland, and gave the region its original name. A remarkable group of stalactite caves can be found around the town. The largest of these, extending over a length of 400m, is the **Binghöhle** (*guided tours only, Mar–Nov daily 8–5; adm DM4*).

From Muggendorf the road rambles on past the villages of **Gößweinstein** and **Behringersmühle**, around knobbly hills and on to **Pottenstein**, a pretty village with a fancy Gothic church and a 10th-century castle. The nearby **Teufelshöhle** (*guided tours only, Easter–Oct daily 9–5, Nov–Easter Tues and Sat 10–12; adm DM4.50*) is a 1500m-long cave with stalactites even finer than those of the Binghöhle.

In the neighbouring hamlet of Tüchersfeld is the **Judenhof**, an old Jewish stronghold which now houses the **Fränkische Schweiz Museum** (*April–Oct Tues–Sun 10–5; adm DM4*), where you can see an array of local history exhibits, including the belongings of the former Jewish occupants.

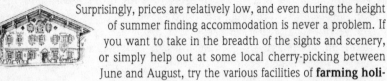

Surprisingly, prices are relatively low, and even during the height of summer finding accommodation is never a problem. If you want to take in the breadth of the sights and scenery, or simply help out at some local cherry-picking between June and August, try the various facilities of **farming holidays** on offer in the region. In many ways the best bargains of all, a number of farmhouses provide full-board rates from as little as DM30 per day. A list is available from: Verein Urlaub auf dem Bauernhof, Löschwöhrdstr. 5, D-91301 Forchheim, ℰ (09191) 65070.

Ebermannstadt

Hotel-Gasthof Resengörg, Hauptstr. 36, ℰ (09194) 8174, ℰ (09194) 4598 (DM110–120). A rustic half-timbered house (including two outlying guesthouses) with commodious rooms, good cheer and hearty wine and beer tavern.

Gößweinstein

Scheffel-Gasthof-Distler, Balthasar-Neumann-Str. 6, ℰ (09242) 201, ℰ (09242) 7318 (DM36–41). An atmospheric Baroque mansion, now a jolly, traditional inn.

Muggendorf

Hotel Feiler, Oberer Markt 4, ℰ (09196) 322, ℰ (09196) 362 (DM120–330). An elegant, quiet, family-run hotel with some romantic timber-framed bedrooms. The restaurant offers excellent sole and fillet of lamb.

Abtei	abbey
Altstadt	old town—usually the medieval part of the city
Bad	spa town (precedes the name of the town, e.g. Bad Berneck)
Bahnhof	railway station
Berg	mountain
BRD	German initials for Federal Republic of Germany
Brücke	bridge
Brunnen	fountain, spring, well
Bundes-	federal, hence Bundestag (Federal Parliament)
Burg	castle
Bürgermeister	Mayor
DDR	German initials for German Democratic Republic (ex-East Germany)
Denkmal	monument, memorial
Dom	cathedral
Dorf	village
Evangelisch	Protestant
Fachwerk	half-timbered
Fasching, Fastnet	alternative names for Carnival in Bavaria and Swabia
Feiertag	holiday
Feierabend	hometime, used by shop assistants to refuse service 10 minutes before closing.
Festung	fortress
Flughafen	airport
Fluß	river
Funk	radio—hence Funktaxi and Funktelefon are not what might be expected.
Fürst	prince
Gasse	alley
Gastarbeiter	foreign labourers (literally, 'guest worker'). Some have been in Germany for decades, yet even their children are denied citizenship.
Gasthaus/hof	inn, guest house
Graf	count
Hafen	harbour
Hauptbahnhof	main railway station
Hauptstraße	main street
Heide	heath
Heimat	homeland, hometown—capable of releasing waves of sentiment and loyalty

Glossary of German Terms

Herzog	duke
Höhle	cave
Hof	court (e.g. of a prince); also courtyard or mansion
Insel	island
Jagdschloß	hunting lodge
Jugendherberge	youth hostel
Jugendstil	German version of *Art Nouveau*, later tending towards Expressionism
Junker	Prussian landed gentry
Kaiser	Emperor
Kammer	room, chamber
Kapelle	chapel
Kaufhaus	department store

Kino	cinema
Kirche	church
Kloster	monastery, convent
König	king
Kunst	art
Kurhaus	central clinic of a spa town or health resort
Kurort	health resort
Kurverwaltung	tourist office in a spa town
Land	state in the Federal Republic (pl. *Länder*)
Landgrave	count (in charge of an important province)
Margrave	count in charge of a March (frontier district)
Markt	market, market square
Meer	sea
Münster	minster, often used of any large church
Naturpark	protected natural area
Palast	residential part of a castle
Pfarrkirche	parish church
Platz	square
Prinz	prince, but since 1918 used as a general aristocratic title
Rathaus	town/city hall
Ratskeller	restaurant in cellar below the Rathaus
Reich	empire
Reisebüro	travel agency
Residenz	palace
Ritter	knight
Saal	hall
Sammlung	collection
Schatzkammer	treasury (e.g. of a cathedral)
Schickie-Mickie	yuppie (often shortened to *Schickie*), collectively the *Schickeria*
Schloß	palace, castle
See	lake
Stadt	town, city
Stadthalle	not the city hall (Rathaus), but communal sports/conference hall
Stammtisch	table in a pub or tavern reserved for regulars; invade at your peril
Stift	collegiate church
Strand	beach
Straßenbahn	tram
Tal	valley
Tankstelle	filling station
Tor	gate (usually once part of a medieval wall)
Tracht	traditional costume
Turm	tower, ditto
Verkehrsamt	tourist office; also *Verkehrsverein* or *Fremdenverkehrsamt*
Viertel	quarter, district
Volk	people, folk—soured by Hitler's abuse of the word, but still a powerful concept
Wald	forest
Waldsterben	disease (caused by pollution) which is killing German forests
Wallfahrt	pilgrimage
Wasserburg	castle surrounded by water (usually more than just a moat)
Zeughaus	arsenal
Zimmer	room

German has never enjoyed a particularly good press. Holy Roman Emperor Charles V considered it as fit only for speaking to his horse. Mark Twain sends it up wickedly in his essay *On the Awful German Language*, and the narrator of Anthony Burgess's novel *Earthly Powers* calls it 'a glottal fish-boneclearing soulful sobbing sausagemachine of a language'.

It is a language of devilish complexity. There are three, rather than two, genders; nouns *and* adjectives decline; it is full of irregular verbs and deceptive conjugations; and the syntax is ornate, and often littered with parentheses that lead the inexperienced astray. The verb often comes only at the *end* of one of these arduous syntactical journeys. *Punch* once carried a cartoon of 'The Man who Died of Boredom while Waiting for a German Verb to Arrive'. More recently, simultaneous interpreters at an international conference were struck dumb during one long, impassioned outburst by a German delegate, as they too awaited the elusive particle. (All one section of the audience heard through their headphones was 'I missed the bloody verb').

But there are some advantages. Nouns are capitalized and easy to spot. This helps you to make some sense of written passages, even if your knowledge of German is scanty. Spelling is phonetical, so once you have grasped the basics of pronunciation there are few surprises. German is a precise language. Numbers of words can be combined into a single new one that hits the nail right on the head (such as *Mitbürger*—literally 'with-citizen'—a foreign permanent resident). Sometimes, though, this gets out of hand. 'These things are not words,' lamented Mark Twain, 'they are alphabetical processions'.

Pronunciation

Consonants: Most are the same as in English. There are no silent letters. *g*s are hard, as in English 'good', but *ch* is a guttural sound, as in the Scottish 'loch'—though *sch* is said as 'sh'. *s* is also pronounced 'sh', when it appears before a consonant (especially at the beginning of a word), as in *stein*, pronounced 'shtine'. Otherwise the sound is closer to 'z'. *z* is pronounced 'ts' and *d* at the end of the word becomes 't'. *r*s are rolled at the back of the throat, as in French. *v* is pronounced somewhere between the English 'f' and 'v', and *w* is said as the English 'v'.

Vowels: *a* can be long (as in 'father') or short, like the 'u' in 'hut'. Similarly *u* can be short, as in 'put', or long, as in 'boot'. *e* is pronounced at the end of words, and is slightly longer than in English. Say *er* as in 'hair' and *ee* as in 'hay'. Say *ai* as in 'pie'; *au* as in 'house'; *ie* as in 'glee'; *ei* like 'eye' and *eu* as in 'oil'. An **umlaut** (¨) changes the pronunciation of a word. Say *ä* like the 'e' in 'bet', or like the 'a' in 'label'. Say *ö* like the vowel sound in 'fur'. *ü* is a very short version of the vowel sound in

Language

'true'. Sometimes an umlaut is replaced by an *e* after the vowel. The printed symbol *ß* is sometimes written *ss*, and is pronounced as a double 's'.

Here are some practice sentences:

Verstehen Sie Deutsch?	*fairshtayen zee doitch?*	(Do you understand German?)
Nein, ich verstehe kein Wort.	*nine, ich fairshtay kine vort*	(No, I don't understand a word)
Haben Sie Zimmer frei?	*haben zee tsimmer fry?*	(Do you have any rooms free?)

The standard of English in Bavaria is pretty good—though restaurants off the tourist track seldom have an English menu. In rural districts, however, you are advised to go armed with essential German phrases.

Useful Words and Phrases

yes/no/maybe		*ja/nein/vielleicht*
excuse me		*Entschuldigung, bitte*
it doesn't matter		*es macht nichts*
I am sorry		*es tut mir leid*
please		*bitte*
thank you	(very much)	*danke (schön); vergelt's Gott* (in rural Bavaria)
it's a pleasure		*bitte(schön)*
hello		*guten Tag; hallo*
hello (in Bavaria)		*grüß Gott*
goodbye/bye		*auf Wiedersehen; tschüss; pfüat di* (in rural Bavaria)
good morning/evening		*guten Morgen/Abend*
good night		*guten Nacht*
how are you?	(formal)	*wie geht es Ihnen?*
	(informal)	*wie geht es Dir?* or
		wie geht's?
I'm very well		*mir geht's gut*
I don't speak German		*ich spreche kein Deutsch*
do you speak English?		*sprechen Sie Englisch?*
do you understand me?		*verstehen Sie mich?; host mi?* (in rural Bavaria)
I don't know		*ich weiß nicht*
I don't understand		*ich verstehe nicht*
how do you say...		*wie sagt man...*
my name is...		*mein Name ist... ; ich heisse...*
I am...	English (man)	*ich bin Engländer*
I am...	English (woman)	*ich bin Engländerin*
	American	*Amerikaner(in)*
	Australian	*Australier(in)*
	Canadian	*Kanadier(in)*
	a New Zealander	*Neuseeländer(in)*
I come from...	England	*ich komme aus England*
	Scotland	*Schottland*
	Ireland	*Irland*
	Wales	*Wales*
	the United States	*den Vereinigten Staaten*
	Canada	*Kanada*
	Australia	*Australien*
	New Zealand	*Neuseeland*
leave me alone		*lass mich in Ruhe*
with/without		*mit/ohne*
and/but		*und/aber*
is this table free?		*ist der Tisch frei?*
the menu please		*die Speisekarte bitte*
the bill please		*die Rechnung bitte*
I would like...		*ich möchte...*
how much does this cost?		*wieviel kostet dies?*
cheap/expensive		*billig/teuer*
where is/are...?		*wo ist/sind...?*
who		*wer*
what		*was*
why		*warum*
when		*wann*

how do I get to...	(town)	*wie komme ich nach...*
	(building or place)	*wie komme ich zur/zum...*
how far is it to...		*wie weit ist es nach...*
how long does it take?		*wie lange dauert es?*
near/far		*nah/weit*
left/right/straight on		*links/rechts/gerade aus*
help!		*hilfe!*
can you help me?		*konnen Sie mir bitte helfen?*
I am ill		*ich bin krank*
I am lost		*ich weiß nicht, wo ich bin*
I am hungry		*ich habe Hunger*
I am thirsty		*ich habe Durst*
I am hot		*mir ist warm*
I am cold		*mir ist kalt*
in this year		*heuer*

Notices and Signs

open/closed	*geöffnet/*	hospital	*Krankenhaus*
	geschlossen	pharmacy	*Apotheke*
closed (literally: rest day)	*Ruhetag*	post office	*Post*
no entry	*eingang verboten*	airport	*Flughafen*
(emergency) exit	*(Not) ausgang*	customs	*Zoll*
entrance	*Eingang*	railway station	*Bahnhof*
toilet	*Toilette*	train	*Zug*
Ladies/Gents	*Damen/Herren*	platform	*Gleis*
bathroom	*Badezimmer*	reserved	*besetzt*
push/pull	*drücken/ziehen*	rooms to let	*Fremdenzimmer*
bank	*Bank*	pedestrian zone	*Fußgängerzone*
bureau de change	*Wechselstube*	picnic area	*Rastplatz*
police	*Polizei*	way round/circuit	*Rundgang*

Days and Months

Monday	*Montag*	March	*März*
Tuesday	*Dienstag*	April	*April*
Wednesday	*Mittwoch*	May	*Mai*
Thursday	*Donnerstag*	June	*Juni*
Friday	*Freitag*	July	*Juli*
Saturday	*Samstag*	August	*August*
Sunday	*Sonntag*	September	*September*
		October	*Oktober*
January	*Januar; Jänner*	November	*November*
February	*Februar*	December	*Dezember*

Numbers

one	*eins*	seven	*sieben*
two	*zwei*	eight	*acht*
three	*drei*	nine	*neun*
four	*vier*	ten	*zehn*
five	*fünf*	eleven	*elf*
six	*sechs*	twelve	*zwölf*

thirteen	dreizehn	ninety	neunzig
fourteen	vierzehn	hundred	hundert
seventeen	siebzehn	hundred and one	hunderteins
twenty	zwanzig	hundred and forty-two	hundertzweiundvierzig
twenty-one	einundzwanzig	two hundred	zweihundert
twenty-two	zweiundzwanzig	thousand	tausend
thirty	dreissig	three thousand	dreitausend
forty	vierzig	million	eine Million
fifty	fünfzig	billion (thousand million)	eine Milliarde
sixty	sechszig	billion (million million)	eine Billion
seventy	siebzig	1995	neunzehnhundert-
eighty	achtzig		fünfundneunzig

Time

watch/clock/hour	Uhr	month	Monat
alarm clock	Wecker	year	Jahr
what is the time?	wie spät ist es?	season	Jahreszeit
one/two o'clock	eine/zwei Uhr	spring	Frühling
quarter-past two	Viertel nach zwei	summer	Sommer
half-past two	halbdrei	autumn	Herbst
half-past three	halbvier	winter	Winter
quarter to three	Viertel vor drei	century	Jahrhundert
morning	Morgen; Vormittag	today/yesterday/	heute/gestern/
afternoon	Nachmittag	tomorrow	morgen
evening	Abend	this/last/next week	diese/letzte/nächste
night	Nacht		Woche
week	Woche		

Driving

car hire	Autovermietung	no parking	Parken verboten
filling station	Tankstelle	driver's licence	Führerschein
petrol/diesel	Benzin/Diesel	insurance	Versicherung
leaded/unleaded	verbleit/bleifrei	one-way street	Einbahnstaße
my car has	mein Auto hat	except	außer
broken down	Panne	(on no-entry signs)	
accident	Autounfall	get in correct lane	einordnen
garage (for repairs)	Autowerkstatt	junction	Kreuzung
parking place	Parkplatz		

Food and Drink

breakfast	Frühstuck; Brotzeit	glass	Glas
lunch	Mittagessen; Vesper	bottle	Flasche
	(in rural Bavaria)	salt/pepper	Salz/Pfeffer
dinner	Abendessen	milk/sugar	Milch/Zucker
supper	Abendbrot	bread/butter	Brot/Butter
menu	Speisekarte	filled roll	belegtes Brötchen
bon appétit	guten Appetit	mustard	Senf
cup	Tasse	home-made	hausgemacht
pot (e.g. of coffee)	Kännchen	à la	Art

fresh	*frisch*	clams	*Venusmuscheln*
boiled	*gekocht*	squid	*Tintenfisch*
steamed	*gedämpft*	eel	*Aal*
baked	*gebacken*	vegetables	*Gemüse*
roasted	*gebraten*	salad	*Salat*
smoked	*geräuchert*	tomatoes	*Tomaten*
stuffed	*gefüllt*	cucumber	*Gurke*
stew/casserole	*Topf; Eintopf*	peppers/capsicums	*Paprika*
starters	*Vorspeise*	onions	*Zwiebeln*
soup	*Suppe*	garlic	*Knoblauch*
main course	*Hauptgericht*	chives	*Schnittlauch*
meat	*Fleisch*	herbs	*Kräuter*
sausage	*Wurst*	jacket potatoes	*Pellkartoffeln*
ham	*Schinken*	mashed potatoes	*Kartoffelbrei*
cold cuts	*Aufschnitt*	chips	*Pommes frites*
pork	*Schweinefleisch*	boiled potatoes	*Salzkartoffeln*
knuckle of pork	*Schweinehaxe*	rice	*Reis*
bacon	*Speck*	beans	*Bohnen*
beef	*Rindfleisch*	(red) cabbage	*(Rot) kohl*
lamb	*Lammfleisch*	mushrooms	*Pilze, Champignons*
veal	*Kalbfleisch*	maize	*Mais*
oxtail	*Ochsenschwanz*	peas	*Erbsen*
hare	*Hase*	cauliflower	*Blumenkohl*
rabbit	*Kanninchen*	spinach	*Spinat*
liver	*Leber*	leeks	*Lauch*
game	*Wild*	lentils	*Linsen*
venison	*Hirsch, Reh*	chickpeas	*Kichererbsen*
ham	*Schinken*	dumplings	*Knödel; Klösse*
mincemeat	*Hackfleisch*	asparagus	*Spargel*
steak	*steak*	aubergine	*Aubergine*
meatball	*Boulette*	dessert	*Nachtisch*
chop	*Kottelett, Schnitzel*	tart/cake	*Torte/Kuchen*
poultry	*Geflügel*	ice-cream	*Eis*
chicken	*Huhn; Hähnchen*	(whipped) cream	*(Schlag) sahne*
duck	*Ente*	nuts	*Nüße*
turkey	*Truthahn; Puter*	almonds	*Mandeln*
goose	*Gans*	chocolate	*Schokolade*
fish	*Fische*	cheese	*Käse*
trout	*Forelle*	fruit	*Obst*
carp	*Karpfen*	apple	*Apfel*
salmon	*Lachs*	orange	*Apfelsine; Orange*
haddock	*Schellfisch*	lemon	*Zitrone*
perch	*Zander*	grapefruit	*Pampelmuse*
pike	*Hecht*	banana	*Banane*
cod	*Kabeljau*	pineapple	*Ananas*
sole	*Seezunge*	pear	*Birne*
flounder	*Butt*	cherry	*Kirsche*
plaice	*Scholle*	peach	*Pfirsich*
herring	*Hering, Matjes*	plum	*Pflaume*
tuna	*Thunfisch*	grapes	*Trauben*
lobster	*Hummer*	raisins	*Rosinen*
prawns	*Garnalen*	raspberry	*Himbeere*
mussels	*Muscheln*	strawberry	*Erdbeere*

redcurrant	Johannisbeere	beer	Bier
drinks	Getränke	red/white wine	Rotwein/Weißwein
(mineral) water	(Mineral) wasser	brandy	Brandwein
fruit juice	Saft		

Menu Reader

Aal	Eel—popular in the north. Served smoked or grün, cooked in creamy herb sauce
Ausgezogene	Flaky pastry dessert with a sweet soft centre
Bauernfrühstück	Literally 'peasant breakfast'—ham, egg and potatoes—or any large, hot breakfast
Bayerische Creme	Vanilla-flavoured whipped cream served with raspberry or strawberry purée
Blaue Zipfel	Pork sausages marinated in spiced vinegar
Bohnensuppe	Thick bean soup
Brägenwurst	Sausage made with brains
Braunkohl	Kale
Bratwurst	Grilled sausage (usually pork)
Dampfnudeln	sweeet steamed dumplings
Eintopf/Topf	Stew, casserole or thick soup
Flädlesuppe	Soup with strips of pancake cut into it
Forelle	Trout
Gaisburger Marsch	Thick beef soup with noodles and potatoes
Grünkohl	Cabbage
Gulaschsuppe	Thick, peppery beef soup
Halbes Hähnchen	Half a chicken (grilled)
Hopfensprossen	steamed hop-shoots, tasting something like asparagus; available only in spring
Kasseler Rippchen	Pickled loin of pork (named after a Berlin butcher called Kassel, not the town)
Leberkäs	Bavarian-style meat loaf
Leberknödel	Doughy bake of minced meat and smoked bacon
Leberknödel	Liver dumplings
Lebkuchen	Traditional spicy gingerbread, made with honey and nuts
Maultaschen	Giant ravioli, stuffed with meat and usually spinach too
Mettwurst	Pork and beef sausages
Mehlpüt	Pear and butter sauce dessert
Nürnberger Bratwurst	Grilled pork sausage about the size of your little finger
Obaazta	A blend mix of Camembert and butter, bound with egg yolk; called Gerupfter in Franconia
Pfefferpotthast	Spicy boiled beef
Pumpernickel	Dark rye bread
Reiberdatschi	Potato cakes
Sauerkraut	Pickled cabbage
Schlachtplatte	Platter of various meats, usually including blood sausage and offal
Schweinshaxe	Roast knuckle of pork
Schweinepfeffer	Jugged pork
Semmelknödeln	Bread dumplings
Spargel	Asparagus
Spätzle	Noodles
Speckkuchen	Substantial bacon quiche
Tellerfleisch	Minced beef preparation served with horseradish sauce; also known as Tafelspitz and Ochsenbrust
Weißwurst	Veal and pork sausage, sometimes with brain
Zünger	Pig's tongue
Zwiebelbraten	Beef in brown onion sauce

800 BC–400 BC	Celtic tribes settled in the area that comprises modern Bavaria.
From 15 BC	Roman invasion of the land between the Alps, Dolomites and the Danube. Provinces of *Raetia* and *Noricum* are protected by forts at Augsburg, Kempten, Regensburg and Passau.
488	Roman control of lands north of the Alps collapses under the onslaught of the Germanic *Baiuvarii*.
555–788	Frankish dukes of the Agilolfing family rule lands south of the Danube. Capital established at Regensburg.
8th century	A Merovingian dynasty establishes crown lands north of the Danube (modern Franconia).
7th–8th century	Irish and Scottish missionaries convert central Bavaria to Christianity.
788	Tassilo III, the last of the Agilolfing dukes, is deposed by Charlemagne and the Bavarian duchy is absorbed by the Carolingian Empire.
843	Bavaria comes under the control of Louis the German, king of the eastern Franks.
907	Margrave Luitpold, founding father of the Schyren dynasty, is killed at the hands of a Magyar army at the Battle of Pressburg. His son Arnulf takes over and defeats the Slavs.
937	Arnulf is demoted to his ancestral margravate by Emperor Otto I. The duchy becomes a bone of contention between the Welf and Staufian families.
1156	Emperor Frederick Barbarossa gives his cousin Henry the Lion, the powerful Saxon duke, the Bavarian duchy.
1158	Munich is founded by Henry the Lion as a salt-trading centre on the River Isar.
1180	Henry the Lion loses his Bavarian lands. Frederick Barbarossa invests the Count Palatine Otto of Wittelsbach, descendant of the Margraves of Schyren, with the duchy.
1183–1231	The adept Duke Ludwig triples his lands by inheritance, by purchase, feudal acquisitions and force.
1214	The Palatinate of the Rhine is secured for Bavaria.
1231	Duke Ludwig is murdered by a cloaked assassin at Kelheim.
1231–53	Otto II (the Illustrious) chooses to relocate his residence to the newly founded Landshut and expands his holdings by purchasing individual patches of land.
1247	The Wittelsbachs adopt the armorial bearings of the white and blue rhombuses (formerly held by the Counts of Bogen) as their family coat of arms.
1255	Territorial division into the separate duchies of Upper Bavaria and Straubing.
1392	Renewed fragmentation into four autonomous duchies (Landshut, Straubing, Ingolstadt, Munich).
1475	Landshut Wedding between Prince Georg and Jadwiga, daughter of the king of Poland, marks wealth of the Landshut branch of the Wittelsbachs.
1506	Duke Albrecht IV (the Wise) paves the way for territorial union and brings in primogeniture. He establishes Munich as main ducal capital for the Wittelbachs.
1508–50	Duke William IV reunifies Bavaria. He champions the Counter-Reformation.
1550–79	Under Duke Albrecht V the Protestants are persecuted. The Jesuit order gains the upper hand.
1555	The Peace of Augsburg establishes religious equality for Protestant and Roman Catholic faith—but subjects have to assume the faith of their rulers.

Chronology

1609	Duke Maximilian I sets up the Catholic League in response to the Protestant Union.
1623	Maximilian becomes Elector of the Holy Roman Empire of the German Nation and seizes the Upper Palatinate for the Wittelsbachs.
1631–48	The Thirty Years' War (1618–48) devastates Bavaria. Following the defeat of Johann Tilly, the military champion of the Catholic armies, Augsburg and Munich are briefly occupied by the Swedes.
1679–1726	Elector Max II Emmanuel embarks on a building plan under the guidance of the Baroque masters the Asam and Zimmermann brothers.
1701	Emperor Leopold I of Austria turns against Bavaria and unleashes the War of the Spanish Succession.
1704	Battle of Blenheim. A Franco-Bavarian army is defeated by the Habsburgs and British under Prince Eugene of Savoy and the Duke of Marlborough. Bavaria is occupied by the Austrians for 10 years.

1743	After the Austrian Succession, an Austrian Army of occupation arrives in Bavaria.
1745	The young Maximilian III Joseph is forced to retire from the war and concentrates instead on domestic reforms. The Academy for the Arts and Sciences is founded in Munich and the Jesuits banned from Bavaria.
1778–9	In the War of the Bavarian Succession between Austria and Prussia Frederick the Great of Prussia ensures territorial integrity for the Wittelsbachs.
1805	Following the French occupation of Bavaria, Elector Maximilian IV becomes Napoleon's ally and his title is augmented to King of Bavaria. Bavaria is doubled in size, receiving Franconia and large parts of Swabia.
1813	Maximilian switches loyalties again and becomes a member of the Germanic Confederation.
1815	At the Congress of Vienna Bavaria rises to 3rd largest power in Germany, after Austria and Prussia.
1825-48	King Ludwig I promotes Bavaria's political and commercial standing and embarks on a Neoclassical rebuilding of Munich under the aegis of court architect Leo von Klenze.
1837	Ludwig I creates the provinces of Upper, Middle and Lower Franconia.
1848	Ludwig I is forced to abdicate because of an affair with one of his mistresses. Political unrest in Munich.
1848–64	King Maximilian II brings Bavaria into an alliance with Saxony, Hannover and Württemberg to establish a strong third force in Germany.
1864–86	King Ludwig II supports Austria against Prussian Prince Otto von Bismarck. He sets out on an ambitious and costly building programme in Bavaria.
1866–7	Seven Weeks' War. Prussia defeats Austria and Bavaria. Ludwig II is coerced into paying financial remunerations and into a defensive alliance with Prussia.
1870–1	Franco-German War. Bavaria is absorbed into a greater German Reich under Prussian domination. Bavaria keeps own army, postal service, railways and embassies abroad.
1918	Germany defeated in the First World War. King Ludwig III is deposed and Bavaria is proclaimed a breakaway Soviet-style republic.
1919	After revolutionary councils spearheaded a 'Red Terror' in Munich, the Bavarian Republic is quelled by the *Freikorps*. Bavaria becomes a constitutional state in the Weimar Republic.
1923	Failure of Hitler's Munich *Putsch*. He is imprisoned at Landsberg Prison.
1927	First all-German Nazi rally in Nuremberg.
1933	Hitler appointed Chancellor. Bavaria loses state privileges. Dachau Concentration Camp opened.
1935	Nazi Racial Purity Laws enacted in Nuremberg.
1938	Berchtesgaden and Munich provide the backdrop for the Munich Agreement, paving the way to the German occupation of the Sudentenland in Czechoslovakia.
1939–45	Bavaria's industry fuels Hitler's war effort from deep inside the Third Reich.
1942–3	The White Rose Society circulates a number of resistance leaflets at Munich University. Most members are tried and executed by the Nazis.
1944–5	Bavarian towns and cities suffer from incessant Allied carpet-bombing.
1945	Bavaria becomes part of US zone of occupation. Nuremberg is the location of the Allies' main war crime trials.
1946	Bavaria re-established as a constitutional *Land* of the Federal Republic of Germany, but does not ratify its constitution. Thousands of eastern refugees are absorbed by Bavarian communities.
1947–1994	The right-wing Christian Social Union (CSU) emerges as pre-eminent political party in Bavaria.
1978	Franz-Josef Strauss heads Bavarian state.
1980	Strauss stages his candidature as all-German Chancellor at general elections.
1988	Strauss dies without a successor. Many party members switch their allegiance to the extreme-right *Republikaner* party.
1990	Reunification puts Franconia back in the heart of Germany.
1991	During the parliamentary debate about the return of the seat of government to Berlin, members of the CDU speak out against such a move, arguing that it would upset the political balance between the Federal government and its *Länder*.

History/General

Fulbrook, Mary, *A Concise History of Germany* (C.U.P 1990). By far the most compact and accessible account of German history—from murky beginnings to the 1989 revolution.

Mann, Golo, *The History of Germany since 1789* (Penguin). Hefty tome, but a good read. Insider's account of the paradoxes of the nation—in history, philosophy and art—ending just after the Second World War.

Tacitus, *The Germania* and *The Annals of Imperial Rome* (Penguin). Amusing, perceptive and at times delightfully personal account of the Germanic tribes knocking about in Roman times.

Blunt, Wilfred, *The Dream King* (Hamish Hamilton 1970). Thorough, intriguing biography of Ludwig II, builder of fairytale castles and patron of Richard Wagner.

Ardagh, John, *Germany and the Germans* (Penguin). Far-reaching insights into a multifarious people, based on personal experience.

Applegate, Celia, *A Nation of Provincials—the German Idea of Heimat* (UCL Press). A scholarly and absorbing study of one of the dynamos of the German psyche.

Schneider, Peter, *The German Comedy—Scenes of Lfe after the Wall* (Farrar Straus Giroux. First published in German as *Extreme Mittelage*). Essays and anecdotes that get under the skin of the new Germany.

Huber, Heinz, with illustrations by **Ronald Searle**, *Haven't We Met Somewhere Before?* (Heinemann). A knowing, often funny, though at times dated view of the nation written in the 1960s. Searle's cartoons are timeless.

Mikes, George, *Über Alles* (Allan Wingate). An opinionated and amusing personal account of the humorist's journey through a Germany recovering from the Second World War.

Schulte, Michael, *Karl Valentin* (Hoffmann und Campe). A picture-a-page biography of Munich's odd comedian.

Art and Architecture

Toman, Rolf, *The High Middle Ages in Germany* (Benedikt Taschen). Lavishly illustrated series of essays on different aspects of medieval art and culture.

Anzelewsky, Fedja, *Albrecht Dürer—Malerische Werk* (Deutsche Verlag für Kunstwissenschaft). One volume of sumptuous illustrations and another of careful analysis of Dürer's paintings. Two further volumes—*The Complete Woodcuts* and *The Complete Etchings, Engravings and Drypoints* (both published by Dover)—make up an excellent record of the Master's work.

Greindl, Gabriele, *Barock in Ostbayern* (HB Bildatlas special series, no.21). A splendid survey of the work of the Asam brothers in eastern Bavaria.

Franz Prinz zu Sayn-Wittgenstein, *Schlösser in Bayern*. An insider's view of the castles and grand houses of Bavaria.

Further Reading

Simplicissimus (Haus der Kunst). The pick of cartoons and articles between 1896 and 1944 from Munich's famous satirical magazine.

Ranke, Winifred, et al, *Franz von Lenbach* (Prestel). A good biography and a well-illustrated survey of paintings by Munich's prince of the portrait (in German).

Watkin, David, *German Architecture and the Classical Ideal* (Thames & Hudson). Sets German Neoclassicism in a European context. Good chapter on Leo von Klenze.

German Literary Landmarks

Grimmelhausen, Johann Jacob Christoffel von, *Simplicius Simplicissimus* (Dedalus). Epic novel written and set in the early 17th century, and one of the most important German works of its time.

Goethe, Johann Wolfgang von, *The Sorrows of Young Werther; Faust; Selected Verse* (all published by Penguin). With these you have the core of the work of Germany's most prominent literary figure.

Hoffmann, E. T. A., Heinrich von Kleist, Ludwig Tieck, *Six German Romantic Tales* (Angel). A handy anthology of tales by masters of the art.

Schiller, Friedrich, *The Robbers, Wallenstein* and *William Tell* (Penguin). Main works by Germany's most respected dramatist after Goethe.

Büchner, Georg, *Plays* (Methuen). *Woyzeck* and *Danton's Death* are perhaps the most extraordinary and powerful plays to come out of Germany—certainly the ones most frequently performed in other countries.

Mann, Thomas, *Buddenbrooks* (Penguin). A semi-autobiographical novel that charts the decline of a wealthy German merchant family.

Hesse, Hermann, *Narziss and Goldmund* (Penguin). The adventures of a beautiful medieval monk—some say suffused with repressed homo-eroticism.

Remarque, Erich Maria, *All Quiet on the Western Front* (Picador). The book that has become the classic tale of the First World War, for German and English readers alike.

Brecht, Bertolt, *Poems* and *Plays* (Methuen). The influential 20th-century dramatist also wrote fine poetry, which has been sensitively translated.

Grass, Günther, *The Tin Drum* (Picador). Gripping and fantastical novel about the curious Oskar, whose scream can shatter glass. Grass digs about in the German psyche to unearth the causes and effects of the success of the Nazis.

Böll, Heinrich, *The Lost Honour of Katharina Blum* (Penguin). Familiar to most non-Germans as a film. The best-known work of one of Germany's most fêted modern novelists.

Note: Page numbers in *italics* indicate maps. **Bold** entries indicate main references.